THE LUFTHANSA HEIST

THE LUFTHANSA HEIST

Behind the Six-Million-Dollar Cash Haul
That Shook the World

Henry Hill and Daniel Simone

Guilford, Connecticut

An imprint of Rowman & Littlefield

Distributed by NATIONAL BOOK NETWORK

British Library Cataloguing in Publication Information Available

Library of Congress Cataloging-in-Publication Data

Hill, Henry, 1943–2012.
  The Lufthansa heist : behind the six-million-dollar cash haul that shook the world / Henry Hill
and Daniel Simone.
    pages cm
  Includes bibliographical references and index.
  ISBN 978-1-4930-0849-0 (hardcopy : alk. paper) — ISBN 978-1-4930-1896-3 (ebook)
  1. Robbery—New York (State)—New York—Case studies. 2. Organized crime—New York
(State)—New York—Case studies. 3. Deutsche Lufthansa (1953–) I. Simone, Daniel. II. Title.
  HV6661.N721978 .H55 2015
  364.16'209747243—dc23

                                                                                          2015012908

∞™ The paper used in this publication meets the minimum requirements of
American National Standard for Information Sciences—Permanence of Paper
for Printed Library Materials, ANSI/NISO Z39.48-1992.

*This is dedicated to my soul mate BJ
and to my dearest son.*

*I reserve deep thoughts for the late Henry Hill,
without whom this story would be lifeless and colorless.*

CONTENTS

Authors' Note ix
Foreword xi
Acknowledgments xiii
The Lufthansa Heist 1
Epilogue 345
Afterword 347
Notes and Sources 349
Glossary of Italian Slang 355
Index 359
About the Authors 367

"I had this theory about reportage," Truman Capote told Newsweek. *"I've always felt that if you brought the art of the novelist together with the technique of journalism—fiction with the added knowledge that it was true—it would have the most depth and impact."*

—TRUMAN CAPOTE (1924–1984)

Authors' Note

THE PRINCIPAL EVENTS AND FACTS CONTAINED IN THIS STORY ARE TRUE. Its narrative is founded on extensive research, interviews, and informed judgment. In many segments, scenes and dialogues have been re-created with literary technique combined or imagined to plausibly reflect the documentary record. The names and identities of some of the characters are fictitious, though these changes do not in any way compromise the integrity and accurate portrayal of the event.

Foreword

When I began reading Daniel Simone's manuscript, it instantly reeled me back thirty-seven years, the time that has passed since the Lufthansa robbery. An extraordinary event that deviated the course of my life. I still think about it almost every day. The investigation was one of the most fast-paced I'd ever conducted, and its course shifted wildly day-to-day. Certain aspects of it, for sure I might've done differently, but in the end justice was served.

As it is vividly portrayed in this book, the times were different time: The era of glory of "Omerta Rules," the days when gangsters were mob stars, and the period when Jimmy *the Gent* Burke was at the top of his game. It was the perfect storm for the Gent. A group of low-level criminals, who were mostly illiterates, as Daniel accurately and in a comedic way dramatizes, somehow pulled off an enormous score, and there were no witnesses but the participants. All the victims at the airport were mute, because of either ignorance or fear. And Burke had his own method of silencing people, a point keenly illustrated in this tome. He was responsible for over thirteen murders. While we, the FBI, chased down the witnesses, he murdered them. Though all the accomplices saw nothing but riches in their futures, they all looked back and rued their involvement in this caper, losing their lives as a result of it.

A case of this magnitude needs witnesses or evidence. With these two essentials missing, we relied on techniques that were still in their infancies, electronic surveillance, wire taps, and electronic bugs. Unfortunately, neither was sufficiently sophisticated to be foolproof. Burke's home was occupied 24/7 and guarded by his criminal associates. The only bug we could install was in a 1979 Thunderbird, owned by Angelo Sepe. Knowingly or not, he neutralized the bug by playing his radio at the highest volume. We encountered many difficulties with these crude devices, simplistic equipment wrought with problems. If we had some of the once imaginary techniques you see today used on CSI, the Lufthansa investigation might've ended with a resolution.

But in May of 1979, the odds reversed. Henry Hill, one of the mob's most trusted servants, opted to cooperate with the FBI. And through our efforts and Hill's testimony, Burke and fifteen top ranked mob figures found new homes in federal prisons.

Moreover, Hill provided the goods to convict Burke for the homicide of conman Richard Eaton. This combined with the Boston College basketball fix sent Burke to prison for the rest of his life. The Gent, above all, suffered the most because of this robbery.

And as I look back, having been the lead investigator, I'd love for another chance but with the assistance of today's technology; sometimes, though, there are no second chances. Life goes on. However, Daniel Simone has deftly immortalized the 1978 Lufthansa robbery, the largest *unrecovered cash* theft in history.

—Steve Carbone, Supervisor FBI Special Agent, retired

ACKNOWLEDGMENTS

IF I WERE TO ASSEMBLE EVERYONE WHO CONTRIBUTED TO THIS PROJECT—and you know who you are—I'd be compelled to rent Madison Square Garden, and my publisher might've had to add another hundred pages to this book. And I thank immensely all of you.

I wish to mention my appreciation to my agents, Marianne *Mimi* Strong and Colin Campbell, for their devotion and unshakeable beliefs in this tome, and the relentless pursuit they embarked on to see it published.

Most deserving of special thanks are US Attorney Emeritus Ed McDonald, former FBI Special Agents Steve Carbone and Ed Guevara, and retired Port Authority Captain Henry Degeneste. They readily availed themselves to me and endured my bothersome inquiries. These gentlemen filled the gaps and lapses that otherwise might've remained as gaping holes in the storyline.

I thank Jon Sternfeld, who spent endless hours tolerating my writing peculiarities throughout his editing of the manuscript, and whose keenness as an editor is superb.

I assign a great deal of credit to Keith Wallman and his supporting staff at Rowman & Littlefield. Their charge of enthusiasm during the development of this endeavor was encouraging.

Last but not least, I take this opportunity to express my gratitude to Henry Hill's common-law wife, Lisa Caserta, for supplying me with indispensable photographs and documentation pertaining to this book.

And for all the gratuitous labors of everyone named herein, any mistakes or inconsistencies you may find are solely my fault.

Kennedy Airport was the solution to all our problems. Money, I got it at Kennedy Airport. If the wife found out about the mistress, and a fur coat might keep her calm, I got it at Kennedy Airport. If our girlfriends were gettin' impatient about wanting a color TV, we went to Kennedy. When the cigarette supply dried up, we'd go to Kennedy and rob a truckload of cartons. The airport was our private bank, and when it all came crashing down, my wardrobe turned from a walk-in closet of silk suits to a cardboard box of cheap jeans and two-dollar T-shirts.

—HENRY HILL (1943–2012)

1

April 1967.

I could never manage time. The night before, I'd been playing cards and drinking 'til the light in the windows turned gray. The next morning, shaking off a hangover, I nursed three cups of coffee and five Marlboros. Still in my boxer shorts, it dawned on me I had to meet Frenchy. He'd been lining up a score that, I later found out, could solve all our money problems—I hoped. The loan sharks and bookmakers were done with me, and every minute I stayed alive was a gift.

Frenchy had said to meet him at The Bamboo Lounge. I picked up my friend Tommy DeSimone, and we drove there, darkening skies raining cats and dogs. Frenchy was at the bar, and as Tommy and I strolled in, he saw us and waved.

"Henry, Tommy, over here."

Tommy and I hopped on the barstools next to him. He cleared his throat and bent in close to us. "OK, Henry, Tommy, listen. This is the story," he shushed, looking left and right for snoopers. He folded his arms on the bar.

"Air France just finished building a new money storage room in the cargo bay. It's thirty feet from my office." Frenchy was getting all worked up, and slapped me on the back of my neck. "Just thirty fuckin' feet," he kept saying. "It's nothing more than a huge closet made out of cinder blocks. I heard they're going to put in an alarm system, but right now there ain't none. Get it?"

Robert "Frenchy" McMahon elbowed me in the ribs and again perused here and there as if he was afraid somebody was listening. He drew another swig of ale and almost had me and Tommy hypnotized. At this point, though, we didn't understand where he was going with this, and mouths open like two five-year-olds listening to a bedtime story, we nodded along.

Once Frenchy felt at ease that nobody was eavesdropping, he went on. "Can you believe it? No alarms, no closed-circuit TV, and they're keeping hundreds of thousands of dollars in that bullshit vault. Those assholes are insane."

Frenchy shook his head as if he couldn't believe how lax the security was at Air France. "The steel door is the only thing stopping anybody from getting inside. And that's it!"

He snickered and paused, grabbed a handful of salted nuts out of a bowl and popped them in his mouth. Chewing, he nodded at the ceiling with his chin.

"The Air France bigwigs in the offices upstairs—the moron *executives*—call it a vault. Shit, it's as much a vault as my house is Fort Knox." We broke out laughing, and Frenchy winked at the bartender. "Mickey, bring my buddies a couple of beers," he said.

Frenchy had a smoker's cough and hacked for a few seconds before he slurped his beer.

He squeezed my forearm as if to say, *hang on, more is coming.* "Only two people have the darn key to this money room."

Now he had my attention. "Who?"

Frenchy, a blond, curly-haired Irishman, licked his lips. "A dumb-ass security guard has one key and never, never leaves sight of it. Mike Nolan's got the second key. He's the supervisor of the whole joint."

It was Friday, and the airport blue-collar laborers had piled in for the five o'clock happy hour. I reached out for a handful of nuts and asked Frenchy, "How the hell can we get our hands on the fuckin' key?"

Frenchy sucked in a dose of nicotine, pointed at his chest, and the joker that he was, came up with one of his rhymes. "Moi. *Your* man's got a plan." Frenchy had a head start on the happy hour. He'd already swallowed three brews and two rye chasers—but somehow liquor never hindered Frenchy from thinking straight.

"Ah! Now we're gettin' somewhere. *Salut.*" I raised my glass, toasted, and we drained our drinks.

Tommy, too, was fired up. "*Salut*, Frenchy. You're our man."

Mike Nolan never took the key off his belt hook. No problem, though. Nolan had a weakness, Frenchy said, an addiction that, as most

2

men do, made him think with the wrong head. Nolan was a half-witted hillbilly; he liked to swing with one-night stands, and sometimes he'd get so stoned his brain ran on half the cylinders.

So we concocted a plan. Frenchy hooked up Nolan with Clementine, a church organ player who moonlighted as a hooker. Not to prick Nolan's ego, we told him she was my sister. Frenchy, Tommy, and I talked it over with Clementine, and she thought the best way for us to steal the key was for her and Mike Nolan to spend a night at the Jade East, a hot-sheets motel near the airport. Clementine knew how to wrap a hot dog like Nolan around her finger. She was to meet Nolan in the bar of the Jade East; Frenchy thought it wise for him and me to be there as well. Nolan found it odd when we showed up; but drooling over Clementine and, dying to screw her in the bubbling spa, he didn't give it a second thought. He whisked her off to his room for a change of clothes.

Frenchy and I stayed at the bar. Halfway into our second martini, we caught a glimpse of Nolan and his rented date. They were headed to the spa salon, holding hands like high school kids. I couldn't help but laugh.

"Frenchy, I think Nolan swallowed the hook."

The couple went on down the stairs to the sublevel and faded out of sight. The reek of chlorine from the Jacuzzis must've been awful—personally, put me in a king-size bed and I'm happy. To each his own.

"Henry, let's go, let's go." We sprang off the barstool and put down the martinis, Frenchy carelessly dropping his, nearly cracking the stem of the glass.

We ran outside to the parking lot to hook up with Tommy, who looked uptight, and jittery. "What the hell took you guys so long to come out?" he screamed. "It's gettin late, and you're not gonna find any locksmiths open."

As we're running toward him, Frenchy was waving his arms to keep Tommy from attracting attention. "Cool it, man. Just now they went down to the spa. I had one of the housekeepers open the window in Nolan's room. One of you guys should be able to get in from up there. You only got an hour to get back here. Get going!"

Frenchy, too, was getting worked up, and I was afraid someone might get suspicious. "OK, take it easy. We'll take it from here. Go back in the bar, Frenchy."

Frenchy went back to the lounge and finished his cocktail, one of many to come.

It was nightfall, and Tommy crouched his six-foot-two heavyweight frame and knelt on his fours. "Henry, you're lighter. Put your feet on my shoulders, and I'll hoist you up as far as I can."

I stared up at the second-floor window, and it looked too high. I got dizzy and couldn't see too good in the dark. I had on a pair of brown wingtip shoes and was having trouble with my footing. "If you can get me close to the ledge over there, I can step on it and open the window."

"You're gonna tear my jacket with those shoes. Why didn't you wear something with rubber soles?"

Here I was about to break my neck, and Tommy was bitching about me tearing his damn black leather jacket, one he wore year-round. Three missteps and my heart was beating as fast as Buddy Rich's drums. Definitely not dressed for these acrobatics—I had on a tan turtleneck and a brown tweed sport jacket, and I was sweating as if I were in a sauna. Panting, I climbed into Nolan's room, and got a whiff of stuffiness.

A light on the night table was on, and Nolan's pants were lying folded on the bed. A ring with eighteen keys was hooked to the belt loops, and I unclasped it. I ran out through the door of the suite and down the stairway. I had ten minutes to hustle to a hardware store before it closed. Tommy waited in the parking lot, hiding behind the garbage bins.

No matter which street I took off the main road, everywhere was congested. I kept checking my watch, and I got more nervous by the second. I felt it in my bones I wasn't gonna make it.

Luck was with me. One hardware store was still open. I doubled-parked my car and ran inside. I didn't know which of the keys fit the Air France money storage locker, so I had the locksmith duplicate all of them. Out of eighteen, he couldn't cut three; he didn't have the blanks. I left in a hurry, just as a cop was writing me a parking ticket. Damn! I didn't need this. Clementine might start playing with Nolan's dick while in the Jacuzzi, and they might bolt to their room for a quick tumble in the hay. "NO, NO, Officer," I begged, "please cut me some slack. I gotta get home 'cause my six-year-old is alone by herself."

"Sorry, I already started writing it. Next time, don't double-park."

4

I was tight on time, and it took this asshole fifteen minutes to hand me the darn ticket. Now I had to tear ass like a bat out of hell, and it got me crazy. Fifteen minutes of wild driving, my face sweaty, I pulled into the Jade East parking lot. I screeched to a halt and gave Tommy the bad news.

"What do you mean, you couldn't make three of the keys?" Tommy nagged in his nasal, high-pitch twang. He was big and rough and tough, but his voice sounded like Frankie Valli's.

I turned up my palms to make a point. "What was I gonna do? Ram a gun to the guy's head? He didn't have the blanks. We just gotta hope one of these is the right key." Tommy was thick skulled and could be annoying. I lit a cigarette. "Help me up there and lemme get Nolan's keys where they belong. I'm praying he's still down at the spa."

Tommy let his arms drop to his sides and shook his head as if it were my fault. "With our luck, one of the three missing keys is gonna be the one to the money room. Why didn't you try another locksmith?"

"It's six o'clock on a Saturday night," I yelled, tapping my Rolex. "Where the fuck was I gonna find another locksmith this late? Man, think positive. Go to church tomorrow and say a novena, and maybe one of the keys will be the right one." Tommy only went into a church to rob the donation box. He was something; if he could, he'd steal the nuts from a bull. I stuck a cigarette between my lips and rushed him on. "C'mon, c'mon, lift me up. Let's get this over with."

I strung the key ring on Nolan's belt loop and got the hell out of the room. Tommy and I drove to The Bamboo Lounge, a hangout on Rockaway Parkway, and by now Frenchy was soaking in liquor. The bar was noisy and packed with the usual characters—bookies, loan sharks, drug dealers, alcoholic airport cargo handlers, and foxed-up divorcés looking to hook the big fish. A tent of smoke hung in the air, so foggy it could've choked King Kong. I handed Frenchy the set of keys for him to test the next morning, and hoped one might work.

"Let's hope one does the trick," Tommy moaned.

"Eh, c'mon Tommy. You gotta have the right attitude. Right, Henry?" Frenchy egged on, his speech slurred. With his irking habit, he slapped me on the back and called out to the bartender. "Mickey, what kind of service you got in this joint? C'mon, bring us a few rounds." Frenchy coiled his forearm around Tommy's neck—one the thickness of a tree trunk—and in a lighthearted way said, "Tommy, you have to take what's handed to you the way I do. You ever see me serious? I take life lightly because nobody can change *intestiny*." We didn't understand what he meant; maybe he wanted to say *destiny*.

The following Monday, I drove to see Frenchy at his Air France office, a cluttered cubicle with empty cans of Schlitz all over the place and smelling as if it were a brewery. I had been wishing for one of those keys to do the job, and I was so tense it must've been written on my face.

At Kennedy Airport, Air France operated from the Air Cargo Center, the largest in the world, and the night foreman was none other than Robert "Frenchy" McMahon. Frenchy had a college education and spoke intelligently—when he had to. As far as vices, he had them all. And talk about gambling—he was worse than a junkie.

The instant Frenchy and I locked eyes, he flashed a big grin.

"Guess we got lucky, eh? *Please* say one of those keys is the right one," I said.

Frenchy, tall and stocky, cuffed me on the back. He hugged my shoulders and laughed like a hyena. "Oh, yeah. Yes, yes, yes, we got lucky, all right." We giggled, and my anxiety loosened.

Frenchy rubbed his palms together. "Henry, all we gotta do is hang in for a good size shipment of dough." Frenchy got into a boxing stance and punched my biceps. He looked around to see if someone was watching and pulled me into him. "I want you to tell Jimmy Burke this is the start of what's to come. You hear? We're gonna be partners for life, pal, 'cause it's impossible to get caught." Frenchy hit my arm again.

I threw my cigarette butt on the ground and snuffed it under the toe of my shoe. "When are we gonna do the job?"

Frenchy placed his hand on my shoulder and said what I wanted to hear. "Could be as early as next week, Henry, baby. Make sure you guys are ready when I give you the word." Frenchy scoured the right pocket of his trousers and fished out the magic key. He dangled it six inches from my face and warned, "*Don't* lose it. OK?" And Frenchy smacked the key into my palm. "Let me get back to work. I'll get ahold of you guys the minute a load of cash lands here, one big enough for all of us to sink our teeth into."

Six days passed, and on the evening of April 8, 1967, a Saturday, the time for the sortie rang. At 11:40, Tommy and I got out of our car and eased the doors shut. We scanned the near-empty parking lots around us and started on foot in the direction of the Air France cargo bay, a warm breeze heating my cheeks.

"Henry, you took your gun out of the glove box?" Tommy asked.

"Yeah, yeah. I shoved it in my back pocket. I don't have to ask, but I'm sure you're carrying your two." He and I trekked with fast strides, our faces beaming straight ahead. "Let's have an understanding, OK? The guns are just for looks in case somebody gets in the way, but we're not using guns to shoot nobody. If somebody sees us, we use our legs to run with, not our guns. And I mean it, Tommy. No shooting!"

"All right, don't give me a sermon."

I stopped. "I'm telling you, if you shoot anybody, expect a bullet in your head *from me*."

We had left our car—a Chevrolet Impala rented under a bogus name—in the parking field next to the Lufthansa air cargo terminal, and we were striding toward the Air France loading dock.

Frenchy and I had agreed on a cue. If he could bait the guard to leave the Air France hangar, Frenchy would leave a note taped to the glass door of his office with the message "Back in Two Hours."

We raced up the freight ramp, and Tommy was out of wind. I was lugging a large suitcase, and I saw a white sheet of paper pinned on the door of Frenchy's pigpen. "OK, Frenchy took the security guard to The Bamboo Lounge."

The area was sixty feet wide with a gray, antiskid cement floor, and lighted with day-bright fixtures. Fifteen to twenty people were hanging around, employees in Air France uniforms and passengers hunting for lost luggage.

We shuffled nonchalantly up to the cinder-block safe room, and nobody stopped us. "OK, Tommy, hold your cool." Peering over my shoulder, I wiggled the key into the lock tumbler, turned it clockwise two circles, and pushed open the green steel door. I peeked inside. Darkness. Mustiness stung my nostrils. We pulled penlights out of our pockets and soft-stepped into the room. The yellow cones of light beams flashed out eight white bags tied with red tags, just as Frenchy had said. They lay on the floor against a wall with mountains of parcels. In each sack was a carton packet of $60,000 bundles. Three feet or so to the left of the bags was a two-foot-square box full of gleaming jewelry and gems.

Tommy pinched his cheeks. "I must be dreaming." He gazed at the booty and poked me. "C'mon, hurry. Open the suitcase."

Hyper and confused, I grumbled, "Shit, man, I hope all this stuff fits." I was born with dyslexia, a wall of mental blocks, and it screwed up my thought process. I couldn't figure out how much space I needed to pack so much money in small bills. So I had only brought one suitcase.

"What were you thinking?"

"Don't worry, I'll squeeze it all in. I'll get it all in." I got into a frenzy stuffing the white bags into the valise, Tommy foaming at the mouth.

Suddenly, music blared from speakers in the ceiling of the hangar. It jolted us, and we upped on our feet.

"What's that?" Tommy blurted out, wide-eyed and spooked. He went for one of the pearl-handle .38 Colt Magnums in his waistband.

I saw Tommy's reflex and gritted my teeth. "Take your hand off your gun. We're not gonna be pulling out heat."

We stood paralyzed for two to three seconds.

"I don't see nobody," I said in a hush. "Wait, don't move." I tiptoed, stuck my neck out the door, and heard footsteps in the distance on the far end of the hangar. My breathing restarted, and Tommy let out a puff of air, oily perspiration bubbling on his forehead.

"I think some joker piped in the radio through the PA system," I said. "Let's get the hell out of here."

We came out of the doorway of the money room, and I, cool as a dozing lion, locked the door. We bopped to the loading platform and bolted down the six steps to the parking lot level, the bulging suitcase swinging at the end of my arm.

Tommy swiveled his head, looked behind him at the terminal, Air France Cargo Building-86, and huffed, "I wonder who the son-of-a-bitch is that's blasting the goddamn radio. Scared the shit out of me. Damn it, my heart can't stop pounding."

"You scare too easily, man. Just make believe we're tourists trying to find our luggage."

Pulses still racing, we trotted across the parking field to where the Impala stood. I didn't know how much money we grabbed, but judging by the weight of the loot, we must've cleaned out the airline's pockets of a lot of cash and a box full of gems and gold.

"All right, all right. Thank you, Air France, baaai-by," Tommy sing-sang, pumping his fist in the air.

"Tommy, shut the hell up. You don't know who could be watching us. What're you, a moron? You're a real *test'e minghia*. Keep goin' and stop acting like an ass-less asshole."

Twice a week, Air France transported US currency from Europe, dollars American travelers exchanged for French francs. Until the armored car company picked up the cash, the brainless freight handlers stored it in a room not far from the shipping ramp. Save for the steel door, there were no safeguards or alarms. Worse yet, the area was *not* off-limits to the public, and believe it or not, those dumb fucks at Air France allowed commuters to freely roam the area to search for missing baggage.

The Passover holiday lasted through the weekend. The earliest the armored car company could've come for the shipment of money was the following Monday afternoon. It meant nobody would know the sacks were gone before then, and it'd be an impossibility to pinpoint when we had clipped them. And if the dockhands had seen strange faces, recalling the incident two days later would've been hazy—a perfect combination of coincidences.

While jogging to our getaway car, we reached the next hangar, the Lufthansa cargo terminal, the yellow sign stretching across the top of the building, its high walls silvery from the full moon. Three hundred feet to go, and we'd be in the clear—the rock music echoing from the cave-like Air France warehouse. *C'mon baby light my fire . . .*

9

I loved to wear classy outfits. I was all spiffed up, as usual, in a light gray suit and a maroon shirt, and nobody would've taken me for a stickup man. Tommy was another story. "Lemme ask you, Tommy. Why didn't you dress in threads that don't make you look as if you just got out of the can?" I shook my head in disgust. "With that leather jacket and black shirt, you remind me of those Puerto Rican hoods from the South Bronx."

Tommy, a thug with more bad habits than a chimpanzee, put on a humiliated face. He bent forward, as if to check out his clothes, and snapped, "What're you talkin' about? This is expensive stuff, man. And it's not like we went to a wedding. We went to rob an airline. So what's the big deal?"

"As I said, you could pass for a bum who don't belong here. Right now, forget about it. Keep goin' 'til we get to the car. Take my word for it, you're a spitting image of a parolee who just got out of jail." I passed a hand over my suit and said, "You have to dress for the occasion and look respectable. Know what I mean?"

"Ouh! Stop breaking my balls," Tommy griped, wheezing from the fast trot. He sucked on his teeth and unlocked the driver's door of the Impala. I threw the brown luggage in the trunk, and we drove toward Boundary Road for the northbound lanes of the Van Wyck Expressway.

Driving under the fifty-five mph speed limit, Tommy shifted his eyes from the lighted road ahead to the rearview mirror; no flashing emergency lights, no one chasing us. Air France was under ether as to what had happened—its largest rip-off ever.

We got to Ozone Park, and Tommy ditched the rented Chevy on a dark street. We walked east two blocks to his girlfriend's apartment, a messy two-room chicken coop. Swaggering and feeling rich, we marveled at what we'd done. Incredibly, we had made off with the biggest cash theft to date without waving a pistol. And although I felt good, a bad sensation hit my gut. We weren't strangers to the NYPD and the Port Authority. And considering the odds against Tommy and me—both with a mere seventh-grade education—was it possible for a pair of schmucks to steal so much money and not get caught?

What if a closed-circuit camera was outside the storage vault? And if so, it was likely Frenchy didn't know it, or else he would've warned us about it.

It'd gnaw on my stomach for the next month.

2

Tommy and I, still wound up over the Air France mission, had to catch up with the skipper of our crew, Jimmy Burke, a talented earner. Everybody knew him as "the Gent." By now, it was past midnight, and we had a one o'clock meeting with Jimmy at a Manhattan comedy club, The Improv, on the corner of West 44th Street and Ninth Avenue. Jimmy must've been counting the minutes, if not the seconds, to find out how the Air France job had turned out.

Two floors above The Improv, Jimmy leased an apartment, an adult playpen. We hustled up the stairs, and Tommy knocked on the door. I heard the clanking of the safety chain and the unclamping of the three dead bolts.

From the other side of the door Jimmy's voice, low and curt, asked, "Who is it?"

"It's Henry and Tommy, Jimmy."

I'm sure Jimmy had recognized Tommy's preadolescent pitch; otherwise he wouldn't have unlocked the door, especially at one o'clock in the morning. He called us his surrogate sons, and I didn't understand what he meant. I thought surrogate had to do with sugar.

"What the hell took you guys so long?" Jimmy complained, swirling the ice in his bourbon. "Jesus, all you had to do was pick up a few bags of money." He glanced at the suitcase I'd set on the rug. Ages ago it had been burgundy, but the dust and dirt lightened it to a shade of gray. Jimmy couldn't stop eyeing the suitcase, and I saw him lick his chops.

"Hard to believe you two bums actually did it," he said.

Jimmy, an Irishman, tall and stocky with blue eyes and dense black hair, had known me since my twelfth birthday, and Tommy from the time he was five years old. The Gent went way back with the DeSimone family. Tommy's older sister had been Jimmy's girlfriend for twenty years. She was fifteen when they started dating. Talk about robbing the cradle. Then again, the Gent robbed anybody and anything. And because we practically grew up with him, he was sort of a father figure to us—though the only subject Jimmy could teach us was crime, mapping out the road of our lives.

That night, even though we made a hell of a score, Jimmy seemed pushy. I could tell he'd had a few shots of liquor and didn't pay mind to his *always* demanding more. "Jimmy, we had to wait until the night guard took his meal break." I slipped a pack of Marlboros from my shirt pocket and lit a cancer stick. "Plus, we had to wait 'til Frenchy took the guard to The Bamboo Lounge."

A man who had no time for elementary talk, the Gent wiggled his fingertips as if he were sharpening them to handle an item of preciousness. "OK, let's count the dough and see how much we got here."

Jimmy, Tommy, and I stacked six-inch piles of cash on the dining room table. We sorted out 164 heaps of twenties, fifties, and hundred dollar bills. The tallying took an hour; when we finished, we clapped hands, and hugged one another like three little kids in a sandbox.

"Wow! Four hundred and eighty grand, and we probably got, oh, . . . I'd say, about three hundred thousand in jewels and stones." I was howling, my smirk growing wide into an open clam. It was by far the our biggest score yet. And to the best of our knowledge, none of the other crews, even the ones running with the big dogs, ever had so much meat to bite into.

Tommy was in the clouds. "Not bad, eh . . . not bad."

Jimmy smacked the tabletop and let himself fall back onto the sofa. "Man, I gotta hand it to you. You've done real good. Real good! You guys got a big future ahead."

I looked straight at the Gent. "By the way, Jimmy, Frenchy wants you to know this is just the beginning." I raised my index finger. "He's got one condition. Should he get pinched, he's gonna want your help."

Jimmy gulped the bourbon, his eyeballs glassy. "Of course, of course! If something goes wrong, I'll do what I can," he promised. "And if I can't, I'll make sure Big Paulie does. Paulie's got a judge in his pocket in every courtroom from Maine to Florida."

"Big Paulie," as he was known, was Paul Vario, one of the Lucchese crime family crew chiefs, a *capo regime*. He made sure the Burke squadron was shielded from independent wiseguys who'd try to move in on us—an everyday happening in the Italian Mafia. And if I had a beef with somebody, I'd go to Paulie. He'd represent me at a "sit-down" with the other side, and Paulie always won at sit-downs.

We stood around the loot and gazed goofily at the size of the Air France haul, eyes twinkling with greed. When the hot flashes started cooling, Jimmy took charge. "I'll give Paulie his cut, about a hundred and fifty grand." Whenever we scored, Jimmy had to pay tribute to Paulie.

Jimmy flipped through one of the hundred dollar stacks as if it were a poker deck. "I'll stash the money at a safe house. When you two want your end, lemme know, and I'll get it to you. Right now, none of us should be holding it. If the Feds look us up and find all this cash, they'll pin this Air France lark on us before you can count to three." Tommy glanced at me.

"I'm fine with that."

Jimmy sandwiched my cheeks with his palms and kissed me on the forehead. He did the same with Tommy, and the Gent grinned, reminding me of a dog with a big bone. Jimmy shredded the packets the cash bundles were wrapped in and repacked the money in a black acrylic garment bag. "I'm gonna get going. I'll take the money and the jewelry to where nobody can get to it. How much youse want in the meantime?"

"How much can you get by with for now?" Tommy asked me.

I counted in my head. "Fifteen grand will do, *for now*."

"Yeah, give me fifteen, too," Tommy said. "It'll hold me a while."

Jimmy tossed six rubber-banded five-thousand-dollar bricks in my suitcase and zipped up his garment bag. "There's thirty grand. Lemme know when you need more. Oh, another thing," and he jerked his forehead toward the fireplace. "Start a fire in there, and burn these torn wrappers and cartons. We don't want this stuff here with Air France stamped all over it."

"OK, but first we're goin' downstairs to The Improv and get a quick bite. I'm starved. Oh, before you forget, give me the key to the apartment."

At my mention of food, Tommy patted his stomach. "I *am* starved. Could also go for a beer or two."

Jimmy flopped his forefinger like a wiper blade. "Ah, ah, ah. You're gonna do it *now* before you start drinking. Understand?"

He knew how Tommy and I could easily stray and forget to button up the little details.

The evidence was burned to ashes; Tommy and I walked downstairs to The Improv just in time for Rodney Dangerfield's final set of his routine. Dangerfield was soaring to stardom and often performed at this club, the launching stage of many celebrity comics: George Carlin, Richard Pryor, Joan Rivers, Jay Leno, Bill Cosby. The Improv was the oldest and most renowned in Manhattan, and that night, before a full house, Rodney Dangerfield was on a hot roll. Garbed in his calling card—the black suit, white shirt, and red tie—he was at the end of his closing jokes. The spectators' laughter quieted, and the comic, as if he had a nervous condition, tugged at the tie and jiggled his neck to the side.

"I tell you, I get no respect." In his New York accent, Dangerfield streamed out jokes one after the other. "My son and the milkman spent last weekend together for a father-and-son reunion."

Applause rumbled, and cheers from the audience shrilled in the dimly lit nightclub, a medley of men's colognes and women's fragrances in the air.

While waiting for a table—no matter how crowded, there was always a table for the big tipper, Henry Hill—we stayed at the bar and dug our elbows into the black vinyl-padded edge. Tommy was checking out the crowd, starstruck tourists from bordering states and some loudmouthed ones from the Jersey shore.

The bartender served us red wine, and we drank on Air France. "*Salut.*" I chugged the vino and said to Tommy, "*Cent'ann,*" an Italian toast meaning a wish for a hundred years of good fortune. I had picked up Italian words here and there from my mother.

Tommy and I were hunched over the bar, and the maître d' tapped me on the shoulder. He resembled a penguin in a long tail, black tuxedo, and a snow-white shirt. "Gentlemen, your seating is ready," he said, sounding like a professor. "Leave your drinks here. The waiter will take them to your table. Please follow me."

We weaved through the tightly positioned tables, and after ten yards or so, the penguin stopped on his toes and swept the air with his hand as if he were unveiling the Mona Lisa. "Eh, Mr. DeSimone, Mr. Hill, will this do?"

"Yeah, these are good seats," I said automatically. I was busy eyeing female targets.

"Happy to be of service. Enjoy dinner."

I unfolded a one-inch wad of Franklins and Jacksons and pasted a twenty-dollar bill in the penguin's palm.

At the next table were two babes sipping cognac. They wore skin-tight evening gowns, sheathing their curvy bodies as tight as the casing of a sausage. The one inside the green dress was a blonde with honey-tone skin and had a short hairdo draping the sides of her cheeks, a WASPish look. Her girlfriend had flowing black hair and a tawny tanned face. The brunette's ebony irises reminded me of women with nickel-size eyes from Catania, Sicily, where my mother was born.

We were trying to figure out the menus—never mind that neither one of us could read words longer than three letters—when the blonde's napkin fell to the floor and landed near my feet. I swooped it up and handed it to her. Well, she couldn't stop thanking me. I mean, she carried on to the point that it was an embarrassment. The dark-haired broad also complimented my manners and came right out with, "We'd love to buy you handsome boys a drink."

The blonde checked us out, too. "I'm Alana, and this is Roseanne." Alana thrust her arm at me, hand bent down, her perfumed wrist wound in bracelets, jingling louder than chimes in the wind.

I was flattered. I stood, and tilting my head forward, gently grasped Alana's velvety fingers. "Pleased to meet *you*. I'm Henry Hill."

Tommy got up and clumsily knocked his chair into the table behind him. Humiliated and turning red, he said to the people sitting there, "Eh, sorry . . . sorry."

I'd never seen him get red in the face. His dusky coloring made him seem as if he had a year-round tan. Tommy could joke about this and that, and here he was in front of these beauties fumbling and stammering. "My . . . eh, my name's Tommy." That aside, his towering height, the combination of wavy, black hair, and square jaw, nailed the template of a Hollywood star from the 1940s. He reminded me of Errol Flynn.

"Oh, nice to know you, Tommy," Roseanne said with phoniness. I had pegged her for a Sicilian.

I shifted my eyes to Tommy. "Tommy, this really is our lucky night."

Alana put up her arm and waved at the waiter.

"Yes, madam."

"Give these fellows whatever they're drinking."

His hands behind his back, looking like an English butler, the waiter bent over and asked in a low voice, "What will it be, sir?"

"We'll have some red wop." I opened two fingers and added, "Oh, and we also want two bottles of Dom Perignon." And the illiterate me pronounced it *Don Perig-nin*.

"Red wop, and Don what, sir?" The butler's eyebrows rose, and his forehead creased.

Covering her mouth with a hand to squelch a cackle, Roseanne rescued me. "The gentleman wants red wine and Dom Perignon." Of Italian descent, she understood the meaning of the slang wop. Originally, it stood for "With Out Papers." Illegal European immigrants at Ellis Island were classified "undocumented." And because Italians were the most common immigrants sneaking into the country, the mostly Irish officials slandered them as wops. Then, little by little, everybody started calling cheap burgundy wine red wop.

"Yeah, yeah. That's what I meant. Red wine. And don't forget the French champagne," I said to the waiter. I gave Tommy the eye. "Tonight, we might as well have everything French."

We were all warming up to one another, and the four of us joined our tables together for coziness. Before I could count to three, champagne and appetizers cluttered the red tablecloth: jumbo shrimp cocktails, lobster salads, cubes of sautéed Chilean sea bass, and whatever else Aldo could truck out of the kitchen. Tommy and I tapped more wine, and in no time, we got into friendly hugging, wooing, and cheek kissing with Alana and Roseanne. Too excited to end the party, we talked them into staying upstairs at Jimmy's pad for a while. We were pickled in alcohol, and it was a head-spinning climb up the steep stairway two floors above The Improv.

Roseanne and Tommy scurried to one of the bedrooms as quickly as two squirrels chasing each other. I was hot to get into a tumble with Alana on the convertible couch in the den. The woman was making believe she wasn't a loose floozy, but as I started massaging her neck, she gave in.

Having been awake for twenty hours, plus the wine, the champagne, the cognac, the partying, *and* burglarizing Air France, I was feeling sleepy, but I still bragged. "I'm really good with my hands. Let's go in the den and sit on the couch." By now, her fragrance had raised my warhead onto the launch pad.

All of a sudden, Alana slipped into drowsiness and kitten-like talk. "Oh, Henry, your . . . fingers feel so . . . strong. You're . . . making me feel so . . . relaxed."

I loved it!

The romp under the sheets was short; we were exhausted. I could no longer hear rustling from Tommy's room. He had probably fallen out, and I was just as cooked—my eyes couldn't stay open. Not a good thing with two strange broads in the apartment.

3

It was nine o'clock in the morning. In blue plaid briefs, scratching his testicles, Tommy hobbled his body—the frame of a hulk—out of the bedroom, on his way to the bathroom.

"Damn. Henry, wake up. We left the suitcase out on . . ." He opened the lid and, "Holy shit." Tommy banged his sledgehammer-like fist on the tabletop. "Them fuckin' rat bastard, thieving whores. I'll turn the whole fuckin' world upside down 'til I get my hands on those two miserable, stinkin' bitches."

Tommy's rant got me to my feet. The air in the cramped apartment was stale with stenches of body odors and a tang of sex. Eyelids drooping, I stood by the doorway of the den in my underwear and a wife beater. I rubbed my eyes to shake the cobwebs. "Why the hell are you screamin'?"

"Why?! Those two sluts cleaned us out. They took every fuckin' dime out of the suitcase. Everything! Everything! Wait 'til I get my hands on those *puttane*." Enraged as if he'd gone mad, Tommy thumped his fists on everything in his way.

I was puzzled, but once I understood, I cracked up laughing. Frankly, this was exactly the kind of fuckup that made Jimmy lose sleep.

Tommy, on the other hand, turned into a 250-pound beast, his eyes untamed resembling two chunks of coal. "Henry, is there somethin' wrong with you, or are you a shithead? I mean, what the hell is so funny? We got robbed, you understand, man?" He came up in my face. "Those two whores are as good as dead." His cheeks reddened hotter than hot pepper, and spit spewed from his mouth. "That . . . that black-haired bimbo is the real bitch. I bet it was her idea to rake us."

We should've known they weren't singles with careers in advertising. Deep in my gut, I had a feeling Alana and Roseanne were hookers. And our clue should've been their advances and overkill praise for picking up the napkin.

Giggling, I plopped on the velour sofa and said, "Oh, c'mon, Tommy, it's no big deal." I shrugged off his craziness. "Let it be a lesson not to trust nobody. It's just money, Tommy. Just money." He was taking it so seriously. "Tommy, Frenchy came through with Air France, and you know what? He'll line up heist after heist. There's gonna be an Air France job every week. See how simple it was?" I yawned and garbled out. "Ahhh . . . for all we know, next week we could be hitting Alitalia, Air Lingus, KLM, or any of those European airlines with their noses in the air and fingers up their asses."

I opened the refrigerator, an antique that reminded me of an old-fashioned icebox, and grabbed a Rheingold. With a rusty can opener I punctured two triangular holes on the top of the can. "Stop gettin' all worked up over a lousy thirty grand, Tommy. Money will be comin' in from left and right." I chugged half the beer.

Tommy, always a hothead, clenched his teeth. "I can't understand how you can make light of it. Thirty thousand bucks, man. They swiped thirty fuckin' grand!" He bit his fingers and brayed, "Ohhh. I hope when those *troias* get their next period, they bleed for twenty years. Hurry up and get dressed. Let's go find them." Tommy punched the wall, and his knuckles put a paw print in the plaster.

"Shit, look what you did. Jimmy's gonna go nuts when he sees this."

"Right now, I ain't thinkin' about Jimmy. I wanna go find those two hustling streetwalkers. I can't stand a thieving whore."

I slapped my knee and couldn't believe he was such a stubborn guinea. "Get real. Where the hell are we gonna start looking? You think they're sittin' downstairs at The Improv having brunch?" I reached for a pack of cigarettes on the lamp table. "Or maybe they're up the block at Sardi's sipping mimosas, waiting for us to join them. Get over it. They're long gone. They're probably on the moon by now."

Two days went by, and we forgot Alana, Roseanne, and the $30,000. We packed up our wives, children, and girlfriends, and we were on a flight to Las Vegas for a week of relaxation. For our families, we reserved two suites on the twenty-second story of the Flamingo Hotel and Casino, and two double rooms on the nineteenth floor for the mistresses. I loved the bright neon lights of Las Vegas Boulevard and wouldn't think of staying at the joints off The Strip.

Despite losing $20,000 playing craps, everyone had a great time, except I felt guilty. I had spent the good part of the vacation with my girl-friend, coddling her with gifts and gambling chips that she squandered in the lifetime of a mosquito. I had also broken a promise to my kids, who so badly wanted their daddy to sneak them inside the casino and drop just *one* quarter in a slot machine. Next time. To make up for my selfishness, when I'd get back home, I'd buy the old lady the new T-Bird they just came out with and get nice toys for the kids.

Back in our rooms, my wife finished packing, and the phone rang. "Hello."

"Henry, is that you?"

"Hey, Jimmy. Yeah, it's me. You're lucky you caught us. We're just leaving the Flamingo to catch a cab to McCarran Airport. What's up, pal?"

"There's a lot of heat on Frenchy. I'm afraid he's about to break down. The cops didn't waste any time going straight to him for the Air France hit."

A rush of heat ran to my head. "Uh . . . Frenchy is tough, Jimmy. He . . . he won't give into the pressure. No way."

"I sure hope not, kid."

4

The telephone rang in my bedroom, a grub filled with fancy shit and done up in a bordello style. My vision blurred; I looked at the digital clock: 7:20 in the morning. Knowing I slept late, nobody called me early in the morning unless there was an emergency.

"Hello," I answered faintly, and my better half curled up under the blanket. The light-headedness from the previous night's liquor spun the room, and I felt I was on a carnival carousel. I lifted the receiver, my fingers buttery, and it fell to the floor. I hoisted it up by the cord and pressed it to my left ear, a headache pounding.

"Hello, Henry, it's Jimmy. Wake up and get to my place fast."

"I got home at four o'clock last night on a red-eye from Vegas. What's so important for you to call so early?" I bitched, coughing.

"It's almost 7:30. So get going. By the way, on your way in, go and get Tommy."

"What's so darn important, Jimmy?"

"Frenchy. That's what's important. This is all I'm tellin' you. I don't wanna say nothin' on the phone. Hurry to my joint."

I crawled out of bed, yawning and staring aimlessly around the bedroom. The furnishings were tasteless with gold-colored trimmings, and my wife, Karen, had covered the walls with velour-like purple wallpaper. Worse yet, she bought a violet and yellow shag carpeting, all too shocking to the eye, especially with a hangover. Not even four hours back from Vegas, and I had to handle a problem—maybe a big one.

I gazed in the mirror, and seeing strands of gray in my sandy hair ruined the morning. My eyes, normally hazel, were a pair of pink marble balls. Too much fuckin' boozing. I threw on a mint green silk shirt, a beige worsted wool sport jacket, and a pair of brown pleated slacks.

The Easter holidays and the Air France celebrations had ended, and it was time for Burke & Company to jump-start business. But I was dying to find out what the hell would make Jimmy call and get me down to his joint, Robert's Lounge, so damn early.

Jimmy Burke, Tommy DeSimone, and I were outlaws. Our livelihood was the product of crime after crime. The thought of earning an honest living was far from our minds—we didn't know how. Cargo truck hijackings, selling untaxed liquor and cigarettes, loan-sharking, bookmaking, gambling, and manipulating union contracts were the roots of our income.

The Robert's Lounge gang, as the cops labeled us, was a rather odd bunch. We were a posse of felons guided by self-imposed rules. We didn't rob the poor, the old, or the weak. We cheated the government, defrauded multibillion-dollar corporations, high-interest credit card companies, banks, and those price-gouging airlines. According to Jimmy, wealthy conglomerates took advantage of naive consumers, and he saw justification in stealing from "that horde of crooks." This was the Gospel he taught us, and I for one believed Jimmy "the Gent" Burke was a model citizen.

I was crafty at rigging sports betting and screwing hoodwinked bookmakers. They were nothing but backstabbers anyway. And Tommy swindled loan sharks, who chose violence to collect from strapped borrowers. Many of the shylocks had the balls to charge five points a week.

That morning, Tommy and I drove to Jimmy's seedy bar, a front for the Gent's sources of illegal revenue. We slid out of my '63 maroon Chevy Impala Super Sport and moseyed into the shadows of Robert's Lounge—a stink of stale beer souring the air.

"How you doin', Don?" I said to Jimmy's bartender.

"Hey, Henry, Tommy. What's new? How was Vegas?" he asked.

"We won big time, Don. Got back late last night. Is Jimmy here yet?"

"He's downstairs waiting for you."

We went down to the lower level, a basement set up for card games, loitering, planning "the swindle of the day," and general bullshitting. Jimmy also used this dungeon-like sublevel as a tomb. On one side was a bocce court, and beneath it, he had buried four or five bodies of the unfortunate who "had done him wrong."

An octagonal game table took up most of the cement slab floor, and a ten-foot bar was on the opposite wall. Jimmy was at the table reading numbers sheets, tallies his "runners" had taken in the night before. Skipping any greetings or pleasantries, he gaped absently at Tommy and me. "Sit down, will you."

We dragged out two chairs and sat with anxiety to hear the urgency of this early morning powwow. Jimmy seemed to sense our nervousness, but didn't lift his eyes from the numbers tapes. "You two had a good time in Las Vegas?"

I put on a fake smile. "Oh, yeah. We won a slew of money playing craps. A lot of money! Ain't that right, Tommy?"

"No doubt, no doubt. A lot of cash. Oh, yeah," Tommy said.

"I know you're full of shit, and who knows how much you really lost," Jimmy guessed. "But it don't matter to me. It's your money. Just make sure you keep telling yourselves you won a lot of cash, and let everybody know it. And make sure your wives keep the story straight. So when you spend some of the Air France pesos, and the cops start X-raying your assholes, you can brag you busted Vegas. Understand?"

"Oh yeah, we filled in the women on what to say. Right, Tommy?"

"Sure did."

"So what's the hurry to meet so freaking early?" I nodded at the small basement window and groused, "The sun ain't even up yet."

Tommy folded his arms, bracing for the worst. "Yeah, what's up, Jimmy?"

Jimmy stood, paced around the green felt-topped card table, and ruffled his hair, flakes of dandruff sprinkling on his shoulders. "They're all over Frenchy. FBI, Port Authority, DA's detectives, Air France private investigators. You name it."

I upped off the chair and turned up my hands. "So what? They can't pin anything on Frenchy. Nobody knows we had the key to the storage room. Frenchy's got nothin' to sweat over."

Jimmy clasped his roundish chin and bobbed his head. "I got a feeling he'll crack under pressure. I'm thinking of whacking him before he starts talking. He could rat us all out, and then it'd be too late."

Nausea came up in my throat. I put my hand on Jimmy's shoulder. "You don't gotta worry about Frenchy. He's been there before. He's a stand-up guy. Believe me!"

Jimmy shook his head. "I don't know . . . I don't know."

I patted Jimmy's biceps. "Here's what we'll do. I'll get word to Frenchy for him to meet Tommy and me at the Jade East. We'll get there ahead of time and hang out in the lounge. So if he's got a tail on him, it'll seem as if we just happened to run into each other."

Jimmy shrugged and chewed on his lips. "Then what?"

"We'll find out where his head is at, but I know Frenchy's no pushover."

A man of firm nerves, Jimmy stared squarely at me. "I hope you're right. Otherwise, I'd hate to do it, but I'd have to whack him." This hung there, Tommy and I peering into Jimmy's eyes to see how serious he was.

Overall, the three of us were heartless criminals with hair-trigger tempers. Tommy was a tough guy, and I didn't put nothing past him. Once, he went on a date with a black broad, and he had the balls to take her to a redneck bar. Some wiseass insulted him; he got into a fight and leveled everybody in the joint. That was Tommy. And me, though a certified sociopath, I was a nice guy who avoided hassles. My felonies, so far, amounted to a string of burglaries, bookmaking, and peddling swags—but never violence.

I rolled my eyes at Tommy. Should Jimmy go ahead with whacking Frenchy, Tommy would be only too glad to carry out the hit. He got pleasure from shooting people. A sick boy. Some people never leave home without their American Express. Tommy DeSimone never left home without his matched pair of revolvers. He had an obsession for guns.

5

Tommy and I went to the Jade East to hook up with Frenchy. The Air France investigators had put him under the hot lamp, and the heat was radiating too close to the Jimmy Burke tribe—especially on Tommy and me. Frenchy swore he had no idea what might've gone down with the robbery and who had done it. But cops and detectives from all corners of the planet were ratcheting up the pressure cooker on him.

We plopped on the barstools in the lounge of the Jade East. Halfway into our beer, Frenchy shuffled into the bar. He sat between us, and I saw a scared look in his blue eyes. Frenchy didn't seem to know where to begin. "Oh, man, you don't know what's been going on."

"OK, let's hear it," Tommy pushed on.

Frenchy held up his hand for the barmaid. "Lemme get a glass of wine."

The spicy brunette, ass wiggling, toddled to our side of the bar. "What will it be, my Frenchy?"

"Red wine. On second thought, make it a double scotch on the rocks."

It sounded as if Frenchy needed a stiff drink, and I joked, "It's that bad, eh?"

"The day after you guys left for Vegas, all hell broke loose." Frenchy looked around the bar. "Air France security was all over Mike Nolan. They figured he must've given the key to whoever broke into the vault." Again Frenchy scanned left and right, front and back, the fear of a trapped animal on his face. "Then they came to their senses. Nolan has no prior record of any kind, and he's too clean-cut."

Tommy seemed edgy. "So what's the bottom line? Where does it all stand now?"

Frenchy waggled his head. "The night guard—the one I'd dragged to The Bamboo Lounge—when they questioned him, he almost had a heart attack. And it's clear that the old man—who probably made his last payment to his undertaker and is ripe to be embalmed—is not going around robbing airlines."

Now *I'm* starting to get antsy. "OK, Frenchy, so where does it stand now?"

"Henry, I wish I knew. The heat is on me. The fuckin' detectives from the 113th haven't let up for one goddamn minute."

"You're shittin' in your pants over nothing, Frenchy." I dropped my hand on his shoulder. "Think it out. No matter what the cops say, they got nothin' on any one of us. Nothin'! If we keep our mouths shut and don't make asinine moves, we got absolutely nothin' to be afraid of. Let them think whatever they want. They can't prove shit."

Tommy nodded at me. "Yeah, Henry, we gotta keep our heads low. So don't even think about buying your wife that T-Bird. You're better off gettin' her a new pair of sneakers."

I took the last drag on my cigarette and finished the beer. "Tommy, you're right, but didn't *we* come back from Vegas with a lot of money?"

"I don't know about that."

We bought another round, drank up, and left the Jade East. On the way out, Tommy kept busting my chops. "Henry, don't buy that fuckin' car for your old lady. I got a bad feeling, man."

6

Henry Hill didn't know it, but Frenchy McMahon held a distinction: he was the only suspect in the Air France burglary. Lieutenant Brian O'Malley, a detective from The Loft, Sale, and Truck Squad, was dead set that McMahon must have been behind it. That afternoon, after his liquid lunch, McMahon resumed his shift at the Air France cargo terminal; the gray-suited O'Malley was waiting for him. The Loft, Sale, and Truck Squad was a special unit instituted in 1911. Its elite corps of sixty-four police officers probed high-stakes thefts, truck hijackings, safecrackings, and bank hold-ups. But the Air France heist was unprecedented; to O'Malley's chagrin, he didn't have a single lead.

"You know why I'm here, Mr. McMahon, don't you?" O'Malley began.

"I know why you're here." McMahon swiped his brow, straining to control the jitters. "Lieutenant, let's not play games. You can see that whoever did this got into the vault with a key. I *never* had a key. When I had to go into the money room, Mike Nolan or the night-shift watchman unlocked the deadbolt, let me in, waited 'til I finished what I had to do inside, and relocked the door."

Sitting in front of McMahon's desk, legs crossed, Lieutenant O'Malley shut his black notepad and gazed at him. "Sure, it's obvious the burglars got in with a key," O'Malley said. "And sure, everybody in this investigation knows you *didn't* have a key to the vault; but, hey, there's lots of ways how you could've helped out the perps." Unaccustomed to losing, O'Malley cocked his head to the side, and out of discomfort, it seemed, shifted from the right buttock to the left. He sighed wearily, knowing he couldn't verify his suppositions. "Who knows, you could've taken pictures of the lock barrel and had an expert cut a key."

McMahon was squirming. But as he sorted out his thoughts, he started to breathe easier. The notion of reproducing a key from photos of the lock might've been the detective's last-ditch bluff. Then, in a brightening moment, an indisputable circumstance slackened Frenchy McMahon's tension—the absence of proof. There were no concrete facts or signs he'd had a hand in robbing Air France. Period. Then, unexpectedly to O'Malley, McMahon reeled on the offensive. His cheeks heated to a red blush, and he pummeled his fist on the desk. He sprang to his feet. "You can make up whatever you want, my mick friend. I told you the truth, and unless you got anything to arrest me for, you'll have to leave my office, or I'm calling my lawyer."

McMahon understood his reputation as a thief; but he rationalized that less any circumstantial or material evidence, the district attorney couldn't mount a prosecution against him.

The lieutenant didn't answer, and with a nod that said, *I know and don't like your kind*, scowled at McMahon. So far, McMahon had neutralized O'Malley.

And for effect, palms firmly on his desk, McMahon leaned into it, and changed his mien to a deadpan stare. "Lieutenant, I got nothing to do with this," he stated, as if he truly believed it himself. "I repeat, I don't know anything about whatever happened here. You're barking up the wrong tree like a dumb dog. And *I know* you're not dumb." McMahon smirked and listed his head. "Maybe it was a ghost that got in there. Eh?"

"You're in no position to be funny, Mr. McMahon. I don't think you'll find it funny when we haul your ass out of here in handcuffs."

"And you're in no position to tell me not to be funny, because you don't have an inkling how this job was pulled off. So do me a favor and stop your useless threats. You're not talking to a schoolboy."

7

O'Malley slapped his notepad with his left hand and backpedaled toward the exit. He scratched his temple and seemed to ponder prolonging the inquiry, but opted to end it, slamming the door behind him.

McMahon opened the white utility cabinet next to his desk, whipped out a white towel, and dried his forehead of sweat. He groped in the bottom compartment for a bottle of J&B and guzzled a mouthful.

McMahon had survived six grueling days of sizzling by a legion of pushy detectives and pestering FBI agents, rising above Burke's wavering confidence in him. None of the investigators had the Air France robbers in their sights. And McMahon's mock comment to Lieutenant O'Malley, "Maybe a ghost got in there," though an absurdity, dangled with the jeering of a haunting specter.

The law enforcement agencies were not in doubt that Jimmy Burke and his gunmen, with McMahon's guiding hand, were the bandoleros who had ransacked the Air France high-value vault, not the supernatural. The mystery was how or who passed the key to the burglars. McMahon? Unlikely. He was a fitting suspect, but on paper the detectives' theory had holes and cracks. The investigators' gut feelings, though, tempted them to revisit their initial hunch: It had to have been Frenchy McMahon.

Could he have photographed the locking mechanism and given the picture to an expert to fabricate a key? This was science fiction. Port Authority interrogators had consulted three locksmiths, who flatly rejected it as undoable.

Barring a sensible explanation, the Air France burlap bags of money had simply vanished. Seemingly, the money disappeared into thin air, and penetrating into the vault might've been . . . well, who knew?

And how was it possible for the night guard not to have witnessed anybody sniffing around the terminal? This churned a curdling foreboding in the old watchman's innards. On the evening of the robbery, McMahon's friendly gesture to invite him for a drink at The Bamboo Lounge, he thought, might've been a ruse to lure him in leaving his post. Now it all made sense to the poor geezer; McMahon was the insider in cahoots with the burglars. And to preserve his job, and his health, he smothered his suspicions—and he'd drag them to his grave.

Mike Nolan, the sex-addicted supervisor, too, felt a queasiness, as if his date with Hill's sister, the enchanting Clementine, hadn't been random. It dawned on Nolan that he'd served as the patsy in a diabolical stunt. *Was Clementine really Hill's sister?* He had partied with her for three evenings before she disappeared. Nolan's reflections on those romps now brought out crystal-clear signs of the woman's falsities, vibes he hadn't discerned while under her inebriation. A thought bolted him. *Had he been the seducer? No, she seduced him. And, he recollected, her love making felt as though she were a programmed robot. Was she a call girl McMahon and Hill hired?*

In one of those escapades, Nolan was convinced, McMahon or the devilish Hill might've somehow stolen his keys to the money room. But how was this possible? His key ring had *never* been lost or missing.

However confounding this mishap was, he had been derelict and couldn't report it.

8

To me Jimmy Burke brought to mind Cary Grant. He spoke with charm and authority, and he was protective of those close to him. Aside from his ruthlessness—a trait he excused as the business side of him and shouldn't be taken personally—Jimmy stretched to great lengths to help one in need, if only to be admired and thought of as a wonderful guy. He could be confrontational, but in a smart way, though he paid everyone his due. It didn't matter who you were or what kind of reputation you might've had in the underworld. But that wasn't why we called him the Gent. He was a big tipper and gave gifts to friends and partners as if there were no tomorrow. Believe it or not, he'd tuck a hundred dollar bill in the wallet of a driver whose truck he'd be about to hijack.

Jimmy would say, "The way I see it, I'm taking the man's license so I know who he is and where he lives. The least I can do is to give the poor bastard a few bucks for his troubles so he can get a duplicate driver's license." And as strange as it sounds, this made sense. This is how he'd explain it: "Should the son-of-a-bitch give me up to the cops, knowing where to find him, I'd show him how miserable life could get when someone doesn't mind his own business and keeps his mouth shut. Know what I mean?"

When I was a kid, I got under the skin of the Lucchese *capo regime*, Paul "Big Paulie" Vario. Because I was half-Irish, I couldn't be *made* into Paul Vario's crime family. But for a slice of the profits, Paulie took me in as an associate and backed my mixed bags of thefts and cons. Jimmy, too, got in with the Lucchese clique and took advantage of the strength and connections of Vario's many rackets.

To ride on the Mafia Ferris wheel of schemes and scams, Jimmy and I simply needed Vario's approval. Once under his wing, Vario shielded us wiseguys from the district attorney's crooked detective squad and protected us from rival gangs, making the hijackings, robberies, gambling, and so forth a daily routine. At times, plots went haywire beyond Vario's control, and the cops and the Burke crew bumped heads. And because of those scrapes the NYPD, the FBI, the Port Authority, and the DA's robbery squad constantly had Jimmy and his cocky raiders in their crosshairs.

The Suite, a bar/restaurant on Queens Boulevard in Forest Hills, Queens, was twenty minutes from Manhattan, fifteen from Kennedy Airport, and twenty from Nassau County, Long Island. The owner, Joey Rossano, a wiseguy wanna-be, was a friend of mine. He was a horse gambler and womanizer, a way of life that had financially crippled him. He dug himself in a deep hole and got into a loan shark, Anthony "Fat Tony" Salerno. And when Joey's debts swelled to a head, the spill was as messy as a pimple full of pus.

Joey finally came to terms that he'd gotten his balls caught in the lion's mouth and sent me a Mayday call.

The minute I got Joey Rossano's distress call, though I didn't know what his problems were, I had a hunch and turned into a hound scenting blood. I rushed to see that *disgraziat*, one of those degenerates who's got every bad habit and doesn't change 'til he dies.

I'd timed it right. It was cocktail hour, and The Suite was crowded with crass, boozing drinkers. The noise was unbearable: clanking glasses and loudmouth rowdies. The odor of free bar food was in the air, as were grams and grams of cocaine dust. And of course, wherever there's free food, you'll find freeloading NYPD cops.

Joey saw me come in and called me over.

"What's wrong?" I asked.

We stood at the bar, and Joey tried to get into the knee-deep shit he'd gotten in without sounding he was on the balls of his ass.

"Henry, you wanna beer or coffee?"

"Yeah, I'll have a Guinness stout."

Joey threw up his hand and called out to the bartender. "Teddy, get us two bottles of Guinness." Joey opened a pack of cigarettes and let me take one.

The bartender poured my Guinness, and Joey vomited his woes. "Henry, I'm into these fuckin' blood-sucking shylocks for about eighteen grand, and this guy who's with Fat Tony Salerno . . . this guy, Sal the Shank. You know him?"

"Yeah, I know that prick. What about him?"

"Well, yesterday, he came here and put the arm on me. I don't know if he's bullshittin' or not, but he said Fat Tony wants me to pay off the whole eighteen thousand by this Friday." Joey drank a swill of his beer and owned up, "I ain't got that kind of money, Henry."

"Ouh!" I said groaning. "If Fat Tony wants you to close out the loan, and you don't pay him, Sal *will* whack you without thinkin' twice. Fat Tony is a crazy fuck, but Sal is not only crazy, he's also a *baccalà*, a moron."

I touched my temple with a finger to mean Sal was not too sane. "He's *stoonat*. Understand?"

"I know. What do I do?" Joey looked as scared as a five-year-old about to get a spanking. His jet-black hair started in a peak half an inch above his eyebrows, and he slicked it back with an oily cream as slimy as axle grease.

I guzzled two-thirds of the beer and gazed at Joey with sad eyes. "I hate to say it, but your only way out is for someone to take over this joint and work out something with the *shylocks*."

"I know, I know."

I stayed quiet a while, and I could feel Joey's nervousness. "Henry, what're you say? C'mon, tell me you're interested. I mean, this is a good place. I swear it makes money. My problem is . . . well, you know my problem. This year alone, I burned a hundred grand on the ponies. Then, you know, I've been running around with a few wild broads, and with them kind of women you can piss away money as if it's water. My wife's ready to leave me."

"You know what, Joey? She shouldn't leave you. She should throw you the fuck out on your ass." I stared at him the way you'd look at a lowlife. "You're a piece of shit," I added. The truth is, I wasn't any different.

Joey squeezed my forearm. "So, what're you say? I swear, you run this place the right way, and you can make a good living here. You can do it, Henry. You got more common sense than me. Besides, you have Paulie's muscle, and you'll probably wind up paying Salerno a third of what I owe him."

Joey slung his head back, eyes closed, put his palms together as if in prayer, and rocked them. "*Madonn*, I've been giving that fat bastard three points a week for the past year and a half." He held up three fingers and twisted his lips. "*Three* points a week, Henry. All the *vig* I paid him, I probably gave that fuck twice what he'd loaned me. That's why you can tell him to take a walk. And if Paulie is behind you, Salerno will have to settle for whatever you wanna give him. C'mon, Henry, help me out? I got nowhere else to turn. Please say you'll do it."

"I might . . . I might. Lemme think it over. All right?"

By June of 1967, Frenchy, Tommy, and I stopped sweating out the Air France heat. The FBI and the NYPD closed up shop and stopped snooping; I could poke my head out of the sand and invest my cut of the Air France loot. I twisted and finagled until I got ownership of The Suite. I negotiated the transfer of the lease from Rossano to me. I had to leave Joey on the liquor license as the owner of record—no way I could get one. The deal was simple. I had to pay him eleven grand and take over his obligations to Fat Tony Salerno—and as sure as shit I wasn't going to give Fat Tony a dime. And Joey was right; Paulie's strength was the key to sending the loan sharks running for the hills. After all, Salerno and his enforcer, Sal "The Shank," don't want an all-out war with the powerful Lucchese *capo regime* over Joey Rossano's measly eighteen thousand dollar loan. Know what I mean?

Paulie gave his blessings and called for a sit-down with Tony Salerno. Not surprisingly, Paulie won.

"*Fattà nah camminat,* Tony. *Capisci.*" Take a walk, the arbitrator said to Salerno. And Joey's loan was wiped out.

We walked out of the sit-down, and Paulie slapped me on the back. "Congratulations, kid. And lots of luck with the new joint. Now you gotta pay me two bills every Friday. Is it OK with you?"

OK or not OK, I'd have to fork over to Paulie two hundred bucks a week as "consulting" fees. This is how it worked.

In no time, I turned The Suite into a roost of Mafia circles. The restaurant played host to shylocks, prostitutes, and other undesirables. The 255-seat supper club soon became the nerve center and boardroom of our rackets.

The unholy trinity of Jimmy Burke, Henry Hill, and Paul Vario bonded, and we carried on our lives of crime as if we were running an expanding enterprise. Sacks of cash started flowing in from all angles, making it easy for Jimmy and me to get into a lifestyle of wild spending and costly vices—so costly you eventually wind up with your back against the wall—as Joey Rossano found out. And if anybody bothered us, Paulie was there to handle the problem. Paul Vario, a multimillionaire with income topping thirty-five grand a day, to fuck the IRS and anybody else who snooped into his affairs, on paper did not hold any assets. None! Nor did he have a telephone in his home; an underworld figure who spoke on the phone, he believed, was easy prey for the cops.

At last, I was getting into a quasi-normal schedule, and life was good. My struggle for money was over; I wasn't under indictment, no pending cases were weighing on me, and none of the blue boys were after me for anything. It felt as if it were a dream—too good to be true. Somehow, it didn't feel right.

9

By 1970, Henry Hill's restaurant was a second home to union administrators whose reputations were, in some way or other, under scrutiny. The president of Local 71, Casey Rosado, practically lived at The Suite. The name of his amalgamation was The Waiters and Commissary Workers at Kennedy Airport.

Rosado phoned Burke and spoke with him about a situation.

"Jimmy, remember Johnnie Ciaccio, the guy with the restaurant down in Tampa?"

"Yeah, I think I do."

"We gotta go see him."

"Does it have to do with money he owes you?" Burke asked in a cadence that said, *I already know the scoop.*

"Yeah, but I don't foresee any hassles with Ciaccio. That goddamn *disgraziat!* I'm gonna need two or three guys to go with me."

"You got it, Casey."

Rosado had an understanding with Burke, a reciprocal pact. Rosado strong-armed the laborers of his union for tips and information on cargo shipments of value that, in turn, Burke's crew hijacked. As a rule, trading favors is the glue of a well-founded association. On occasions when Casey Rosado needed Burke's mob troops to bridle the troublemakers at

Local 71 or to intimidate into surrender employers of the union members, Burke flexed his muscle and fought for Rosado.

10

"Henry, I gotta talk to you."

I was at the bar in The Suite. I had a mug of beer between my hands, my trademark, I turned toward the door, and there was the Gent. "Hey, Jimmy. How you doing?" I hollered out. He came over and sat on a stool next to mine.

"Have a cold one with me." I signaled with two fingers for the bartender to lay out the chilled steins.

Jimmy tossed a ten-dollar bill on the bar. "Listen Henry, we have to do Casey a small favor."

"Here we go again." Whenever somebody mentioned Casey Rosado's name, trouble was on the way.

"Nah, nah, nothing that's gonna be a hassle. We have to go to Tampa. First class. All expenses paid by his union. We'll do what we gotta do and then relax over the weekend on a beach. Can't wait to get out of this shitty snow."

I dragged on a Marlboro. "I don't know. Casey is a jinx, a *scaronnia*. Remember when . . ."

Jimmy fanned his hand. "Oh, forget the past. You're always living in the goddamn past."

"And when are we supposed to go?"

"This afternoon," Jimmy answered, his eyes slanted, knowing I wasn't gonna like the short notice.

"This afternoon!" I threw up my hands. "I can't drop everything and go. I got a million things to deal with. I mean, I'm running a restaurant, Jimmy."

"I would've had Tommy go with me, if that mammalook hadn't gotten arrested yesterday. I told him not to get involved in that fuckin' hijacking. So get yourself ready. It'll be fun. Casey is already down there gettin' a head start on his suntan. I'll give him a call and have him send his driver to pick us up at Robert's Lounge, say, at . . ." Jimmy slid up his cuff and peered at his watch. "Around one o'clock. All right?"

Little by little, I found out why we were going to Florida.

Jimmy and I got our luggage off the carousel in the Tampa Airport terminal and spotted Rosado.

"Hey, there's Casey," Jimmy hollered, his arm up and waving for Rosado to see us.

The squatty Rosado, a man you could easily buy with flattery, saw us. "Hey, Jimmy, Henry. Over here." We strutted toward one another, dropped our luggage, and shook hands. He kissed Jimmy on the cheeks, then me—the old, queer Mafia greeting. Eh, I couldn't stand it. I could never understand those Italian men, who were supposed to be so macho, kissing each other.

Jimmy took off his camel-tan coat and draped it over his left arm. "We made it. A bit of a rough flight. Bumps and shaking, but we're here. Thank God." Jimmy looked up to the Lord in humbleness. He was a believer in God—when he was in trouble.

I couldn't wait to peel off my three-quarter-length overcoat. My neck and armpits felt sticky. The moment we'd gotten off the plane, I smelled warm humidity as if I were in a room that's been shut tight for a whole summer. "Jesus, we're not even out of the air-conditioning, and it's hot as hell."

Clad in white shorts, sandals, and a flowery, red Hawaiian shirt, the heavyset Rosado remarked, "What did you expect? You come to Florida wearing Eskimo clothes."

The terminal was sleepy, a change from the franticness at Kennedy Airport. Unlike New Yorkers, the travelers, mostly from Middle America, seemed unhurried and mellow—*and* naive.

"Casey, these people look spaced out as if they're from Mars."

"Tell me about it. Down here, they're all *baccalàs*."

That night, Jimmy and I had dinner with Rosado at The Colombia on East Seventh Avenue, Tampa's restaurant row. Rosado had rented a car for us in his own name—the first mistake. We strolled up to the smoked-glass doors of The Colombia and stepped inside, the coolness of the air conditioning instantly drying my face. We heard utensils clanking as they dropped into dishes—the reaction to our presence, we hard-nosed New Yorkers. We scanned around for Rosado. "Jimmy, he's over there." And we went to his table.

Rosado stood and hugged Jimmy and me. I sniffed a men's cologne on him and commented, "Casey, you're lookin' good. You're smellin' even better." For a second, not understanding if I had meant to offend him, he gave me a pitching stare. I quickly said, "Hey, hey, hey, Casey, don't read into it . . . I mean it, I love your cologne."

Rosado grinned, his teeth the size of a horse's. "Glad you made it. Everything OK at the hotel?"

"Everything's fine," Jimmy answered cheerily. "We got a nice room right above the pool."

We sat across from Rosado, who, with a fork in hand as a pointer—another Italian quirk—outlined the evening. "After we're done eating," he said, "we're goin' to Johnnie Ciaccio's joint. This *stroonz* is one of them arrogant Cubans who thinks he's got it over on everybody. He's got a joint, The Temple Terrace Lounge, a few miles north of here in Ybor City. We'll rough him up a bit. Nothin' serious, a few stitches, maybe a broken nose. A love pat, you know. And hopefully, we'll squeeze my money out of this prick."

Rosado's plan made me a bit jumpy. "Is he with anybody we gotta be on the lookout for, Casey?"

Rosado pressed his lips together, forming a huge doughnut. "Nahhh! He's got nobody he can run to. Nobody! It'll be a piece of cake."

Johnnie Ciaccio's restaurant was nothing more than a lounge with a bar menu. The setting was fit for a singles' nightclub with red lighting and cocktail waitresses with see-through panties up to their crotches. No shame at all! Rosado asked one of them to send for the manager, who came to our table in thirty seconds. Rosado shoved a ten-dollar bill in the man's lapel pocket and said, "Tell Johnnie someone's here for him."

Ciaccio didn't think of asking who might want to see him. He had the manager take the three of us to his office, a six-foot by six-foot square wedged under a staircase next to the kitchen. We stooped forward to pass through the low doorway, and Ciaccio saw us. His body stiffened, eyes darting here and there as if he'd been ambushed. A look of surprise iced on the man's face, jaw slack and mouth open. In a near slow-motion wave, he warily motioned us in.

"Why . . . why didn't you call me to lemme know you were comin' to Florida?" Ciaccio swallowed harshly, his Adam's apple rising and falling as he looked pleadingly at Casey Rosado. "I mean, I'm glad you're here, but . . . but what . . . what's going on? You should've called."

Rosado drilled into Ciaccio's pupils, a pair of shit-brown marble balls. "Call *you* to tell you I was coming? You didn't return my fuckin' messages, you son of a bitch. As if you're the king of Cuba, I had to fly twelve hundred miles to get hold of you. Who're you think you are, Fidel Castro? You think I got nothin' else to do but chase bums like you?" Rosado snarled. And to Ciaccio's angst, he moved in closer, jabbing a forefinger inches from the Cuban's face.

Ciaccio's lips were quivering. "Casey, I . . . I didn't mean no disrespect. Business has been pretty tough down here. There's . . . there's a recession goin' on."

The union president leaned over Ciaccio, now meek as a spring lamb. Rosado screamed out, "What recession, you *disgraziat*? This dump is full of customers, and it's only Tuesday night. So who're you bullshitting?"

Four or five minutes into this, and all of a sudden Jimmy clutched Johnnie Ciaccio in a headlock, Rosado clobbering him with the butt of a revolver. An uneasy look must've come on my face, and I think it made Jimmy and Rosado back off on the beating. The sun-blackened Cuban lay on the floor in a sprawl of arms and legs, his nose, lips, and ears bloody as if they'd been ground by the blades of a high-speed fan.

Two kitchen helpers had witnessed the assault, normally a Class E felony and usually reduced to a misdemeanor. Someone read the license plate of our rented car, and the next morning a bunch of hillbilly cops arrested us all. In a cruel coincidence, Ciaccio's sister, Maria, was a clerical employee of the South West Florida FBI outpost. She ran crying to the agents in her office, and out of sympathy they took over and bumped up the charges against Jimmy, Casey, and me to a federal extortion case. It was a knife through my heart. I couldn't believe of all the shit we'd done that went unpunished, we got a federal rap for smacking around that fuckin' Cuban.

We sat with our attorney, and Jimmy laid it out in simple terms. "I've been thinking about it day and night," he moaned to me. "We should've killed Ciaccio. At least we would've gotten our money's worth for our legal costs." He rocked his head in frustration at our lawyer, who was slumped in a green leather chair, at a loss for advice.

We were going through a string of bad luck. Twelve months after Johnnie Ciaccio's beating, the trial began, and to everybody's shock Casey Rosado keeled over and died of a heart attack. He wasn't even forty-eight.

Jimmy, a man with a stomach of stainless steel and genes borrowed from the devil, never sweated. This one, though, frayed his nerves. He couldn't resign to a long stretch in prison for a little assault. Jimmy didn't mind a long sentence if he deserved it. Then again, look at the slew of people the Gent had killed without paying for it; but in his psychopathic mind, as he saw it, "they had it coming." He'd say, "Somebody's gotta keep the lowlifes in line. Otherwise, every day a new crook comes out of the woodwork and hustles or hurts you in some way."

Rosado's croaking took the wind out of me. Without his testimony, I'd be convicted as if I were a murderer. And I never touched a hair on anybody's head.

I had a knot in my throat, and with trembling fingers I lit a cigarette. "He was our only ticket out of this," I whined to Jimmy. "With our records, you and me can't take the stand and convince the twelve talking baboons on the jury that this case had been blown out of proportion."

In the past, Rosado had miraculously dodged indictments; his criminal record was clean, and it would've shut the door for a prosecutor to tear him apart on the witness stand. Now he was dead.

For the first time in my life, I was looking at years in the joint, and not in a county jail, but a real prison.

Jimmy was uptight, as I had never seen him before. He asked me the same question over and over. "Did you hear from Paulie if he reached out to a judge in Florida?"

"He hasn't gotten to anybody yet, and it don't look good that he's gonna be able to squash this mess."

Paulie's political tentacles reached deep and wide, but he couldn't rig this one, not even for his two most dependable producers. The way the law reads, ". . . a bodily assault for recovering a debt is a federal statute classified as an *extortionate extension of credit* . . ." the very charge weighing on Jimmy and me. The wheels of justice went around; and with the casualness of a priest giving a sinner ten Hail Marys, a prick of a judge mercilessly sent us to prison for ten years.

"A totally unfair decision" was the only thing our lawyer, Cy Roth, could say. Despite this outrageous punishment, there was a consolation. Paulie had pulled some strings, and the judge let Jimmy and me stay out on bail pending the outcome of our appeal.

As if it were his doing, our lawyer held up his arms in victory and put on the grin of a goofball. "For now, you're still free. As I said, we're appealing, and when I'm done with my tactics, two years will go by before there'll be a ruling."

Jimmy and I, as you might guess, didn't share Roth's sense of triumph.

11

Our appeals for the extortion conviction dragged out into a two-year roller coaster of doom and hope. Meanwhile, it was business as usual; we even stepped up our thievery. Knowing the ten-year sentence might stand, we had to save cash to last our families through the long prison stretch. And Jimmy and I did not pass up any action.

A hundred feet to the west of The Suite, between a gym/spa and a boutique shop, was a hair salon for bald men. The sign above the front door read FOR MEN ONLY, and it sold and serviced wigs. The owner was

Marty Krugman, a short, drum-shaped man who could aggravate you if he just looked at you.

At first, I thought For Men Only was a goldmine; not quite, though. Krugman, sharp in street math, couldn't help but dabble in the "numbers racket." He was forced into hustles that had nothing to do with men's hair. Morning, noon, and night his wife hung out in expensive department stores and burned his hard-earned cash faster than you can count to three. And as the man in a Jewish marriage, he'd bellyache, "No matter how much I bring home to my wife, it's never enough to keep my mother-in-law from *kvetching*."

I'd see Marty Krugman in The Suite when he came for lunch or just to bullshit. We got friendly and pretty soon took a liking to one another. In no time, Marty and I became friendly, and he wasted no time putting a deal on the table.

"Henry Boy," as he'd call me, "mazel tov on you taking over this joint. It's a good location. You're gonna knock them dead here." We clinked glasses. "Listen, pal, I heard you're with Jimmy Burke, and I found out you two are with Paulie Vario."

"Uh, uh," I hinted unclearly. I didn't know him well, and I didn't want to say something that might get me in a tight spot with the law. I mean, for all I knew, he could've been an undercover vice cop.

"I can talk to you straight, right?" Marty chanced.

"Yeah, yeah. Go ahead."

"I've been taking a little action. Some numbers, sports betting, and a bit of shylocking. Nothing big. Just small potatoes," Marty said, rattling the ice cubes in his drink, eyes blinking out of nervousness. He braked as if he might've had second thoughts. "Eh . . . Sometimes you know how it goes. When you're into those rackets, you can run into hassles; the guy who don't pay you, the one who tries to flimflam you. You know what I'm talking about."

I chuckled and sipped my beer. "Tell me about it. Once a day there's a sit-down with somebody. Every day there's a beef. Every day somebody's lookin' to swindle you out of somethin'."

Marty laid down his drink. "I'm just a little Jewish guy from East New York. I don't have anybody behind me. I guess what I wanna say is, well . . . if you back me up when the day gets rough, I'll cut you in on a percentage of the action."

My decision was quick. I put out my arm for a handshake.

The Suite was building the reputation as the showcase for stolen merchandise that the Burke crew, me included, plucked out of Kennedy Airport. We got our hands on clothes, shoes, fur coats, cosmetics, appliances, cameras, stereos, drugs—I mean legal drugs, the ones you buy at a drugstore. The joint had the vibes of a bazaar. My restaurant customers went from drinkers and diners to shoppers of stolen stuff.

Speaking of drugs, Tommy DeSimone and I had hijacked a truck loaded with penicillin. When I read the bill of lading—it was above the driver's sun visor—I had second thoughts. "Tommy, check this out. This penicillin is for the American G.I.s in Viet Nam." And it was badly needed there.

The jerk that he was, Tommy shrugged. "So what?"

"What're you mean, so what? We gotta bring this truck back."

"Bring it back! Are you nuts? We can get at least ten grand for this load."

In the end, I won. We drove to a shopping center and left the truck there.

Word spread The Suite was now a one-stop department store. Unbelievably, the roguish detectives from the district attorney's unit came in and bought hot merchandise.

"So what's the swag of the day, Henry?" they'd tease. Soon, the Robert's Lounge gang and the cops got cozy, and the shady policemen made The Suite the last bar hop of the night. Quite often, the detectives drank and hung out at my place until dawn to get away from their wives. After a while, I got tired of this routine, and to free myself of babysitting these party animals, I lent them the key to the restaurant. You don't need an imagination to understand how far this went with those cops.

At The Suite, police brass, politicians, and robbers fraternized and cooked up all sorts of swindles. We ate, drank, gambled, did business, sang, danced, had our choices of women, stole, and always covered each other's asses. With these dudes practically living in my joint, they all got involved in the scheming. The politicians let us know where it was safe to steal, and the cops tipped us off when somebody filed a complaint or when the heat was getting too close. How could we go wrong?

12

1974.

Our appeals did not overturn the conviction for the Johnnie Ciaccio beating in Florida. An appellate court held up the ten-year prison sentence that son of a bitch, the trial judge, had handed Jimmy and me. Cy Roth called us and said he wanted to talk to us in his office right away. I sensed it'd be bad news. And though it had been two years since we lost the trial—lots of time for me to clean up my affairs and get ready for prison—nonetheless, the unthinkable worst-case scenario that now knocked at my door was a hair frizzing jolt. For the first time, I'd be locked up in a real joint, a federal penitentiary. About to be a convict, the color drained out of my face, and sharp jabs tore at my intestines.

It seemed absolutely crazy. Ten years in the joint. I'd be forty-one by the time I got out. I rose from my chair and started pacing around Roth's desk. For Christ sake, my kids are gonna be grown by then.

"What am I gonna do, Cy?" I begged. "Ten years is a long time. And all for smacking around that miserable spic."

"What're you complaining about?" Jimmy said, pounding his chest. "Look at me. I'm gonna be a great-grandfather by the time I get out."

Cy Roth loosened the knot on his yellow tie—one so bright it could've blinded you—and cut in. "You know, the system has a lot of purging valves, and if you play your cards right, you could be home in about five to six years."

"What'r you mean?" I barked.

"Yeah, what exactly *do* you mean?" Jimmy asked in a calmer voice.

Roth smiled and leaned back in his chair, tinkering with a letter opener. His office was so small you could spit from one side of the room to the other, and because he was a pipe smoker, an odor of stale tobacco siphoned oxygen out of the air.

He drew a long breath as if he needed the wind for a long story. "I wasn't confident an appellate court might overturn your conviction. I guess I hoped for a miracle and didn't prepare you for the worst." Roth shook his head and sucked his teeth, as if this jam we'd gotten ourselves in was a tough situation *he* had to face. "The Feds want to make an example out of you guys." His eyes went to the ceiling. "Not even Moses and Jesus Christ together could've helped you two." But then he said, "Luckily, in the federal prison network, you can participate in programs and work details that will give you credit off your sentence."

"Really?" Jimmy and I said almost in a chorus, our eyelids now wide open.

"A lawyer friend of mine has a paralegal working for him," Roth explained. "An ex-inmate, who did about eight years for sodomy. While in prison, some of these felons study law and learn more than us attorneys. And they're certainly up on all the latest rules of the inside world. So they can be helpful to someone going in for the first time. He can make your life easier during your confinement." He riffled through a Rolodex on his desk and found the phone number to his colleague's office. "Here ... here it is. Jimmy, Henry, take down this phone number. I'm going to call him and let him know you'll be in touch with his prize paralegal."

My wife, Karen, a brunette with neck-length hair and a slender but curvy body, couldn't imagine living alone for ten years.

"How am I gonna pay the rent, Henry? And what about all the other bills?" She was going nuts like a sixteen-year-old girl, the whites of her eyes red from a crying marathon. Karen and I were at the table in our dining room, her beautiful legs crossed, and I could see she was beside herself. She upped off her chair and circled around the furniture, a gaudiness of ultra-modern chrome and glass.

"Karen," I said in a pacifying way, "I won't be gone for ten years." I stood and clasped her arms. "I spoke to this guy who did a long stretch. He works for a lawyer and said there are all kinds of ways to get out early. We figured I'll be home within five and a half years." I put on a warm smile as if with a few words I had fixed the direness of this lousy sword hanging over our heads.

Karen threw her hands in the air and went berserk, her squarish nose twitching. "Oh, this *really* makes a big difference," a blue vein swelling on her neck. She stormed up to me and came nose to nose. She kicked me in the shin. "Don't you see, it doesn't solve anything. You're only leaving me enough money to last a year and a half . . . maybe two. What do I do then?" And the sobbing went on and on. "I wanna kill myself. Oh . . . oh, I hate you."

"What'll you do then? If I don't get something goin' in the joint, I'm sure Paulie will lend a hand."

"Oh, Henry, Paulie's not gonna help, and you know it. Damn it, I wish I never met you."

I bent over and massaged my bruised ankle. "Stop talkin' that way. You never complained when I gave you whatever the fuck you wanted. You forgot about that, eh?"

"Yeah, but it didn't last too long, did it? Look at where you got me now," she scolded, her eyes round with madness, wide apart and black as onyx.

"Oh, yeah. Daddy's only as good as his last paycheck. Ain't that the sayin'?"

The instant I said it, I felt bad. I listed my head to the side and drew Karen into a hug. I whispered in her ear, "Let's stop screaming at each other. The kids are gonna wake up." I glanced in the direction of the children's bedroom door. "Look, I'm handing over my sports-betting book to Marty Krugman, and I made a deal with him. Until I come back home, he's gotta give you forty percent of the action."

Karen broke out of my arms and grabbed my chin. "Is that true?" she asked excitedly. Her excitement, though, quickly dimmed to a frown. "Wait a minute, wait a minute. How do you know Marty'll keep his end of the bargain? None of youse can be trusted."

I looked up and sighed. "Are you kiddin'? Marty? Of course, I can trust him. I'd trust him with my life."

Karen swung around, her back to me, and gazed out the window, the streetlights veiled in a summer night haze. "I don't know . . . I don't know," she uttered.

"There's no doubt I can trust Marty. But let's say he *does* fuck me, I'd get Paulie to straighten him out in a minute. Understand?"

Karen must've felt a bit of relief. She turned from the window and held her stare at me. "You're making me feel a little better, honey. Ahhh, I'm sorry, I'm all stressed out," her lips parting and smilingly curving upward. She wiped her tears, narrowed the eyes, and clenched her teeth, two perfect rows of pearls. "I hope you're not just saying all this to keep me quiet."

"Everything's gonna work out. C'mon, let's get ready for the party. I want you to put on your nicest dress and look your best."

"Don't you always say I look good in anything *and* even nothing?"

"Don't be a wiseass, Karen."

She hugged and started kissing me, her fingers kneading my nuts. She pulled me onto the bed, and we got into it as never before.

I dressed in one of my Armani worsted wool suits, light tan with white pinstripes, and a mauve custom-tailored shirt. No tie: It'd be an informal dinner, and I'd be more cozy; I had little tolerance for the August heat. Karen poked around her closet and chose a black dress with a cleavage-plunging neckline and a mid-thigh length. She clasped diamond-studded earrings to her earlobes—compliments of a jeweler Tommy had robbed at gunpoint—and slipped on white spike heels. She decked out her neck with three strands of mother-of-pearl and an emerald pendant. And for a woman who for years to come would be without a husband, she looked ravishing.

August 18, 1974, was my last day—for a long time—as a free man. The boys had planned a farewell party at a restaurant in Queens, and I welcomed a final evening of barhopping. The night first included the wives. Later, we had set on connecting with our girlfriends, cavort with them for an hour or two, and for a grand finale, the guys, less the women, might carouse about town. Should we run into a few loosey-gooseys, well, then, the rest of the night was in the hands of fate.

But I couldn't come to terms this was my last night out as a wiseguy. I was the king of all, the man guaranteed a table anytime at any restaurant; the man who was admitted into the hottest discos and spared the humiliation by the bullying doormen, the clowns who handpicked those who should or shouldn't be let in.

We were roughly twenty in all and met at this Italian joint, Salvatore's. Joe "Buddha" Manri was standing by the doorway and practically bear-hugged me. "Henry, *che si dice?*" he greeted me in Sicilian. He was a South American trying to pass as an Italian in the hope we'd accept him in our circles.

"All right, all right, Joe," I saluted. Everybody was coupled with the wives. We sat at this long table and studied the menus. Joey Rossano was there, too, and, the *cafone* that he was, asked the waiter if the chef could make him some *pasta e fasool*, an old peasant dish of pasta and chickpeas.

"What's the matter with you, *scemoneet?*" Jimmy hollered across the table to Rossano. "You can't get pasta e fasool here. Where do you think you are, at your grandmother's house?" The whole table sprung into laughter, and the noise got louder and louder. It was fun. The guys made me feel like they cared.

We drank a lot of red wop and ate a good lasagna, nice brasciols, and lots of minestrone. In the back room, a four-piece rock band played hit songs from the sixties. After a dozen flasks of wine, we all loosened up and drifted to the dance floor. A few seconds later, I freaked out. The band started playing a Doors number. I didn't know what it was called, but the last line was something like "Love me twice, I'm going away . . ."

I couldn't figure out if it was a coincidence, or if the musicians knew this was my last bash. Karen started crying; it freaked her out, too. I asked if anybody had mentioned to the singer that I was headed for prison, and the answer was no. It must've been an omen, and it upset me. But a couple more drinks, and it passed. The guys were anxious to meet up with their girlfriends, so we dropped off the wives at home, picked up the mistresses, and carried on at Maxwell's Plum on the East Side of Manhattan.

We were drinking and raising hell. The music was great; the disco sound had just become popular, and Donna Summer was the Disco Queen. The nightclub was filled with Ms. Summer's voice singing her song. In those days, that damn hit, "I Heard It on the Radio," was played a million times a day. "Someone found a letter you wrote . . ."

My girlfriend, Linda, started getting emotional. I wanted to spend time with her alone, and we sneaked into a corner. She cried and cried 'til it was time for me to go. She was sad, thinking she'd never see me again.

"Why do you say that? There's no reason why you can't visit me," I said to her. Then to keep it light, I joked, "Maybe you can hitch a ride with my wife, and on the way keep one another company." Smack. She hit me with her purse. "Just kiddin'... just kiddin'," I said, half apologetically. I gently pulled her head into my chest, the fragrance of her shampoo whiffing from her auburn hair. We stayed at Maxwell's until eight o'clock the next morning.

From the time Jimmy and I had lost the trial, I'd been busy making preparations for the day I had to turn myself in. I collected most of the money I had on the street; once a loan shark goes to prison, all loans are automatically forgotten—so I had to salvage as much as I could. I also had been buying a lot of provisions to stock The Suite—food and beverages that I resold and didn't pay the purveyors. I beat the IRS, too; I hadn't been paying the quarterly employer contributions and payroll taxes. I pocketed the money. The New York State Tax Treasury also joined the list of stiffed creditors. As we used to say, I busted out the business.

The Sales Tax Commission foreclosed and padlocked the place. A date was set to auction everything inside my supper club. On the eve of the sale, I removed the heavy steel locks by melting them with an oxyacetylene blowtorch. I then picked apart the joint and burglarized my own restaurant. I stripped it of every fixture, table, chair, glass, knife, fork, and lightbulb. And before ransacking it, I threw a party there with a mix of guests from every profession and social class. A mingle of corrupt NYPD detectives, Queens DA investigators, questionable labor union delegates, crooked New York City politicians, and underhanded building inspectors. On the colorful end of the scale, Mafia chiefs, bookmakers, fences, schlock lawyers, and flashy prostitutes were also on hand.

But all of that was over, and I was supposed to turn myself in at 8:00 a.m. sharp. At last, rain falling and wind gusting, my legs wobbly from the booze, the limo driver drove me to the Manhattan Correction Center at 9:30, and I was late. I mean, what were they gonna do to me?

Jimmy was already there, but he'd been assigned to the Atlanta Federal Penitentiary, and not where I was going.

As if I had blanked out, or maybe *blocked* it out of my mind, I don't remember walking in, but I found myself in the processing room of the MCC. "Empty out your pockets, and take off your belt. Put your wallet on the table, here," said the corrections officer, a six-foot *mouleenian*.

"I ain't got a fuckin' wallet," I said in my curt way. My lawyers suggested I not carry a wallet, cash, credit cards, and personal documents. This was to make sure things such as a driver's license or important paperwork wouldn't get lost or stolen. It was par for the course for the lowlife guards to confiscate prisoners' belongings—an initiation rite for virgin inmates.

Henry Hill was confined at the Federal Bureau of Prisons check-in facility for seventy-two hours in an eight-by-ten cell, its walls plated with quarter-inch steel armor. The facility, formerly a hotel on Park Row at Foley Square, was on the eleventh floor of the MCC. The strip-down area measured twenty by twenty-two feet. The grayish-green cinder-block walls and slate floor lent an air of dourness and, darkened by the screen mesh on the dust-coated windows, depressed one into the mind-paralyzing realization of losing his freedom. An odor of urine emanated from the stainless steel sink/toilet component standing in a corner of the pen.

The next and last stop of Hill's journey was the Lewisburg Federal Penitentiary in Lewisburg, Pennsylvania. It's a maximum-security prison 130 miles west of Long Island. The marshals at the check-in housing assigned convicts to penal complexes far from their hometowns to make it, at best, an inconvenience for friends, family, and cohorts to visit and communicate with the inmates. This could be a big problem for Hill.

13

"Hey, listen, you," Jay Boone, an assignment officer at the MCC, shouted at me. "I'm the guy who calls the shots to which joint you go to, you hear?"

The inmate adviser, whose guidance I had been relying on, had mentioned to me this guy, Boone, and how he shook down new convicts.

"Can I have a choice?" I asked dimly.

"Come with me. Leave your belongings here," Boone said in his deep voice. "Follow me."

I took this as *the invitation*. I walked ahead, turning left and right through a maze of dungeon-like hallways. We came to an area that in the previous life of the hotel must've been a visiting room. "Sit down," Boone said, and I did. Seated face-to-face at a splintered wooden table, we stared at one another for what seemed an eternity. Boone looked behind him to make sure we were alone. "*Technically*, you don't have a choice where we ship you off." He winked. "If there's something you wanna say, talk to me."

I felt as if he'd let out the leash a bit. "I wanna go to Lewisburg."

"Lewisburg, eh?"

"Yeah, Lewisburg."

"No problem, Mr. Hill. It'll cost you two hundred dollars, and it has to be in five-dollar bills. I gotta have it before I fill out the commitment and confinement sheets."

"What happens if you don't come through?"

"Now look, here. I don't need you making all kinds of noise over two hundred fuckin' dollars. I'd lose my job." Boone lowered his voice to a whisper and inched into me. "Listen to me, Hill. I'm a family man with three kids. Two of them are about to go to college, and I'm gonna make sure they get a goddamn education so they won't have to do the kind of shit work I'm doing handling scumbags of your type. I don't have the balls to do what you done. Let's keep it straight; you're the criminal, not me. Understand?"

I listened with my lips twisted to mean I wasn't taking him seriously. "Whoa! All right, all right, bro. Don't get your black ass gander up."

Boone didn't think I was too funny, and I thought he was going to belt me one. He leered at me. "Now you either do it my way or I'll find a nice, cold prison to send you off to somewhere in north Alaska. And the only way anybody will be able to visit you is by spaceship. Or they'd have to go through Siberia in a Russian submarine."

I got the point. "All right, all right. I gotta call my wife and have her bring the dough."

"OK. Lewisburg it'll be, Mr. Hill. Let's get back to the inventory room and finish up the paperwork."

Boone and I started walking back to the check-in room. "Hey, CO," I said jokingly, "if you don't come through, you don't gotta worry about me dropping a dime on you. But I'll guarantee you this, you're gonna have to buy yourself a special wheelchair."

Boone's rubbery mouth stretched. "And why so?"

"Why? 'Cause when I'm done with you, my *mouleenian* friend, you're gonna be a paraplegic." I gave him the punch line with a deadpan gaze.

A rough and tough guy in a three hundred pound body, Boone chuckled with a sneer. "I didn't know you're a comedian, Hill."

Had they sent me to a federal joint farther west, Karen's commute could've been far longer than the 136-mile trip from Long Island to Lewisburg. The relatively short distance simplified her hauling and smuggling of narcotics into the prison. I sold the contraband to fellow convicts, and for a blind eye paid graft to correction officers. This made it easy for me to carry out my shenanigans: drug distribution, the sale of liquor, wine, seafood—Alaskan king crabs, jumbo shrimp, lobster, and scallops. I fancied myself a purveyor of fine Italian salamis and high-quality olive oil. My wife and I had built up this business to the point where we were supporting the family in the same style we had when I was hustling in the streets. I, too, was eating large, and so were the guards on my payroll.

I not only made money from the goodies Karen was sneaking in, I also made new friends and contacts that went hand in hand with my schemes. I was in the company of gunrunners, controlled substance lords, high-tech burglars, and contract killers—and though I didn't like hit men, they became my customers for weapons and ammunitions.

Less than four years passed, and despite my cons and bootlegging, the warden endorsed my early parole and labeled me "a model prisoner." I guess he wasn't playing with a full deck. In mid-September of 1978, I proved to the parole board a job was waiting for me on the outside—a "no-show" job set up by Vario—and the three commissioners at the hearing cut me loose.

But I was penniless. Throughout my time behind the wall, taking care of my family and the payoffs to the prison guards had been sucking my earnings. And as if starting over totally broke hadn't already devastated me, I owed my lawyers a huge sum, and I couldn't waste time. I had to put together a score sooner than now.

Within three weeks of my homecoming, prospects were on the horizon. And in a month, Jimmy also was to get paroled.

14

Marty Krugman had honored the pact he had made with Henry Hill by sharing the bookmaking proceeds with Karen while her husband was in the shade at Lewisburg. Krugman expanded Hill's small operation and managed to crank up the income tenfold. His pushiness and the access allowed to him by the Air France shipping foreman, Frenchy McMahon, cleared all obstacles for Krugman to do business inside the hangars at Kennedy Airport and hook addicted sports bettors—cargo handlers who squandered paychecks badly needed to put food on their tables. They were all mottled with vices and on the brink of bankruptcy—if not personal ruination. They borrowed from Peter to pay Paul, and satisfying their gambling debts was last on their list, choking Krugman's cash flow. McMahon was the bookie's ears and eyes at Kennedy Airport and collected Krugman's past-due bets from the stragglers—freight handlers who dodged their exasperated creditors.

One such individual, Louis Werner, a supervising shipping clerk at the Lufthansa cargo depot, owed Krugman $20,000. Fed up with carrying the long-standing delinquency, Krugman threatened Werner. One day, the phone call Werner had been dreading came, and the bookmaker tested him. "Lou, are you gonna clean up this money you owe me or what?"

"Marty, I'm in a slump, but my luck is bound to change. I'm not gonna beat you. I'm good for it. Hey, where am I going?"

"I'll tell you where you're going, Lou, because I'm the one who's gonna send you there. You're gonna wind up in a grave in Spikey's backyard."

Krugman's enforcer, Spikey, a mean-spirited chap, repaired lawn-mowers in his basement. He had a heavy-duty vise bolted to a work-bench. Spikey dragged Krugman's debtors to his cellar and squeeze their hands in the vise until bones crackled. The delinquents could scream at the top of their lungs. It was no use because Spikey's house was half a mile east of Floyd Bennett Field, the Air Naval Reserve Station in Brooklyn. He could slaughter cows in his basement, and nobody would hear a thing. Werner's excuses incensed Krugman, whose eyeballs resembled two hard-boiled eggs. The light brown toupee glued on his head could've been mistaken for a bird's nest.

Werner's troubles were the product of alimony to his ex-wife, a three hundred dollar a day gambling addiction, and a girlfriend with champagne taste. His income from Lufthansa Airlines was only fifteen thousand dollars a year. And Krugman now riding him hard was Werner's breaking straw. This jarred the Lufthansa shipping clerk into reality; doomsday was at his heels, and he couldn't possibly erase his liabilities. Realizing this, Krugman wasn't counting on Werner paying him the $20,000, though the bookmaker was relying on an ace card, a trade-off. The bookie understood that someone in Werner's capacity—who was privy to security schematics in the Lufthansa building—could be the insider to assist in pulling off rackets of all colors. Krugman was waiting with the patience of a vulture perched on a tree branch. Someday this downtrodden gambler, bartering to wipe out his outstanding losses, might come up with a tip-off, leading to a lucrative larceny. This was why Krugman had let Werner slide until his debts surged hopelessly beyond recovery.

It happened. Louis Werner and a coworker, Peter Gruenwald, had been polishing a design to plunder a large haul of cash from their employer, Lufthansa Airlines. Gruenwald was in search of burglars who could put it in motion. It had to be someone with the tenacity and experience to ambush the airline's night staff and storm the high-value vault where Lufthansa stored sacks and sacks of US dollars it transported for international banks. Gruenwald spoke with a group of wannabe gangsters to assess their abilities and relayed his findings to Werner. "Lou, those boys can't even pickpocket a dead man without getting caught. They're nothing but kids in diapers."

Louis Werner, a puny man with unwarranted self-importance, was disheartened. "Pete, it's a year you let pass, and you haven't found anybody worth his salt. And I'm tired of going along with you. I'm under a lot of heat, and I need money in a hurry."

Drained by Gruenwald's procrastination and caving under pressure from Krugman, Werner's desperation was growing by the hour. He tossed and turned on sleepless nights, and on a wintry dawn, the answer to his problems rang in his mind.

Keeping Gruenwald in the dark, Werner cranked up the courage to confide in Krugman and advance a daring proposition, one that could simultaneously slay two dragons. He'd ask Krugman to forgive the $20,000 debt and connect him to a squad of gunslingers who could raid the Lufthansa vault. In turn, Werner would pass on to Krugman's source his "foolproof strategy." Simple. Werner phoned Krugman and asked the bookmaker to lunch with him.

Krugman accepted, but warned, "Listen, and listen good, you lying kraut." Aside from Werner's grossly past-due balance, another note strained the rapport between them. The Jewish Krugman clung to a dislike for Werner, whose ancestors were Germanic. "The public is either ignorant or insensitive to the pains us Jews suffered at the hands of those fuckin' Nazis," Krugman admonished anyone who'd listen.

In a fawning approach, Werner sidestepped Krugman's contempt. He placed his hands in prayer and implored, "Marty, I'm not bullshitting you. Not this time. I know I've been jerking you around, and I know you think there's no way I can come up with twenty grand all at once. And you're right. But I've got . . ."

The bookie interrupted. "All I wanna know is *how* are you gonna straighten me out?" When Krugman spoke, his speech accelerated as if he were running out of time. Excitement or rage sped up his talking and you could only grasp half the words.

"If you got ten minutes, let's go to the Airport Diner. We'll have a cup of coffee, and I'll tell you what I got in mind." Werner scanned the surroundings. "I don't wanna talk here. There are a lot of ears around this fuckin' hangar."

"All right, this better be good." Krugman peeked at his watch and pretended to be disinterested. By nature, he was always hurried, fretting as if he had to skin all the rabbits before sundown, for tomorrow might never come.

The Airport Diner, a fixture from the sixties with a decor of that era, was a landmark on the South Conduit, the service road of the Belt Parkway nearby Kennedy Airport. Air cargo workers, gangsters from Queens and Brooklyn, prostitutes, truck drivers, and bookmakers patronized the old-fashioned slop house. Werner and Krugman settled in a white booth, and in less than a minute a waitress with rust red hair and blackened dentures stood over them, chewing gum.

"So what'll it be for you big spenders?"

Krugman gave her a look of inferiority. "Two coffees."

Werner raised his finger. "Yeah, that'll do it."

"Okaaay!" she chanted, as if wishing she were elsewhere.

The waitress had balloon-size breasts, and Werner teased, "Miss, you carry an air gauge to check the air pressure in those jugs of yours?"

She shot the bespectacled Werner a killer look and harangued, "Fuck off, you four-eyed kraut."

"How'd you know I'm German?"

She fluffed the back of her hair in an air of detachment. "Honey, you couldn't look more of a kraut if you had a swastika pasted on your forehead."

Krugman managed not to laugh. "So, what's the story, Lou?" He rolled his hand for Werner to move on. "C'mon, I ain't got much time."

Werner bent into the table and again peered about to see if anyone was spying. "Marty," he said in a hiss, "remember when Henry Hill robbed Air France and made off with a half million bucks?"

Krugman tittered. He sensed the rest of the story was going to delight him. Maybe this German might not be so bad. "What about it?"

The dark-toothed waitress reappeared with the two coffees and hurled them onto the tabletop, splashing a few drops of the mud water on Krugman's lap, her jaws chewing faster than a cow with a nervous condition.

Werner restarted, his eyes shifting left and right. "I've got something bigger than Air France. A couple of million. Maybe three."

Krugman whistled. "So what are you putting on the table?"

"I'm talking about nabbing a load of cash in unmarked bills. It's gonna come in at the Lufthansa cargo bay."

Krugman glared at Werner in disbelief. "From what I hear, it's impossible to get anywhere near the Lufthansa high-value vault."

"That's right. It's pretty hard, but nothing is impossible."

Krugman sneered. "Nothing is impossible, eh?"

"Marty, I wouldn't be fuckin' around if I was shooting from the hip."

"For a guy who's down to the balls of his ass and owing more money than he's worth alive, you're fuckin' cocky."

"Yeah, I am cocky, 'cause I got everything it takes for a stickup team to pull this off. *Everything*!" Werner's blue eyes sparkled, and Krugman could see in them the smugness of someone sitting on a golden egg.

"I don't know, Lou. It's too risky. Chances are that anyone who tries it will get nailed."

"Marty, it took me a long, long time to figure it all out, and now I got it all together."

"OK, let's assume you do know what you're doing, what do you want from me?" A sudden glow brightened Krugman's face; the question was mechanical, and he whiffed a windfall.

Werner slithered closer to the table and ran a hand over his dirty-blond hair. "All you gotta do is link me with some of your contacts who can pull this off. That's all."

Krugman slumbered in his seat. "That's all, eh?" he nodded at Werner's minimizing the enormity of his request. "Lemme ask you, why are you coming to me with this generosity?"

Werner slanted his neck to the side and pushed the eyeglasses up his nose. He shook his head. "Oh, no, no, no. This is no generosity, my friend." He eyed Krugman with a slight smile. "I want you to wipe out the twenty grand I owe you, *plus* I want ten percent of the take from the heist." Werner gazed timidly at Krugman, expecting a rejection.

Instead, the bookmaker seemed interested. "I reckon it can be worked out. Lemme talk it over with my people. I'll let you know tomorrow."

Krugman already felt rich as if he'd inherited a million dollars—though he did not know that a Peter Gruenwald was also attached to Werner's plot to loot the German airline.

15

My phone rang. "Hello, who's this?"

"Henry Boy, it's Marty."

"Heeey, what's doing, pal?"

Marty Krugman and I had a tight friendship, and after a four-year prison stretch I was glad to get a call from my old buddy.

"Henry, listen. I'm onto something big. I gotta talk to you."

I figured Marty might've been onto a truckload of stolen merchandise, "Oh, yeah? What is it, Marty?"

"I can't go into it on the phone. We gotta talk face-to-face. This is big. *Real big*!"

"Why don't you and Fran come to my house for dinner Saturday night." Fran was Krugman's wife. "I'll have Karen buy a whole bunch of stuff from the kosher deli, and we'll eat 'til we burst at the seams. We're better off ordering out. Remember, she can't cook for shit, and I ain't got the head to do any cookin' right now."

"That's fine, that's fine. But it can't wait 'til Saturday. How about tonight?"

"That important, eh? Lemme check with Karen and get back to you in twenty minutes."

On Marty's insistence, and insistent he was, we set the dinner date for that evening. At eight o'clock, my doorbell rang.

"Come on in, Marty, Fran. You look good, Fran. Marty must be treating you like a queen."

"Yeah, a drag queen," Fran remarked. She hugged Karen, and out of habit her bony hand swatted the air. "You should know, Karen, you keep a neat home," she said in her Jewish way.

Karen was so proud. "Oh, thanks." She was in bliss because we'd just rented and furnished a new apartment, a two-bedroom in Valley Stream, Long Island. "The kids will grow up in a good neighborhood," Karen said.

I also was proud as hell. "Here, lemme take you through all the rooms, Marty."

As usual, Marty couldn't hold still. "No, no. I gotta talk to you." He grabbed me by the arm and whisked me into the hallway out of earshot of the wives.

He kept tugging at me, and I said to Karen, "Show Fran our new entertainment console. Marty and I gotta talk business."

The console was an ugly, black Formica furniture contraption with a hidden television and a stereo set, a novelty that popped up at the touch of a finger. Karen turned on the stereo to let Fran hear it: "Nights in white satin, never reaching . . ."

The high-fidelity sound overly impressed Fran, a miniature woman with a screechy speech, the bark of a Chihuahua. Nosiness was her make-up. Fran was one of them spoiled women who'd go to the beach in a fur coat just to show it off.

"Wow, what a stereo. And I love the Moody Blues," she said, going into personal questions. "This must've cost Henry an eye, Karen."

"Not really. It came off a truck Tommy DeSimone hijacked right after Henry came home," Karen answered with the openness of a kindergartener.

Once Marty and I were apart from the women, I was dying to know, "What's so pressing that you won't even take time to look around our new house?"

"Yeah, yeah, it's a nice pad. Mazel tov. This is more important. The score of a lifetime, Henry Boy," Marty trumpeted, looping my neck with his arm.

"So what is it?"

Marty started stuttering. "This . . . this will make your Air France job look like kids stealing bub . . . bubble gum in a candy store."

"C'mon, Marty. You're exaggerating," I said, throwing my head back in doubt.

"Listen to me, you schmuck. I came across the same setup with Lufthansa, but mmm . . . much, much bigger." Marty let go of my neck and spread his arms for me to picture the size of the sting. "See Henry, this guy, I think you know him, Louis Werner, a kraut. He's into me for twenty big ones."

"Yeah, I know him. He's some sort of a foreman at Lufthansa. Same kind of job Frenchy's got at Air France."

"That's him, that's him. He told me they're waiting for a shipment of money to come in, and it's gonna be to the tune of, give or take a few hundred thousand, two million bucks."

"Who's waiting for a shipment of money?"

"Henry, weren't you listening to me? Are you meshugna or what? I said Lufthansa's gonna be bringing in a fat sum of cash. Unmarked bills!"

"You gotta understand," I said. "I'm under a lot of stress. Fours years in the joint, bills up the ass, the kids need clothes, and all kinds of stuff. Plus I've been drinking the whole afternoon."

"This . . . this could straighten out all your problems. All of *our* problems, Henry."

My face lit up, but quickly shrank to a sulk. "It's all different now. The airlines learned a lesson from Air France. Today they got state-of-the-art alarms and surveillance equipment."

"Oh, I know, I know. You can't just walk in and out the way you and Tommy did back then. This has gotta be different. Werner's got a damn good plan. It's gotta be a holdup with armed men who got balls. Werner can't do it himself. He's got chestnuts for testicles."

I waved my palms back and forth. "Count me out, Marty. I'm out on parole and don't need another pinch. If I get another felony, they'll hang *my* balls on the horns of a bull. Armed robbery's not my bag. Besides, I wouldn't put much faith in this 'plan.' You know *everybody* says Lufthansa is the toughest to fuck with."

"I hear you, pal." Marty kept bringing his face into mine. "All I want you to do is sell Jimmy Burke on it and have him coordinate it. He can do it. Problem is, I can't reach out to him. You know Jimmy and I don't get along." Lightly, Marty ran a hand over his hairpiece as if to check if it was still in place. "And no offense to you, them fuckin' Irish hate us Jews."

"Well, I'm sort of a Jew, too." When I married Karen, who is Jewish, her mother, that pushy bitch, made me convert and renounce my Catholic religion. It didn't bother me. I wasn't a practicing Catholic and didn't care one way or the other. So I became a Jew.

"Yeah, but no matter what, your genes are still half mick and half guinea, and that'll never change. I love you anyway." And Marty kissed me on the forehead.

On his own, Marty didn't have the clout to put together Werner's deal. Then there was another hurdle: the Lucchese and Gambino families had planted stakes at Kennedy Airport and often fought over it. But Jimmy and I had a stronghold; we had Paul Vario's backing. And although Marty and Jimmy *did* know one another, because of the Gent's distrust for the bookmaker, the connection between them was frosty at best. I couldn't get it into Jimmy's head that Marty was an OK guy.

That night, Marty, Fran, Karen, and I gorged on kosher food: corned beef on rye, potato knishes, sour pickles, hot pastrami, coleslaw, smoked salmon, gefilte fish, and lots of matzos. The whole house smelled like a deli.

Even before finishing dinner, Marty was bugging me to reach out to Jimmy at the halfway house. A paper plate in hand, scavenging the table for more food, Marty was talking a mile a minute. "I gotta know if Jimmy can handle it, *and* if he wants to do it. Let's not wait until the morning. C'mon, Henry, let's get a jump on it."

Fran and Karen were yapping about bargains and junk they'd bought at a 99-cent store. I stuck a cigarette between my lips and shook my head at Marty. "What's wrong with you? I *can't* call Jimmy at the halfway house," I said in a hush. "The halfway house is not a hotel. It's a prison. Stop *kvetching*, will you! There's no doubt Jimmy can get it done." I inhaled a drag of smoke and blew it to the side. "And of course he'll be interested."

"How do you know that? I mean, what if . . ."

"Stop, stop. What if nothing. Jimmy's gonna need a score. He hasn't had a stitch of income since we both went in. And while he was in the can, his crew, those numbskulled *chitrools*, haven't made a dime. Not a fuckin' dime. Jimmy's fuming. After four and a half years in the joint, he's got no cash. And none of the crew has any action goin' on." I pulled another drag on the cigarette and gulped the last of my Miller; I was ready to step up to vodka. "Jimmy desperately needs a win."

To Marty, this was as calming as a shot of anesthesia. "Oh, Henry Boy, for a *goyim*, you got such common sense. Such common sense." And he pinched my cheek.

The dinner party broke up, Marty and his wife drove home, and Karen coaxed the children to bed.

I was too wound up to call it a night and drove to my *commara*'s house. I celebrated Marty's good news with a bottle of Smirnoff and a few lines of coke. At just about midnight, the phone rang, and my girlfriend, Linda, answered it. "Hello. Oh, yes, here he is."

She handed me the receiver and brushed aside her hair, a silky flow of auburn. Stoned and glassy-eyed, I gazed at Linda, her tresses glowing red under the high-hat lights. "Who the hell is callin' at this time of night?" Sleepy, Linda shrugged and laid her head on the arm of the couch.

My mind started racing. Then I recognized the baritone voice of the caller.

"What's goin' on? I'm trying to relax, Marty."

Marty tended to overreact, and I could hear it in his voice. "Werner called. He sounded drunk and said if I don't give him an answer by tomorrow, he's got somebody else who can do the job."

"So?"

"*So?* I don't wanna lose this deal, Henry. You gotta get Jimmy to give you the green light tomorrow morning. This guy, Werner, is a desperate man, and desperate people make bad moves."

"Jimmy's not gonna make a decision on the spot, Marty. He's first gonna run it by Joe Manri."

Manri, a phony as far as I was concerned, had Jimmy believing he was a genius when it came to scams. But Manri couldn't piss and shit at the same time. And I would've bet my last hair that a four-year-old could've counted higher than him. He was just a yes-man, and Jimmy loved yes-men.

Like a woman who's had her period for a month, Marty kept nagging, "How am I gonna hold off Werner?"

I was dying to get some papaya from Linda, and I couldn't wait to get him off the phone. "Here's what I'll do, Marty. I'll send Tommy to pay Werner a visit and tell him to keep his cool. You know Tommy; he's good at keeping people cool and quiet. Tommy won't let Werner know his real name, and he'll never connect Tommy to any one of us."

"I don't know, Henry. Werner sounded he meant what he said. He's past desperation and may go to another crew."

"Keep calm, and go to sleep, Marty."

16

The following morning, my brain cells not quite dried out of vodka, I went to see Jimmy in the basement of Robert's Lounge. My mouth was parched from the alcohol of the night before. "Jimmy, do me a favor," I said, "call upstairs and have them send down an ice-cold beer."

"Jesus Christ, Henry. I got more important hassles to deal with than your dry throat." Jimmy seemed annoyed; nonetheless, he called the bartender on the intercom. I could sense he was uptight and had headaches on his mind. Sure enough, Jimmy let fly, and I got trapped in it.

"So what's the story? We gotta get somethin' going. And soon! I'm broke." The more Jimmy ranted, the more steamed up he got. "These asshole bastards haven't taken in a cent while I was in the shade."

The only way to muzzle Jimmy's tirades was to nod along and pretend to be pitiful and apologetic. While he vented, a waitress came down the stairs and handed me a tall glass of lager.

"Jimmy, I wanna fill you in on something I got from Marty Krugman. I think it's gonna make your day."

"Well, let's hear it, kid." Jimmy crossed his arms on his chest and lay back in the chair.

I dragged my seat nearer to him. "Jimmy, Air France was a hell of a score, wasn't it?"

"Damn right, it was."

I rocked my head, dived into the beer mug and kept my nose in it for a few seconds.

I had gotten Jimmy's attention. "Talk first, drink later."

I repeated to him everything Marty had said to me.

Jimmy's eyes said he wasn't going for it. "What're you thinking?" I asked.

"I don't buy it." He pouched his lips and put on the look of a naysayer. "Nope. It can't be so easy. Everybody's sayin' to stay far from the Lufthansa building; they got the tightest security. And you think they're gonna leave millions of dollars to be plucked by a few holdup men?"

I doused my cigarette butt in the sink on the wall. "I didn't say it's a snap. This guy, Werner, has been working on this for a year. You should at least talk to him."

"Hell, no. I don't wanna see him. Why should I talk to him, so later when he gets busted he can pick me out of a lineup?" Jimmy rubbed the back of his neck and bit his lower lip. "Want some coffee?" he offered. He had a taste for espresso coffee with anisette, an Italian custom that had brushed off on him from Vario and me.

"Why not," I said.

We poured the coffee into white porcelain demitasse cups, and I sipped. The Gent downed a shot glass of the clear, sweet liquor and wiped his mouth with a paper napkin.

"Ahhhh!" Jimmy smacked his palate and kissed the tips of his fingers, looking at me with eyes half-closed. "I'll send Joe Manri to find out what Werner's all about and listen to what he's got to say. If Manri thinks it's doable, we'll take it from there."

Joe Manri was fat with a bloated potbelly and a blocky face. We called him Buddha. He was a hijacker and a veteran stickup man. Manri was in the know as far as the inner workings of the cargo hangars at Kennedy Airport, and Jimmy relied on his intuition. Manri was the quiet type and did not mince words; when spoken to, he listened intently before asking questions. His low-key attitude made everybody think he was smart, and those who knew him, who for the most part were loose-lipped quacks, took him for a shrewd cat. But I knew better.

Jimmy and I were hanging around in Robert's Lounge when Manri walked in. The Gent called him over and told him about Werner's scheme.

"This guy, Werner, is dreaming, Jimmy," Manri said, his club-like arms folded and resting on his stomach as if it were a pullout table. "You can't get anywhere near the Lufthansa terminal. Are you kiddin'? It's a fortress. Werner could be blowing smoke up Krugman's ass in the hope Krugman gives him breathing room on the money he owes him."

Despite Manri's refusal to put stock in Werner's "air-brained scheme," Jimmy—who wouldn't rule out anything—didn't discard this Lufthansa idea.

It was twenty minutes into cocktail hour. At the bar in Robert's Lounge, Jimmy opened the drinking with a snifter of cognac. "Joe," he said to Manri, "I want you to look up this Louis Werner. And don't let him know your last name or mine. Understand?" Burke tapped his fingers on the bar top and stared into Manri's eyes, a pair of gray olives. "Remember, *do not* say who you're working with."

Manri nodded in a way that said, *rest assured, I'm the right man for this.*

I phoned Marty and clued him in on the Manri fact-finding mission.

"Oh, shit. How long is this gonna take, Henry? We're gonna lose this hit. And this is the biggest score we'll ever see. It'll never happen again. Never!"

"Calm down, calm down. Jimmy's taking this seriously. And you can't blame him for covering all the bases. Keep in mind, he just got out of prison and can't afford another scrape with the law. If he racks up a new felony, they'll lock him up for life."

"We're gonna lose this. I feel it in my bones. We're gonna lose it. You gotta push Jimmy."

"Get yourself together, Marty. Nobody pushes Jimmy Burke. Besides, didn't I say I was gonna send Tommy DeSimone to knock some sense into Werner's coconut kraut skull. And Tommy *did* go see him. So stop losing sleep over it. *Please!*"

A constant worrier, Marty was always antsy and neurotic and could bite off all his fingernails in one night.

17

In the bookmaking hustle, a runner picks up money the bettors owe the bookies. He also delivers the gains to the winners. Frank Menna was one of Krugman's best runners, and Krugman entrusted him to present Manri to Werner.

It was a bone-chilling mid-November evening, and an early snow-storm was in the air. Lowering as though it were a dark blanket, the sky, thick and clouded, seemed to stifle Queens County.

"Where is this jerk?" Manri thought out loud. He had been waiting in his Buick at the Airport Diner parking field, engine running and heater fan at maximum speed. Fifteen minutes had passed, and Werner hadn't yet arrived. Louis Werner was consistently late for his appoint-ments. Manri, on the other hand, was as punctual as the ocean tides. Disquieted, he was thinking about going inside the diner to phone Burke. An ill thought had stirred him to abort the meeting; maybe, he began surmising, this was a police entrapment.

But as Manri reached for the door handle, from the corner of his left eye he saw a hand rapping on the window. Jarred off guard, he glanced up, and standing next to his Buick was a shaky figure with small blue eyes behind rimmed glasses. Manri lowered the window about three inches. "Lou Werner?"

"Yeah. Joe?"

"Get in, get in. You're fuckin' late, and it's cold as a bitch." Manri unlocked the passenger door.

"Sorry I'm late," Werner apologized, vapor swirled from his mouth. "I had some problems with my girlfriend," he said offhandedly. He unbut-toned his navy blue wool coat, its collar up high, enfolding his neck and part of his balding scalp.

"Uh-huh." Manri acted aloof. The steering wheel was wedged in his stomach, and to clear it he had to shift sideways and face Werner, an ordeal when taking into account his 360 pounds. "So what're you wanna talk about?"

Werner behaved somewhat tentative; he hadn't expected someone of Manri's grotesqueness. "I can get my hands on a lot of money, all unmarked. And maybe five to six hundred thousand in diamonds and jewelry. The thing is . . . well, I need a few professionals."

"Where's this loot, and how can we grab it?"

"I've been working on this for a year. I got it down to a science. And the . . ."

Manri stopped him and passed a hand through his hair, a curly bush of black frizz. "Man, you're not giving me a hint where this money is." He rolled his hand as if to say, *Let's have it.*

Werner coughed and stared out the windshield. He sensed Manri's patience dwindling. "The . . . the Lufthansa cargo building."

This awakened Manri, who wheezed when he breathed. "Lufthansa! And how much is supposed to be there?"

"Around two million in cash and a few hundred thousand in gems."

"*Minghia*! Are you sure?" Manri's wheezing was the whistling of a teakettle. "They don't keep so much money lying around."

"Oh, you can bet your bottom dollar they do." Werner's cockiness was getting zesty. "The shipment with the money will get here on a Friday. Usually, Brinks picks it up at five o'clock in the evening. Here's where I come in. I'm gonna make sure Brinks walks out empty-handed and leaves the money in the high-value vault over that weekend."

"And how are you gonna do it?"

"That's my business. All I'm gonna say right now is this: The job has to be done on a Monday morning right before dawn, at exactly ten minutes to three."

At a loss, Manri wrinkled his forehead and narrowed his eyes. "Why at ten to three?"

"These details are beyond the scope of this conversation," Werner crowed. "Don't think I'm a complete fool. If your people have *real* interest, then I'll give you the whole scoop." Werner rested his arm on the door padding and gaped out the side window, snowflakes beginning to dance in the darkness. "Not for nothing, if I give you everything now, what stops you from doing it on your own?"

The Lufthansa cargo terminal was reputed to be the most secure hangar in the world. And this runt was assuring a veteran holdup man that *he's* figured out the means to practically excavate the whole German airline compound off its foundation and cart it away.

"You're sayin' to me . . . let me get this straight," Manri said, "we're gonna walk in *and* out of the Lufthansa cargo terminal with a couple of million bucks? Just like that!" Manri snapped his fingers. "My people aren't gonna believe this shit so easily. And if I say to move on it, they'll think I'm a nut. So you gotta give me some details to go back with."

"No way." Werner stood his ground. "When you're ready to go, I'll lay out everything, starting from how to rob the money, to how to skate off without a hitch."

Werner smelled Manri's perking curiosity, though a queer feeling dawned on him. *Whoever this fat man is, he didn't give me his last name, and whom he's with.* Werner decided not to pry. Judging from Manri's line of questioning, Werner figured this Michelin man look-alike was a leathered-skin burglar who knew his apples.

Manri swung his body and faced forward, the steering wheel digging into his belly. Werner glanced at him, and for the first time noticed Manri had no neck. Manri's head looked as though it rested directly on his chest. With nothing else to discuss at the moment, Manri said, "OK, Lou, I understand. We'll let you know."

Unceremoniously, Werner exited the Buick and slammed the door, and Manri drove to Robert's Lounge.

"Lounge" was too elegant a name for Burke's "gin mill," a dilapidated shack with a brew of nostril-wrenching odors. Burke, who by now had fueled up on five shots of rye with beer chasers, anxiously awaited his emissary. Manri saw the Gent on a stool in a corner of the bar, and with elephant-like steps strutted in his direction. A party of rowdies, airport cargo handlers, crowded the floor; despite the temperature outdoors hovering near the freezing mark, they stood in T-shirts, drinking watered-down beer and laughing rousingly.

Burke glanced over his shoulder and hollered at Manri, "Over here, Joe." He was soused in liquor, Manri detected, though, Burke, a certified alcoholic from the age of eleven, functioned sharper than a sober man ever could. "So what did you come up with?"

A smile parted Manri's lips, a rarity, and he was glad to report his assessment. "This Werner dude, he's a fuckin' wimpy creep. But he's got it down to a science, Jimmy. He didn't give me details but said that if we're gonna be in on it, the next time I see him, he'll fill me in."

Burke hollered out to his bartender and asked for two new rounds of firewater. His mouth gaped to a broad grin, a twinkle shining in his eyes. "You think so, eh?"

"Hell, yeah," Manri verified, sipping his cognac. "Sounds as though Werner's worked out all the angles. Says he's been at it for a year."

"But . . . but explain to me." Excitement fumbling his speech, Burke couldn't wait another second to know the specifics. "So what's all this about the Lufthansa hangar having all kinds of alarms? Everybody says it's as safe as Fort Knox. *And* I thought they don't keep a lot of currency at the cargo terminal. Because if they do, they're stupider than I imagined."

Manri recapped his conversation with Werner, and Burke listened without missing a beat.

Mulling it over, the Gent said, "Joe, tell Werner we're definitely on board and get him to give you the step-by-step play."

The next day, Manri set out to see Werner. "I got the green light, Lou."

"All right, all right. I'm happy to hear it, Joe."

"Now let's have it all."

Lou Werner fed Manri the whole aspect of his conspiracy—particulars of a well-thought-out assault on Lufthansa. It astounded Manri, though he did not lift the curtain of his steely stare. Werner, short and bespectacled, didn't appear to have the astuteness to think of so an infallible caper. On first meeting him, Manri had detested Werner's shiftiness and conceit; he saw him as a dreamer, a loser. If it weren't for Burke's interest in Werner, and had Manri run into him on a dark, lonely street, he might've pummeled him until "the snobbish little bastard's cheeks turned to bratwurst."

That aside, Werner totally sold Manri on Lufthansa.

Manri huddled with Burke and recounted the obstacles to the robbery and how Werner's ploy could overcome the hurdles. "I say we do it, Jimmy."

"What makes you so sure?"

"I asked Werner all kinds of questions, trying to punch holes in his plan, and it sounds airtight."

Burke called for another round of alcohol, held his glass high, and toasted, "To the Red Baron."

Even in this happy moment, Manri's ever-fixed eyeballs appeared as if they were locked in a permanent stationary setting.

18

At 7:30 in the morning, the goddamn phone woke me up. I grabbed the cordless receiver, and with a throat full of spit, I said in a scratchy voice, "Hello."

"Henry, it's Jimmy. Come down to my joint as soon as you can." And the Gent hung up.

I dropped the phone on the bed. That insomniac always called before the sun came up.

The moment I set foot in Robert's Lounge, Jimmy said to me, "All right. We're gonna do it."

For a moment, my mind went blank. "We're gonna do what?"

"Lufthansa," Jimmy whispered, looking behind him as if someone might be listening. Out of habit, because we always talked about something underhanded, we'd look around for spies.

I wanted to hug him. "Good, good, Jimmy."

"So far, you're the only one who's trying," the Gent praised. "There's gonna be a good payday in it for you, Henry." He stared at the cracked plaster on the wall, and I could see he was calculating numbers in his head. "If everything works out, I'm gonna give you fifty grand. All right?"

All right or not, I didn't have any choice. "OK, thanks. Whatever works for you."

Jimmy's eyelids formed a V, and his voice dropped. "What does that Jew want for his cut?"

"Who, Marty Krugman?"

"Yeah."

"Seven hundred and fifty grand?" I said, knowing Jimmy would protest.

I was right. The Gent jumped up, his forefinger pecking the tabletop. "He's out of line. That fuck isn't taking any risks whatsoever, nor investing a dime, and he wants $750,000. He's way off. Tell him . . . tell him I'll go for four hundred. And that's a gift."

Sour negotiations went into the next month, and as a settlement Jimmy gave in to paying Marty five hundred thousand, which he accepted bitterly. But this wasn't the end of it.

"See, Henry," Marty raged, "Burke is no damn good."

When Marty spoke to me, because of his excited mannerism, he'd slant his head and nearly tuck his face under my chin. "Burke talks about us Jews wanting it all and having greed. Meantime, nobody's more greedy than him, the shanty mick that he is."

"Everybody wants the most they can get, Marty. Nobody wants to leave a dollar in the other guy's pocket. I think he's givin' you a fair shake. You got no risk of gettin' pinched; you're not putting up any money. So don't make waves. Take his offer and go home." With a jerk of my chin, I said, "You know, without me asking, Jimmy's paying me fifty grand just for bringing you to him. And he didn't have to do it."

Marty got as red as a tomato. "Burke wants to put it up my ass. He must think my anal canal is as wide as the Panama Canal." He rubbed his eyelids. "My snag is that I'm in no position to fight with him. I'm gonna have to be happy with a lousy five hundred grand." Marty gritted his teeth, and I never saw him so boiling mad. "Henry, I swear, I'm gonna make him pay for it." He spat on the floor and pointed to it. "See that? Burke's lower than spit. And I got a way to fix his ass. From now on, I'm no longer Marty Krugman the nice schmendrick Jew."

And he left, a plume of smoke puffing out of his ears, or so I thought. Ten paces later, he turned back to me, his finger angrily stabbing the air. "Mark my words, Henry, I'm gonna take care of that mick bastard because he's screwing me. And *you* know it!"

19

Henry Hill had sensed that Jimmy Burke saw Lufthansa as the chance to jump-start his dying dynasty. The Gent had unflinching tenacity, a flair burning in him since his teens.

Burke's immediate challenge was to cast the characters best suited for the Lufthansa sortie—and characters they were. Also, he had to clear it with Lucchese capo Paul Vario and pitch to him the financing needed to lay the groundwork of the heist. Burke treated Vario to dinner at Don Peppe, an Italian restaurant on Lefferts Boulevard in Ozone Park, Queens. The eatery featured a coarse southern Italian cuisine, and the furnishings were from the 1950s, rickety chairs and bright fluorescent light fixtures. One could smell an overpowering stench of garlic, not only inside the place, but also in the vicinities outdoors—a needling nuisance to the thoroughbred trainers at the nearby Aqueduct Racetrack. Their grievance was an odd one; the unbearable reek wafted onto the track and sickened the horses. Don Peppe, though, was Vario's favorite. "Fuck them horses," he cursed. "All they're good for is dog food. You have any idea how much money those motherless bastards have cost me?"

"Paulie, forget about the horses. We got a big fish on the hook." Burke shoveled a spoonful of black beans in his mouth. "I'm gonna need some seed money to get it out of the water and into the frying pan."

In public, whenever Burke discussed business, he spoke in coded terms. He presented the Lufthansa undertaking, and the six-foot-three, 280-pound Vario didn't seem too attentive; at the moment, he was salivating to hear the specials. "I don't know, Jimmy. It sounds too good to be true. I can't see Lufthansa keeping millions of dollars in their terminal for a whole weekend."

If Vario didn't front the start-up costs, Burke could not shift the Lufthansa wheels in gear, and nervousness stiffened the Gent's face. "Paulie, I checked and re-checked Werner's idea. I know it sounds far flung, but it's gonna work. Listen," he leaned into the table and toned down to a whisper. "If something goes wrong, I'll *personally* guarantee your money back. Besides, you stand to make a hell of a lot of dough."

"Who you got for this job?" Vario was chewing his meat ravioli sopping with Milanese sauce, and something struck him. "Jimmy, every time we come here, why do you always eat black beans?"

"If I could get corned beef and cabbage, I'd have it. These guineas here, no offense to you, Paulie, don't know nothin' about Irish cooking."

They both chortled. Vario quipped, "Yeah, well, you're used to the Irish seven-course meal, a boiled potato and a six-pack. Ha, ha, ha!"

Burke side glanced Vario and sipped his merlot. "Real funny, Paulie. Back to what I was saying—Henry don't want no part of it. I still have to give him a piece because he's the one who made this happen."

The Lufthansa broker, Henry Hill—for whom Burke had a soft spot—did not intend to be on hand for the robbery itself. He didn't want to chance another long stint in a federal prison. On the second time around, the stars would have to fall from the sky before he'd be granted an early parole, so Hill thought it best to stay out of the trenches. Burke sympathized with Hill and respected his judgment. Moreover, Hill was not prone to violence. The armed robbery could spin out of control, and cold-blooded stickup artists had to be on hand to take drastic action, if necessary, even if it meant injuring the hostages, or worse, shooting it out with security guards or the police. This was not for Henry Hill.

Vario gobbled the ravioli, slipped the napkin out of his shirt collar, and wiped the red sauce off his mouth and chin. "Who else are you gonna use?"

"I'm not sure."

"How much you think you'll need?"

Burke poured wine for Vario and slurped a swig on his own glass. "In total, I'll have to pump out forty to fifty grand. And you stand to make ... eh, less any promises ..." He raised his palms and curved his neck. "You stand to make, ... eh, a hundred and fifty grand, Paulie."

Vario came alive. "*Minghia*! All right, Jimmy, if that's the way you want it, I'll go for it." With the crudeness of a caveman, he ripped a piece of Italian bread off the loaf, and working it as if it were a sponge, soaked up the splotches of tomato sauce in his dish—a custom among low-class Italians. Chewing on a mouthful, Vario pointed at Burke, and said severely, "Remember, come hell or high water, I don't wanna know nothin'. I'll be looking to you for my money, Jimmy."

The Lucchese *capo regime* consented to the cash advance, and the next day Burke called his glacier hearted disciple, Angelo Sepe, and the not too warm hearted Tommy DeSimone.

Sepe, wiry and unkempt, and though a short man with a welterweight frame, could stare down a gorilla. Malevolence lurked in his eyes, a pair of murky holes. If the occasion arose, he'd murder a human but never an animal; Sepe loved cats, dogs, birds, squirrels, and ferrets, sheltering all the strays in his cramped quarters. And not unlike many Italian Americans in New York's five boroughs, he had built a pigeon coop on the rooftop of his apartment building. There he housed racing pigeons, a popular pastime among his *paesani*. The flying races of those birds were high-stakes contests, and the wagering often surpassed twenty thousand dollars. Hill tried to fix the competitions. He and Sepe, though, had to scrap the idea; the exotic birds, apparently more honorable than Hill and their owner, couldn't be trained to throw the matches.

Angelo Sepe had the savagery of a jungle animal, but he'd only kill for gain. As for Tommy DeSimone, his predisposition to murder weighed in differently. He was a breed unto his own. A penchant for destruction— humans not exempt—prowled in his self; and he inflicted harm out of sheer pleasure, as though it were a sport. When he calibrated the sights of a weapon, you couldn't put it past him to test it by shooting at whoever happened to be in proximity, friend or foe.

To train his commandos for the Lufthansa attack, Burke had outfitted the basement of Robert's Lounge with an oblong table and a display board mounted on a wall. On the board, he posted, as a visual aid, classified material Werner had passed on to him through Manri. In a classroom-like setting, the Gent hashed out with his henchmen the siege on the German airline.

In the second week of November 1978, one of Burke's briefings of his star murderers, Sepe and DeSimone, was underway.

"From the looks of things, a big score is going down," DeSimone guessed.

"Yeah, what's going on, Jimmy?" Sepe asked, swaying his palms horizontally, an Italian gesture of confusion.

"OK, settle down and pay attention," Burke said. "I'm gonna get right to it."

Everybody sat, and DeSimone and Sepe slumped in their chairs, arms hanging on the backrests the way lazy, uninterested students count the minutes for the class to end.

Burke said with sternness, "Listen good, cause there'll be no room for mistakes."

Sepe remarked, "Man, whatever it is must be big."

"We got an Air France situation on our hands," Burke announced, his pupils suddenly bright-eyed.

"All right, all right!" DeSimone shouted.

"We got somethin' on that order with Lufthansa, and this time the take will be a lot bigger." The Gent bulleted the main steps of how the robbery had to flesh out and demanded DeSimone and Sepe's commitment.

Burke never briefed the troops as a group, and as does an air traffic controller, separated them, imparting particulars *specific* only to the function each individual man would play in the burglary. This was so no single robber knew every detail, a safeguard against their flapping mouths.

The next warrior Burke sat with was Manri. "Joe, you're gonna stay as my go-between with Werner. Anything you see or hear, I mean *anything*, you tell me and only me. Understand?" Burke underlined.

Eyelids hooded, Manri nodded. "Uh-huh. I understand, Jimmy. Nobody's gonna find out nothin'."

Burke held reliance in Joe Manri; nonetheless, the Gent tirelessly reminded him, "Any talks with Werner, go see him in person. No telephones. And Joe, never go where he works." With greater emphasis, Burke said, "Oh, don't give Werner your address. And I can't say this too many times: don't let him know *I'm* the one running this gig, or who's gonna be doing the job. OK?" The Gent paused and suggested, "Hey, shouldn't you be writing this down?"

"I can't read or write too good, Jimmy."

"Oh, great." *I'm dealing with illiterates*, Burke must've thought as he poured bourbon in his glass. "Joe, set up your meeting with Werner. Tell him his cut's gonna be ten percent." Burke aimed two fingers at Manri and said, "If he squawks and wants more, here's what I want you to say to that worm. Either he takes the ten percent or the deal is off. And say that if he goes with another crew, he won't live long enough to count his money."

Manri rapped the tabletop twice with his knuckles. "Sounds fair to me." He hugged Burke, lumbered up the steps, the treads creaking under his feet, and left Robert's Lounge, the Gent's bunker.

A day passed, and Manri met with Werner, who unfolded his Lufthansa blueprints.

Barring unanticipated illnesses, injuries, arrests, or enforcements of outstanding warrants, Burke's chosen few were a cast of six gunmen and a driver. They all had backgrounds with rap sheets thicker than a prostitute's black book, and temperaments, so unpredictable, one might've thought the Gent had kidnapped them from a circus of freaks. In all, Burke's brigade was a combustible blend of varied nationalities: Italian, Irish, African American, German, and Hispanic, a reflection of the New York City melting pot.

His front line ready and in formation, Burke was now equipped to strike at the Red Baron. He felt a knot dissolve in his stomach and plowed on, plotting and rehearsing. Burke, a realist, was keen to his bandits' handicaps; their collective intelligence equated to a flickering lightbulb. One was dyslexic, another could hardly read or write, and three were illiterate. And DeSimone—aside from his stunted intellect and IQ of a seven-year-old—personal grooming, hair care, and polished shoes took precedence; he'd often miss the overall prize. On the other hand, Burke's mind was a calculating machine. Thus, knowing his stumblebums were "brain-dead," and could easily stray, he was resigned to shortening their leashes until the Lufthansa showtime.

20

Jimmy hinted to me he'd cleared the start of Operation Red Baron.

"Henry," he said, "let Krugman know we're gonna do it, and tell him to keep his mouth shut about it."

Hopped-up on adrenalin, I drove like a nut to Marty's wig salon. I trotted into his barbershop, a place for people with fake hair, and whiffs of lotions and hairsprays swamped my sense of smell. Marty was talking to a client and saw me come in. He excused himself from his customer and practically ran to greet me.

He put his stubby arm around my shoulders. "Henry Boy. I feel it in my bones. You got good news, eh."

Mindful of the nearby stranger, I spoke in riddles. "The fat man's gonna be the go-between to the German," referring to Manri and Werner. "That's how Jimmy wants to handle it. The Gent doesn't want himself, you, or me to have any ties to the German. So stay out of his sight and where he works."

Marty's face lit up. "So he's doing it. Oh, Henry Boy, he's doing it." He planted a kiss on my forehead. "All right! All right!"

"And do us all a favor, Marty." I held my words 'til I was eye to eye with him. "Don't say a word of this over the phone to no one. No one!"

"Sure, sure, sure. Hey, give me fifteen minutes to finish up here, and we'll go down the block to Stratton for a drink. OK, Henry?"

"Yeah, I'll wait. There's something else I gotta talk to you about."

Marty strutted to the far end of the salon and was almost singing. "Oh, Henry Boy. You made me so happy. So happy!"

Stratton was a nightclub on Queens Boulevard in Forest Hills, two blocks north of Marty's shop. It was a "meat house," the singles' scene of the 1970s. Leopard-patterned leather was all over the inside of the joint, and every furnishing was upholstered or lined with it. Mirrors were everywhere, and above the dance floor was a giant crystal ball shooting strobe lights, sometimes shining on a dancer's bald head and blinding his date.

All kinds of weirdos hung out in the nightclub, some to drink into a stupor; and those who were gluttons for punishment listened to eardrum-puncturing disco music. Others came to find a lonely soul hungry for company—company meant sex. The unmarried girls hoped to catch an older, rich prince who could still get it up, a blend you only see in the movies. The unattached men stalked for one-night stands—much easier to find. And the guys cheating on their wives hunted for horny divorcees—Stratton was a beehive of those boiling vaginas.

Marty and I sidled up to the bar, and the barmaid, Juliet, who had a puffed up ball of red hair, slid a beer bottle and a glass of red wine in front of us. She always remembered what we drank—Marty and I were regulars at Stratton. The multicolored spotlights lighted Juliet's head, and her electrified mane resembled cotton candy. "Anything else, Henry?" She feigned a kiss to me and put on one of those teasing smiles to make you feel as if you got a chance with her, though she was just plugging for a bigger tip.

"Bring a plate of gefilte fish for Marty."

She looked at me with her head stooped to the side. "What?"

Juliet didn't get it. "Just kiddin'. Just kiddin'."

Marty certainly got the joke. "Oh, Henry Boy. Always trying to make fun of this little Jew boy."

I chugged half the beer and changed the subject. "Marty, I need your help."

"Whatever you want, pal."

"Through my connection in Pittsburgh, this old pal of mine, Paul Mazzei, we latched on to a couple of college basketball players. They're on the Boston College team, the Eagles, and we talked them into fixing the games by shaving points."

Marty's mouth opened wide, his eyeballs popping out of their sockets. "Henry Boy, do you know what this means?" He thought this was the greatest day of his life. Burke was gearing up to rob Lufthansa, and at the same time I had another sting going on in Boston.

"Oh . . . Hen . . . Henry, this is go . . . going to be a hell of a year—Lufthansa and Boston College. You're a genius." He twirled his pudgy body on his feet for a full turn and sang, "Oh, happy days are here again . . ." In two seconds, though, Marty turned serious, a troubled look on his carbohydrate-fed face. "I'm gonna be in on it, right?"

"That's what I wanna talk to you about. We wanna put a lot of money on the games, and we need you to place our bets with all the bookmakers you know from here to California. You gotta spread out and edge off the bets so when we plunk down heavy money on an underdog team, the bookies won't get wise to our game. You understand?" I gave Marty a wink.

"Henry Boy, of course I understand." He swilled his wine, and again launched into the cheery tune, "Oh, happy days are here again . . ." He touched his glass to my beer bottle. "It's brilliant. We're gonna rake in millions. MILLIONS!" And Marty slapped me on the back.

21

A week had passed since I'd spoken to Marty when he phoned me at home. He didn't sound good.

"What's the matter?" I asked.

"Henry, I got a problem with one of my bettors, this fuck, Remo Visconti. The young punk owes me six grand, and the bastard's stringing me along for three months. He said he was gonna pay me half of it today. And here I am with my dick in my hand. He disappeared. I want you to round up Tommy and go to his house with me. Maybe he's hiding out there."

I got a hold of Tommy DeSimone, and we drove to Visconti's house. Marty had gotten there before us and was waiting in his Cadillac. Remo Visconti lived with his mother in a black neighborhood in Jamaica, Queens. I rang the doorbell, and this little old lady opened the door, her gray eyes wet with tears. "We wanna talk to Remo, ma'am." Her bluish-white hair was sparse, and, I could see her pink scalp. She looked as if she might've had a tough life and seemed frightened, or upset over something.

Granny gave us a tired going over and spoke in a faint voice. "Remo is my son. I don't know where he is. I haven't seen him in a . . ." and started sobbing, her shoulders shuddering.

"You must be Mrs. Visconti."

"Uh-huh." She scarcely had the strength to speak.

We all felt terrible, and I was as polite as I could be. "Is there a problem, Mrs. Visconti?"

She wagged her head. "No, no. There's nothing wrong."

Marty, too, felt pity for the tiny grandmother. "You seem upset. Why?"

We pressed her, and she broke down. "He . . . he took all my savings I had in my nightstand. He probably spent it on the horses."

I eyed her to figure out what she was saying. "Who took your money?"

"My son."

"Who, Remo?"

She tipped her head, and I patted her back. "How much did he take?"

"Forty-five hundred dollars. It was all I had. I'm on Social Security and can't buy any groceries 'til I get my check on the third of next month."

I turned to Marty and Tommy. "The third of next month? That's two weeks from now." Mrs. Visconti backed up a couple of steps to let me in the doorway. "You have no food in the house and no money at all?"

Ashamed, she stared at the ground. I dug in my pocket, counted out five grand in fifty-dollar bills, and tried giving it to the poor woman. "Here, take this for now."

"No, no. I can't . . . I can't," she said louder, pride uplifting her.

I reached for Mrs. Visconti's hand, opened it, and stuck the wad of cash in her palm. "Nah, nah. You need it. I'll be damned if I'd make you go without eating for two weeks." *They'll find you dead by then.*

I stomped toward the car, and Tommy and Marty followed. Marty looked upset. "Henry, what the hell is the matter with you? We didn't come here to be Good Samaritans. We're here to collect a debt."

I stopped in my tracks. "Marty, how the fuck could you let a sweet old woman go without food?"

Tommy cut in. "What if she was conning us?"

"C'mon, Tommy, she's a nice old lady, for Christ sake," I said. And it ended there.

Tony Perla was a Pittsburgh bookmaker, and his younger brother, Rocco, had been a high-school classmate of Rick Kuhn, a basketball player with the Boston College team. The Perla Brothers had swayed Kuhn to recruit two additional team members who, in concert with him, could fix the outcome of the games.

Their objective was to restrain the scoring under the point spread of the Las Vegas oddsmakers. Once Kuhn was on board, the Perlas asked Mazzei to search for investors and strong arms. The aim was to seek out someone who had access to a network of bookmakers and the financial strength to wager heavily on the games. The one who popped into Mazzei's mind was his New York connection and partner, Henry Hill. Hill and Mazzei had been trafficking heroin and cocaine interstate, and there weren't enough hours in the day for the two ex-convicts to count the enormousness of their profits.

Hill, however, had to tiptoe with his drug emporium, leaping to great lengths to keep it a secret from Paul Vario. Vario forbid anybody allied with him to handle controlled substances. This was not because he disapproved of drug use, nor did the distribution of such destructive narcotics touch on his morals. Rather, his point was for his soldiers not to risk a conviction that packed a long, sometimes life stretch in prison. Facing a sentence of eternity, Vario rationalized, could melt the most hardened criminals into frightened little girls, informants.

"I couldn't give a shit if these fuckin' kids of today's generation wanna fry their brains with drugs," Vario acknowledged. "But any unlucky son of a bitch facing a long, long time in a six-by-eight smelly closet is bound to rat out even his own mother. And I don't care how badass you think you are. Anybody can break down. Anybody!" Then Vario closed his damnation without mincing words. "So let's get it straight. I don't want any of youse, or anybody in your crews to ever touch drugs. If you do and get caught, you're on your own and won't get no help from me."

Meanwhile, the Hill-Mazzei heroin/cocaine wholesaling was thriving, as does a well-lubricated machine.

22

The next day Paul Mazzei called me from Pittsburgh to give me the latest on the college basketball-game rigging that we were cooking up.

"When's the next time you'll be making a trip here to Pittsburgh?" Mazzei asked.

"Why, you got a package ready for me to pick up?" I answered in our lingo. "Because I got one for you." The package "to pick up" was the heroin Paul supplied me; the "one for you" was the cocaine I bartered for it.

"Not yet, but you can bring whatever you got for me, and I'll owe you. I gotta talk to you about somethin' else. Come to Pittsburgh as soon as you can."

When I got there, Mazzei introduced me to the Perla brothers, Tony and Rocco. Rocco, striking and manly at six-foot-two, had a heavily bearded face and a black Afro. His eyes were hidden behind large, fashionable sunglasses, and he had a lighthearted way about him, a charmer and lady killer. Tony, slightly shorter, was cool-looking with his black, curved mustache, thick nose, and tough-guy features. They arranged for us to meet with Rick Kuhn and the Boston College team captain, Jim Sweeney. I met with the Perlas in Pittsburgh at Paul's condominium. There a distraction paralyzed my brain—a cute, freckle-faced redhead, Marley Carr, one of Paul's drug couriers. Within seconds, Marley and I were smitten with one another.

This gathering, though, was supposed to be strictly business, one that could potentially roll in a lot of dough. And Paul's focus was to steer me clear of interferences. He was aware of my tendencies for dalliances and wanted to keep me on track. Paul and the Perlas understood I'd be the cornerstone of the basketball point-shaving con. I could provide the means: piles of money to bet with and a national web of bookmakers to break up the lofty bets into smaller, unnoticeable wagers so as not to raise eyebrows. When the oddsmakers see massive bets in favor of an underdog, and all the action is in the hands of two or three bookies, it's a giveaway of foul play. That's why it was important to sprinkle the action throughout the country. Paul and the Perlas had to rely on my clout, the power to force a bookmaker to pay even if he suspected the games were rigged.

As crazy as it sounds, despite the promising Boston College basketball sting, a new fling with a broad always sidetracked me. After an hour of Marley Carr and me ogling one another, Paul lost his cool. "Henry, why don't you do us all a favor?"

"What?" I muttered.

"Why the fuck don't you take her to my bedroom, close the door, and get her out of your system?"

To the amazement of Tony and Rocco Perla, Marley and I locked ourselves in Paul's playpen for a romp.

Thirty seconds later, from the bedroom I heard one of the Perlas say, "Are you sure Hill's got what it takes to do this? We got a hell of a bang here. I mean, it's not often that you come across basketball players willing to fix games."

Now I wanted to know what else they were saying about me. I opened the door a crack, and with one eye I was watching and listening to Paul and the Perla brothers.

"Nah, nah," Paul assured, fanning with his hand to cast aside Tony and Rocco's reservations. "He just goes bongo when he runs into fresh pussy."

"Hope you're right," Tony Perla said with a cagey look, joggling his head. "Cause we don't wanna blow this."

The following day, Marley and I, as if attached at the hip, came up for air. We showered together, and along with Paul and the Perlas, boarded a flight to Boston. We had reserved a suite at the Boston Sheraton, a swanky hotel on the corner of Dalton and Belvedere Streets. The Sheraton is snuggled in a cluster of modern high-rise buildings and stands a few blocks south of the Harvard Bridge, which spans the Charles River basin. At the hotel suite we hosted the college basketball stars, Rick Kuhn and Jim Sweeney. The two athletes knew the Perlas; Kuhn had been their friend from his childhood years. Three weeks earlier, the Perlas had hooked up Sweeney and Kuhn with Paul Mazzei, and as for me, the basketball stars had a hunch why I was in the middle of this.

I signaled the two college boys to follow me into another room of the suite and closed the door. "All right, and this is nothing personal. Just makin' sure you boys are on the open-up."

Suddenly tense, Kuhn glanced at Sweeney, who asked with alarm, "What's this about?"

"I don't know you guys, and I gotta make sure you're not wired," I said apologetically. "It won't hurt. Take off your sweaters and drop your pants."

Until now, my New York talk had amused Kuhn and Sweeney, but this security frisk unnerved them.

I finished the pat down, and the jocks and me walked back to the main room. Marley, freshening up her purple lipstick, was giddy, presumably at my prying around the athletes' privates. "Henry, you should've asked me to help you. I would've gone over them inch by inch." She was the only one giggling; nobody else thought it funny.

I later found out Kuhn and Sweeney had made an admission to Rocco. My way of talking big as if I owned all of New York frightened the shit out of them. These studs—tall with muscles everywhere, except in their brains, and Waspy faces less standout features—had milk-fed skin. They didn't have an ounce of emotion. In short, Kuhn and Sweeney were the collegiate American male devoid of expression. On the other side of the coin, I was a braggart, cursing and talking with my hands and mouth. I was the Brooklyn/Bronx roughneck, sending out vibes of a shady hoodlum whom you couldn't put anything past. And it shocked them.

Rocco, easier going than brother Tony, said, "Henry, you gotta tone it down with these kids. You're making them shit in their pants."

"I want these snot noses to know they gotta take this seriously and not to fuck us."

Rocco, who dressed in classy sport jackets, took Kuhn and Sweeney aside. "Don't make too much out of Henry's rough and tough talk. I mean, he's nobody to mess with, but he's not an irrational maniac either."

Everybody's stomachs now settled, we got down to talking turkey. I was on a couch—skinny Marley on my lap—and Kuhn and Sweeney, like two mopes, sank into two brown club chairs across the coffee table. Paul and the Perlas stood and sipped coffee. Everyone was embarrassed; me squeezing my date as if she were a stuffed doll must've looked awkward. Of those there, I was the expert on sports betting, and I mistook Kuhn and Sweeney for a couple of kids who hadn't seen raw neighborhoods and had no street smarts. "What you guys have to keep in mind is this," I said, "we're gonna be bettin' against the odds, and all you have to do is . . ."

Sweeney, the talkative of the two, grunted out of his drowsiness and cut me short, his thick Fu Manchu mustache twitching. "Yes, yes. We have to make sure the final score is under the point spread. And we can't make it seem as if we're faking it."

This surprised Paul and me. How did these two wholesome mama's boys, who hadn't yet learned how to wipe their asses, know about underground sports betting? I mean, shaving points was totally against the grain of their collegiate upbringing. I glanced at Paul, and with my palm facing up I pointed at the two Yankee Doodle boys. Chuckling, I said, "Well, well, what're you know. They're in the know." I caught Kuhn and Sweeney nodding with arrogance, their lips curving downward in a wily grin that says, *we're above the low class you come from.*

Paul, short, and stocky, with a bald scalp, was taken aback. "For your sakes, I sure hope you're *experts* at controlling the games."

Paul's rough talk seemed to have shaken Kuhn and his teammate, and sensing a thickening of the air, Tony Perla butt in. "All right, all right. Let's lighten up and talk money." Sweeney gave an ultimatum that woke up everybody. "We want thirty-five hundred a game, and we want you to pool our money with yours and bet it for us."

I folded my arms across my chest. "You do, eh? You kids are fuckin' nuts with these stupid demands."

Kuhn, more uppity than Sweeney, kept quiet.

Rocco stayed cool and mediated. In the end, we left it at twenty-five hundred dollars per game each for Sweeney and Kuhn, and should they need a third player to help them get results, he'd be paid the same way. Cocaine came into the picture. Kuhn and Sweeney were to get it as a bonus for the games they threw. I looked long and hard at the pair of all-American apple pies and said through my teeth, "I want you to take this arrangement very, very seriously. Behind me are some heavyweights who are gonna gamble a lotta cash. Make sure . . . and I mean *make sure* there ain't no screwups. Understand?"

Paul and the Perlas muttered in support, and thinking I might've been too harsh, Paul said, "I don't know about youse, but I'm hungry. What're you say we call for some food, Henry?"

Everybody had worked up an appetite; Marley wrote down the lunch order and called for room service. Sweeney and Kuhn picked out a gourmet salad, lobster and Alaskan king crab—the most expensive combo on the menu. Wouldn't you know it! The food came, and letting go of their shit-don't-stink mind-set, they chomped it like two Stone Age men who had been fasting for a month. Everyone finished eating, and we all shook hands.

This basketball point shaving was hot, and I couldn't wait to talk to Jimmy about it. It was a Sunday morning when I phoned him, the day of the week he didn't want to be bothered. He sounded pissed off, and I got right to the point. "Jimmy, I gotta talk to you. Can I see you at Robert's Lounge?"

"Christ, it's ten o'clock on a Sunday morning. I got a heavy schedule ahead of me. Word is the Red Baron is probably gonna be comin' in next week."

"Jimmy, this *is real* important. You're gonna love to hear it. I've been kicking it around with my friend from Pittsburgh. I didn't wanna say nothin' to you 'til we had it all together. And now we do."

"All right, Henry. Why don't we meet at the Airport Diner?"

"OK. I'm at Linda's apartment. I had a fight with Karen, and I've been here since Friday night. It's gonna take me a half hour to drive to the diner."

"I'll see you there, Henry."

23

On Sunday mornings, I craved eggs with hash browns. Jimmy had no appetite, though a thirst for a beer always tickled his throat. The waitress came back with my breakfast and a Miller for the Gent.

"So what's this business in Pittsburgh about?" Jimmy asked. The Airport Diner was overcrowded, and everyone was talking at the same time. It was loud, and to have a conversation in privacy was as hard as talking in a hurricane.

I dug my fork into the hash browns. "It's got nothin' to do with Pittsburgh. I said it's my friend from Pittsburgh who came up with the scam."

"Well, let's hear it." Jimmy looked irritable; Lufthansa was jumbling his mind. The chance his elves could bungle the robbery was gnawing at his ulcers. Such a huge theft could drag every law enforcement agency into the investigation. They'd look under every rock and inside cracks even mice and rats didn't know existed. The slightest slipup could leave behind smoking evidence, and the cops would pick it apart. Worse yet, too many light-headed people knew Jimmy was about to fry a big fish—something to do with Lufthansa—and these whispers could come back to haunt us.

I shoveled a forkful of hash in my mouth. "Jimmy, you know Paul Mazzei, the guy who's gettin' me the guns and the heroin."

"Sure, it's all you've been talkin' about lately. And by the way, if you don't keep your business a little quieter, this drug dealing is gonna blow up in our face. I don't wanna be too close to you when it does. So watch your ass."

"Yeah, yeah. I know. Anyway, Paul is on to something with a couple of players on the Boston College team, the Eagles." I spotted the waitress and flagged her down.

"Want anything else, dear?" she asked with a put-on.

"The same. Two eggs with hash browns." I turned back to Jimmy and went into the swindle. The crowd inside the Airport Diner was growing, smoke from the kitchen hovering beneath the ceiling.

He swatted the air and admitted, "I like this point-shaving thing, Henry." Jimmy poked his left temple and winked. "I always thought that out of all the clowns in the crew, you're the sharpest."

Flushed, I said, "Thanks. If nothin' else, you can rest assured I'm scheming even when I'm sleeping. Hey, it rhymes. Scheming when sleeping."

Jimmy didn't think that was funny. "What're we gotta do to get this point shaving off the ground?"

On December 2, 1978, a Saturday, the first fixed game got underway, Boston College versus Providence on Boston's home court, the Roberts Center in Chestnut Hill, Massachusetts. Chestnut Hill is a preppy community in the Brighton section of Boston. The streets are lined with Victorian homes whose clapboard sidings look as if they'd been freshly painted ten minutes ago. I was one of the forty-five hundred in the stands, and to my shock, Jim Sweeney wasn't playing the way he and Rick Kuhn had worked it out. Kuhn looked on, his face muddled, while Sweeney was bagging basket after basket as though he were taking shots at setting a record. On the court, Kuhn seemed dazed like a groom stood up by his bride.

After the game, he told me he had whispered to Sweeney, "What the hell are you doing, Jim? You're blowing the twenty-five hundred dollars. And Hill is going to be pissed."

"I'm on a roll tonight, and I'm going for the win," Sweeney replied in his *I do what I want* wisecrack. When the ball swished through the net, the fans roared cheers and applause, rousing Sweeney's adrenalin, bypassing his commitment to me.

The odds favored Boston to win by seven points, but when the digital clock up in the rafters clicked the final second of the match, Boston had won by nineteen. Jimmy and Paul Vario, who had bet Providence to fall short by less than the seven-point spread, were stung by the loss—a $43,000 disaster; and you could've made book that Sweeney and Kuhn would have to answer for it. We were beside ourselves, and Jimmy was ready to bury them under the bocce courts of Robert's Lounge.

24

Henry Hill was overseeing the point-shaving racket up in Boston, never letting go of his new toy, Marley Carr.

At the Airport Diner in Queens, Louis Werner and Joe Manri were eating cold grilled cheese sandwiches. Werner had gobbled half of one and washed it down with ginger ale. Manri was devouring his fourth toasted grilled cheese and wolfing down a second plate of pasty French fries—his appetite rivaled the hunger of a pregnant horse. Werner dropped the remnant of the soggy sandwich in his dish. "Damn, you can't get a hot dish in this filthy hole."

Manri generally didn't care for elementary talk. "So what'd you get me here for? I hate the cold." The air had a stinging chill to it, and the meteorologists were forecasting snow accumulation.

Werner removed his eyeglasses and cleaned them with a paper napkin. "I got news that's gonna warm you up. Yesterday the day supervisor got a Telex from Germany."

"What's a Telex?"

"You *don't know* what a Telex is?" Werner exclaimed comically, his jaw dropping in an exaggerated gape.

Manri, infuriation distorting his mouth, pointed at Werner with his fore and index fingers, subliminally symbolizing a double-barreled shotgun. "Listen and listen good, you fuckin' kraut. I didn't come here for your bullshit. Understan'?"

Werner held up his palm and pumped the air, eyes blinking in startle. "Take it easy . . . take it easy. Touchy, aren't we?"

Manri leaned the mass of his torso into the table as though he were about to grab Werner by the neck. "You better get this straight; *nobody* makes a monkey outta me." Spittle dribbled out of the corners of his lips. "And if you ever . . . if you ever try again, I'll stuff your mouth with your own dick."

"OK, OK, I didn't mean to insult you," Werner excused, his voice two octaves higher. He inhaled a long breath and continued with caution. "Anyway, a Telex is more or less a typewriter. You can type something and send it to anybody who has a Telex, too. That's how we communicate with the Lufthansa headquarters in Germany." Werner gulped. "We got notification of a large shipment of cash and jewelry. It should land here in about two weeks."

"How much?"

"Probably one to two million. The jewelry, well, I can't begin to guess how much."

"Uh-huh!" Manri grunted.

"Get your people on the go because when I give the word, you'll have twenty-four hours to pull it off. Twenty-four hours and not another minute."

Manri threw a five-dollar bill on the table. "No problem. You just lemme know." He lifted his whale of a body out of the booth—the assistance of a crane might've helped—and ambled out into the night, a frigidness crisping the air.

Werner sucked in a deep breath, thankful to have deflected a harrowing moment.

Manri drove to Robert's Lounge, parked, and went into the bar. Inside, the off-tune, squeaky twangs of an electric guitar made it unbearable for one to think. The musician was an African American, Parnell "Stacks" Edwards.

Manri scanned the bar area and saw Burke perched on a barstool. He sat next to the Gent, and to overcome the screechy guitar spoke into his ear. "Werner is sure that a big cash shipment should be coming in around fourteen days."

Burke put down his drink and rotated on the barstool to face Manri. He smiled. "Really?"

"Uh-huh," Manri mumbled with an air of aloofness, and not out of disinterest; his detachment typified the man's disposition. Manri had emigrated from one of the third-world countries of South America and was born José Miguel Manriquez. Above all, he yearned to be a "made man" in the Mafia—he abbreviated his surname and adopted the guise of an Italian American. He mimicked the mannerisms, body language, and manner of speech of the stereotypical New York Sicilians and acquired a palate for their cuisine, a delightful bonus.

Burke waved his arm for the bartender to refill his cocktail and to build one for his newest hero, Joe "Buddha" Manri, when a disruption ensued.

One of the regulars, a blond, goateed, tattooed drunkard, berated the musician, Stacks. "I'm sick of your black ass and your nigger music. I don't know why they let you play here on Friday nights? And guess what? Time's up. You got ten minutes to pack your shit and get the fuck out of here."

The known neighborhood racist stood in the center of the floor, feet apart, beer bottle in hand, unstable and wobbling.

Burke, not surprised, for these outbursts were common disturbances in Robert's Lounge, upped off his stool and nudged Manri's forearm. They both accosted the unruly heckler, whose name was Cody.

"Joe, let's bounce this drunk out the door." Burke clasped Cody by the shirt, and as he wound his right arm to clock him in the nose, one of Cody's pals, also blind drunk, lifted a chair above his shoulder, and in the stance of a baseball batter, he swung and walloped Burke across his spine. The Gent felt as if a thunderbolt had struck him, and he couldn't breathe for a second or two.

Three yards to the right, Manri clamped his hands around Burke's attacker, raising him off his feet and, as if he were a rag doll, sailed him over three tables. Two more of Cody's friends, whiskery types, seized Manri by the shoulders, a trunk the span of a mountain. As he fought to shake them off his back, Tommy DeSimone stepped through the doorway of Robert's Lounge. He walked into the melee and eagerly joined in. DeSimone clenched a handful of hair belonging to the ones who were struggling to hold onto Manri and pulled the rednecks' heads fast into his fist.

Burke had recovered his wind and charged Cody, who was recklessly dismantling Stacks' musical instruments. The Gent clutched Cody's neck in a chokehold. "Listen to me, you white trash. This time I'm gonna let you leave here with a small inconvenience, a broken nose. If your money's good, you can come back in my joint anytime. But the next time you get loud with anybody in here, black or white, you won't be stumbling out of this bar. You'll wind up under the cement floor in the basement."

Cody seemed to be sobering quickly, his eyes pleading with fright. Burke propped Cody's head so to steady it and fired a knuckled hand into his face, bones cracking.

DeSimone overheard somebody say, "Jimmy, I think somebody called the cops."

Startled and out of breath, Burke was glad to see him. "When did you blow in here?"

"Thirty seconds ago."

"Just in time, eh?"

Droplets of blood splotched the scuffed wooden floor of Robert's Lounge, drippings from Cody and his shaggy dogs. Burke, DeSimone, and Manri, to avert a confrontation with the police, absconded through the basement door. The Gent didn't want to jeopardize his posse's readiness for Lufthansa. For any one of them, an arrest meant an automatic parole violation, forestalling the burglary.

The African-American musician, Stacks, had been DeSimone's high school truant companion. In their adulthood, DeSimone had introduced him to Burke's buccaneers. Hill, too, befriended Stacks, and the aspiring blues artist was grateful for the gigs Burke and Hill set up for him. Stacks reserved Friday evenings for Robert's Lounge and also played in restaurants and nightclubs under the control of Hill, Burke, and Vario. Stacks' easygoing character was his entry into the Robert's Lounge clubhouse, though his day job was the incentive for Burke & Co. to let him loaf about their haunches. Stacks was a "plastic dealer": a peddler of stolen credit cards, a common pilfering of the sixties and seventies. Hence, his asset to Burke and his crooks.

The Gent had also entrusted Stacks with disposing of the Lufthansa getaway van. Stacks was honored, and rightfully so. Called upon by an organized crime figure of the likes of Jimmy "the Gent" Burke was a privilege and a mark of respect for Stacks. However, such a responsibility, if mishandled, could plunge him from the greatest exhilaration to the blackest day of his life.

25

I found out that Werner got a message to Manri. "Lufthansa is about to take a shit, and a big one. So make sure you guys got your act together."

Jimmy had to un-wrinkle one last glitch, coordinating the robbery with the Gambinos. Through a *farfalla*, a messenger, the Gent made an appointment with one of their "captains," John Gotti, who oversaw the family's larcenies at Kennedy Airport.

Although I was up to my eyes in the narcotics wholesaling *and* recouping from the Boston versus Providence point-shaving flop, I made time to tag along with Jimmy. Gotti was in Long Island City at an Italian restaurant, Prudenti's Vicin' O'Mare, a place buzzing with Mafia VIPs. Most of these guys were garbed in Al Capone costumes: chalk-striped, double-breasted black suits and loud ties. The high-flying wiseguys flashed gold watches and rings that often outnumbered their fingers. It might've looked to outsiders as if they were competing in a pageant for most fashionable goombah.

That evening, the winner of the fashion show would've been John Gotti. He wore an ash gray single-breasted jacket, a powdery violet tie, and navy blue pleated slacks. I could've been a runner-up. I was clad in one of my Armanis, but with the name Hill, I wouldn't have been eligible as a contestant.

What is it with Mafia people and their flashy outfits? And what about those Lincolns and Cadillacs?

In the mid-seventies, a bunch of psychiatrists studying Italian gangsters diagnosed them as sociopaths. But mobsters did not think of themselves as lowly citizens. And to inflate their big-shot syndrome, they believed in flaunting designer suits and long Cadillacs to set them apart from the common outlaws. The majority of the so-called wiseguys, though, could hardly scratch a living. Jimmy and me, because of our brashness and skills to earn large, were one in a million.

A blonde hostess lugging super-sized breasts led Jimmy and me to Gotti's table.

"Henry, whoa! Get a load of this broad!" the Gent said, whistling in amazement. The woman's tits, sloshing under her knit blouse, were so heavy that the pull of their weight rounded her shoulders.

Gotti was with three or four dumb-looking bruisers. Taking into account the gold chains missing from those baboons' necks and wrists, and their undersized cheap clothes, they were probably gophers who handled low-level errands, fifty-dollar bone-breaking jobs. Gotti saw us coming into the dining room and snuffed his cigarette in an ashtray, smoke pouring out of his mouth. He stood, spread his arms, and threw them around Jimmy.

"Jimmy! How you doin'? Long time no see." They kissed on the cheek. In my childhood, I'd seen it when my mother's side of Sicilian immigrants got together: uncle kissing uncle, aunt kissing aunt.

I moved in, and save any corny cheek pecking, a limp handshake was all I gave the Gambino captain. We sat, and Gotti offhandedly named each of the goons in his company: Bruno, Mickey, Silvio, and Marino. Then he snarled at the four imbeciles. "Ouuh! Take a walk. Go have a drink at the bar. Tell the bartender it's on me."

A waiter, pen and pad in hand, parked himself close to the table. Gotti wagged two fingers at him. "Bring my friends here whatever they want."

Jimmy and I ordered chardonnays and got into reading the menu. Tricolor salad, Caesar salad, buffalo mozzarella with tomatoes, chicken and veal Marsala, eggplant and chicken parmigiana, meat ravioli, linguini with clams in a red sauce, mussels in a garlic broth. I'm a damn good chef, so I didn't think anything was worth eating. Every Italian restaurant I went into had the same dishes, and I was sick and tired of them. Plus everything was loaded with garlic, a condiment so overbearing you can't taste anything else. Believe it or not, authentic Italian cuisine isn't spiked with a heavy hand of garlic. In Italy, if your guest can smell it in a plate, it's an insult to his or her palate. And the same goes for onions. I wanted to say, *John, you got no class? How can you eat this garlic-stuffed shit?* But I didn't want a "fiver," a beating that might've landed me five days in a hospital; a "tensky" was twice that.

Gotti shifted sideways in his chair, crossed his legs, and held up his glass. "*Salut*, Jimmy, Henry."

Jimmy and I joined in. "*Salut.* To you, John."

"So what'r you got?" Gotti asked, a smirk widening on his lips.

Jimmy tapped me on the back of the neck. "Henry here came up with a hell of a score."

Gotti gazed at me, smiled, and bowed his head. "Ah! *Buona salute*, Henry."

Jimmy began talking to Gotti about Lufthansa, and I cut in here and there to take credit for my part.

Gotti squeezed his lips. "It's a good shot. I like it." He finished his wine and leaned forward, elbows firm on the table, hands folded under his chin. "What can I do to make it go smooth?"

"Well, John, we need some cooperation."

It was ten o'clock, and the restaurant was alive with customers, the noise level heightening by the minute. The stench of cigars and two-dollar men's cologne overpowered all scents—good and bad.

Gotti smoothed the sides of his ashen hair, a coif styled in a pompadour, and volunteered like a wolf about to sink his fangs into a piece of meat. "You say it, and you got it, Jimmy."

Minus any long-winded discussions, John Gotti granted his stamp of approval, and before the end of the evening, he and Jimmy sealed the terms. Gotti was to lend a warehouse where the Lufthansa haul was to be reloaded to "a switch car," and he'd work it out for an auto-wrecking yard—one indebted to the Gambinos—to crush and destroy the getaway van. Jimmy was to share with Gotti two hundred thousand dollars, 10 percent of what we figured might be a two-million-dollar theft.

Gotti poured wine, raised his glass, and we drank. Jimmy had the veal Marsala, but I didn't eat. I was glad not to have to chow down two dinners in one night, with my wife, Karen, and then with my girlfriend, a tiring shuffle. I had promised my *commara*, Linda, to take her to an after-hours Manhattan bistro, and later to Regine's, one of the hottest discos in the seventies. The single dinner was a welcome change. Some people think it must be nice to keep two women, but it's a lot of work. In the end, it's not worth it. Believe me!

The owner of the restaurant, a Sicilian American, walked to our table and rested his hand on Gotti's right shoulder. "Everything OK, John?"

Taken by surprise, and not recognizing the voice, Gotti looked up and quickly connected the raspy growl to the man standing over him.

"Ouuh! Anthony, it's you. Yeah, yeah, everything was terrific. Terrific." Gotti swept his arm from Jimmy to me. "Oh, this here's a friend of mine, Jimmy Burke. They call him the Gent. And this is Henry Hill. He's a half mick, but he's all right in my book." Gotti jabbed the air with his pinkie and said, "Anthony, whenever you see my buddies here, treat 'em right. They're friends of mine."

If Jimmy and I were made men, and Gotti introduced us to another made man, he wouldn't call us friends of *mine*. Instead, he'd say, friends of *ours*. Those are codes to single out Mafia members from outsiders.

Fawning over Gotti, Anthony guaranteed, "Sure, sure, John. They'll get the VIP treatment in my joint." He thrust a hand at Jimmy and then me, a gold bracelet with diamond initials, *AP*, glaring on his wrist.

The waiter brushed past us and left the check. Mr. Gotti swooped it off the table. "I got it, I got it. It's on me." He was quite the sport.

In the parking lot, waiting for the valet to fetch our automobiles, Gotti, a cigar between his fingers, moved in eye to eye with the taller Jimmy. The Gambino captain then said something, and I couldn't believe my ears.

"You know, Jimmy. You're a stand-up guy and a hell of an earner. What're you doing with that fat fuck Paul Vario?"

Gotti, a criminal with dangerous ambitions, had known Jimmy as a top earner. Why should Vario, and not he, reap the lion's share of the Jimmy Burke cash machine? For years, this bugged Gotti.

Mafia rules don't allow a made man to recruit an earner of another faction, unless at a sit-down the capo regimes of both parties approve of it. Jimmy and I stood on a gray line. Not of pure Italian lineage—and barred from the Cosa Nostra inner circles—we were freelancers without ties to any of the five crime families. And because Jimmy was a crafty profiteer, the New York Mafia syndicates often negotiated, and even fought, for a partnership with him. Nonetheless, Gotti's slick move stunned Jimmy, and he couldn't find words to turn down the Gambino captain without offending him. He hung his head and studied the ground.

"All due respect, John. I got no problem with you. And I got no problem with Paulie either. Right now, I have unfinished business with Paulie." Jimmy rustled the gravel with the tip of one shoe, and leveled his eyes with Gotti's. "John, it's not the end of the world. At some point we'll do some scores together."

I, too, was scuffing at the pebbles under my feet.

His baboons waiting in the Lincoln, Gotti waved at them, signaling he'd be there soon. He shook his head at the Gent and snickered with a wily grin. "Uh-huh. No doubt, Jimmy. One day, you and me, *and* Henry, we're gonna do a real big hit. Like stealin' the Verrazano, takin' it apart, and sellin' it for scrap. Now *there's* a score!" He laughed brashly, rapping Burke's chest with the back of his hand that held the cigar. For a few moments that seemed endless, he glared into Jimmy's eyes, then moseyed to his white ocean liner.

Gotti paraded with an overconfidence about him, a swagger that said, *if you got a problem with me, come and say it to my face.* He strutted with his legs slightly parted, his shoulders bobbing to the left and to the right, arms swinging, as if to say, *fuck off*. Before crouching into the car, he looked back at the Gent and hollered, "Jimmy, I'm gonna send my boy, Paolo Licastri, to talk to you. I want him to help you out with the job we just talked about."

Gotti and his jackasses drove out of the parking lot, and the darkness swallowed the Lincoln, the Manhattan skyline blinking in the background with a billion lights.

In the Mob world, the Gent was fearless—and feared. Yet, at Gotti's mention of Paolo Licastri, I had sensed a shiver bolting through Jimmy's spine. We'd heard of this bloodthirsty fanatic, whom even the two-pistol-packing Tommy DeSimone shuddered in his presence. And Gotti's message, "I'm gonna send my boy, Paolo, to talk to you," meant he had chosen who'd be seeing after the Gambinos' cut of the Lufthansa bonanza. It left Jimmy and me speechless.

26

"You know, it's pretty hard to play basketball with broken fingers. And if you two fuck up *again* with the Harvard game, that's what's gonna happen." I poked a finger at Kuhn and Sweeney. "You're gonna wind up with your hands in a vice. We took a hell of a hit on the Providence game last week. Now you better listen. Saturday night don't blow the Harvard game; otherwise you're gonna have a problem with me."

Sweeney side-glanced me to figure out if I was bluffing. Red-faced, he looked at Kuhn to read what *he* was thinking. I had ruffled the two athletes, and their laid-back Irish coolness thawed.

"Henry, we . . . we can't play under this pressure," Sweeney begged.

"Oh, really! When we went over this at the Boston Sheraton, you said you could easily get a grip on the games. Let's see, how did you put it? Oh, yeah, *it'd be a snap*." I snapped my fingers for drama. "And now two weeks later, you call it pressure?" I screamed, my arms flailing madly. "And today you got no answers. What happened, you lost your *shit-don't-stink* attitude?"

This was all going on in the lobby of the Boston Sheraton for the hotel guests in the lounge to hear and see. Kuhn and Sweeney, sticking out at six-five, looked as if they were looking for a hole to hide in. Plus they were shitting in their pants that my rumrunners might give them a beating.

Sweeney collected himself and spoke in a hush, hoping to snuff out the growing attention around us. "What we need is another man on the team to work with us," he said quietly. He saw the anger falling off my face and was smart enough to know he could deal with me. "See, Henry, if the other players are running hot, it isn't easy for us two alone to have a handle on the final score. There's only so much we can do without making it seem obvious we're throwing the game."

"Why didn't you say that from the get-go? Now I gotta go back to my people and tell them we need a third player. And lemme guess, he'll wanna get paid the same as you two. Right?"

Sweeney was squirming, and sat on a barstool. "Henry, when you look at the big picture, what's another twenty-five hundred dollars a game? Because then we can make sure the scores wind up the way we want them to."

I glared at both of them, venom in my eyes. But in all fairness, they were making sense. "You got somebody in mind?"

"We can get Earnie Cobb on our side," touted Kuhn. "He controls the ball, and he's our top scorer." By Kuhn's steadier voice, I could tell his pulse must've slowed. "We talked it over with Earnie, and he's all for it."

The Boston Eagles/Harvard game was a sensation. It was played before sixteen thousand spectators at the old Boston Garden, where watching the matches ran electricity through you. The Eagles were the favorite with the oddsmakers by a twelve-point spread. Through Marty's bookmakers, we bet twenty-five grand on Harvard to lose by less than the twelve-point spread. It worked out. Sweeney, Kuhn, and Cobb—the black guy of this trio—bungled plays, gave up easy shots, and though Boston won by three points, it was far short of the point spread.

Jimmy and Paul Vario were thrilled, and Marty was as happy as a child on Christmas morning—in his case, Hanukkah. And as one of the bookies in on the scheme, he lined his pockets with a piece of the winnings, plus the usual 10 percent vig.

For the next two games, the three kids rolled the scoring under the spread, and profits rolled in.

Three weeks from now, the Boston Eagles were expected to trounce Fordham, and surely the oddsmakers might pick a fifteen-point lead. It'd be a cinch for Kuhn, Sweeney, and Cobb to win by fewer than fifteen. Boston versus Fordham was the matchup Jimmy and I had been praying to happen. It'd be a lock, and we could make a lot of dollars. The returns might outweigh everything but Lufthansa.

The Fordham game was marked for February 3, 1979, and Sweeney pressed, "Bet the farm on Fordham. Henry, it's going to be a sure shot."

27

Henry Hill was still lost in his own world in Boston, frolicking morning, noon, and night with the fleshless, pointy-nosed Marley Carr. Somehow, he held tight to the reins of the fixed basketball games.

In New York, Joe Manri rushed into Robert's Lounge and trotted up to the bartender. "Where's Jimmy?"

The Wurlitzer jukebox from the late fifties was playing "Black Magic Woman" at full volume.

"What did you say, Joe?"

"Where's Jimmy?"

"I'll call him on the intercom, Joe. This jukebox is gonna make me go out of my mind."

"You're lucky," Manri quipped. "You don't have to go too far. You're halfway there."

In a minute, Burke came up from the cellar and shook Manri's hand. "What's happening, Joe?"

"I spoke to Werner."

"Not by phone, I hope."

"Jimmy, c'mon. Give me some credit. Anyhow, the Lufthansa money shipment came in. We gotta do the job early Monday morning at three o'clock."

A hard stare chilled Burke's aspect. "Good." Though an irresolvable circumstance troubled him: The misfits in his gang were not of sound mind. Amid Burke's psychotics roosted the bipolar, the manic-depressive, the sociopathic, the dyslexic, the narcissistic, and the sadistic. To add to the list of defects, they tended to stray off track. Those volatilities and weaknesses were as sensitive as the fuse of a bomb, and Burke was well aware he couldn't be too prudent.

In the late afternoon of December 10, 1978, less than twelve hours to the 3:00 a.m. Lufthansa exploit, although the dance routine of the robbery had been practiced exhaustively, Burke felt "with these morons" a thorough last-minute going over was a must. That evening, he rounded up his crew. A string of eleventh-hour movements had made for a hectic day, and Burke could feel that weariness was impeding the focus of his stickup men. They gathered at the table in the cellar of Robert's Lounge and were rapt by their shepherd's last session of instructions. The Gent concentrated on the final review of the Lufthansa hangar footprint, the alarm-disabling schematics, the names and number of the night-shift workers—information Louis Werner had compiled and relayed to Manri.

"Pass it around and look at it 'til you memorize everything in your heads," Burke insisted, instilling a final caution to his bumblers not to ignore any details.

At 8:20 p.m., Burke and DeSimone had to check themselves in at the halfway house. Before leaving, Burke stood tall above the table, and as a pastor blesses his apostles, preached, "I think we covered it all. If something isn't clear, speak up now." Truly a mock image of da Vinci's *Last Supper*. The Gent gazed at his sheep, or rather wolves, locking his stare on Paolo Licastri. "Because if you run into a problem, I don't wanna hear, 'oh, I didn't know what I was supposed to do.'"

They nodded respectfully, all except Licastri. Burke rapped the tabletop with his knuckles. "All right, we'll see each other afterward at the Maspeth warehouse. Good luck."

Burke and DeSimone trekked up the stairs and left Robert's Lounge. The others stayed and began the countdown to 3:00 a.m. One of the gunmen, Louis Cafora, was to drive Burke and DeSimone to the halfway house for their nightly check-in. Afterward, they'd sneak out, Cafora would return DeSimone to Ozone Park, where the Lufthansa hit team was waiting. Owing to his 360 pounds of blubber, Cafora's nickname was "Roast Beef." Cafora backed his Cadillac Coupe DeVille out of the parking spot behind Robert's Lounge and wheeled around to the front entrance.

Burke and DeSimone were donning black overcoats and carried toiletry totes under their arms. It was cold with a penetrating humidity, and smoke seeped from their mouths. DeSimone opened the passenger door, folded the leather seat forward, and to straighten his long legs stretched sideways on the rear bench seat. Burke sat in the front next to Cafora and shut the door.

"Tommy, are you all right back there? Or should I pull up my seat a bit?" Burke asked. Coupe DeVilles were short of legroom.

"Nah. It won't make no difference. I got my legs up across the seat."

Burke turned to Cafora. "Mind if I smoke?" There was no sense in asking permission; Burke had already lit a cigarette. DeSimone, too, fired up a Camel. A mile down the road, the air in the Cadillac was as smoky as the inside of a chimney.

"Should we take the Midtown Tunnel?" Cafora asked, coughing and spitting phlegm out the window. Burning cigarettes revolted him, though out of respect for the Gent tolerated the smoking.

"Yeah, the Midtown is a good shot this time of night. And step on it, 'cause we wanna get there early," Burke hastened.

He and DeSimone had planned to arrive at the halfway house earlier than the eleven o'clock curfew. From eleven on, the only living soul there was a lone correction officer, a lethargic, easygoing black man with creases on his skin dating him back to the Civil War. His memory was shorter than short, and should he be called upon to verify the entries in the logbook as to Burke and DeSimone's check-in, in his fogged recollection he might not remember if he were alive that far back. Their purpose was *to be seen* at the halfway house before it was too late. Until ten o'clock, a cleaning porter and three guards were still on duty and could solidify Burke and DeSimone's alibi for that night.

Registering in the logbook was a quick step, but Burke and DeSimone made a lengthy to-do of it. Rather than going directly to their cells as they ordinarily did, they loitered in the lobby, and in his clownish way DeSimone joked with the guards. "What the hell does the cleaning man use to mop the floors? It smells worse than piss," he said, crinkling his nose.

The shorter of the correction officers volleyed with a crack. "When we do urine tests on you prisoners, we throw your piss in the wash water. It's so full of liquor and drugs that it's good for scrubbing floors."

Burke cut in with a quip of his own. "Well, it can't be my piss, because it sure wouldn't stink like this crap. It'd smell like Johnnie Walker Black."

Except for the elderly guard, who hadn't understood the pun, everybody laughed boisterously. This was a ploy to underscore the moment so the correction officers and the porter would not forget the incident. DeSimone and Burke ultimately bid them good night and went upstairs to their rooms/cells. All the while, Cafora was parked two blocks to the east on 54th Street.

A month prior, Burke and DeSimone had been transferred from their penitentiaries and remanded to the halfway house, the Community Treatment Center. The CTC was where inmates transitioned from incarceration to freedom. It was a high-rise on 54th Street near Times Square. The Federal Bureau of Prisons had leased this ramshackle edifice and converted it to a minimum-security lockup. Amid the contemporary skyscrapers, it was an eyesore, galling the property management companies in the area.

For the privilege of completing his sentence at the CTC, an inmate had to comply with rule number one: be gainfully employed. This was not a difficulty; "phantom jobs" could easily be arranged.

Second, the Bureau of Prisons imposed an 11 o'clock curfew. On the ground floor, near the entrance of the CTC, stood "the bubble," a three-sided glass-enclosed booth from which the correction officers oversaw the traffic of convicts. The guards were not the beefy types you'd find on detail at the harsh jailhouses. This quasi-prison was staffed by hunched-over, slow-shuffling seniors on their way to pasture. Incredibly, a half dozen of these older gents were the whole force guarding homicidal prisoners with the brutality of Tommy DeSimone and Jimmy Burke.

The plaster on the walls in and around the bubble was peeling, and two of the four fluorescent light fixtures were burned out. On the upper floors were the prisoners' cells, and many of the windows could not be locked. The three-foot-square casements led onto a fire escape in an alleyway at the rear of the CTC. To flee unnoticed, one didn't have to be Houdini. Correction officers at most prisons carry out body counts several times during the night. At the CTC this precaution was not practiced. The one-time daily count occurred at 11:00 p.m. when the inmates were due in. If a convict wished to stroll down 42nd Street or rendezvous with a hot date, or *rob an airline*, he could do so at his whim. Sneaking out was simple: through a window, onto the fire escape, and into the alley. And as long as you returned by the same route no later than 7:00 a.m., when the inmates checked out, no one would be the wiser.

"Everything all right?" Cafora asked, DeSimone and Burke sinking into the plush seats of the Cadillac.

"Piece o'cake. It's gettin' easier and easier to sneak out of the joint," DeSimone said, lighting a cigarette.

"Ouh! Enough of these fuckin' cigarettes," Cafora protested. "You're gonna choke me to death."

Burke didn't balk.

They drove in silence for three quarters of an hour, and the Cadillac stopped in front of a brick warehouse on a dead-end street in Maspeth. The whole block was lightless and night-still. Burke got out of the automobile. Before shutting the door, he pointed at DeSimone, and said with firmness, "Remember, I don't want nobody gettin' hurt. OK?"

"No problem," DeSimone said unconvincingly.

Burke gave him a steely-eyed stare that said he wasn't having it any differently. He slapped the roof of the car and disappeared through the side door of the warehouse.

Cafora steered the Coupe DeVille onto Metropolitan Avenue, and three miles east the headlights flashed on a sign indicating the Interboro Parkway Eastbound. "We should get to Ozone Park in about fifteen minutes. I'm kind of hungry."

"We just ate dinner. How many times a day you gotta eat? Jesus!" DeSimone complained.

"I just want something to kill the appetite. Let's go to Don Peppe's for a bowl of scungilli and fried calamari. Or maybe a nice deep dish of pasta e fasool." He glanced at his passenger for a look into his thoughts. "It'll only take ten minutes."

DeSimone threw his head back. "What the fuck, you're like a pregnant cow. Every fifteen minutes you're chomping on something. We ain't got much time, man."

Cafora won. Burping, he gobbled a combo of scungilli/calamari in a fire-breathing sauce and a two-foot loaf of Italian bread he dunked in olive oil. Perhaps, it was the intake of hot sauces that had blemished Roast Beef's round face with black-cherry colored patches, resembling a soccer ball. "I got *achità*, can you believe it?" he groused.

"Can I believe it?" DeSimone exclaimed. "You ate like a fuckin' pig for the fifth time today. One day, your belly is gonna tear apart like a sack overstuffed with rotten eggs."

They drove on to Robert's Lounge to link up with the rest of Burke's mercenaries.

28

The stage was set, the curtain rose, and the performers readied for Act One.

In this predawn hour of Monday, December 11, 1978, a black Ford van with six passengers is entering Kennedy Airport from the northeast end, a zone with a chain of cargo hangars. A silver Pontiac Grand Prix, the chase car, is trailing the van. The two-vehicle motorcade continues to travel southbound on the JFK Expressway, and at the Federal Circle intersection it veers off the ramp and heads east on Nassau Expressway. Within a half mile, the driver of the Ford van, Angelo Sepe, has in his sight the Lufthansa yellow florescent sign atop Cargo Building-261.

"It's a quarter-to-three. We're five minutes early," Sepe says.

DeSimone glances at his wristwatch. "You better slow it down, Angelo. We shouldn't get there before ten to three."

Sepe steers into a maze of parking lots until he reaches the targeted hangar, the German airline freight complex. The chase car passes the van, idles to the rear of the three-story Lufthansa building, and parks in front of a loading dock. The Ford van then stops near the main entrance, and everyone inside hardly breathes as they peruse the environment. White lighting splashes out of the third-floor office windows, at this restful hour, though, Kennedy Airport is dormant, and even a watchdog can find peace. The six armed robbers can hear the sound of a truck and the swishing tires of a courier panel-van somewhere in the distance. The takeoff and landing of aircrafts is non-existent, an eerie contrast to the frenetic daytime traffic at the world's busiest airfield. The quietness and stillness is strange to the marauders; they've never roamed the inner roadways of the airport at three in the morning. It spooks and confuses them.

"Shit, I hope we don't run into ghosts," Sepe says. But in the perimeter of the Lufthansa compound no phantoms are in sight, and the burglars' breathing restarts, their hearts throttling back to a slower beat. Sepe then shifts the van into drive and eases on a hundred yards to the east of the hangar, where the chase car has been waiting. He brakes to a halt twenty feet from a chain-link fence. A padlocked gate encloses the loading ramp.

A square, man-size gaping hole opens widely on the side of the van as the door slides open. Four of the six men, Frenchy McMahon, Joe Manri, Tommy DeSimone, and Louis Cafora, have been in a squatting position on the metal floor. Sepe throws the selector lever into park. "OK, it looks clear. Get out now." He and the gunman seated to his right stay put in the vehicle, and their four compatriots, in a disguise of black ski masks and dark clothing, disembark. Two of them hop out with agility; overweight Manri and Cafora roll out as if they are two giant pillows bouncing off a bed.

In case someone spots them, Sepe waits three or four seconds—poised to scamper away—but the seas are at peace, and he climbs out of the van. The man in the front passenger seat, Paolo Licastri, also bails out. A short Sicilian immigrant without a visa, Licastri is on hand as John Gotti's envoy. Licastri and his bunch clump in front of the van.

McMahon peers at his watch. "OK, guys. Mr. Hychko should be coming soon."

Mike Hychko, a shipping clerk, is due back from collecting air bills from various airlines that, through Lufthansa, forward shipments to Europe. He regularly finishes these errands in time for the 3:00 a.m. meal break.

And here he pulls up with punctuality. Hychko, medium built with a square jaw and refined facial features, parks his pickup truck next to the Ford van, and the half dozen people grouped near it unnerve him. Five of the shadowy figures, he notices, are wearing wool caps. Hychko's eyes blink with alarm. "What're you guys doing here? And . . . and you can't park this van here by the gate."

The sixth interloper, Sepe, head and face uncovered, tackles Hychko. With the butt of his Colt .45 Gold Cup semiautomatic, a marksman competition firearm, Sepe thwacks the Lufthansa clerk on the skull and restrains him in a headlock. Hychko's wound gushes blood, tinting his light, wavy hair, and he roars out a piercing scream. "Rolf, Rolf, c'mon out here. Call Port Authority. I'm getting kidnapped. Call 9 . . ."

Manri rams his shotgun into Hychko's stomach. "Shut the fuck up, or I'll put a couple ounces of lead in your temple." Hychko's hollering is echoing, and he's writhing to break free from Sepe's forearm hold. The gash on his scalp is deep, and his face is sodden with blood. DeSimone pitches in and grapples Hychko from Sepe, who's fumbling to slip on his mask.

Too late. Hychko's memory bank has photographed a snapshot of Sepe.

Sepe puts on his ski cap. He plucks Hychko's wallet and waves it in front of the man's eyes. "OK, Mr. Hychko, I got your wallet, and now we know where you live. Somebody's gonna be parked on your block. If you rat on me, you can kiss your family good-bye. Got it?"

Anguishing over his fate, and more immediately, the life-threatening loss of blood, Hychko doesn't answer but nods in full understanding. DeSimone then handcuffs Hychko and bullies him. "Where's the three-sided key?" He raps the wounded man on his head. "Gimme the key. In which pocket do you have it?" DeSimone grabs the lapels of Hychko's coat and shakes him. "I said, gimme the fuckin' three-sided key."

The three-sided key? They have inside information, Hychko perceives. Panting, he mumbles, "It's . . . it's in my left side pocket."

DeSimone gropes in the pockets of Hychko's trousers and finds the specially shaped key that deactivates the loading ramp motion detectors, a system wired to the Port Authority headquarters at the airport. "Mr. Hychko, where's the switch for this key on the gates?"

Hychko's wincing contorts his face. "It's on the right post of the gate. Right there, you see it?"

DeSimone slides the key into the cylinder and switches the tumbler to the "off" position. "You better not have lied, Hychko. 'Cause if the alarm is still on, you're gonna be a bag of broken bones."

Hurriedly, with a bolt cutter Cafora swiftly shears the thick chain that's padlocked to the gates. He pushes them inward. DeSimone prods the wounded Hychko inside the fenced grounds, manhandling him to the top of the loading platform, the rest of the gunners following with soft steps. Sepe quickens his pace, trots ahead of DeSimone and Hychko, and reaches the small service door to the hangar. He presses the handle downward and steps indoors, everyone else at his heels. Werner had informed Manri that this door, the one used for foot traffic, will be unsecured. So far, Werner's input has been accurate, and the pirates are hoping the upcoming sequences will be faultless.

They storm inside, and a Lufthansa shipping agent, Rolf Rebmann, hears the shuffle of feet and a commotion of energetic movement. Rows of steel shelving stacked to the ceiling grid the ground level of the warehouse, and Rebmann's workstation is at the end of those lanes. He cranes his neck into the open space, and on seeing the charging gunmen, tenses. Rebmann's lips freeze, and he can barely speak. "Hey . . . hey, what's going on? Who are you?"

With the snap of a lisping snake, Licastri leaps at Rebmann's throat, and Sepe binds the man's wrists behind his back.

Rebmann struggles futilely and succumbs, his knees shaking. "Don't hurt me. I'll do whatever you want. I got two kids and a sick wife."

"Join the club," DeSimone replies. "I got a wife who plays sick, too. I've never known a married woman who isn't sick. The minute you marry them, they get sick and stop fucking."

Sepe says, "Take it easy, take it easy, Mr. Rebmann. Keep your mouth shut and nothin's gonna happen. And if any of you steps out of line, you'll all get it." To stress the threat, Sepe, in mock, raises the barrel of his semi-automatic to his temple. "See? Get my drift?"

The gunmen were clued in that at the end of the shelf rows, somewhere near the high-value vault, a security guard may be loafing out of sight. Up to now, the lone watchman has not yet detected the intrusion. Manri, whom Burke appointed in charge, directs the assailants, and in a whispery voice says, "Frenchy, you and Cafora go find the guard. He's an old dog, so go easy on him." Manri indicates the direction where the watchman may be stationed. "He's probably goofing off back there next to that pile of pallets. Go get him; we'll wait here."

McMahon and Cafora, crouching, walk stealthily down the aisles. They turn a corner and see the guard slurping hot soup from a Styrofoam cup and listening to a radio broadcasting the weather. His face is gaunt and gray. His frame, tall and fleshless, is curved forward, and from a side-view it forms a "C." He's a dozen years past his golden days and doesn't belong on the night shift protecting Lufthansa's cargo hangar.

The two commandos rush the watchman. He glimpses at them, and in a delayed reaction his body flexes, and the soup spills onto the floor. Cafora, his gun aimed at the wrinkled geriatric, says, "It's OK, Granpa. It's OK. Nothin's gonna happen. Come on with us." McMahon and Cafora each gently clasp one of his arms and walk him through the maze of shelving to reunite with their compatriots.

Petrified out of his wits and vibrating faster than a tuning fork, the brittle guard doesn't know how to react. His job calls for him to arrest trespassers and detain them until the police respond. How can this senior, who's in pain from a slipped disc and rheumatism, enforce security? He can scarcely stand upright, never mind wrangling 250-pound armed robbers.

For his will, though, he deserves an "A." "What'r you think you're doing? We got cops all over the airport. You don't know it, but the loading dock outside has an alarm, and you probably tripped it. And ... and Port Authority will be here any minute."

McMahon chuckles. "We know about it, Pop. As we said, it's all gonna be all right. And because you're the oldest here, when we get upstairs tell everybody there to behave and not to do anything stupid. OK? And nobody will get hurt."

"Or killed," adds Cafora, and the watchman gasps, his freckled hands trembling.

Manri sees that McMahon and Cafora have the guard in their custody. "Good. You found the old man." Under his breath, out of earshot of the captives, he calls out, "Frenchy, Tommy, Roast Beef, and me will take these three with us and go upstairs to round up the rest of the night workers. Angelo, Paolo, you two stay down here. If anybody shows up, tie the fuckers and take them to the lunchroom."

Werner had instructed Manri to locate and account for the night supervisor, seven employees, and one guard. Nine in total. And Werner specified that at 3:00 a.m., the night shift groups in the lunchroom for the meal break. This was the significance of initiating the raid at 2:50 a.m.

Paolo Licastri questions Manri's directive, and in his thick Italian accent suggests, "Why I no go with you? If you gotta kill somebody, I can do easy."

"The Gent don't want nobody killed here tonight. And if you do, you'll be the next one to go. Got it?" Manri promised.

"Whatsa matta? Burke no have big *collioni*, eh? Ah, ah, ah."

Manri exhales heavily, bellies up to Licastri's chest, and hovers over him. "You just do what I say, you little prick." Inches from the Sicilian's eyes, Manri rams the air with his finger. "Because if you don't, we'll send you back to your boss, Mr. Gotti, in tomato sauce jars." This silences Licastri—for the moment.

Manri motions with his sawed-off shotgun for McMahon, DeSimone, and Cafora to follow him up the stairway. DeSimone and Cafora are dragging along the two Lufthansa cargo expeditors and the old gent, jabbing the younger two in their spines.

Manri flips off the light switch in the stairwell; he and his co-holdup men, flashlights in hand, nudge along the three captives, and they all file up to the third floor.

29

They're climbing two flights of stairs. Leading, Cafora stops on the landing and signals with his hand for everyone to halt. "Hold up." He can smell microwaved food, and murmurs are rumbling from one end of this floor.

"They're supposed to be in the lunchroom," McMahon says under his breath.

The melody of a song is seeping from the cafeteria. Faintly audible, the lyrics are escaping into the hallway: "Monday, Monday, can't trust that day . . ."

Handcuffed and standing between the watchman and Hychko, Rebmann informs them, "They're all in the cafeteria. The supervisor, Rudi Eirich, is the only one who doesn't come up here." This submissiveness is Rebmann's way of ingratiating himself in the hope the brutes will spare him harm.

Suddenly, a chirping of rubber soles, then the jolly whistling of a man nearing the stairwell.

"I guess they're not *all* in the lunchroom. Are they, Mr. Rebmann?" DeSimone chides. "Listen, Rebmann. Don't try to be cute, because you're gonna get your ears cut off. You're already a donkey, and you'll look even stupider without ears. So who the fuck could be walkin' around in the hallway?"

Rebmann's intent to cooperate is misconstrued and reeks of deception. He explains, "No . . . no. That . . . that could be the supervisor, Eirich. I . . . I told you he's the . . . the only one who doesn't come to the lunchroom on his meal break."

"Shut the fuck up and don't say another word," Cafora shushes, tightening his jaws.

Manri prods DeSimone to step out into the corridor with him and grab hold of whoever is wandering outside the cafeteria. Guns up high, the two robbers spring into the brightly lit hallway and plant their feet two yards from Cargo Agent John Murray. Not to draw the attention of those in the cafeteria, DeSimone says quietly but harshly, "Put your hands up. What's your name?" His .38 Magnum pearl-handle Smith & Wesson is aimed at Murray's midsection.

The abrupt images of the masked gunmen terrify Murray. Only because adrenalin is anesthetizing him, he dares to ask, "Who are *you*?"

Manri and DeSimone move in, flanking Murray, the shotgun and the Smith & Wesson scraping his temples.

"We're asking the questions, not *you*." Manri's eyes are spearing Murray's through the eyeholes of the ski mask. He jams the barrels of the shotgun into Murray's forehead. The cargo agent twitches, the veins in his temples now blue and swelling. "If you wanna be a wiseass, a blast from this thing will make a tunnel through your head."

DeSimone has ten pairs of handcuffs in a satchel strapped to his shoulder. He pulls out one set and fetters Murray's hands, while Manri holds the shotgun inches from him. "Mr. Murray, where's everybody else?"

Murray points with his chin at the doors of the lunchroom. "Some of them are in there."

"Where's everybody else?"

"The supervisor is downstairs in his office. Rolf Rebmann, Mike Hychko, and the security guard are somewhere in the warehouse," John Murray answers genuinely, unaware three of his coworkers have already been corralled.

Werner had said the night supervisor, Rudi Eirich, often stays in his office on the warehouse level. Manri does some math in his head. "Mr. Murray, how many people should be in the cafeteria?"

"Probably seven." Murray assumes he is the only one captured; otherwise, he would've confirmed only four workers in the lunchroom.

Werner had also spoken about a cleaning service. "Where are the porters, Mr. Murray?"

Murray is shaking as loosely as a leaf in the wind. "They're . . . they're gone. They leave early." Judging by the scent of fresh wax and the high luster of the blue vinyl-tiled floor, Manri and DeSimone believe him.

Manri knows of the independent contracted porters, the number of personnel in the building, and their identity. It's clear, Murray thinks, a

Lufthansa employee must've spelled out the indispensable facts to the robbers. And though the sight of Manri's shotgun is short-circuiting Murray's brain, he's convinced the ring leader of this holdup is Louis Werner.

Everyone in the building now accounted for, Manri and DeSimone walk Murray to the stairwell, and Manri nods at his companions to take the captives into the cafeteria. He touches his nose as a reminder to maintain silence. "We got everybody who's supposed to be in the building. There should be four more in the lunchroom down the hall."

Single file, the four thugs herd the hostages down the tunnel-like corridor. They stride up to the swinging doors of the lunchroom; DeSimone kicks them open and hurls Murray inside. McMahon gives Hychko and Rebmann each a hard push, and Cafora and Manri lurch in with the watchman.

In this moment, the four in the cafeteria are unflustered by the incursion. "Oh, c'mon, what kind of a joke is this. You guys got nothin' better to do?"

"It's . . . its no joke," warns Rebmann, his mouth quavering.

"Oh, please. Get the fuck outta here. Who do you think you're fooling?" says one of the workers.

Manri flaunts his weapon. "This ain't no joke, and if you don't believe this shotgun is real, lemme put a shot in your fuckin' head."

The harrowing invasion nearly ceases the heartbeat of the Lufthansa night shift, and the leisurely meal break erupts into bedlam.

His shotgun sweeping side to side, Manri shouts, "Get on the floor face down, and don't look up."

Two of the Lufthansa staffers had been dozing. Having been jarred from sleep, but not quite fully awake, their grogginess sees this head-whirling moment as the absurdity of a dream.

The seven hostages do as they're told and scramble to the floor.

Manri yells out, "Like I said, everybody keep your fuckin' eyes down and don't look around the room."

One of the detainees, Wolfgang Ruppert, can't seem to concentrate on keeping his gaze on the pavement; his eyes rove from Cafora, to McMahon, to Manri.

Cafora goes up to Rupert and presses his booted foot on the man's neck. "We told you not to look around. If you lift your head again, you better say your last prayer."

Ruppert complies and starts weeping. "I have a family of five. Two of my sons are three and four years old. They need me."

Cafora grins. "Yeah, well, everybody needs their fathers."

One by one, the captors rifle through the pockets of the prisoners, take their wallets, and hurl them at DeSimone for him to keep in his satchel. The robbers then take turns addressing the Lufthansa staff. This tactic is to lessen the chance for the gunmen to leave traits or clues of their identities. McMahon is in rotation to speak. Mimicking a professional master of ceremonies, he clears his throat. "You all must've heard the story of the unsung hero. The message I'm trying to drive home is this; we're as concerned for your safety as you are yourselves."

Burke had chosen McMahon to give this speech because his manner was the exception within the Robert's Lounge gang; his pronunciation was indistinct, unlike the rest of them, whose New York Brooklynese accent could be singled out even by a foreigner. "We got your wallets, and we know who you are and where you live. So please do what we say. If any of you doesn't obey, *remember*, we can find you. You should also understand that the damage we're going to do tonight to Lufthansa, a corporation with millions and millions of dollars, will be as minute as a mosquito bite on a horse. But if you try to be a hero, well . . . it may cost you your life. Now that's a big loss. So no heroes, please!"

Manri and DeSimone lift Murray to his feet and shove him into the corridor. "Mr. Murray, pay attention," Manri says. "I want you to call your supervisor and have him come up here."

"You mean Rudi Eirich?" Murray asks.

"Yeah, him."

Supervisor Rudi Eirich is responsible for the high-value vault and the alarm keys.

"You want me to get him up here? What do you want me to say to him?"

Cafora is up at bat to do the talking. "How about telling him he's got a call from headquarters in Germany. When Germany phones, he's gotta take the call. Right? So don't play stupid. If you don't get Eirich here, I'm gonna mix your brains in your dinner." Cafora glances at his watch. "Germany is six hours ahead of us. Let's see, it's 3:15 here. There, it's 9:15 in the morning. So it's likely they could be calling. Right?"

Holding Murray by the arms, Manri and Cafora take him to his workstation. Cafora unshackles him so he can dial. The cargo agent picks up the phone on his desk and punches in Eirich's extension.

Manri grasps Murray's wrist and interrupts his dialing. "Before you call Eirich, lemme warn you. Don't get the idea to use tricky words to give your boss a heads-up. Remember what we said in the lunchroom: no heroes, please."

Murray bobs his head and redials. "Rudi, it's John Murray. Listen, I . . . I got a call on hold from Germany. They wanna talk to you. Said it's important."

Manri and Cafora assume Eirich to be saying, "Switch the call to my extension."

"No . . . no, Rudi," Murray stammers. "The call . . . the call came in on the open line." The open line is a dedicated telephone toll cable for overseas communications.

There's a lapse in the phone conversation. Seconds pass, and Murray hangs up the receiver. "Mr. Eirich's coming." He's perspiring but is relieved.

Cafora removes his gun from Murray's temple. "Good, good."

Manri, too, bows with appreciation. "Good job, John." By now, they're on a first-name basis.

Towing Murray along, Cafora and Manri go to the far end of the hallway where the steel door to the stairs is. They keep Murray standing against the wall, and the two holdup men position themselves out of sight on the sides of the stairwell.

Manri says to Murray, "Don't make a move." Forty seconds clicked, and Eirich hasn't arrived. Manri frowns at Murray. "I hope you weren't foolish enough to have said something to give Eirich a hint."

Murray's forehead douses to a drench. "Hell, no! He . . . he'll be here. It's a long walk from his office. He'll be here . . . soon."

He isn't lying. In ten seconds, Eirich pushes open the fireproof door and urgently emerges from the stairway. To his dismay, a mouth-fluttering dread, Eirich runs into the deadly end of a high-caliber pistol and a stubby, double-barreled shotgun. And so sinister are the sizes and shapes of the felons toting the artillery.

"What the hell . . . ," Eirich utters, and his body braces.

Cafora wiggles the tip of his gun on Eirich's cheek. "Relax, relax. You missed the speech in the cafeteria. The bottom line is we don't want you to be a hero. Everything's gonna work out, and nobody will get harmed. *Or killed*." Cafora nods. "Let's have your wallet."

Hands trembling, Eirich promptly produces it.

"In the next half hour," Manri forewarns, "a couple of hot-headed guys, who have no respect for a human life, will be parking themselves in front of your house. Know what I mean?" He nods, and Manri says, "I know you do, Mr. Eirich. Now let's go to the cafeteria."

Envisioning a prelude to death, Eirich lowers his head, and the two robbers pull him by the arms for the hike to the lunchroom.

On seeing his staff sprawled on the cafeteria floor with an armed, hooded burglar standing over them—a heart-skipping picture—Eirich wets his underwear. More wrenching, he sees blood dripping from Hychko's scalp, leaching onto the pavement as though it were a red, slow-moving river.

Manri bumps Eirich's back with the shotgun barrels. "These are eight of your people. Is everyone here, or is someone missing? And don't bullshit me."

Eirich counts eight pathetic men, one's hair bloody and tangled. "Yes, they're all here." His fingers unsteady, he indicates Hychko. "Eh, he's losing a lot of blood. He needs an ambulance." The supervisor feels his urine warming the left thigh and frets that the expanding stain on his pants might be noticeable.

"Yeah, yeah. The sooner you get the money room opened and closed, the sooner we get out of here, and the sooner you'll be able to get help for Hychko. OK?" Manri waves the shotgun in the direction of the stairs. "Let's go downstairs."

Manri, Cafora, and McMahon take Eirich two floors below to his glass-enclosed office, where the alarm control panels are mounted on a wall. Cafora tugs roughly at Eirich's sweater. "You got the key for the alarm?"

Shivering from fright, Eirich straightens his collar and points to a safe anchored under the control panels. "When I'm in the building, I keep it in there."

With his forehead, Manri nods at the safe. "Get it."

Burke's orders to his field marshal, Joe "Buddha" Manri, are not to injure anybody. And unaware of such considerateness, these hell-bent raiders portend a fatal ending. Hand trembling, Eirich works the combination dial, opens the safe door, and reaches in for the key.

All the while, Licastri and Sepe have been standing by on the loading platform. Earlier, Licastri removed a key from Rebmann's pocket, and with it, he, Licastri, turns on the switch next to the overhead door. It opens, and Sepe backs the Ford van into the cargo bay. The van now indoors, Licastri switches the door shut.

Manri instructs Eirich to disarm the alarm, a delicate procedure. The position of the switch must be precise, a deliberate exactness intended to trip unauthorized tempters. Eirich steadies his thinly fingers, huffing and wiping his brow. He sets the knob to the supposedly correct setting. "The alarm is off."

"Hear me out, Eirich, before we go and unlock the door to the vault, let's get one thing straight. If you're doin' some kind of trick and an alarm goes off at the Port Authority, we'll . . ."

Eirich loses his composure and bangs on the alarm panel. "Oh, stop this shit. I don't want to be no hero, and I don't want any trouble. I got a family to go to. All I want is for you people, whoever you are, to take what you want and get the hell out of here. And leave my workers unhurt. God damn it!"

Eirich's outburst surprises the robbers, and Manri doesn't want to test Eirich's sincerity. "Here's what I'm gonna do. If you got nothin' to worry about, then when we leave here, you won't mind coming with us until we're out of the airport. All right?" Manri squares his shoulders and speculates, "If you did what you weren't supposed to do, and we get a tail of cops on our asses, well, then we can kill you right then and there. How's that?"

Cafora breaks out into a laugh. "That's a good one, Joe."

Eirich doesn't see the humor, his knees as rubbery as overcooked linguini, and feels he's about to faint.

30

McMahon and Joe Manri leave Eirich's office, and Cafora stays to guard him. McMahon and Manri huddle in a corner to mull over the supervisor's fate.

"Joe," McMahon says, "I don't think it's a good idea to take Eirich with us."

Manri crimps his lips. "Why not?"

McMahon shakes his head negatively. "Let's say we make it out of the parking lot, and somewhere down the highway we get into a chase with the cops. You know how DeSimone and that nut-job Licastri are. They got balls but no brains, and the common sense of a two-day-old spic."

The common sense of a two-day-old spic! McMahon's disparagement incenses Manri, a South American himself, though he can't defend against the slur. It must remain secret that he isn't of Italian descent. Inwardly, he's boiling with rage and would love to strangle McMahon.

"If things get hairy," McMahon reasons, "with Eirich *and* those two empty-headed nitwits in the van, anything can go wrong. Then we'd have a murder rap on our hands." Affecting a psychological dominance, he palms his gloved hand on the wall above Manri's left shoulder. McMahon's uniqueness to the Robert's Lounge gang is one of value; though he's a schizophrenic, his cleverness and keenness are talents Burke needs to restrain the rest of the louts in check.

Seething, Manri glares fiercely at McMahon and doesn't answer.

McMahon pauses and lets four to five seconds linger. "Me, I'd rather take my chances with the cops. I mean, Sepe is a hell of a driver." McMahon senses he's mollifying Manri.

Manri studies the cement floor, and McMahon recaps, "I believe Eirich is playing it straight. He doesn't seem the type to risk it all. And for what? So when he retires, Lufthansa will give him a twenty-dollar watch?"

Manri isn't the sharpest knife in the drawer, though his smarts are a notch above the rest of Burke's flock. He mulls for a moment or two. "All right, Frenchy, I'll go along with you on this, but if something goes wrong, it's on you. Let's get Eirich to open the vault."

The high-value chamber is built as two separate vaults, an outer and an inner. The cartons of money are stored in the inner room. To access the second vault, after deactivating the alarm, one must unlock the door (Door-1) to the outer chamber. Once inside there, Door-1 must be closed before opening the one to the second vault (Door-2), a critical step. If Door-1 and Door-2 are simultaneously left open, a warning sounds off at the Port Authority.

Settled on trusting Eirich, Manri and McMahon trot back to his office.

"Are we taking him with us?" Cafora asks.

"No, we ain't," Manri answers with an air of finality.

"Why not?"

"Let's just get this done," Manri says.

McMahon looks severely at Eirich. "OK, the moment of reckoning is here."

Manri presses the barrels of his weapon against Eirich's spine, and they fast-step to where the vault is, McMahon following them.

Again, Manri prods Eirich with the shotgun. "Open it. So far you've done good. Don't blow it now, Eirich." The four-inch thick cast-iron door can only be unlocked by turning three handles to the left and to the right in a preset sequence, and Eirich does so. No alarms or sirens, so far.

"Thank God!" Eirich mutters, his inhalations slowing.

The faces of Manri, McMahon, and Cafora are glistening with perspiration, and their pulses have suddenly quickened. They seem to be wondering if a silent alarm is alerting the police. A battalion of cops could be here in two to three minutes and surround the Lufthansa complex.

"Get inside." Manri jostles Eirich through the doorway of the vault. "There's supposed to be an alarm button somewhere on a wall. Where is it?"

Eirich points to a red knob next to the light switch. "It's right there."

"OK, Eirich, sit down in the middle of the floor."

Listening for sirens, a torrent of misgivings rushes through Cafora's mind. He's been keeping watch on Eirich; McMahon snaps him out of his anxieties. "Pay attention and make sure Eirich don't go near that red button over there."

"How many times do I have to say it? I don't want trouble," Eirich appeals.

"Yeah, yeah, we believe you, but we can't take chances," Manri says. "Now you're the man of the hour, Mr. Eirich. Stand up and shut the outer door airtight before you open the second one."

They know about the distress call knob and how not to set off the alarm when opening the door to the inner vault, strengthening Eirich's belief. Definitely inside information.

Only a handful of Lufthansa managers know that coded succession, and a name booms in Eirich's mind, *Louis Werner.* The robbery isn't yet over, and two employees of the German airliner have already pegged blame on Werner.

Eirich gives the gunmen access to the inner vault. Hundreds of packages in a variety of dimensions and sizes are piled on steel shelving. A clipboard hangs on a shelf post, and a sheaf of invoices and bills of lading are clipped to it. Manri leafs through the paperwork to pinpoint the parcels with the cash. Werner's data has been on point; one-night's work, at last, is about to make everyone flush.

But what if there isn't any money? Well, then, Mr. Werner should buy a ticket to the far end of the world because Jimmy Burke will hunt him until the end of time.

In the outer vault, from where he's standing Eirich can spy Manri sifting through the tissue-thin freight manifests rubber-banded to the clipboard. The tale-tell signs of an insider's role are plain, and Eirich can't contain his curiosity. "One thing I'd like to know."

"Yeah, what's that?" Cafora says, his gun pointed at Eirich.

"I'd love to know who's your inside man." Another spell of panting, and Eirich feels his pulse thumping.

"Maybe we'll send you a postcard with his picture," Cafora jokes. "We *do* have your address, you know."

McMahon snaps the clipboard from Manri and quickly isolates the money packets. "Here, Joe! I think these are what we're looking for."

Teeth gritting, Manri reproves, "Watch yourself! Don't call me by my fuckin' name in front of Eirich."

McMahon covers his mouth, glances slyly around him. "Shit, I'm sorry." Unfazed by the blunder, McMahon speedily unravels one of the bundles, and the content is green. "Yeah! These are the ones," he gloats, his broad grin flashing through the mouth opening of his ski mask.

Sepe has been in the driver's seat of the Ford van, waiting for Manri's cue to back it close to the vault. His heart is racing; he's imagining a SWAT team staking out the loading dock outside, waiting to ambush the robbers. In the interim, Licastri joins Cafora in guarding Eirich. Manri motions for Sepe to start the engine; Sepe glances at him through the side-view mirror and rolls the van so the rear bumper is four to five feet from the vault. He jumps out of the cab and helps his confederates transfer the one-cubic-foot boxes from the inner room, across the outer vault, and into the van. The engine is running, and the exhaust fumes are fouling the cargo bay with carbon monoxide.

"Shut off the motor before we all get gassed," McMahon squawks.

The stickup men need six minutes to load the loot.

Manri and McMahon practically lift Eirich by the armpits. "This is your final act, Mr. Eirich," McMahon jibes. "Now look into my eyes. Without fuckin' around, close the doors of the vaults, *the right way*."

Eirich first closes Door-2 and then opens Door-1. Despite Eirich's assurances, McMahon and Cafora fear the unknown, an automatic signal going off at the Port Authority. McMahon prompts, "C'mon, Mr. Eirich, let's make this fast and finish locking Door-1. We wanna get out of here."

Eirich completes securing the outer vault door, and Licastri and Sepe board the Ford van, now laden with three hundred pounds of treasure. McMahon, Cafora, and Manri haul Eirich upstairs to the lunchroom. DeSimone has the cargo agents sitting quietly on the floor, and he's been hankering for one of them to provoke him.

Cafora and McMahon are prodding Eirich, Manri strutting ahead. They bound into the cafeteria, and DeSimone seems glad to see them. He slides the ski mask over his forehead and wipes his cheeks of perspiration. "Did you find what we came for?"

"Pull down your damn cap, man," shouts Manri. "What're you, a moron?"

McMahon glances at two of the Lufthansa shipping clerks, who are in a direct line of sight to where DeSimone is standing. He stews, realizing a second gunman has revealed himself to the Lufthansa workers.

Rebmann and Murray surely will not forget DeSimone's visage. Hychko also has locked Sepe's face in his mind from the glimpse he caught of it earlier.

McMahon points his gun to the floor and draws an imaginary ring with the left hand. "All right, everybody. Sit on the floor in a circle with your asses inside the circle."

The armed men string together the cargo agents, arms behind their backs, and DeSimone gags everybody's mouth with silver duct tape, a well-thought-out drill.

DeSimone is about to strap the tape on Eirich's mouth, and the supervisor recoils, his face red and filmy. "This is not necessary, goddamn it! Even if we wanted to scream for help, nobody can hear us. We're too far from the other buildings. We've been gentlemen all through this."

DeSimone hurls the tape at Cafora and pats Eirich on the shoulder. "You're right. You have been gentlemen. If you weren't, by now you'd be at the pearly gates talking to St. Peter."

Eirich gazes pitifully at Hychko, though he can't make out the seriousness of the man's lacerations, a sickening flesh of blood and pulp on his cranium. Eirich implores the robbers, "Hychko is in bad shape. He needs medical care. Immediately!"

"He'll get it soon enough. First we gotta finish our job," Cafora says with the callousness of a hangman.

Of the nine hostages, eight are handcuffed. The burglars do not cuff Murray and loosely rope his wrists, enabling him to free his hands and phone for assistance.

Manri scowls at Murray, his jaws clenched. "Wait twenty minutes before you call 911. Even if you get free, WAIT twenty minutes. GOT IT?"

The Port Authority can block the four airport exits within fifteen minutes. Three days ago, during the same early morning hours, Manri and McMahon drove from the Lufthansa cargo hangar and out of the airport in six minutes. Ample time to escape.

To ensure the victims are tied snugly, McMahon checks each one. "Remember, no heroes, please! When you're asked what we sounded like, be smart, say you were too shook up and don't remember a thing. We're going to remind you again. We know where you live."

McMahon and DeSimone are ready to follow Manri and Cafora to the stairway. They quick-step four or five paces, and then turn around to face the lunchroom. Unscripted, McMahon bids, "Good night, and have a nice day tomorrow. You're going to be on TV and in newspapers, so dress up in your Sunday clothes."

"Let's get out of here." DeSimone taps McMahon's forearm, and they scurry to the stairway.

They catch up with Manri and dash below to the ground level. Cafora remains on the landing, slams the door, and counts to sixty.

". . . fifty-eight, fifty-nine, sixty." He plows his 360 pounds into the door and forcefully reopens it, bursting into the corridor, an intimidating effect. "Didn't I say not to move for fifteen minutes?" Cafora shouts, his voice lasting in the hallway as he fades down the staircase.

Burke's highwaymen regroup on the loading ramp and pile into the Ford van. McMahon presses the "Up" button on the wall, and the corrugated roll-up door of the warehouse starts to open. The van exits, and he walks out the side door of the cargo bay. McMahon jogs to where the chase car, the Pontiac Grand Prix, is parked, and folds his six-foot-one frame into the bucket seat on the passenger side. He tears off the woolen ski mask, and a gust of wind refreshes his cheeks. The engine is idling, and the heater fan is blowing warm air.

"Turn off the damn heater," McMahon complains. "I'm sweating like a pig."

"How did it go?"

"All right. We got it, Frank." McMahon vents his face with a hand and lays his head on the headrest. He lets out a sigh of relief and shuts his eyes.

Licastri engages the "Down" switch, and the twenty-four-foot-wide door begins to lower, its rollers screeching loudly, fracturing the complacency of the early dawn. With Sepe at the steering wheel, the van turns left into the driveway of the Lufthansa compound and onto the Nassau Expressway.

"Stay close behind the van and keep checking for cars that might be following us," McMahon says to his driver, Frank, Burke's oldest son.

Duly respecting the 45 mph speed limit, Sepe decelerates and shifts his eyes from the solitary road to the rearview mirror. "Oh, shit!," he exclaims.

"What's wrong?" Manri asks.

"Some kind of car with flashing lights is creeping up behind the Pontiac. Could be cops."

Everybody becomes rigid and stares through the rear windows of the van.

"Fuck," Cafora curses, "an alarm must've gone off."

"Hit the gas, Angelo. Floor the goddamn pedal," DeSimone yells out, gritting his teeth.

Panic breaks out inside the van. Manri looks at the closely tailing Pontiac carrying McMahon and Frank Burke, and squints to focus three-hundred feet farther back on the vehicle with the orange emergency beacons, flashes careening in the darkness.

They scramble for their weapons. "Cool it, cool it," Manri yells out. "They're not cops. Those lights are orange. It must be a tow truck or somethin'. Only ambulances, fire trucks, and police cruisers have red emergency lights. Everything else got orange lights."

"Whew!" The desperados exhale heartily, releasing a surge of breath they'd been holding in, and bellow in unruly laughter, palms slapping with one another.

"A close one," cries out Cafora, wheezing and winded.

"You ain't shittin'," Sepe remarks.

A tune comes on the radio, and Paolo Licastri amplifies the volume to the maximum. It's a new hit, "Gonna Fly Now," from the soundtrack of the film *Rocky*. The music incites Burke's scholars to a rocking mood; they're richer than an hour ago and clap to the beat of the song. Manri quells the excitement. "Whoa, whoa! Cool it. Paolo, turn it down. You can hear it from outside. Let's not attract attention at the last minute."

"It's all under control, man. I got an eye on the rearview mirror. All is quiet, and the seas are calm," Sepe wisecracks. "Just Frank and Frenchy in the Pontiac. We're home free. WE'RE HOME FREE!!!!"

Sepe veers onto the entrance ramp of the northbound lanes of the Van Wyck Expressway and hums in sync with the radio.

DeSimone is sulking over the ultra-foolish move of removing his ski mask in the Lufthansa cafeteria, but rises above it, dreaming about to-morrow, the heftiest payday of his felonious career. And to forget the dark thought of that stupider-than-stupid move back there, he jokes, "How can you go through life with a name like that Lufthansa worker, Wolf-gang Ruppert?" DeSimone was a bully from the moment he'd sloshed out of his mother's womb, and in his school days, had he come across a boy named Wolfgang, he might've slapped him just for laughs.

"If my old man named me Wolfgang, I'd kill the bastard," Sepe as-sures.

Rowdy guffaws crackle in the crowded van, and foul odors from per-spiring bodies taint the air. And though the temperature is at the freezing mark, the passengers feel as if they're broiling in an oven—it's been a nerve-racking night.

Paolo Licastri, though, has been moping; he can't relate to the humor in DeSimone and Sepe's heckling. His English isn't much better than that of a retarded parrot. Moreover, he's stewing over Manri's orders back at the Lufthansa hangar not to harm anybody, offending him in the company of his equals, a discourtesy he will not ever bury.

31

In the dawning hours of December 11, 1978, the Lufthansa cargo complex underwent two cleaning services, one by the contracted porters, and the second, a costly scrubbing by the Jimmy Burke company of convicts. Afterwards, as John Murray unshackled his wrists, he bolted to his workstation and sent a Mayday call to the Port Authority headquarters a mile to the west of Lufthansa.

Fingers fluttering, Murray dialed the Port Authority. "Eh, this . . . this is Cargo Building-261 re . . . reporting an armed robbery. I'm, eh . . . Shipping Agent John Murray. One of us is bleeding badly. Please send an ambulance."

"Emergency response units will be on the way, Mr. Murray."

In the next twenty minutes, as the magnitude of the theft flew over the wires to the regional and federal law enforcement agencies, a fleet of police autos, unmarked vehicles, ambulances, crime scene trucks, and Brinks patrol cars swooped into the Lufthansa parking field.

Nine miles from Lufthansa ground zero, traveling south on the Van Wyck Expressway, exhaustion was weighing on Sepe's eyelids, and the Ford van swerved slightly, riling McMahon, who was watching the zig-zagging getaway vehicle from the chase car. "Damn, look at this jerk Sepe driving all over the road. He's gonna get stopped."

Indeed, if the gunmen attracted the interest of a cruising patrolman, a shootout could definitely ensue.

"Ouh!" Cafora yelped. "Angelo, what're you, sleeping at the wheel? Paolo, give'm a smack before he falls asleep."

Paolo Licastri refrained; nobody could slap Sepe and go on unscathed.

Sepe shook off his doziness. "I'm OK. We only got a few blocks to go."

"You sure?" Manri second-guessed. "'Cause I can drive the rest of the way."

"Nah, nah, I'm all right."

They were headed to Metropolitan Avenue in Maspeth, Queens, where an industrial park with factories and commercial buildings spanned blocks on end.

"Slow down, Angelo. It's the second building on the left," Cafora said.

"Are you sure?" Sepe questioned.

"You're a real mammalook. Wasn't I here just a couple of hours ago to drop off Jimmy?"

Sepe decelerated. "I see it." He nosed the van into the driveway of the warehouse, and Manri bounced out. He banged on the roll-up door, and in seconds it began rising. The warehouse was John Gotti's contribution.

The gangly black man, Stacks, was waiting inside, his finger on the button of the electric opener. "All right! All right! C'mon in. You got plenty o' room," he directed, waving on the Ford van. Sepe drove it in, the Pontiac chase car immediately behind.

Outdoors the street resumed its stillness. Inside the warehouse, the lighting was dusky at best, and everyone spilled out of the van. Draped in a black, full-length wool coat, its collar and a white cashmere scarf enveloping his neck, Burke came forth from the shadows, seemingly in a slow motion, soundless stroll, hands deep in his pockets. He smiled at Manri. "How did it go?"

"Smooth, Jimmy. Smooth," Manri informed him, kissing his thumb and index fingers. To feel accepted, he overcompensated in mimicking the Burke gang of Italians.

A flush warmed the Gent's face, and he had the look of a child who couldn't wait to unwrap a gift. "What're you waitin' for? Unload the cash and lemme get it out of here."

This startled the robbers. "Jimmy," Licastri spoke out, "why we no count the money now?"

Everyone else gazed at the floor, and Burke stared at Licastri. "You think we're gonna stand here counting for the next three hours? I wanna be off the streets in case the cops put up roadblocks."

"How I know how much we steal?" Paolo Licastri clucked his tongue, his rotting teeth as pointy as a pitchfork.

"You're gonna have to trust me. And if you don't, tough shit. Now let's get this cash out of the van," Burke said.

In a minute, the warehouse changed into a setting reminiscent of Santa Claus's shop of elves. Everyone lined up, forming a human conveyor belt. They unloaded the cartons of money from the van, and reloaded them into a switch car, a second vehicle for ferrying the booty to where it'd be hidden—a precaution if perchance a witness had seen the black Ford van on the Lufthansa property. Burke and his stickup men packed the bundles into the trunk of the switch car, a white Toyota Corona. As a decoy, they added twelve pounds of foul-bagged bluefish over the packets of cash. This tactic, Burke's idea, served two objectives; it hid the money, and if an inquisitive cop started searching the trunk, the nostril-gassing odor would fend him off from digging further. Who'd conceive of cash camouflaged under rotting fish?

Sepe pinched the tip of his longish nose, the outline of a ski jump. "Whooh! Sure as shit, nobody's gonna wanna go near this car."

"Pheeew. Jimmy, after this run, you're gonna have to junk it," Manri said. "You'll never get the stink out of this car."

"OK, we're done," Burke said, wired energy in his speech. "Frenchy, let everybody squeeze into the Pontiac and drive them back to Robert's Lounge. Frank and me will go stash the loot." The Gent's son, Frank, a tall, skinny nineteen-year-old, would be inhaling the putrid fish fumes, and Senior . . . well, he'd be basking in the defeat of the Red Baron.

The Toyota loaded, Burke said to Stacks, "Listen carefully." He dropped his hands on the black man's shoulders. "This van's gotta disappear faster than immediately. Understand? You know where to take it. Change the plates and go there now."

"I got you, Jimmy," Stacks said.

The gunners changed their clothes. Manri threw the outfits and ski masks into the van. John Gotti had arranged for an auto-wrecking yard in the Flatlands section of Brooklyn to crush-compact the getaway vehicle and all the paraphernalia used in the robbery.

Burke's thieves huddled around him. "All right," he coached. "After we all leave here, I want you to do whatever you've been doin' and don't change your routine. I don't want none o' you to phone each other. If you got something to say, do it in person. NO PHONE CALLS. Got it?" The Gent peered at them one by one. "Five days from today, Joe Buddha's gonna come to see you all and square up with your cut." Burke leered at Licastri. "Paolo, tell John that I myself will be straightening out with him." The whole crew gave signs of understanding, and disbanded. Licastri, though, wore a glare of disdain for Burke.

Frank and his father drove to their house in Howard Beach and pulled into the driveway, the black, overcast sky losing its darkness and streaking to a violet hue, shades of the new aurora. The Gent got out of the Toyota, took a remote control out of his coat pocket, clicked it, and the garage door opened. He waved Frank on to roll the car in. In the middle of the garage floor was a four-foot by twelve-foot wooden hatch. Beneath it, the Gent had dug a pit two yards deep, originally for a mechanic to work on the undercarriage of an automobile.

Into that hole, an oily and grease-saturated trench, Burke ditched the Lufthansa haul.

32

Minutes after Burke and Frank had driven out of the warehouse, Stacks snuffed out the lights, backed the Ford van out onto the sidewalk, and the electric overhead door closed automatically. He was headed east on Metropolitan Avenue and tuned the radio to an FM jazz station. He hummed, floating into a reverie while listening to the fast-skipping blues notes of the sax musician, Sonny Stitt. Stacks glanced at the digital clock on the dashboard: 5:54 a.m. "I gotta get this van to the junkyard before it gets light out," he muttered to himself. A distraction titillated his thoughts, Shelly, a "fine sistah" with whom he curled up from time to time. She fashioned a claret-dyed Afro, a cushiony fluff in style with the one Angela Davis trended in the late sixties. Shelly had had four children with four different men, or possibly five. She herself had lost count.

Stacks was cruising at forty-five mph, careful not to speed; the license tags on the van, number 508HWM, were stolen. Sonny Stitt's saxophone was lulling Stacks into the mood, and he suddenly longed to stop by Shelly's; he'd stay with her for a couple of lines of cocaine, a romp in the sack, and then scram to the flatlands quarters of Brooklyn to dump the van.

At the auto-wrecking yard, the operator had been waiting to crush the Ford van into a bale of scrap metal. Stacks, instead, boarded the westbound lanes of the Belt Parkway at the Cross Bay Boulevard intersection. He traveled on the Belt for seven minutes and exited on Rockaway Parkway. He then swung north for two miles toward Canarsie until reaching East 95th Street. Shelly lived in a garden apartment, a drug exchange center, crack leading the neighborhood commodity. The tenants were five-dollar prostitutes, drugrunners, social assistance scammers, and addicts. A balanced blend of citizens. On the grounds outdoors, weeds were littered with trash and newspaper debris, empty bottles of Gypsy Rose wine strewn here and there.

Clunkers with rotted fenders lined both sides of the block. The late-model Ford van, clean and shiny, was bluntly out of place on this ghetto street. Stacks absentmindedly parked it near a fire hydrant; he locked the door, and traipsed to Shelly's doorway.

Nailed to the door was a piece of cardboard with a handwritten message, "Bell No Work." Stacks knocked. No answer. He knocked again, and after thirty seconds in the frosty climate he heard the jangling of a safety chain and the clanking of the doorknob.

"Who is it?"

"It's Stacks, baby. Open up."

The door opened, and Shelly appeared, yawning and sleepy, a brown infant crying in her arms. "Stacks, it's five o'clock in da mornin', honey. Whatchu doin' here so late?"

He hugged "his lady" and kissed her, the baby howling louder. "I wanted a snort o' coke, baby. And I know you got a little stash," he said, plugging his nostril with a thumb, a hint of his craving.

"C'mon in," Shelly mumbled with reluctance, her hand shielding the child's scalp. "Hurry up and close the door. The cold be comin' in." Rocking the tot in her arms, she went into the tiny kitchen. Sprinklings of cat litter on the tattered vinyl flooring crackled under her sandals, and a mountain of crud-plastered dishes covered the sink, a chipped and dented basin. In the den Stacks sat on a red velour couch, the edges of the armrest frayed and stained with a rainbow of spillages from chicken soup to urine. An acidy smell of sour milk fouled the air.

Awake for the past thirty hours, Stacks rubbed his eyelids. Shelly plopped a ceramic sugar bowl on the glass coffee table, and in it was a dusting of cocaine. Stacks coiled his arm around Shelly's caramel-toned thigh and giggled. "All right! All right, baby. I knew you'd come through for your Stacks." He kissed her upper leg, inching closer to the vagina. "I goin' come through for you."

Shelly pushed Stacks's head aside. "Whatchu mean?"

His pulpy lips widened and, teeth missing, his mouth opened to a gaping hole. "Baby, we just done a big, big score, and I'm gonna be comin' into a piece o' change."

"Oh, Stacks, nobody goin' give you nothin'. You been sayin' this since I know you. It never be happenin'."

"It be happenin', baby. You'll see."

"Don't be a fooh, Stacks. Stop believin' them white boys. They like to keep everythin' for themselves. And you gotta watch out for those Aital-ians. They be bad people."

Stacks didn't care to dwell on this. "Baby, they won't be messing with this nigga." He enfolded his arms around Shelly's buttocks, a pair of bas-ketballs, and lapped at her navel. She hugged his cheeks, and they began snorting the cocaine. At some point, Stacks, ever the lover, lifted Shelly off the couch and carried her to the bedroom, a darkish room with news-papers on the windows. They tumbled in the hay for an hour; Stacks fell asleep, the baby shrilling in the background, and the Ford van—stolen plates and all—illegally parked at the fire hydrant.

By daybreak, law enforcement agencies understood the enormity of the theft, and more and more representation from the NYPD, FBI, the

Queens district attorney, Port Authority, New York State troopers, and Brinks detectives were teeming into the Lufthansa cargo hangar.

Dense pewter clouds were spitting out watery snowflakes, and within minutes into the inquiry the scene of the robbery underwent a transformation; a cargo shipping plant had turned to a boxing ring. Ranks of investigators from the many police forces were growing uncivilized, hostility mounting by the hour. The sparring for top command of the investigation was brewing antagonism, and blows were about to fly, literally.

33

Minutes after John Murray's Mayday call, Port Authority Captain Henry DeGeneste and his detectives were the first investigators on hand at the Lufthansa administrative offices. DeGeneste sat at a desk and opened an interrogation with Rudy Eirich. Sipping coffee from a ceramic cup, DeGeneste, a tall, tawny-skinned African/American with the well-proportioned built of a Cruiserweight, got the queasy feeling he'd have to endure "one of those days." "How much did they get?"

Eirich dabbed his forehead with a linen handkerchief. "I don't really know, Captain." He looked up at the ceiling and said, "They're trying to figure it out upstairs."

The baffled Lufthansa executives were huddled in the managerial offices on the top floor, reviewing their paperwork and totaling how much money was supposed to have been in the vault. This chore wasn't progressing well; disruptions and humiliations were interfering. Officials at the Lufthansa headquarters in Frankfurt mercilessly disparaged their American counterparts for, "*nachlassig*" (carelessness) and "*dummheiten*" (stupidities). And as if the New York-based managers had themselves let the thieves into the vault, the overseas bosses were condescending. "*Wie können Sie das Geld verlieren? Sie Amerikaner sind alle idioten*" (How can you lose all that money? You Americans are all idiots). The most degrading insult was, "*Alles, das Sie tun möchten, ist, bis fünf Uhr zu warten und zu trinken zu beginnen. Und wir wissen, daß Sie degenerierte Spieler sind*"

(All you want to do is wait until five o'clock and start drinking. And the whole world knows you're a bunch of degenerate gamblers).

Eirich, meanwhile, couldn't expound on the facts DeGeneste had already gathered, though Eirich reaffirmed his belief that it was an inside job, and had no reservations in naming Louis Werner as the insider. When asked for proof, he gaped at DeGeneste with a stupefied look. "I myself don't have proof, but I'm *damn* sure Werner's got something to do with this."

"Are you saying there are others who know that this . . . eh, what's his name?" Captain DeGeneste fumbled.

"Louis Werner," Eirich answered positively, waggling his head with the assurance of an accuser who had seen the eyes of the guilty.

"Right. Louis Werner," DeGeneste copied, jotting the name on his pad. "So, are you stating that, maybe, other people in here have some way of connecting Werner to this perpetration?"

Eirich squinted his eyelids. "Per . . . perpetration?"

DeGeneste, soft-spoken and minus the lingo of southern blacks, waved a hand about the room. "Mr. Eirich, don't you see what's going on here? There's been a robbery. Perpetration means a crime has been committed. Got that? Now who's got the goods on Mr. Werner?"

"I . . . I don't know, Captain. I don't think anybody does. It's just my hunch," Eirich chanced, staring at the captain with a look that said he wasn't guessing.

"Tell me why."

Eirich sucked in a long breath. "Well, they knew everything about this place: how many men were on tonight, their names, their jobs. Everything."

DeGeneste was recording this in his notes, and Eirich slowed to allow him time to transcribe it. In a few seconds, the captain caught up. "Go on, let's hear more."

"What got me is this: They knew the steps to open and close the doors to the outer and interior vaults without setting off the alarm in your office." Eirich shook his forefinger at DeGeneste. "They must've known the meal break is at three o'clock, and everybody hangs out in the lunchroom for an hour."

DeGeneste smoothed his mustache with a thumb when he saw one of his deputies, Detective Lloyd McClaren, coming toward him. "You need me, Lloyd?"

"Yeah, Cap. Lemme have a word with you," Lloyd said, his finger raised at eye level, a sign this wouldn't take long.

"Excuse me, Mr. Eirich." DeGeneste rose from the chair, pulling McClaren by the arm. In a discreet voice, the captain said, "What's the latest?"

"The lab techs are going over every inch of this place for fingerprints. So far, zip. The only consistency is that just about all the perps had heavy Brooklyn accents. It had to be a local group of hoods."

"You're right," DeGeneste said.

"Something else, Captain," McClaren said. "See the paramedics over there working on Mike Hychko, the one who got his head bashed in? Well, he said he saw the perps standing outside by the gate near the loading platform. They had a late-model black Ford E-150 van. And here's the riddle. They knew about the silent alarm that goes off at our office when the gate is unlocked."

"Definitely an inside job," DeGeneste deduced, loosening his taught lips in anticipation to an early closure of this inquisition.

"And, Cap," McClaren added with the enthusiasm of a novice, "Hychko said he thinks the inside man is one of the cargo shipping supervisors. Louis Werner, a guy with all kinds of vices and debts."

"Damn! This is the second time this morning that name has come up," DeGeneste exclaimed. He tapped McClaren's chest with the back of his hand. "Lloyd, we got two, maybe three of the Lufthansa workers who can ID two of the perps, and more interesting, they're fingering this, eh, Werner." DeGeneste swept his hand from side to side. "I'm sure the lab techs will find fingerprints somewhere in this building."

McClaren drummed on his notepad with a pencil. "No doubt, Cap. The hostages estimate the robbery lasted about forty-five minutes. Somebody had to have left a fingerprint."

"Not to mention, the money must've been marked," DeGeneste speculated, rippling with optimism. "I think we're gonna wrap this up fairly fast." The captain walked back to Eirich, and as an afterthought turned and instructed McClaren, "Oh, Lloyd, put out an APB on the van."

"I was going to bring that up, Cap. Problem is none of the victims saw the plate number."

"It wouldn't have done any good," DeGeneste corrected the rookie. "Most likely they changed the plates with stolen ones as soon as they got out of the airport. But that's OK. When we put Mr. Werner under the hot lamp, he'll spill his guts. And he'll point us to the perps who did this." DeGeneste smiled and winked at McClaren. "As I said, Lloyd, we'll have this case closed in no time."

34

In the time frame of an hour, DeGeneste's buoyancy deflated quicker than a punctured balloon. The lab techs had combed the cargo complex and hadn't discovered anything; no fingerprints, no tire marks in the parking lot, and no footprints. The APB out on the black Ford van had not yet been fruitful. Six hours had lapsed since the burglary, and De-Geneste was resigned to the probability the getaway car was already a compacted ball of scrap metal.

He knocked on the open door to the office of the head bookkeeper, Hans Beck, who looked and breathed as if he had spent an hour on a treadmill. The man's nostrils were as wide as those of a cow, and the under-arms of his white, starched shirt were stained with brown spots of sweat. Beck looked up and surmized the visitor was a cop. From the moment the bookkeeper had started his shift, he felt as though he had stepped on a hornet's nest. He slowed the rhythm of his respiration and invited DeGeneste in. Palpably uneasy, Beck indicated a black cloth-padded chair at the side of his desk. "Please sit here, sir."

DeGeneste must've seen this blue-eyed German as the epitome of an Aryan straight out of a World War II German propaganda film. He flipped open his pad and asked, "Have you tallied how much is missing?"

"Off the bat, I'd say about two million, but we're not finished going through our paperwork," Beck said tentatively, running a hand over his hair, a crop of razor-short yellow bristles. "It could be more."

The captain blew out a whistle. "I trust these are marked bills, right?"

Beck partly closed his eyes. "No."

"The *goddamn* money wasn't marked?" DeGeneste moved forward into Beck's desk. "What kind of an operation are you running?" He raised his palm. "On second thought, no need to answer that. This . . . sounds crazy."

Beck loosened his tie and fidgeted, rotating back and forth in his swiveling chair. "Sir, this was a batch of US dollars American tourists in Germany had converted to deutsche marks. They were small bills." The bookkeeper was feebly excusing an inexcusable folly. "From the practical standpoint, time wise, it's impossible to mark millions of fives, tens, and twenty-dollar bills."

DeGeneste exhaled a long puff. "I've never come across such a thing." He held a prolonged stare at Beck. "This is getting better and better by the minute."

Beck pretended not to hear the captain's exasperation. "We'll have an exact amount of the lost money in the next forty-eight hours."

In compliance with international shipments federal statutes, DeGeneste phoned the satellite FBI office at Kennedy Airport.

"This is Port Authority Captain Henry DeGeneste speaking."

"Yes, Captain. How may I direct your call?"

"Switch me to Agent Yost, please."

"Hello, Henry," greeted Agent Walter Yost. "What do I owe this early morning call to?"

"I'll make it short, Walter. I got my hands full right now."

"Oh. What's going on?"

DeGeneste and the Kennedy Airport FBI satellite office agents had upheld a co-existing cordiality, an unusual accord between law enforcement agencies. "Walter, there's been an armed robbery at the Lufthansa cargo building."

"Why are you calling me?" Yost asked with a trace of surprise.

"The theft's a huge one and has to do with an international shipment."

Yost was silent for a moment. "Ah, I see. And what exactly did this international shipment contain?"

"Cash and jewels."

"Well, the perps can't do a heck of a lot with the cash. I'm sure it's all in traceable bills," Yost trumpeted with aloofness typical of FBI agents.

"Nope," DeGeneste replied. "We're talking about a couple of million dollars in unmarked small denominations."

"Pheew! Where are you right now, Henry?"

"On the third floor of the Lufthansa administrative offices."

"I'll be right over."

Before dashing to the Lufthansa complex, Agent Yost, a towering figure at six-foot-four, telephoned the FBI Rego Park Queens unit and spoke with Supervisor Stephen Carbone, the special agent who directed the policing of federal offenses at Kennedy Airport.

Four NYPD detectives from the 113th Precinct in Ozone Park parked their Crown Vics on the Lufthansa grounds and hurried up to ground zero, the cafeteria. With permission from DeGeneste, one of his clerks provided them the scanty data on the burglary. With that the NYPD cops tempted their luck at interviewing the hostages. Detectives and victims separated into pairs, and two of the investigators paired with John Murray and Rolf Rebmann. The armed robbers had put the Lufthansa employees through a hell of a night, and these policemen were browbeating them into recalling the gunman who had removed his ski cap.

The NYPD investigators suggested hiring artists who'd work with Rebmann and Murray and take a stab at sketching an image of the unmasked captor.

Two Port Authority detectives, DeGeneste's deputies, were persistent on interviewing the injured Mike Hychko. Less hesitation, a medical technician saw fit to intervene. "We have to prioritize procedures. Can't you see this man is in desperate need of medical treatment?"

The EMS strapped Mike Hychko onto a gurney and wheeled him into a service elevator for the ambulance ride to Jamaica Hospital. Hychko's scalp, completely bandaged, was a ball of white gauze, and his sapphire-blue irises were the resemblance of two gems etched in cotton candy.

The morning matured, and all the top-billed lawmen seemed infatuated with the sensationalism of the Lufthansa debacle. Unlike the outlandish crime stories of fiction and films, in real life most offenses are mundane, and attempted by dim-witted criminals. And here, as television stations broadcasted pieces of the news, this event had the ingredients of a Hollywood scripted thriller. Hence, egocentric stars in the upper echelons of police organizations, following protocol, filed their notices of appearance with the Port Authority Commander at Kennedy Airport, Captain DeGeneste.

For the most part, these preliminaries were conducted in an orderly fashion. The Lufthansa saga was another story. It was a one-in-a-million on a level beyond the thousands of ordinary misdeeds congesting the workload of investigators.

The person who resolves a so-called "TV case," moves onto the springboard to an illustrious future. This, however, breeds conflicts. From the onset, the Lufthansa cargo hangar had become the theater for the overly ambitious. The winner, though, was a late arrival, a competitor who didn't have to duel for the Lufthansa case; federal jurisdiction empowered him to assume command.

The FBI Rego Park branch was an extension of the Manhattan New York City regional office. The abbreviated designation of this division was BQ5. Special Agent Stephen Carbone, a supervisor, hailed from there. At 10:20 that morning, Carbone, a native Brooklynite, hadn't had breakfast and felt a taste of hunger. He broke for an early lunch, and as he was slipping on his jacket, the phone rang.

"Yes, what is it?"

The voice of a young woman, his secretary, said Agent Yost was on hold on line three. Carbone lifted the receiver. "This is Steve."

"Good morning. Walter Yost here."

Yost's call was a fateful one; it redirected the course of Stephen Carbone's career—perhaps even his life. A half hour later, rather than lunching at one of the bistros near his office, Carbone was in the Lufthansa lunchroom chomping on a stale doughnut. Besides Yost and him, a league of distinguished policemen were roaming the cafeteria, one of whom was Lieutenant Thomas Ahearn from the NYPD 113th Precinct detective squad.

Then at 11:30, as if it were the procession of a king and his jesters, Borough Prosecutor Francis Tyson's detectives heralded his grand entrance into the Lufthansa cafeteria. Tyson came with his personal photographer and press agent, but in all fairness, every one of these personalities was a self-centered, ego-driven individual. Though as far as their respective agendas—to land a case of national fame—they were all on the same page.

And the first round of scrimmage began.

"I'm Borough Prosecutor Francis Tyson, Captain." He thrust his hand, and to his dismay, DeGeneste did not offer his. Sniffing vibes of disrespect, Tyson, said, "Eh . . . I didn't get your name."

Standoffishly, DeGeneste said, "*Captain* Henry DeGeneste." He disregarded the borough prosecutor and asked one of his detective sergeants to update him.

In the midst of the confusion, Tyson was struggling to piece together the many conflicting accounts of what had gone down. He whispered to his bureau chief, "Fred, this is big . . . real big. I *must* be in the center of this case. It's going to spin a lot of media."

Chief Fred Graff seemed doubtful. "Francis, as I see it, this has to fall in the hands of the FBI."

With the strut of a peacock, Tyson expanded his chest. "Nonsense. This crime was perpetrated in my county, *my* jurisdiction."

"This involves an international . . ."

"I don't care what it involves. I'm the borough prosecutor of the district where this crime happened."

Typifying the core of elected officials, Tyson was a self-serving publicity monger; after all, the press can be a politician's best friend. In the upcoming months, the Lufthansa show would have his bald-headed face on television screens and on the front pages of New York tabloids, the keystone to a reelection. He'd be an admired civic servant, who with impartiality and sound judgment had solved the greatest robbery. Tyson could see himself grandstanding before throngs of cameras and reporters: *My office unraveled the Lufthansa puzzle.*

The Honorable Tyson's vision, however, was a fantasy. He was counting his chickens before they hatched. True, the robbery took place in his territory, but because the theft was an international shipment, it'd fall in the domain of the federal government. And the US attorney for the New York Eastern District was not about to miss spearheading this high-profile opportunity. Publicity was on everybody's mind.

35

Newspapers and TV stations had been updating news of the Lufthansa heist, riveting the early morning commuters to the electrifying story. The five law enforcement agencies tackling the investigation were keeping details close to the vest, and the administrators of the airline stuck to vagueness as to the size of the piracy. At the outset, the management approximated without full commitment, a million, or maybe two.

At 11:20 a.m., en route to his office for his noon tour of duty, Peter Gruenwald, a German native of the Bavarian countryside, switched his car radio to 1010 WINS. A reporter was narrating breaking news, and it boomed in Gruenwald's head. His mouth went dry: "During a predawn raid at Kennedy Airport, a team of masked gunmen forced their way into the Lufthansa cargo terminal and managed to escape with an undisclosed amount of cash. The Port Authority reports that two million dollars was taken and . . ."

Gruenwald despaired in German. *"Dieses Bastardschwein. Ich kann nicht warten, um meine Hände auf ihm zu erhalten"* (That bastard pig. I can't wait to get my hands on him). Gruenwald felt shock and betrayal, and couldn't believe the reports churning out from the dashboard speaker. Did Louis Werner steal his master plan and go forward without his knowledge or permission? He neared the Lufthansa cargo hangar, and a surge of voltage bolted through his body. The grounds were crowded with haphazardly parked police cruisers and unmarked automobiles, emergency lights shooting flashes in all directions. Detectives garbed in ill-fitting polyester suits moved about here and there, their faces surly and sour. Six or seven TV station vans with antenna booms extended thirty feet into the snowy sky took to the airwaves, gripping a nationwide audience. Gruenwald pulled into the parking lot, and jogged to the Lufthansa building, his face discoloring to a paleness.

A police officer guarding the main entrance put up his hand and stopped Gruenwald. "You work here?"

Gruenwald uncovered the laminated ID tag hanging underneath his green plaid scarf, his countenance tart with indignation, and answered in a dense German accent, "Of course, I work here. What's going on?"

"I can't say nothing." And the guard unblocked the doorway for him.

Peter Gruenwald was steaming: his suspicions centering on Louis Werner. The German immigrant stomped into the warehouse, hounding for Werner, who was inventorying a pallet of merchandise. With thumping steps Gruenwald strutted up to the *schwein* and cornered him. His dentures jutting out in a canine snout, Gruenwald demanded, "What have you done, Lou? You did it, yah?" Gruenwald's complexion sizzled to a flaming red. "I wanna know now!"

"Cool your heels, Pete. I got a lot of shit on my mind, and I don't need you coming in here with wild accusations."

"I gotta know if you have anything to do with this, Lou."

Werner clammed up into a distanced stance and went on with his work as if Gruenwald didn't exist. That's when Gruenwald, a tall, gaunt man with a pencil mustache and black-framed eyeglasses, lost his temper. He picked up a shovel lying next to a shelf, held it high, and seemed ready to club Werner. It scared the shorter man, though he masked his fright with a menacing glower.

"If you're gonna get violent, you'd better think it over 'cause I'll have you arrested in a minute," Werner said without moving his lips, striving to seem collected.

A dozen eyes had been witnessing the spat; Gruenwald, panting, rested the weapon on the cement floor. The man's salt and pepper hair was ruffled, sticking to his moist brow. "You're right, Lou. Why should I get in trouble with the law? I'm not the one who did anything wrong.

Yah, I think I'm gonna have a chat with those detectives over there and save them a lot of time and work."

Werner swallowed hard. "All right . . . all right. I wasn't trying to hide this from you, Pete." He nodded to underscore his sincerity. "I can't understand what's the matter with you. I didn't wanna talk about it here. Look at all the people staring at us," Werner shushed. "That's just what I didn't want." He let Gruenwald simmer for several moments. "There's no way I'd cut you out. What's the matter with you? You should know better. You and I go back a long time."

Gruenwald bought into Werner's act. And although Werner appeased him for the time being, Gruenwald was stewing for having been excluded from their dream. Above all, despite Werner's touching speech, Gruenwald was bothered by the pricking thought that Werner must've been toying with the notion of double-crossing him. Gruenwald jabbed his fist inches from Werner's nose. "OK, Lou, if you mean what you said, tonight after bowling we'll sit down, and you gotta tell me how you did this, *and* what's in it for me. Understand?"

Werner patted Gruenwald on the shoulder. "Of course, Pete. That's exactly what I was going to say. You took the words out of my mouth." Eager to change the subject, Werner said, "By the way, are you ready for tonight's tournament? We're gonna have a big win against the KLM clowns. We're gonna destroy those chumps."

Werner and Gruenwald were avid bowlers, a passion that precluded any other interests. Bowling was the bond among cargo workers, and the airlines promoted teams and sponsored matches.

"I'm not thinking about bowling right now, Lou. I wanna straighten out this shit. I put two years into it and don't wanna get fucked." He held up two fingers and, his voice got louder. "Two *goddamn* years, Lou. You hear me?"

"Pete, nobody's gonna get fucked. You're in good hands. I'm your buddy." Werner understood his attempt at duping Gruenwald had been in poor judgment. And after the fact, Werner came to terms with the harsh reality that his coconspirator could be the leaky seal of an otherwise foolproof heist.

"I'll see you at the bowling alley tonight, Pete," Werner cajoled, squirming to hide his slyness.

Gruenwald moped around for the remainder of the shift and couldn't tear his mind off Werner's gumption. Robbing Lufthansa was an enterprise that he, Gruenwald, had dedicated two whole years in perfecting. *"Wie könnte er den mich antun?"* (How could he do this to me?) he kept mumbling under his breath.

Gruenwald fumed hour after hour and began second-guessing Werner's honesty; his connivance seemed transparent. Gruenwald smoldered and made up his mind to extort a hefty bite of Werner's windfall. And, should Werner dare not fulfill his demands, Gruenwald cursed, his retaliations might spark an avalanche of problems for the *schwein*, and hell would freeze before he'd dig out of it—even if an archangel flew to his rescue.

36

Upstairs in the cafeteria of the Lufthansa terminal, Tyson pried open a dialogue with FBI supervisor Stephen Carbone and Agent Yost. "Good morning gentlemen. I'm Francis Tyson, borough attorney. I've heard of you, Mr. Carbone, and am pleased to meet you in person." Tyson was conspicuously endearing himself to Carbone while ignoring Yost.

"Nice to meet you, Mr. Tyson. And call me Steve." Carbone was about to introduce Agent Yost, but Yost, feeling disrespected by the district attorney, turned his back.

Tyson spoke in a fast tempo—hyperactivity in his body movements—unless he stood before a camera. "Thanks, thanks, Steve. And call me Francis. My understanding is the intruders have done quite a lot of damage here. A couple of million, I believe. Do you or your agents have anything to go on?"

Carbone bit into a doughnut. "No, no. Not yet." And if he did, he'd be unlikely to share it. The FBI had a history of not divulging information outside its agency.

Tyson, overly self-impressed, sipped a few drops of coffee. "I'd like to discuss a strategy with you, Steve. A collaborative venture between your organization and my office. I think it may be a good tactic for you and I to hold a joint press conference. This case is a perfect platform for publicity."

"We at the FBI are not elected officials," Carbone retorted tartly. "The last thing we need is publicity." A declaration that wasn't altogether true.

"I understand, Steve. The difference is that the future of we, elected officials, is not as secure as yours is. Let's face it, come hell or high water, you federal employees get your salaries and a guaranteed pension." Tyson put up a palm and tilted his head. "But I don't wish to debate this. We have bigger fish to fry." He peeked at his watch. "Today is hectic. I'm scheduled for a press conference on another matter. How about we meet at my office tomorrow, say, around eleven." Tyson's ploy to crawl under the same public spotlight with the FBI was plain to Carbone.

Carbone, his face taut, asked, "And what is the topic we will be discussing?"

"This case, of course. As I said, I'd like to align ourselves with a strategy which can be of great help to your outfit and mine," Tyson said.

Carbone was on to the borough attorney's motivations: not the best interest of the county; not safety in the streets; not to cleanse the community of criminals. No, it was publicity he wanted—publicity to secure a reelection. "I'll be there at eleven, John," Carbone said with frostiness.

Tyson offered a handshake and his TV smile. "I'll see you tomorrow. I'm looking forward to working with you, Steve."

Fat chance, Carbone thought.

The west end of New Hyde Park lies in the borough of Queens, and the eastern section expands into Nassau County. A quarter mile into the Nassau border, on Union Turnpike, was The Sterling Bowling Alley, the venue of the airline-sponsored tournaments. In the bowling alley, it felt as if you were in a long, low-ceilinged cavern with eighteen bowling lanes, all rumbling as if thunderstorms loomed overhead. There were no windows; it was smoky with stale air and noisy from the loud-talking bowlers, working-class dilettantes whose forms of entertainment were gambling, bowling, and swapping profane riddles.

In the third frame of the first match, Werner, a dogmatic braggart, was next to bowl. He had been posting a 255 average; this evening, he seemed disturbed by a mind-crippling distraction. He wore the team uniform, a navy-blue shirt with the yellow Lufthansa inscription embroidered on the chest pocket and across the back.

Concentrating not to be sidetracked by the ruckus in the adjacent lanes, balls crashing into wooden pins, and rowdies bursting with shouts of laughter, Werner raised his green bowling ball to eye level. He aimed to the right of the alley for the hook-pitch to swerve into the center of it, smashing the kingpin at a thirty-degree angle for a strike. He quick-paced for fifteen feet, bent his knees, hunched forward, and curving his wrist, hurled the cannonball, sending it into the right gutter for the third consecutive time.

"Shit," he groused, swatting the air with a hand. "It ain't happening tonight," Werner grumbled.

Gruenwald and the rest of the Lufthansa team were waiting their turn, lounging on a vinyl bench beside the alley. Their KLM rivals bellowed cheers and jeers. The whole scene revived the trends of the fifties: cigarette-puffing women in skintight pants and teased, lacquered hair resembling dyed cotton candy, and men with oil-slicked pompadours.

One of the KLM bowlers, Vincent Regina, a Lucky Strike propped between his lips, readied for his shot. He swept a gaze at the Lufthansa lineup, then gave Werner a snide grin and heckled, "Hey Lou, what're you thinkin' about? Last night's heist?"

Nobody commented, though Werner felt a rush of heat flaming his face as Vinnie fired and scored a strike.

"Damn! They're destroying us," groaned someone from the Lufthansa side.

Dressed in turquoise shirts with the white and blue KLM logo, Vinnie's pals sprang to their feet with a deafening uproar. By the closing of the tenth frame, KLM, the underdog, had trounced Lufthansa. It was a likely ending; the Red Baron's best bowlers, Werner and Gruenwald, were preoccupied. Everyone scattered, and Werner and Gruenwald went to sit at a table near the bar, a quieter area.

Werner said, "Pete, I'm gonna get a beer. Want one?"

"No," Gruenwald declined flatly. "Lou, all I wanna know is how we're gonna straighten this out."

Earlier that afternoon, Lufthansa had upgraded the theft from about one million to two and a half. And as subsequent announcements increased the loss, Gruenwald bumped up the sum he was squeezing out of Werner, whose constantly irritated temperament had lightened over the past twenty-four hours. And not appreciating Werner's sudden cheerfulness, Gruenwald glared into his deserting partner's eyes. "How much am I getting for my stake in *my* plan, Lou?"

"I'm gonna give you eight grand."

Gruenwald bared his teeth in the enraged snarl of a mad dog. "EIGHT GRAND?" he screeched out, a spray of spit shooting from his mouth. For a moment, it looked as though he were about to flip the table upside down. "Eight grand?! You must think I'm some dumb American. This was my plan, Lou. MY PLAN! They're saying over two million is missing, and you said you're getting ten percent of that. That's two hundred thousand. And all I'm supposed to get out of this is eight grand?! NO, NO, NO!"

"Whoa, whoa, whoa," Werner yelped, pumping his palms and groveling to reel in Gruenwald's appall. "Pete, I took all the risk, and it wasn't just *your* plan. It was *our* plan. And I repeat, I took the risk. You didn't do nothin'. Nothin'! What'r you want me to give you, half?"

"By rights, I deserve half . . . but you did take all the risk. So what's fair is fair; I'll be happy with seventy-five grand."

Werner outspread his arms with fisted hands. "That's fuckin' ridiculous, Pete. And you damn know it. You're shaking me down, goddamn it." He banged the tabletop with his balled fist. "You saw all the cops and FBI all over the terminal, and it won't be long before they hang me upside down with a rat trap clamped to my balls."

"What would they want with you?" Gruenwald asked with blunt puzzlement.

"What would they want with me? You know why there was so much money sitting in the high-value vault?"

"No."

Werner leaned into the table and wiped his mouth with the back of his hand. "Well, lemme tell you why. Since the twenty-two grand we swiped a couple of months back . . ."

Gruenwald clenched his teeth, bent forward, and corrected, "Not that *we* swiped. *You* swiped it. So get it straight, Lou."

"Whatever. Bottom line is that since the twenty-two thousand dollars disappeared, currency packages can only be released to Brinks with the approval of a shift supervisor. Last Friday afternoon, when they came to pick up the shipment of cash that arrived in the morning, I was the shift supervisor. Well, I got lost for an hour and a half, and the Brinks guards couldn't wait any longer and left. You understand?" Werner pecked his temple with an index finger. "That's why the money got held up at the terminal over the weekend. And sure, I can say the fact that I wasn't at the cargo bay when Brinks came was coincidental. Still, you can bet your last dollar they're gonna be looking up my asshole with an MRI machine."

Werner downed his beer. "Just watch and see. The FBI's gonna be all over me."

"Maybe I should be worried, too," Gruenwald said, graveness in his pupils, a pair of steel-gray globules.

"Nah. There ain't nothing to worry about for you or me," Werner snubbed, swaying his hand in dismissal. "Look at it this way. It's not that I knew at what time of day Brinks was supposed to come. They show up at different times. So if I wasn't in the warehouse when they did come, it's just one of those things. As I said, a coincidence."

Werner was correct in believing he was the prime suspect as the insider. Three months earlier, he had been embroiled in a suspicious mishap. A Lufthansa Boeing 707 had landed at Kennedy Airport with a courier on board who delivered a sealed burlap sack. In it were twenty-two thousand dollars, partially in US currency and mostly in foreign exchange. Werner accepted the delivery and signed a waybill, certifying his receipt of the parcel. He then locked himself in a broom closet inside the cargo hangar, unsealed the sack, and replaced the cash with rolls of toilet paper. When his superiors questioned him, his explanation was that the theft must've occurred at the originating airport of the flight prior to the courier boarding the aircraft.

More of a peeve for the investigators was Werner's insolence. He contended it wasn't his duty to solve this larceny, and whatever wrongdoing took place, he had nothing to do with it. The Lufthansa security officers, though, had known beyond the slightest doubt that Werner was the thief; their dilemma was how to prove it.

Werner wisely did not hide the twenty-two thousand dollars in his home, and for a percentage he persuaded Gruenwald to bury it in his backyard, thus Gruenwald's complicity.

Now millions had been stolen, and again it seemed to be an inside job. Less than twenty-four hours had elapsed since this latest theft, and every Lufthansa cargo worker was tossing about Louis Werner's name.

"And because of the missing twenty-two grand, they're gonna be on my ass over last night's heist, Pete."

"I don't care about any of that. Lou, I gotta get seventy-five grand out of this."

"There ain't no way I'm gonna do that. NO WAY."

Gruenwald slammed his key ring on the tabletop, catching the attention of bystanders. "No way! Then tomorrow morning, when they start asking me questions I'll say I know who did it. *Das bringt Ihnen eine Lektion bei* (That'll teach you a lesson)." When Gruenwald became upset, he'd switch to his first language.

"Oh, knock it off with your German bullshit, Pete." Werner slung his head back and sighed. A thousand terrible scenarios were pounding in his mind. Was Gruenwald bluffing? Werner didn't want to chance it. If Gruenwald blew the lid off him, he'd be in a six-by-eight cell for twenty years. Worse yet, he wasn't even in a position to bargain. He didn't have the stolen money, nor could he identify who had actually plundered it. Werner's sole conduit to the burglars had been an obese person whom he only knew as "Joe." And all communications had been in person at the Airport Diner. It dawned on Werner that if he were prosecuted, he'd go down in flames alone, without recourse to anybody else.

"OK, I'll give you seventy-five thousand. All right? Done deal," Werner relented.

They walked up the winding staircase to the street level and left the bowling alley, a subfreezing gust of air stinging their flushed faces. Wary of one another, they shook hands and strutted briskly to their automobiles.

Werner rolled past Gruenwald's Audi and lowered his window. "Pete, remember, you don't know nothin' about nothin'. As long as nobody says nothin', everything will be OK."

Gruenwald nodded his pointy chin and lit a cigarette, his fingers unsteady.

37

Shacked up at the Boston Sheraton with Marley Carr, I phoned Jimmy and reminded him of Sweeney's insistence to "go heavy" on the Fordham game; I thought I fanned his spirits.

"We gotta make this one count," Jimmy goaded. "When are you coming back to New York?"

"I'll be flying into LaGuardia in the morning, and I'm gonna hook up with Marty Krugman around lunchtime." I was juggling a lot of craziness: the narcotics trafficking and managing the basketball sham. "What's happenin' with the Red Baron, Jimmy?"

"Let *me* take care of it. And stop talking about it over the phone," Jimmy scolded. "You should be staying on top of Krugman, and make sure he lines up every bookie he can."

Here I was on parole, mindful of not getting mixed up in anything that smelled illegal, and I found myself in the middle of a point-shaving sting—a felony that could've put me back in the can until all my teeth fell out. But as *stoonat* as I was, I didn't give it a thought. I saw it as a victimless scam, and the only ones breaking the law were the bookmakers—a herd of swine who sucked paychecks from hopeless gamblers, degenerates who couldn't feed their families.

Jimmy pooled his money with Vario, Marty, and me. For good measure, the Gent threw in another 160 grand from his slice of Lufthansa.

I landed at LaGuardia, called Marty, and asked him to wait for me at his hair salon. It was cold and wet, and it felt good stepping into Marty's warm place; but the scent of toiletries that hangs in the air in a barber-shop made my nose itch.

"Henry Boy! What's going on, my friend?" Marty's sense of humor always on duty, he said, "Come into my parlor." He bowed and grandly waved with his hand.

"Listen, Marty. The Fordham game's coming up. It's gonna be a sure shot. We're going in with big money. *Real* big money."

Marty smirked, his eyeballs bulging. "How much?"

"About a hundred and eighty large ones."

"All right, all right," Marty sing sang as he rubbed his palms together. "Fordham it'll be." With the joy of a five-year-old in an amusement park, he shouted, "Hurray for Fordham . . . hurray. I'm gonna start laying off the bets . . . let's see . . ." He looked at the clock on the wall. "Damn! Too late today. I'll start tomorrow morning."

Marty was taken aback when six bookmakers he'd called in the New York tristate area told him they no longer handled college basketball bets, though he picked up suspicion on their part. Telephone calls to a dozen more bookies ended the same way: no college basketball. Bookmakers were never prone to accepting basketball betting, especially if they felt queasy about the odds.

Marty phoned me with the bad news. "Why won't they take our fuckin' bets?"

"Henry, I got a feeling they suspect something."

"Shit," I cringed. "I'm gonna have to see if Paul Mazzei can lay off a good amount of bets in Vegas. He's got a whole string of bookies out there, but I'd hate to trust him with a lot of cash."

I didn't waste time relaying this latest hassle to the Gent. In the basement of Robert's Lounge, Jimmy and his runners were reviewing the numbers sheets they had turned in before the day's post time, and he wasn't in the mood to hear the latest snag. "What's up, Henry? I'm tallying today's take. Make it short."

"Marty can't place our bets. He thinks the bookies figured out what we're doing."

"Shit! After all we went through to put this deal together, and now this fuckin' worthless Krugman can't lay off the bets. What now?"

"Jimmy, it's not Marty's fault."

"I don't give a fuck whose fault it is! Unless we can place a lot of bets, we make no money. So don't just stand there and make excuses for that Krugman. I'm busy right now. What's the next move?"

I let the Gent go through his rant, then I said, "Paul Mazzei's got bookmakers in Vegas, and he says he can lay off about a hundred to a hundred and fifty grand out there. But do we wanna trust him with a valise full of money?"

"I don't see why we shouldn't trust Paul Mazzei," Jimmy said. "He damn well knows if he fucks with me, I'll kill him. Call him, and let's get goin' with this."

I was not as comfy with the idea. On second thought, Jimmy went along with my suggestion, and if Paul did flimflam us, well, the Gent couldn't blame me. Could he? Uneasy, I dialed Paul's phone number. "Paul, you think you can spread out about a hundred and eighty grand in Vegas?"

"Damn right, I can," Paul said, oozing confidence. "The only thing is, I'm not gonna have time to come to New York and pick up the dough. You'll have to get it to me here in Pittsburgh."

"Yeah, but I'd have to drive there. I don't wanna get on a plane with all that green. Know what I mean?"

"When do you wanna come? 'Cause we can kill two birds with one stone. Bring me some golf clubs, and I can give you back a handful of opals," Paul said. Golf clubs meant cocaine, and opals were heroin.

"OK, Paul. I'll be there tomorrow in the early afternoon."

The next morning as it got light, I loaded my green Buick Riviera with a change of clothes, two pounds of cocaine, and the $180,000 Jimmy had packaged for me to place in Paul's hands. My trip from Long Island to Pittsburgh was smooth; the drug-cash swap took twenty minutes.

"Now, Paul," I said, resting my hand on his shoulder, "you're responsible for this money." I squeezed his shoulder blade. "Whatever happens, you gotta account for it to Jimmy. And he's not gonna wanna hear bullshit excuses. So don't pull any nonsense, Paul."

"Nah, nah, Henry. Nothing's gonna go wrong. I wouldn't fuck with the Gent," Paul guaranteed.

He, too, felt safer driving to Vegas with all that cash. We shook hands, and Paul set sail for Nevada to dump our bets on the unsuspecting bookies. It was a big weight off my shoulders.

38

It had been eight days since Henry Hill delivered the $180,000 to Paul Mazzei, whose white, longish Cadillac Coupe DeVille, purring at a fluffy eighty miles per hour, was traveling southwest on Interstate 15. Besides Mazzei, the second occupant of this white steamship was Tony Perla, whose black eyes always cast a sly glint. Three miles back they'd crossed Valley of Fire State Park.

The sun was sinking behind a horseshoe-shaped mountain range, a chain of elevations that a few decades ago had cradled a desert. The edges of the jagged mountain caps were ablaze—an optical illusion affected by the eye-blinding sunrays beaming in the background from the west—and the sky was tinting to a flaming orange.

A consortium of Italian, Jewish, and Irish gangsters had developed a forty-mile radius of this arid land and built the City of Sin, Las Vegas.

Mazzei and Perla lowered the windows and let the wind breeze through the Coupe DeVille—the radio tuned to an oldies station rocking to Steppenwolf's "Born to be Wild." Mazzei pulled down the sun visor and rested his balding dome on the headrest, relaxing the muscles in his meaty jaws, giving way to a serene smile.

In less than twenty minutes, at 3:00 p.m. eastern time, Boston College was warming up to face off against Fordham. Burke strolled into Robert's Lounge and sat not far from the bartender. He nodded at the TV mounted above the bar. "Donnie, switch it to the Boston game."

The starting buzzer blared, and the Eagles/Fordham game was heating from the first few seconds. Kuhn, Sweeney, and Cobb, with subtleness, nimbly coordinated their moves to help Fordham from trailing too far behind in points, harnessing their more formidable team so as not to run off with the scoring. Up to the middle of the fourth quarter, the Eagles hadn't yet surpassed an eight-point lead, a safety net from the fifteen-point spread posted by the oddsmakers.

39

The game opened in Boston, and I couldn't go; I had to handle a thirty thousand dollar drug deal at home in Long Island. For sure, Jimmy was watching the Eagles/Fordham match on television, and so was I.

Two minutes after the heroin customers left my house, the phone rang, and Karen answered it. "Hello." I heard her say, "Henry's right here. I'll get him. Heeeenryyyy, it's for you. Paul Mazzei's on the phone long distance. Says it's important."

I lifted the extension in the kitchen. "Hello, Paul. Everything all right?"

"I ran into a problem."

The first thought that slammed into my mind was: *Is Mazzei gonna make up a story of how he was held at gunpoint and robbed of our money? Or did he blow it at the crap tables?*

"Oookay, let's hear it."

"I got into Vegas last night at about three o'clock, and the only room I could find was in a broken-down motel about forty-five minutes from the strip near Red Rock. I was dead tired from the seven-day trip, and I slept 'til one o'clock this afternoon."

My innards stirred. "Get to the point, Paul."

"The bottom line is that by the time I left the motel, I got caught up in rush-hour traffic downtown Las Vegas and . . . and I missed post time."

I freaked out. "You what?!" My cheeks got hot. "You gotta be fuckin' kidding me! This game is goin' perfectly. It's in the fourth quarter, and it's running the way we want it to." I felt my blood pressure shoot up, and the veins on my temples and forehead must've spelled out Z's and Y's. I hit the wall with the receiver. "I can't believe this, Paul!"

"What could I do? It's what it is." He said it with that's-the-way-it-goes casualness.

"What you could do? You're gonna have to explain it to Jimmy Burke. And you know what, Paul?"

"What?"

"They may call him the Gent, but when he finds out you missed the window, the last thing he's gonna be is a gentleman, you sorry son of a bitch."

I flung the phone, and it cracked the cradle.

40

All fronts were catapulting out of control. Henry Hill shut down the failing basketball point-shaving sting, and the Lufthansa probe was picking up steam. Every day newspapers published segments of the story, and Jimmy Burke, his name in the headlines, was the protagonist of the drama. The investigation was intensifying, and the heat was radiating too close to Burke. And he didn't need Paul Mazzei duping him out of the winnings from Vegas, an unforgivable indiscretion. Burke, however, had to delay serving street justice on Mazzei until the Lufthansa turbulence subsided.

At the 113th Precinct, guided by two Lufthansa shipping agents, Rolf Rebmann and Mike Hychko, an NYPD artist had drawn sketches of Angelo Sepe and Tommy DeSimone, the two numbskulls who had uncovered their faces during the robbery. Port Authority Captain DeGeneste and NYPD Lieutenant Ahearn, however, couldn't match those renditions to the thousands of mug shots in their archives.

A nameless FBI informant had hinted to Carbone's agent, Ed Guevara, that the Robert's Lounge gang were definitely the Lufthansa marauders. Carbone did not pass on this bit of intelligence to the NYPD and Port Authority, placing the FBI one lap ahead of their competitors. He requested from DeGeneste and Ahearn copies of the artist's drawings, but DeGeneste's subordinates fabricated a multitude of excuses why they couldn't deliver the drawings to Carbone's office. One lame lie purported that someone at the station house had spilled coffee on the sketches. Another underling said to have misfiled the folder.

Prepared for lack of cooperation from Ahearn and DeGeneste, Carbone gave up on pursuing that matter. Once the FBI informant had revealed the strong probability of Burke's part in the Lufthansa snag, Carbone could narrow the ring of suspects to those known as chums of the Robert's Lounge gang. Unbeknownst to the other investigating agencies, Carbone sent for Rolf Rebmann and Mike Hychko, the two hostages who had had a peek at the two unmasked stickup men.

Carbone and Guevara hosted Rebmann and Hychko in a carpeted conference room with lavish furnishings and a long, cherrywood table. An oil painting of J. Edgar Hoover adorned one wall, and the toothy grin of President Jimmy Carter hung next to it. An American flag graced a corner of the room.

Everyone sat around the table, and Carbone showed Rebmann and Hychko photos of convicts linked to Jimmy Burke. Rebmann scrutinized a picture of Henry Hill and shook his head. "Nah, that wasn't him." The next mug shot was the fat, melon-like face of Joe "Buddha" Manri. "Nah." The third photo was a smirking Jimmy Burke, a shot taken on a prior arrest. "That's not him either," Rebmann said discouragingly.

Carbone and Guevara were wondering whether their source had double-crossed them and deliberately derailed the investigation to protect the actual culprits. Carbone breathed heavily and held up a headshot of Paolo Licastri. "How about *this* one?" Carbone's FBI monotone was dissolving and his New York accent rising.

Hychko and Rebmann waggled their heads.

"Nope, not this one either," Hychko said.

Exasperated, Supervisor Carbone presented his two guests with a picture of Tommy DeSimone. Rebmann's eyes widened as he examined the photograph; he poked it with his finger and attested, "That's him. He's the one who took off his mask."

Hychko wasn't sure.

"Who is he?" Rebmann asked. "What's his name?"

Carbone and Agent Guevara regarded one another. At last, they were in the right direction. "That's Tommy DeSimone," Carbone informed, "a recidivist felon from Ozone Park."

"What's a recidivist felon?" Rebmann asked, his eyes crinkling with confound.

"A chronic criminal," Guevara set straight.

Carbone tossed a sixth mug shot on the table. "How about this one? Does he look familiar?"

Hychko instantly verified, "That's the guy who hit me on the head. I'm sure it's him." He pointed at the image, "a wiry looking son of a bitch" with uncombed oily hair and black eyes that, as Hychko put it, could frighten Charles Manson. "He walked with a bop, swinging his hips. Who's he?"

"Angelo Sepe," Guevara was happy to say.

Carbone collected the photos and closed the folder. "We appreciate your time, fellows. I'm putting both of you on notice you may have to testify in court."

Hychko looked at Rebmann, and both shook their heads, faces suddenly grim. "I don't know about that," Hychko said to Carbone. "I'd love to see that lowlife guinea, what's his name? Angelo Sepe?" It occurred to Hychko that Carbone was of Italian descent and wished he hadn't let fly with the racial slur. "I . . . I'd want Sepe to rot in jail, but I don't wanna get mixed up in this." Hychko rubbed the back of his neck, feeling shame for his bluntness. "I mean, I didn't hear you say anything about getting us protection."

Carbone didn't reply and shot him a searing gape; Mr. Hychko had denigrated his heritage.

Guevara pointed at Rebmann. "And you, are you willing to help us throw these criminals in jail?"

Rebmann looked at the floor. "I . . . I don't wanna get involved, either."

The FBI agents skirted the subject of security and dismissed the two eyewitnesses. Guevara twisted in his chair, crossing his legs. "Well, I think we hit the jackpot this morning; if only those two will come forward in a courtroom."

Carbone reclined in the high-back chair. "I wouldn't call it a jackpot. Just because two witnesses can pick out the perps from photos doesn't help us. Even if we dragged Hychko and Rebmann into court—and they don't seem too willing—to get a conviction we'd have to couple their testimony with material evidence." He stared past Ed Guevara as if something dawned on him and held up a forefinger.

"Ah! Another problem, Ed," Carbone said. "In the evenings DeSimone had to turn himself in at the Manhattan halfway house, the CTC. And Burke did, too. That in itself is an indisputable alibi." Carbone placed a fist under his chin. "But at least we know where to go from here. The Robert's Lounge gang."

"Steve, you're saying, well . . . technically, they were in prison on the night of the robbery," Guevara pondered.

"Before we start spinning our wheels," Carbone said, "I want you to send Mackey to the halfway house and find out if there's any way to prove or disprove if Burke and DeSimone were in custody there on the night of December 11th."

Guevara dispatched Agent Mackey to the CTC on 54th Street in Manhattan. The FBI was relying on a long shot, the chance there was no documented verification of an inmate's nightly attendance. FBI Agent Christopher Mackey, fresh out of the Midwest Wheatland, was twenty-nine and had an orange-blond crew cut. He cut the figure of a young John Glenn, the pioneer astronaut who in 1961, possibly in a state of insanity, orbited the Earth inside a tin can.

Agent Mackey, green as spinach, and unconscious of the shenanigans New Yorkers are capable of, inspected the logs at the CTC. He spoke with the corrections officers there and inquired about Burke and DeSimone's attendance on the date in question. One of the guards affirmed, "Yeah, I remember them two checking in at about ten o'clock. A couple of jokers."

His coworker thought for moment. "It was a Sunday night."

It was a gain for Jimmy Burke and his bandoleros and a loss for the authorities. Guevara and Carbone had lost a crucial round. The FBI, mighty with resources and far-reaching tentacles with which to slay dragons; at times, a highly intelligent criminal with street smarts can trip the bureau. Carbone and his pinstripe-suited subordinates were in the dark as to the tomfoolery that went on at the CTC—prisoners coming and going by way of the fire escape. And because Carbone couldn't fathom such lax security, he reckoned it'd be pointless to grill Burke and DeSimone on their whereabouts on the night of December 11; they were in prison. Not really, though, and Carbone had a hunch. "Those two customers, like magicians, must've trumped up an illusion and in actuality were not in custody at the CTC; they were out robbing an airline. But how?"

41

On December 13, 1978, two days after The Great Robbery—a coinage the media had labeled the Lufthansa calamity—a police officer spotted a black Ford Econoline van parked four feet from a fire hydrant on East 95th Street in Canarsie, Brooklyn, three miles north of Kennedy Airport.

Officer Marie Santiago, a squatty woman with hips and buttocks the width of a bus, pulled up next to the van and did a walk-around to investigate further. An oddity stood out. This vehicle was out of place on this block; it was too new and too clean. Santiago returned to her cruiser and unhooked the radio microphone. "Officer Santiago requesting license plate authentication."

A scratchy static squelched, and a barely understandable voice said, "Go ahead, Santiago."

Santiago spoke into the mike, "The subject vehicle is a 1977 Ford E-150 Econoline, and the tags read: Five, Zero, Eight, *H* as in Harry, *W* as in William, *M* as in Mary. Over."

The radio crackled, and the dispatcher repeated the plate number.

"That's right," Santiago confirmed.

In less than a minute, the radio squelched again. "Officer Santiago, come in."

"Santiago here."

"Plate number Five, Zero, Eight, *H* as in Harry, *W* as in William, *M* as in Mary is on the hot sheet, reported stolen on December tenth. I'm sending detective backup and a tow truck. Stay with the subject vehicle."

Inside of fifteen minutes, the blue and white police tow truck backed up in front of the van. The driver jumped out, and with the gait of a laborer trudged up to the cruiser. Santiago was sitting inside it, the heater blower on maximum speed; it was an icy afternoon. She lowered her window part way and glanced up at the tow-truck operator. "Hot plates, and the van is probably also stolen. We gonna impound it. Just gotta wait 'til the dicks get here."

Soon thereafter, two detectives—the dicks—were at the scene, hands in their black trench coat pockets, arms tight at their sides, and necks withdrawn into their shoulders to retain body heat. Santiago got out of her cruiser and consulted with the plainclothesmen. "The plates came back hot. I didn't get a make on the van yet."

One of the detectives, the shorter of the two, must've stoked a penchant for meaty Latinas, and stole steamy glances at Senorita Santiago. His partner, all business, asked the tow-truck driver if he could break open the rear doors of the van. Prying with a three-foot crowbar, the tow operator obliged him, and sprang the latch, the part of his job he loved most.

The detectives climbed into the vehicle and immediately construed this was not an ordinary auto theft.

"What the hell are these?" Half a dozen black ski masks with orange rings around the eyes and mouth openings were strewn on the floor.

They also spotted a wallet on the passenger seat, and the billfold contained the driver's license of a Rudi Eirich; an employee photo identification card next to the license revealed who he was. "And look at this," said the second detective. He examined the piece of ID and read aloud, "Kennedy Airport Lufthansa Cargo Terminal-262. Rudi Eirich. Employee number 07-13341."

"Holy smokes, Jimbo. This goddamn van might've been the one used in the Lufthansa robbery this past Monday."

"Let's get it towed to the precinct, Ray. The robbery squad may get lucky and lift some prints."

The tow-truck driver was securing the chains and J-hooks under the Ford van, and a neighborhood teenager, who had happened to watch Stacks park the van two days ago, sprinted three hundred feet to Shelly's garden apartment. He banged frantically on her door. A groggy Stacks answered the knock. "Hey, Damon. Whassup, bro?"

"Stacks, the powleece . . . they be taking youh van, man."

Stacks's bottom lip plunged open. "What?"

"Yeah, no joke. The powleece be hookin' up youh van on a tow truck."

Stacks's mind throbbed with visions of the illegitimate license plates, the ski masks, Rudi Eirich's wallet, and most spine-shuddering, fingerprints.

Since the early dawn following the Lufthansa burglary—the morning he had dropped in on Shelly—Stacks did not leave her apartment and procrastinated driving to the auto-wrecking yard to destroy the van. For forty-eight hours, he loafed around in a drug-induced stupor, strumming his guitar and romping in the sheets with "his lady."

The police laboratory inspection of the van and its contents lasted two days. A spokesperson for the 113th Precinct convened a press conference. At 8:00 a.m., Carbone was en route to his office as a station on the car radio broadcast breaking news:

Detectives from the 113th Precinct found a Ford van believed to have been the Lufthansa getaway vehicle. In it were ski masks and the wallet of a Lufthansa cargo manager. Also four fingerprints found on the vehicle are a matchup to known associates of Jimmy "the Gent" Burke and the Robert's Lounge gang.

Carbone was livid, and a flood of blood warmed his face. "Those lousy snakes. They . . . they found the getaway vehicle and didn't say nothing to us." He smashed his fist on the steering wheel and nearly lost control of the automobile. "Son of a bitch!" He strutted hastily into his office, and as he whizzed past the receptionist he asked, "Is Agent Guevara here?"

"Yes, Mr. Carbone. Should I buzz him?"

"Yes, I wanna see him." Carbone's anger was about to peak, and his New York accent came out. He slammed shut the office door and hurled his jacket at the coat rack, missing it by a yard.

Ed Guevara rapped on the door and stepped inside his boss's office. "Good morning, Steve. Did you hear . . ."

Carbone spoke at the same time. "I guess you heard it, too. Me, I got it on the radio. Some set of balls on those two characters."

"I don't think DeGeneste knew anything about it," Guevara surmised. "Bear in mind the NYPD found the van, not Port Authority. And you can bet your bottom dollar our friend Lieutenant Ahearn is the vermin who kept this to himself."

"Ed, have you spoken to any of those underhanded bastards?"

"No. I was waiting to talk to you first."

Carbone stuck the phone receiver to his ear and dialed his secretary. "Lillian, get Lieutenant Ahearn on the phone. He's at the 113th Precinct. And get some coffee in here for me and Agent Guevara." He gusted a long breath of air, or rather carbon monoxide. "Son of a bitch!" Ahearn had withheld a break in the Lufthansa case, the FBI's taste of its own medicine, and it was bitter.

"What are you planning to do?" Guevara asked searchingly.

Carbone said nothing; he was brewing a strategy, and the intercom beeped. "Yes?"

"Mr. Carbone," the secretary answered, "Lieutenant Ahearn's receptionist said he's at a high-brass meeting at 1 Police Plaza in Manhattan."

"Thank you." Carbone held the phone receiver and pointed it at Guevara. "Is Ahearn avoiding us?"

Carbone and Guevara were not the only ones wrestling with that question. Borough Attorney Francis Tyson also was fit to be tied. "How can Ahearn get such a case-winning break, only to let me find out on TV?" He stood round-shouldered and stooped forward, arms planted firmly on his desk, as two squad detectives sat forlornly before him. Then Tyson pounded his chest with a fist and seethed, "That press conference belonged to *me*. That's right, it should've been *my* press release. All the jokers want to get in on this act. This is *my* show in *my* county."

Four miles south of where the Honorable Tyson was brooding, Port Authority Captain DeGeneste vented, "I'll be damned. Ahearn retrieved the getaway car, and the dickhead doesn't say a word."

"Sure, he's after the spotlight, lieutenant," his sergeant noted.

DeGeneste scribbled absentmindedly on a scrap of paper and uttered, "Who isn't?"

By a quirk of fate, Jimmy Burke, the one man who had been ducking the limelight, was becoming quite the celebrity. Articles about his lifelong crimes—some accurate and some embellished—were ruling the newspapers. To those who rooted for the bad guys with the black hats, Burke was ascending as a legend. This business about the Ford van, though, was disconcerting. It should've been crushed two days ago, and here it turns up parked near a fire hydrant. "They said fingerprints were found. A hundred times I told those morons to wear gloves before they got anywhere near the van," the Gent carped to Frenchy McMahon.

He opened the refrigerator door in the basement of Robert's Lounge and reached for a beer. He thought for a second and put it back, hankering for a more potent anesthetic. "Frenchy, go upstairs and tell Donnie the bartender to give you a bottle of Johnnie Walker Black." He turned to DeSimone and blustered, "How could Stacks, that dumb *mouleenian*, not understand the importance of gettin' rid of the fuckin' van?"

DeSimone stared at the tabletop. "Maybe . . . maybe something came up, and he couldn't get to the junkyard."

"Maybe something came up! What the fuck could take priority over gettin' rid of the van?"

"Who knows, Jimmy?" DeSimone mumbled.

"Who knows! Come to think of it, you ain't a hell of a lot smarter either, chump," Burke reproved, a hand massaging his forehead. "If I live to be a hundred, I'll never understand what you were thinking when you took off your damn ski mask."

Something popped in DeSimone's mind. This detail hadn't been publicized at Ahearn's press conference. "How'd you know about the ski mask?" DeSimone asked, a look of guilt blushing his face.

"It don't matter how I know. What counts is how stupid you were." Burke waved a hand and shifted his concentration to tidying the damage. McMahon returned with the scotch, and the Gent nearly tore the bottle out of his hand. In these moments, Burke preferred to be alone; he'd rehash the Ford van bombshell and debate with himself how to defuse it. It was time to seek the advice of his old mentor, Johnnie Walker, who always brought order to his confusions. "OK, everybody clear out."

"All right, Jimmy. If you need me, you know where to get me," DeSimone offered.

"It'll all work out," Frenchy McMahon added with genuine consolation. "Don't let it get to you, Jimmy. Anything I can do, lemme know."

I wish the hell you all disappeared, the Gent ruminated.

They vanished into the stairwell, and Burke poured the Johnnie Walker into the glass. He fetched a handful of ice cubes from the freezer and sipped. When he had to sort out a troubling difficulty, it was Burke's custom to talk it out aloud, as though his material self mulled it over with his soul.

He sat at the same table where he and his knights had hatched the logistics to duel with the Red Baron. *"Now look, Jimmy,"* Burke said to himself, *"they're saying four different fingerprints were gotten off the van, but they didn't say whose prints they are. Did they? For all you know, they could be anybody's prints. Or maybe the cops are bluffing, and there are no prints."*

Burke drew another swig of scotch and deliberated. *"And even if the fingerprints match up to one of my idiots, it doesn't mean they had anything to do with Lufthansa. Anybody could've touched the van. You can brush past a parked car and touch it by accident. Right, Jimmy?"*

Burke added ice cubes to his Johnnie Walker and gazed at the ceiling as if it might hold a solution. *"As far as the ski masks, the cops said the Lufthansa workers are sure they're the same wool caps the holdup men were wearing. Then again those masks could've been anybody's. Even though they got the van, it don't prove shit."* Burke drained the scotch tumbler and ticked his fingernails on the tabletop, his way to loosen nervousness.

"Now here's the thing, Jimmy. If those fingerprints turn out to be any of your guys', and the detectives start putting pressure on them, well, that could be a big problem. If anyone cracks, he could rat everybody out, and your ass will

*be in the line of fire. To be on the safe side, if the cops found prints belonging
to one of your boys, you gotta figure out who the jerks are that got sloppy. Then
you'll know what you gotta do. As for Stacks, he fucked up big time. He's gotta
go before the cops get to him."*

Burke's chat with his self unloaded a weight. The Ford van quandary
now didn't seem as critical, though he had to act quickly to find out
whom the fingerprints matched up to. If his imbeciles had been so careless, he'd have to eliminate anybody who could be sentenced to a zillion
years. Because a person in so wretched a fix might chuck Mafia *omertà*
laws and throw anybody he could under the bus, as Paul Vario drilled,
over and over. *Somebody who's up against the wall will testify, even against
his own mother.*

42

Carbone kept his appointment with Borough Attorney Francis Tyson.
His office was on Queens Boulevard on the fifth floor above the criminal
courthouse. Tyson's suite was partitioned from the rest of the floor by a
locked glass door. Carbone pressed the bell. A police officer came to the
door and asked him to state his business. Carbone pulled out his photo
I.D. "I'm Agent Carbone. I have an appointment with Mr. Tyson."

The policeman snatched the I.D. out of Carbone's hand, glared at it,
and like a curious gorilla, flipped and reflipped it. "This way. Follow me."
They walked through a maze of corridors to Tyson's private office. The
door was open. "Mr. Tyson," the policeman announced, "this man is with
the FBI. He says . . ."

"Ah! Yes, yes. C'mon in, Steve." The borough attorney waved away
the cop, and said invitingly to the FBI supervisor, "Please be seated."
The Honorable Francis Tyson repositioned one of the chairs in front of
his desk and encouraged, "Steve, sit here so the sun coming through the
window won't be in your eyes."

Tyson's zeal was overbearing to Carbone. He checked his wristwatch.
"Francis, I don't have that much time. What are you proposing?"

Feeling rushed and tipped off balance, Tyson had to reword his rehearsed statement to Carbone. "Eh, understandably, Steve, we're all inundated with an overload of cases." He writhed in his chair and dove into his pitch. "I'd want the Lufthansa investigation headquartered here in my office. I'm centrally located between the Port Authority and your office, and . . ."

Carbone reeled him in. "The theft was an international shipment. It falls in the jurisdiction of the New York Eastern District US attorney, who will assume the investigation and prosecution of the case. And the FBI, meaning me," patting his chest with an open hand, "is the US attorney's investigator. If you wish to assist in any way, well, be my guest. Procedurally, however, you cannot lead this investigation."

Tyson coughed nervousness. He folded his hands. "It's not so simple, Steve. Because the crime was perpetrated in my . . ."

"Francis, this is not for me to argue with you. I'm not the US attorney. I can only state that, if he has to, he *will* serve you with an injunction from a federal judge. And now, I'll excuse myself." Carbone had unofficially banished Tyson from the Lufthansa burlesque. His next bone to pick was with Lieutenant Ahearn at the NYPD 113th Precinct.

Tyson was left to stare blankly out the panoramic window of his office, a view of the six-lane Queens Boulevard, and felt dazed by Carbone's rejection of partnering in a case of such notoriety—a cause célèbre. The enormity of the publicity might've elevated him higher on the white-carpeted stairway to political stardom, and Borough Attorney Francis Tyson would've trended to a household name. He could've been a mayoral candidate or bid for a governorship. And this tough-skinned Italian American from Brooklyn, no less, had curtly snuffed this once-in-a-lifetime opportunity. "Who the hell does he think he is?" Tyson bemoaned.

Carbone stepped into the overcrowded elevator, and Tyson faded from his mind. On landing in the lobby of the courthouse, he headed to a bank of telephone booths and phoned Guevara. "Ed, it's Steve Carbone. Meet me in the parking lot of the 113th Precinct. In a half hour. OK?"

Carbone and Guevara strode to the entrance of the 113th Precinct and went directly to the desk sergeant. "We wish to see Lieutenant

Ahearn," Carbone stated. The purpose was to waylay Lieutenant Ahearn, who had been ducking the FBI.

Judging by Carbone's general demeanor, and the somber black suits he and Guevara wore, the desk sergeant ruled them out as morticians, so they must've been in law enforcement. "And you are?"

The two FBI men displayed photo I.D.s, and Guevara answered, "He's FBI Supervisor Carbone, and I'm Agent Guevara."

"Is Lieutenant Ahearn expecting you?"

"I'd guess he might be," Carbone replied with an air of superiority.

The desk sergeant's higher-than-mighty attitude turned to uneasiness; Whenever FBI agents pop up unexpectedly at a New York City police precinct, it's usually a sign of trouble. The sergeant phoned Ahearn and practically whispered into the mouthpiece, "Lieutenant, two FBI agents are here to see you." He eyed Carbone with obvious resentment, as though an intruder had encroached on his territory.

Ahearn, a personality who didn't rattle easily, nonetheless was taken aback by the uninvited parties. "Sergeant, did they show you ID?"

"Yes, sir."

"Shit," Ahearn muttered. "Eh, sergeant, tell them you have to make copies of their I.D.s." This was a gambit to curb Carbone's FBI snarl. The desk sergeant handed the I.D.s to a clerk and instructed her to make photocopies. When she returned, she gave the originals to the sergeant, who in turn released them to Carbone and Guevara. The same clerk led them one flight up to Lieutenant Ahearn's antiquated space.

Ahearn did not behave as a well-mannered host and didn't bother to ask the G-men to be seated. "Do we have an appointment, Mr. Carbone?" he asked bitingly.

Steven Carbone, an Italian American born and reared in Brooklyn, was a true New Yorker. And although a degree in English and the FBI indoctrination in ethics had professionalized his comportment, beneath his skin lurked a subtle manliness. Carbone spoke with a neutral enunciation and deliberated before passing judgment—as long as a provocation didn't prick him. And here Ahearn's insolence had sparked Carbone's ire.

"I don't need an invitation from you or anybody else in your department, Lieutenant. As I informed your borough attorney, the Lufthansa case is within the boundaries of federal statutes, and that's indisputable. We, the FBI, have the lead role, and you and everyone else are merely assistants."

Ahearn, a taller than tall white-haired Irishman with belligerence to spare, reddened, stood, came to the other side of his desk, and pointed at Carbone inches from his nose. "Now you listen to me, my guinea friend. Don't think that because you're one of the boys of that flaming faggot, Hoover, you're gonna muscle in on my grounds and push me around."

Carbone's skin was an olive tone and did not easily redden. In the next moment, his own finger was inches from Ahearn's face as a screaming match drew half a dozen cops. Fortunately they stormed in; it seemed to Guevara that in those combustible seconds Carbone and Ahearn were moments from a gun-slinging shootout. A police officer with muscles bulging under his uniform stood between the two, holding Carbone by his shoulders. Ahearn fired an overhead punch, landing short of the FBI supervisor.

"Hey, c'mon, take it easy, both of you. You're adults, for Christ's sake. You're acting like little kids," reprimanded one of Ahearn's subordinates, enfolding his arms around the lieutenant's waist. The clash quelled, everyone but two detectives dispersed. Carbone and Guevara were bathing in elation; their ambush had had an impact, and they trundled out of the 113th Precinct.

"Ahearn sure is a fighting Irishman," Guevara said laughingly.

"I'll be damned if he thinks he can pull the wool over our eyes," Carbone swore.

Two days had passed since six masked stickup men had relieved Lufthansa of six million dollars, and Stacks, afraid to walk the streets, was still shacked up with his girlfriend, Shelly. Surely, the lab techs must've dusted the van for fingerprints . . . and Stacks remembered he had fiddled with the rearview mirror. He might've been derelict in his duties, but his mama hadn't raised a fool. It was a foregone conclusion the police were searching for him, and on the day of reckoning he'd have to cook up a fairytale about how he was in possession of ski masks similar to those worn by the Lufthansa holdup men. Worse yet, Stacks felt in his gut the reality he was Burke and Vario's most-wanted man. He roamed back and forth from the kitchen to the toy-littered den, wringing his hands and scouring his cocaine-dusted brain to contrive the next move.

"Stacks, boo, you gotta git out o' here. You gotta go where nobody can find you," Shelly implored, cuddling him.

"I know . . . I know. I just don't know where to run to," Stacks said dimly, his head buried in her bosom, hefty breasts that could've been mistaken for brown grocery bags.

Shelly perked up and stood on her feet. "Stacks, you can stay at mah sistah apartment in Ozone Park. She ain't there. She be with our mom in Jamaica."

Stacks glanced at Shelly, a glimmer of faith in his eyes. "What she doin' in Jamaica?"

"Welfare people're giving her a hassle. They sayin' she got game goin' on. So she stayin' low."

"I goin' call Tommy. He'll drive me there."

Shelly made a face as if she were at a loss. "Tommy who?"

"You know, the big Aitalian dude, Tommy DeSimone."

Shelly wrinkled her nose. "Can you trust him, Stacks?" She grew up in the hood, an ecosystem that instills wariness of white folks and breeds instincts to keep the authorities at arm's length.

"Hell, yeah. Tommy and me go back a long time," Stacks said with conviction.

She shook her head. "I don't want you trusting them white boys too much."

Stacks swatted the air with his palm. "Tommy's good people. He's my best friend." He put on a green baseball cap and wraparound sunglasses—a not-so-clever disguise on a gray, wintry afternoon. He walked three blocks to a phone booth—its glass panels shattered—and hoped the local street kids hadn't broken into the coin receptacle. He slipped a quarter into the slot, and the dial tone hummed, a nerve-settling sound. He punched in DeSimone's number. "Tommy, is me, Stacks."

Stacks's voice threw DeSimone off guard. "Stacks, where the fuck have you been? Man, you fucked up. Why didn't you get rid of the god-damn van when you were supposed to?"

"Ah tell you later, bro. Right now, you gotta come git me."

"Where are you?"

"My lady's house. You know, on East 95th Street in Canarsie."

Stacks went back to his girlfriend's apartment and fretfully peered out the window, scared that someone might've seen him in the phone booth.

He waited in agony for twenty minutes. At last, he saw DeSimone's pink Cadillac slow to a stop twenty yards to the left of Shelly's doorstep. DeSimone honked two short beeps. Stacks jogged out of the apartment with two pillowcases filled with clothes. He dropped them in the rear seat of the Cadillac and sat in the front. DeSimone shifted the car into drive and turned off the radio.

"Man, Jimmy's pissed at you, Stacks. The van's gonna bring a lotta heat on all of us." DeSimone pivoted his head and gazed at the careworn Stacks. "Everybody can't understand why you didn't ditch it after we left the warehouse."

"Ah, you know how it goes, bro. I just shut down, man." Stacks patted the front of his shirt. "Got a cigarette, Tommy?"

"Look in the glove box."

Stacks poked inside there and took out a pack of Viceroys. He lit one, his fingers trembling. "I got caught up with my lady, and one thing led to another. You know how it is, bro."

DeSimone, by and large a jolly prankster, his mood seemed dismal. "Honestly, Stacks, this time I don't know how it is." He was traveling to a hideout with a fugitive, a felon sought by the law. And graver yet, Stacks was wanted by Vario and Burke.

"That's the apartment, over there, bro," Stacks said, indicating a three-story tenement from the turn of the century. DeSimone carried one of the pillowcases as they climbed two flights to a darkish hallway with four independent doors. A reek of urine disgusted DeSimone. Stacks didn't seem to notice. They entered the apartment and near tears, Stacks whimpered, "Tommy, I know I fucked up big time. I know it, and I'm real sorry."

DeSimone glanced at him, his eyes glazed with sympathy. "You better hope this whole thing blows over, man."

Stacks hesitated a moment and pleaded, "Tommy, can you put in a good word for me with Jimmy? Tell him I'm sorry."

DeSimone sighed and pecked Stacks's chest with a finger. "I'm gonna give it to you straight. Best thing for you to do is to call Jimmy and have a man-to-man talk with him." Then he cut it short. "I gotta go, Stacks. Take my advice, pal."

"Tommy."

DeSimone turned back and felt pain for his friend. "What?"

His brown eyes damp, Stacks was on the verge of tears, his purple lips twisted, wrenching not to shiver. "Tommy, don't let nobody know I'm stayin' here."

"You know I won't, Stacks."

DeSimone left the putrid-smelling hallway and clacked on hastily down the stairway, his unbuttoned black leather jacket flapping, the shadow of a crow's wings. Stacks watched his friend's abrupt departure and sensed doom.

On the front pages of the morning papers was a photo of the black Ford-150 van. The bold caption above it read, THE LUFTHANSA BLACK HORSE; the article described it as the vehicle in which the robbers had made off with the cash and jewels stolen from the German airline. One paragraph highlighted the discovery of fingerprints and their connection to the Robert's Lounge gang:

Police detectives confirmed several fingerprints corresponding to a reputed credit card thief, who is connected to Jimmy "the Gent" Burke, leader of the infamous Robert's Lounge Gang. The suspect is a thirty-one-year-old African-American, Parnell S. Edwards, AKA Stacks.

Burke was nipping a cup of caffeine at his Howard Beach home when his son, Frank, stormed in with a copy of the paper. "Look at this shit, Dad." And he chucked the tabloid on the dinette table.

Burke slipped a pair of garnet-framed reading glasses out of his shirt pocket and scanned the newspaper story. He expunged a breath of air. "Frankie, go to Tommy's house and leave word for him to meet me at Robert's Lounge. Then go find Angelo Sepe and have him come also."

Not a good learner, Frank retorted, "Why don't you just call them?"

Burke whipped off the eyeglasses. "Lemme ask you something, Frankie. Don't you remember anything I ever taught you? When things get hot, you don't talk on the fuckin' phone. Prisons are full of assholes who got pinched just because they talked too much on the phone." He leered at Frank and flapped his hand. "Now get goin'."

That evening, Sepe, Burke, and DeSimone gathered in the basement of Robert's Lounge and unwound over a game of bocce.

The Gent pointed at the table. "Let's sit here and talk." He sat at the head and seemed to grope for words.

"You know about the Ford van." He placed his hands at the sides of his head, and didn't look at Sepe or DeSimone. "There's . . . there's just no soft way I can say it . . . you gotta whack Stacks."

DeSimone felt a spike in his stomach. He straightened in his chair. "I can't do it. I'm the only friend he's got. The only one he trusts." Never before he had to tussle with his morals; DeSimone could put a man in a hospital or kill him without losing a minute's sleep.

"Nobody knows where he's hiding. Maybe you do, Tommy, eh?"

"I ain't saying that I don't know, but Jesus, Jimmy, I can't do it."

43

The federal courthouse at 225 Cadman Plaza in Brooklyn housed the United States Justice Department. The official designation of the complex was the United States District Court, a six-story glass building with trimmings of aged limestone. This edifice typified America's solidly built structures. It was an icon of the invincibility and might of a world power, the United States of America, whose poetic personification is Columbia. In 1738, the poet Samuel Johnson coined the name Columbia—extracted from Christopher Columbus—to distinguish the United States from the rest of the Americas.

The third floor accommodated the Eastern District Organized Crime Strike Force and the office of Special US Attorney Edward A. McDonald. From his window he had a view of the Brooklyn Bridge and the East River, a body of water separating Manhattan from Brooklyn and Queens. On this December day in 1978, the agitated surface of the East River reflected the steel-gray dullness of the low, pewter clouds.

It had been a snowy month, and with Christmas in the air, the Strike Force prosecutors, paralegals, secretaries, receptionists, and porters had finished the workweek and were reveling in a holiday party. It was a catered affair with a buffet of delicacies and a worthy list of wines: chardonnay, Chablis, Moscato, Shiraz, Cabernet, Merlot, and Port. The food was inviting: cheeses, salads, cold cuts, dumplings, exotic pates and mousses, morsels of pizza, and shrimp cocktails. The Strike Force pampered its personnel extravagantly. The room bustled with noisy conversations, and the entire floor was decorated with pine-scented wreaths and garlands.

Ed McDonald, a handsome thirty-year-old, welcomed the softer schedule of the Christmas season. His supervisor, chief of the Strike Force, Thomas Puccio, "a workaholic," had not mingled at the party, and not surprisingly, isolated himself in his office behind a closed door. He had a propensity for arrogance, though he was intelligently confrontational. A half hour into the celebrations, Puccio darted out of his think tank, raised his arm high, and caught McDonald's eyes. "Ed, come see me, please." It sounded pressing; then again, urgency was second nature to Puccio.

Ed McDonald, six-foot-two and lanky, was Puccio's favorite of all the youngsters on the prosecution staff. With a goblet of chablis in hand—the one and only drink he'd have throughout the evening—he ambled over to Mr. Puccio. "Yes, Tom, what can I do for you?" McDonald's warmth and charm were always in gear.

Puccio hustled him inside his workplace. "Plenty, Ed."

McDonald, light-brown hair covering the top of the ears, put on quizzical look. He placed the glass on Puccio's desk, a paper-piled jumble. McDonald erected his spine, and with a catching smile held both hands together in his lap. "I'm at your service, Tom."

McDonald couldn't have imagined that what was about to transpire over the next two minutes in Chief Puccio's tiny office would re-route the direction of his career and the outlook of his future.

44

"I know you got your plate full, Ed," Puccio said, "and with Christmas in the wings, this is going to be a heavy burden. And believe me, I've been mindful of it, but you're the only one here in whose hands I can place an investigation of this proportion."

"What is it, Tom?"

Puccio glanced over the rim of his glasses. "Lufthansa. I'm putting you in charge of it."

McDonald's knowledge of the Lufthansa saga went no further than the accounts he had read in the media. He did understand the allure of the case, and his subconscious had been baiting him to it, though only Chief Puccio could have assigned him to it.

Puccio, a fifty-year-old with an ebbing hairline and an air of impatience, had been in conflict with the decision to hand over this big catch, Lufthansa, to his underling. Puccio, a self-absorbed opportunist, had tendencies to hoard extraordinary prosecutions. But it was an impracticality for him to administrate his strike force and allocate time and energy to Lufthansa. Thus, he rightfully surrendered the reins to his top deputy.

Entrusted as the lead prosecutor to unravel a crime of enormous significance weakened McDonald's knees. Soon, though, as the queasiness allayed, the prospect of racing up the ladder stabilized the young US attorney's legs and boosted his will to tackle the dragon.

"Well . . . I must say, your confidence in me is an honor, Tom. I can't guarantee any results. I *can* guarantee that I'll give it two hundred percent of my efforts."

Puccio reclined in his high-back chair and removed his glasses. "You know me well enough by now, Ed. I'm very direct, and if I had the slightest doubt, I wouldn't have thrown this in your lap. So get busy and let's see results."

McDonald didn't hide his enthusiasm and bridged his arm across the desk to shake Tom Puccio's hand. Their palms met with a slapping sound. McDonald then gathered the Lufthansa file that Puccio had prepared for him.

Puccio lifted his jacket off the coat rack, and roped an arm around McDonald's shoulders. "Shall we join the party, Ed? This may be the last intermission you'll enjoy for a long time."

Police detectives are the investigators for district attorneys, as FBI agents are for the US prosecutors. On the morning after the Christmas party, a Saturday, McDonald telephoned Special Agent Steve Carbone. McDonald, his feet floating as if he were on a cloud, waited with edginess for someone to answer. "Hello, FBI BQ5 offices. Nadine Marchesi speaking. How may I direct your call?"

McDonald's restlessness tickled his stomach. "This is Special US Attorney McDonald from the Eastern District Strike Force. I wish to contact Special Agent Carbone."

"I'm sorry, Mr. McDonald, he is not available today."

"Do you have any way of contacting him? Can you beep him, or call his home and ask him to phone me at my office?" McDonald suggested.

"Yes, I can beep him."

"Yes, yes, please beep him. Here's my number: 212-297-4100. My extension is 4113. Oh, please advise him it's urgent."

"I don't know how quickly he'll call back. I do know he's supervising an investigation at Kennedy Airport. If he does answer his beeper, I'll be sure to give him your message," Ms. Marchesi said.

McDonald sat at his desk, then paced back and forth by the window. Carbone's receptionist had said he was at Kennedy Airport; *probably something to do with Lufthansa*, McDonald rehashed to himself. He was thinking, gazing absently out the window but not seeing anything. He was the sole person in the labyrinth of rooms that housed the Strike Force, and the tranquility seemed strange to him. Jarringly, the phone shrilled, snapping McDonald out of his lull. He ran for the handset.

"McDonald here," his heartbeat quickening.

"This is Steve Carbone." From the outset, the US attorney and the FBI agent had trimmed the prefix "Special" from their titles.

"Thanks for returning my call, Agent Carbone." McDonald's hazel eyes glimmered.

"Please, call me Steve."

McDonald discerned modesty about Carbone, and maybe, he hoped, they could tag-team and forge the wherewithal to dispose of the Lufthansa matter. "Thanks, Steve, and to you I'm Ed. I'm one of the US attorneys from the Eastern District Strike Force, and my supervisor, Thomas Puccio, has given me charge of the Lufthansa case." He paused and added, "I guess I'm the unfortunate one."

"Yes, yes, Ed. I know of you and your illustrious chief, Mr. Puccio. 'The Pooch'; interesting man."

"Yes, he is an accomplished lawyer, and I hold him in high esteem. Anyway, I guess the reason for my call is obvious. It behooves us to meet at the earliest and have a reciprocating briefing on the Lufthansa investigation."

"Agreed," Carbone replied.

And the top-gun duo declared war on the Lufthansa ambushers.

Carbone sauntered briskly through the doors of the federal courthouse in Brooklyn. He looked above the archway at an eight-foot statue, a gold-painted eagle clenching a streaming banner in its beak with the inscription, "E Pluribus Unum," a Latin term meaning one from many. This phrase is a reference to the initial cluster of states that unionized to form one nation, the United States of America.

On entering McDonald's office, Carbone shed his overcoat and folded it on the backrest of a chair beside the US attorney's desk, an antiquated metal remnant. Carbone had been snooping at the Lufthansa cargo hangar and interrogating anyone tied to the airline. Although it was a Saturday, he was expected to dress in the standard FBI uniform: the dark suit, gray tie, black wingtip shoes. Carbone was a supervisor—theoretically a desk job—but he couldn't resist diving into the trenches as a hands-on investigator, especially for a high-intrigue robbery. The ulterior motive for Carbone to roll up his sleeves and dredge through the menial footwork of this particular investigation had to do with capturing personal achievement—not an unreasonable ambition.

The suites and furnishings of the assistant US attorneys were stark, unlike the opulence of high-powered lawyers' private practices. Carbone stepped close to the only window in McDonald's office, and the vista of the New York City skyline and the Brooklyn Bridge left him breathless. "This view is relaxing, Ed." He smiled, his body sagging in a chair opposite McDonald.

McDonald was out of uniform, outfitted as if he'd been shooting hoops on a basketball court. He had left the black suit in his closet, and because it was the beginning of the weekend, he was in jeans, sneakers, and a green sweatshirt with white lettering advertising the Boston College Eagles—his alma mater.

"Yes, it's quite the view. When the day gets hectic, I stop whatever I'm doing and take it all in. You should see it when Manhattan lights up. This window is the frame of a painting." He gazed at it, a glint of bliss shining in his eyes.

Carbone returned to the current agenda, and seemingly equipped for this moment, opened the briefcase resting on his lap and read from his notes. He went through an up-to-the-minute progression of the Lufthansa probe—or as the US attorney quickly gathered, the lack of it—at which point Carbone brought up a sore wound: the NYPD holding out on the discovery of the black Ford van. Then he gave McDonald a colorful version of his debate with Francis Tyson, and the man's ridiculous proposition for him to be at the helm spurred a good laugh. "Can you believe the gall of this guy?"

"That's why they're called politicians," McDonald cracked. "County attorneys should be appointed, not elected, but that's another story."

The casualness of their banter brought levity, and Carbone placed the black attaché case on McDonald's desk. "The perps had inside help." He sliced the air back and forth with his left hand—a touch of his Italian American upbringing—and underlined, "No doubt about it! Two Lufthansa shipment supervisors are our primary targets. There's this Louis Werner and Peter Gruenwald. Werner insists he knows nothing.

We've interviewed Gruenwald over and over, and he hasn't yet given in to the pressure. He maintains that when he heard about the robbery, he was just as shocked as everybody else was. But as I said, Werner is the real tough one to crack."

Carbone relayed details of his agents' conversations with Gruenwald and Werner's bug-off attitude. And in a stab at forcing Werner's hand, Carbone propounded, "Gruenwald might crack and give up Werner. And once Werner comes to grips that he won't get out of his fate behind bars, he'll give up whom we believe to have been the ring leader, Jimmy 'the Gent' Burke."

McDonald stopped writing notes. "As you were talking, I was thinking of a possible alternative."

"Which is?"

"I'm considering convening a grand jury and serving, this, eh . . . Peter Gruenwald. I'd like to slap him with a material witness subpoena."

"Good start. Why not serve Werner, too?"

"Because if he's subpoenaed, he'll run to a lawyer . . . and what is an attorney's standard instruction to a client?" McDonald paused for Carbone to comment, but he didn't reply. The US Attorney raised his finger and said, "Don't answer any questions without my presence. That's the customary advice, right?"

"Maybe, or maybe not," Carbone countered.

McDonald rebutted, "We can't take the chance Werner will clam up. But Gruenwald, seems to me, he'll crack at the prospect of appearing before a grand jury."

"I'd still take a shot and send Werner a subpoena. If he's going to clam up, what makes you believe he'll talk later?"

McDonald didn't endorse Carbone's inclination to roll the dice. The US attorney ordinarily dodged risky moves that could jeopardize a conviction. He walked around his desk, a body language to animate his reasoning. "We don't want to take shots from the hip. If we induce Gruenwald to testify against Werner, he'll realize it's hopeless and may cooperate in exchange for leniency. As matters stand," McDonald explained in lawyerly terms, "Werner will stand firm in his denial because he knows we don't have any witnesses or evidentiary exhibits."

"The fact that Werner doesn't seem fazed by the investigation, *which* is leaning toward him, doesn't mean his pants won't fill with diarrhea when he reads the subpoena."

McDonald bent his head and sighed. "That's all well and good, Steve, but we can't use diarrhea as evidence in court. Besides, why take the chance that Werner will run for cover and hide behind a lawyer?"

McDonald won the debate.

45

"You gotta do it, Tommy," Paul Vario said adamantly. "Stacks gotta go. If that fuckin' *mouleenian* gets locked up, he'll give up every one of us."

They were at the bar in Robert's Lounge. Vario, who was not much of a drinker, stood over DeSimone; Burke was on the other side as if he were bartending. DeSimone glanced up at the six-foot-three, 280-pound Vario and groveled to express his feelings for his high school friend and truant buddy, Stacks.

"Paulie, how can you ask me to whack Stacks? I mean, him and me go back before I can remember. I'm the only person on earth he trusts." DeSimone hung his head in grief.

Vario put his arm around DeSimone's shoulders, and counseled in a fatherly way, "I understand, Tommy. I understand. Here's what I want you to know: When the commission opens the books, this can get you your button. You'll be a made man. And I promise you I'll do whatever I can to make it happen."

Nothing in the world meant more to DeSimone than becoming a made man in the Lucchese family. "You mean it, Paulie?"

Vario pointed at his cylindrical-shaped chest. "Tommy," he said in a gravely hush, "don't you know when Uncle Paulie makes a promise, it *always* happens?"

DeSimone gazed uncertainly at the Lucchese capo, and then at Burke, who nodded favorably. Vario tapped DeSimone on the back and smiled weakly. "Do it for me, Tommy, eh? You won't regret it."

And they gulped their drinks.

Once Paul Vario signed Stacks's death warrant, DeSimone, though still wrangling with remorse, chose Sepe as his co-trigger man. It had been eight days since Stacks "had gone to the mattress"—a Mafia slang for hiding out—and only stuck his head out of the apartment when he went to a store to buy food. Out of caution, he'd wear a hat with earmuffs, a scarf around his neck and face, and bug-eye sunglasses. It had been a cold, snow-laden week, and save for the nutty sunglasses, Stacks's apparel was in season, and he didn't seem out of place. He was living on Mexican tacos stuffed with mystery meat and beans, and on his ninth day on the lam he jogged two blocks to buy a bucket of southern fried chicken.

On returning to his apartment, he undressed to his underwear and chomped on a drumstick. Paranoid, Stacks peeked out the window to see if anyone had stalked him. Fresh snow was accumulating on the sidewalk pavement. No footprints. It eased his trepidations. He poured Coke in a red plastic cup, and a hollow knock on the door spooked him. His heart palpitating, Stacks disguised his voice. "Who's there?"

"Stacks, it's Tommy. Lemme in, pal."

46

Waiting for Stacks to let them into his apartment, DeSimone and Sepe tromped their feet to circulate blood, billowing warm breath as they talked. "C'mon, open up. It's fuckin' cold."

Though Stacks was relieved that DeSimone had come to see him, his friend's startling knock couldn't stop his pencil-thin legs from trembling. He unlocked the door and was face-to-face with DeSimone and Sepe. "C'mon in. You scared the shit out of me, man. I didn't know who it was."

Ahead of Sepe, DeSimone advanced into the narrow corridor and smelled fried food. "You havin' lunch, Stacks?"

"Yeah, want some chicken?"

DeSimone sniffed the food. "Nah, I'm good."

"You always eat in your *skivvies?*" Sepe remarked.

"I ain't in no mood for bullshit, Angelo," Stacks said tersely. He rubbed his eyelids as if he'd just wakened. "Tommy, when am ah gittin' a little piece o'change for the job from the other night?"

"You're a real comedian, man," DeSimone replied with scorn. "You fucked up big time, and you want money! You're gonna have to talk to Jimmy about that."

"Jimmy been givin' me the run-around, man," Stacks protested. He sat on the edge of his bed, in front of which stood a night table with the food and a bottle of soda. Stacks turned his back on the visitors to refill the cup with Coke. DeSimone deftly drew a .25 caliber revolver out of his waist holster, and at point-blank range wedged five bullets in the black man's skull. The shots rang out, the explosions reverberating throughout the floors of the tenement. Stacks's head slumped into the chicken bucket, his mouth full of French fries, gunpowder dust clouding the air.

DeSimone slung his head and stared solemnly at his lifeless buddy. "Sorry, pal. I hope it didn't hurt. Sooner or later, I'll see you in heaven or hell. Wherever *you're* going, I'm sure that's where I'll be going."

"I'd love a cup of coffee. Wonder if he made a fresh pot," Sepe said.

"What's the matter with you? We just whacked this guy and you're looking for a cup of coffee. Let's get out of here."

More snow had been forecast as Christmas was sleighing closer, and Carbone, through his agent, Ed Guevara, turned up the heat on Peter Gruenwald and Louis Werner. Gruenwald was increasingly edgy, while Werner stuck to his smugness. Almost daily Guevara haunted Werner. "Mr. Werner, just a few more questions you might help us with. I know you're busy, and myself and the bureau appreciate the time and patience you're taking to assist us." The medium-built, square-jawed Guevara spoke with a neutralizing civility. He was the portrait of a trusted reverend to whom you'd confess your sins.

To Werner, however, Guevara's gentleness was unnerving. It reminded Werner of carbon monoxide, an odorless gas that kills painlessly without detection. It was a late Friday afternoon, the week before Christmas, and Werner was in a hurry to punch out on the time clock and do his holiday shopping. And here came Agent Guevara, with his wavy, jet-black hair, and mustachioed upper lip—a debonair projection. Fast-trotting in Werner's direction, deep in the rear of the Lufthansa cargo bay, the princely Guevara said, "Good afternoon, Mr. Werner. How are you?" I hate to bother you on a Friday night. I only have one small question."

Werner lost it, his thick glasses fogging from the flush on his face, and he engaged his brazenness. "You're damn right you shouldn't be bothering me on a Friday night, or any other fuckin' night. And I ain't answering small *or* big questions. All right? Now unless you got a warrant, get lost." Werner left Guevara, pen and pad in hand, standing in the middle of the busy warehouse.

Werner waited for his car engine to warm, a wool scarf coiled around his neck, and dug into a train of thought: *If these FBI clowns had anything, they wouldn't be tailing me day and night. They'd lock my ass up in a second.* Werner was partially right and partially lost in delusion. He had blabbed to the wrong people how he schemed to rob his employer; it'd be a question of time before someone contacted the investigators and opened a Pandora's box. Or maybe not. Those who knew of Werner's "connections" might be afraid to come forward, and he could skate unharmed.

On the blotter of witnesses who could take down Werner was Gruenwald, the weakest link in the chain. Then there were the three inept thugs whom Gruenwald had contemplated enlisting. He had unloaded on them the particulars of his master design. And should those small-time thieves get arrested for any reason—a likelihood—they wouldn't think twice about informing on Werner and Gruenwald for their own salvation.

Werner's friend Bill Fischetti also posed a liability. Fischetti owned a fleet of taxicabs in dire need of capital. Werner had openly discussed with him his plot against the German airliner, rousing Fischetti's interest. "Lou, when you get your end of the Lufthansa money, I want you to invest thirty-five grand in my taxi cab company. It'll throw off cash, steady income for you. No taxes, just spending money. How about it?"

They were at the bar of the Sterling Bowling Alley, and Werner saw Fischetti's proposition as an upshot. The five beers he'd drunk made it seem even more dazzling. "It's a deal, Bill. The minute I get some of the money, I'll give you the thirty-five grand."

Shortly before the robbery, however, Werner had found out that his pal, Bill Fischetti, a happily married man, was carrying on an affair with Beverly Werner, the ex-Mrs. Werner. And although this hadn't broken Werner's heart, nor it affected his friendship with Fischetti, the underhanded cabbie dealt him yet another low blow. It had been a week since Lufthansa, and Fischetti and Beverly were tumbling in the sheets. At the end of that burst of passion, he whispered in her ear. "Bev, I gotta tell you something about that worm ex-husband of yours."

She rolled off her lover. "What?"

Smoking, Fischetti let out a cloud of smoke, and watched it swirl to the ceiling. "Bev, you heard about the Lufthansa robbery a week ago, right? Guess what? Lou did it."

In a sudden, jerky move, Beverly upped from a lying position, her sagging cantaloupe breasts dangling. The woman's brown eyes, as large as chestnuts, widened. "That son of a bitch missed six alimony payments."

Fischetti grinned goofily, misaligned teeth jutting out of his mouth. "He's gonna have to keep everyone quiet *and happy*. A lot of people know he did it."

"I'll be darned!" Beverly shouted. "In the morning, I'm gonna call that bastard."

"Hello, Lou, it's Bev. Swing by my house after you get off work. I have to talk to you about something. OK?"

Now it's her house. How unfair, Werner mourned. But later for self-pity. "Yeah, yeah. I'll be there, but whatever it is, you gotta make it fast. I have no time to bullshit about the same shit."

That evening, Werner drove into the parking lot of Beverly's condo, a home that was once his kingdom. He trotted up to the front stoop and rang the chiming bell. As Werner waited, he reflected on a biting thought: how much of his hard-earned money he had dished out on this house. A reminder as pungent as rotten lemons stabbed him in his innards. After all those sacrifices, there in the master bedroom Fischetti, "his best friend," had made himself at home, tapping the former Mrs. Werner.

The door lock clanked. Clad in a transparent pink pajama top unbuttoned midway to her breasts, a whorish-looking Beverly opened the door. "Come on in, Lou. Company is coming, so this won't take long."

It didn't take long at all. A half-minute later, Werner exploded in a fit of madness. Arms flailing wilder than a windmill in a hurricane, his ears as red as molten iron, he harangued, "He told you what! That cocksuckin' piece of shit."

"He's just looking out for me, Lou. He wanted me to know you got a nice chunk of money, and there's no excuse for you not to pay me the monthly alimony."

"And what if I don't?"

"Well, I just might call Agent Ed Guevara, the one who's been bugging you about this Lufthansa thing."

Gruenwald, the trio of amateur burglars, Beverly Werner, and Bill Fischetti could all enmesh Werner in the Lufthansa trap. And more of these shakedown artists started crawling out of the woodwork. Werner had boasted to two or three bartenders from different bars in the vicinity of Kennedy Airport how he'd "grab the kraut airline by the nuts" and he'd soon be a wealthy man. He was also vulnerable through his girlfriend, Janet Barbieri, a woman with the emotions of a six-year-old. Janet was frightened of Werner's likely arrest and almost volunteered her boyfriend's confession to the FBI.

Werner reproached her. "Are you fuckin' crazy, Janet? They got nothin' on me. Don't you understand? They got nothin'. Please lemme handle this."

"How do you know the police don't have anything on you? How can you be sure?" She hunched over, sobbing hysterically.

Werner well understood those loose cannons out there might lead the FBI to him, and he could find his wrists in a pair of stainless steel bracelets. But his self-assertions comforted him: he was smart, organized, and never failed to swim to the surface. As for Gruenwald, Beverly, Fischetti, and the three jerks whom Gruenwald had stupidly considered hiring for the heist, Werner toyed with bribing the ones who'd resort to extortion.

A week had gone by, and Lufthansa's loss was growing larger and larger. Day one, the currency that had vanished, according to the airline accountants, started at one million, then two million, and eventually some estimates topped five million dollars. The 10 percent due Werner now totaled $500,000, adequate to upright his life. This sum could silence the barking dogs who were baring their fangs, it'd suffice to wet Gruenwald's beak, and leave Werner with cash to blow town and start a new life somewhere in the tropics. To hell with New York winters.

In no time, things began falling into place. Through Manri, Burke paid Louis Werner the first installment of his 10 percent, $35,000. He cleared his mind of worst-case scenarios and went on a Christmas shopping spree. Feeling rich and untouchable, Werner treated himself to a costly gift, a burgundy, customized Chevrolet van with a color TV, stereo, VCR, a plush sofa, the works.

The festive carols, lighted trees, and garland scents were ushering in the holiday season, and Janet, an anorexic bleached-blonde with crusty makeup, was spaced out on prescription sedatives. The FBI agents had retreated for Christmas and the New Year. And thanks to the medication *and* the intermission in the Lufthansa investigation, Janet was coping with less hysteria. Newspapers and TV reports implicating Werner as the insider of the Lufthansa plotters were no longer much of a bother to her. Janet was also beginning to place credence in her boyfriend's positive viewpoint. He unwaveringly instilled in her, "In time, it'll all clear up and this Lufthansa nonsense will fizzle because they ain't got nothin' on me." Minus whatever payoffs Werner might have to cough up to quiet the wolves, Janet and Louis could relocate to North Carolina, or maybe to one of those beach-and-sand Caribbean islands, and she'd be the second Mrs. Werner. Her Louis was resourceful; he could start a small business, and life would be peachy.

In the opening months of 1979, McDonald fired his first torpedo. He declared Gruenwald a material witness in the Lufthansa international shipment case and tagged him with a grand jury subpoena. At the cargo hangar, Gruenwald was busy tying a sack of parcels, and a process server accosted him.

With a jolly grin, the stranger said, "Top of the morning to you, Peter. I got a feeling this is not your lucky day." He handed Gruenwald the folded subpoena, a serious looking document bound with a blue paper cover. The clownish process server then teased, "You'd better sit down before you read it."

"Oh, Gott. Ich wußte, daß dieses im Begriff war zu geschehen. Ich kannte es! Uhhhh, dieses verfluchte Lou, dieser störrische Ruck" (Oh, God. I knew this was going to happen. I knew it! Uhhhh, damn Lou, you stubborn, hard-headed idiot). Gruenwald felt his intestines melting; and like a horse with a limp, he trotted to the men's room.

47

Stacks was my good friend, and I couldn't get over he was gone. His remains had started decomposing before the family was notified of his death. Jimmy was sorry over the whole situation and sent me to give Stacks's mother and sister money to cover the funeral expenses. I felt bad for his mom, so I added two thousand dollars of my own and went to the church where the funeral services had already started.

I walked in the chapel and saw Stacks's body laid out in the casket. From a distance, I could see his head, and it sucked all the air out of my lungs. The coffin was lined with a brown acrylic veneer that matched Stacks's face. Fifty to sixty people had squeezed in the first six or seven pews. All I could see were blacks and a couple of whites here and there looking like specks of dandruff on a dark collar.

I went up to Stacks's mother and sister, who were sitting ten feet from the altar. I put my arms around the two women, tears streaming down their cheeks, and forked over the thick envelope. Mom didn't stop crying, but sis smiled as I handed it to them. Shelly wasn't there, and gossipers in the hood said she'd already hooked up with "a new brother."

The sweet smell from the three bouquets of white and pink chrysanthemums next to the casket and the arrangement of red roses above it filled the air. Most of the mourners were old, and in the last row a black man with a fuzz of gray hair was snoring, his wife elbowing him to stay awake. The elder ladies wore hats with black veils covering their faces, and everyone was misty-eyed. A short, barrel-shaped congregant limped to the lectern and began eulogizing. She introduced herself as Avonelle.

"Oh, I know da boy since he be ten years old." Avonelle ran out of breath with every sentence and wheezed. "He was a handful, and once in a while he got into trouble with the powlice, you know. But Stacks had a gooh heart, and he was no fooh; if his mama had a way to send him to schooh, he'd be someone we'd all be proud of. The Lord only knows."

A chorus of black women, every one of them fat, sounded out, "All right! All right! Praise the Lord . . . Praise the Lord! Uh-huh . . . Uh-huh."

That as a kid Stacks stole his teachers' credit cards, kidnapped dogs and shook down their owners for a ransom, robbed food supplies from his school kitchen, and fished Social Security pension checks out of mailboxes, all in all, in the view of eulogist Avonelle, it did not make him "a bad kid." He was just a "little mischievous." But that was my old buddy Stacks, and I was going to miss him.

.

48

In February of 1979, six days after Peter Gruenwald had been served with a grand jury subpoena, his superior scheduled him a for three-week vacation. Airline employees had free travel privileges, and Gruenwald, ignorant of the powers and severity of a federal subpoena, requested a pass for a flight to Germany.

The jumbo jet was full. All passengers were seated, hand luggage stowed in the overhead compartments, and flight attendants had finished checking seat belts. The cargo bays had been shut, and the ground support personnel had cleared Frankfurt Lufthansa Flight 405. Gruenwald checked his watch: 10:22 p.m. Seated in an aisle seat, he plopped his head onto the headrest.

A vacation *and* getting away from Werner might be the prescription to hold on to his sanity, Gruenwald thought. He was energized to visit Frankfurt, the city he'd hardly known during his early life as a Bavarian citizen.

Gruenwald closed his eyes and recalled some of the landmarks: St. Paul's Church, the Goethe House in the Innenstadt District, the Alte Oper (Old Opera House), the Museumsufer, the . . . and the quick shuffling of feet oncoming from the fore section of the aircraft disrupted his trance. He opened his eyes and saw a file of people approaching, two flight attendants, trailed by a cockpit officer, and three dark-suited men. They neared him, and Gruenwald caught a split-moment sight of Agent Guevara. He was sure his heart was about to stop and fidgeted not to overreact.

Guevara had directed Werner and Gruenwald's supervisors to notify him if any of their employees requisitioned vouchers to fly out of the country. Sure enough, Guevara and his backup stopped at Gruenwald's row. "Peter Gruenwald, you're under arrest," Guevara decreed, holding a document up to Gruenwald's face. "Here's the warrant. You have the right to remain silent. Anything you say may be . . ."

"Shut up, shut up. Can't you keep this a little quiet? Damn it," Gruenwald protested.

The nearby passengers had heard Guevara recite the Miranda rights to Gruenwald, and rustling nosiness spread through the cabin.

"Please put your wrists together, Mr. Gruenwald."

"You . . . you can't arrest me. I'm going on vacation," Gruenwald said foolishly, mouth fluttering and cheeks purple.

In a demure manner, Guevara said to him, "Mr. Gruenwald, maybe you're too upset and didn't understand me. I repeat, I have a warrant. Here it is. You may read it if you wish." Gruenwald was weighing how to handle the next few seconds as Guevara's colleagues were already patting him down.

The coach class of the 747 withdrew into a vacuum of silence. Gruenwald, frightened and ashamed, raised his hands and gave in to Guevara latching on the handcuffs. Two G-men marching in front of him and one behind, Gruenwald dropped his head, eyes twitching, and shoulders heaving. And the feds transported him to the Eastern District headquarters.

On arriving at McDonald's office, Guevara took Gruenwald to a conference room. One of the marshals remained vigil and stood in a far corner.

McDonald came in and motioned the guard to leave, figuring it might relax the shaken Gruenwald who was trembling uncontrollably, spilling his coffee on the bulky walnut table.

"Good evening, Mr. Gruenwald," McDonald said firmly without forfeiting decorum. "I'm Special US Assistant Attorney McDonald." A faint smile parted his lips. He opened a manila folder and pulled out several documents. He laid the papers on the tabletop in a particular sequence. "Mr. Gruenwald, I know you are not feeling well at this moment. You've never been on the wrong side of the law, and this may be a first."

Gruenwald clamped his hands together to steady them from quivering, and stared at McDonald through his thick glasses. "I've never been in trouble before, and I'm not in trouble now. I know nothing about this crap. Nothing!" Gruenwald's boldness was a product of adrenalin.

"Mr. Gruenwald," McDonald summed up, "right now, we don't know the extent, if any, of your culpability in the Lufthansa robbery. We do know you have breached a federal law."

"I did not break any laws."

"Oh, but you did, Mr. Gruenwald." McDonald sifted through his files and displayed a copy of the warrant. "You were served with this, a material witness subpoena, and yet you were absconding on a flight to a foreign country."

"I didn't know I couldn't go on vacation for the holidays."

McDonald tapped the subpoena with his finger. "Mr. Gruenwald, the stipulations of this writ are explicitly written on its cover page."

"You think I got the time to read all that crap?"

"Mr. Gruenwald, let's not play with semantics," McDonald said. "You can be indicted for contempt, and if convicted, you could be imprisoned for up to three years."

Gruenwald closed his eyelids, retreating into the haven of defiance.

"Sir, prisons are not kind to a forty-four-year-old white-collar inmate."

Gruenwald raised his head just slightly so to look into the eyes of the US Attorney. "I don't care, because I'm not, eh . . . as you Americans say, a law breaker."

"Actually, in this instance you are. You'll be arraigned for contempt, and I will ask the court to hold you without bail. As you've demonstrated, you're a flight risk. You'll be in the county jail until your trial begins. And that could be a year from now."

Gruenwald wagged his head, rejecting McDonald's warnings. "I said I don't know anything about this bullcrap."

"We are aware your coworker, Louis Werner, might've conspired with the perpetrators." Gruenwald's eyes blinked furiously at the mention of Louis Werner. "Whether *you* have any complicity remains to be seen," McDonald said. "But on paper you committed a felony. Here's the saving grace, Mr. Gruenwald, if we can rely on your cooperation to move this investigation forward, we can mitigate the subpoena violation, and you can return to your life."

Gruenwald looked puzzled. "What does mitigate mean?"

McDonald nonchalantly wandered to the opposite side of the table where Gruenwald was sitting. He placed his hands on the back of Gruenwald's chair and bent over him. In a hushing voice, the US Attorney said, "In your case, *mitigate* means to do away with." He paused as the suspect rocked his head. "All we want, Mr. Gruenwald, is for you to reveal the degree of Werner's culpability."

Gruenwald removed his eyeglasses, gawked at the floor, and invoked his constitutional right not to answer any questions.

McDonald nodded at Guevara to step out into the corridor.

Guevara whispered to McDonald, "What do you want to do with him?"

McDonald replied, "He's just plain stubborn, and stupid."

Steve Carbone appeared in the doorway of McDonald's office. "Ed, did Gruenwald confess to anything?"

"Afraid not, Steve."

"I'd like to interview Gruenwald. I'll get him to talk," Carbone said.

"Oh, please, Steve! Ed Guevara and I worked over Gruenwald for an hour. The man is incredibly moronic. Or he doesn't appreciate the seriousness of his predicament. So I don't think *you* talking to him is going to change his frame of mind. He has to get shocked into reality."

"And how do you propose to do so?"

McDonald rubbed his chin and breathed. "Gruenwald lives in Nassau County, right?"

"He does," Guevara said. "What's the difference where he lives?" Carbone asked condescendingly.

McDonald scratched his nose and thought out loud, "Following his arraignment, I can have him remanded to the Nassau County Jail. From what I've been told, it's one of the worst county jails in the country. And I'll wager it won't be long before Mr. Gruenwald will want out of there and beg to cooperate with us."

McDonald had hit the bull's-eye. It took three days, and Gruenwald couldn't have withstood another hour at the Nassau County Jail. The reception officer had placed him in the general population, a dormitory populated by the most vicious low-level criminals and deranged felons awaiting trial or sentencing. The bedding entailed steel double-bunk beds with three-inch foam pads that the jail staff called mattresses. Gruenwald had been assigned a top bunk, a challenging climb for a middle-aged man. The prisoners were permitted a three-minute shower, barely enough time to shed the chill from the reduced fifty-five degree temperature during the night. More of a farce, each inmate was supplied a green blanket as thin as a paper napkin.

Gruenwald's spirit broken, as was his back from sleeping on the steel bunk bed, he went to the recreation room, where two public telephones hung on a wall. He had to wait in line for a half hour behind some scary looking inmates and finally phoned McDonald. He prattled into the mouthpiece, "*Schwarzers*. I'm sleeping, eating, pissing, and shitting with *schwarzers*. Get me out of here. These niggers are crazy. And it's cold as hell in here. I'll tell you what I know. Just get me out of here."

49

The short imprisonment had snapped Gruenwald into reality; he was ready to spill it all. Recuperating from his stay at the badly rated Nassau

County Jail Hotel and Resort, he was coughing pitifully and suffering from a cold he had contracted in his igloo-like prison cell.

In the interview room at the US attorney's suite, Gruenwald sat in the presence of McDonald, Guevara, Carbone, and a stenographer, a cute brunette. McDonald felt sorry for him. The US attorney was accustomed to interviewing felons and discerned that Peter Gruenwald did not have the skin for larceny; he was simply brainless.

"Peter, I'm sorry you've got this terrible cold," McDonald sympathized. "Hope they gave you something for it."

Gruenwald didn't answer and blew his nose between coughing spells, the hacking dry and strenuous.

Guevara was too attentive to the stenographer's artificially tanned legs. McDonald noticed it and mused: *It must be a thing with Hispanics and Italians.*

"So, Peter, where do you want to start?" McDonald asked.

"Well . . . ." Gruenwald's narrative lasted two hours. The FBI and the US attorney became fully apprised of Gruenwald and Werner's Lufthansa master plan. Moreover, Carbone and McDonald now knew of the three rookies Gruenwald had considered recruiting for the heist. He had also brought into the picture Frank Menna, Werner's go-between to a fat individual by the name of Joe. Gruenwald made known Louis Werner's best friend, Frank Fischetti, who was currently screwing the former Mrs. Werner. And though these witnesses could complicate Werner's plight, none of them were privy to who had *actually* taken part in the robbery. True, Menna was the conduit to "Joe," but the trail to the Robert's Lounge gang ended with him, an unknown.

Jimmy Burke was paying close attention to the behind-the-scenes developments. He damn well realized that if Carbone and McDonald confronted Joe Manri, he might be coerced to talk. Manri though, a Burke loyalist, confided, "Jimmy, even if Menna picks me out of a mug shot and the FBI ties Werner to me and me to you, that alone don't mean shit. Menna got a rap sheet as long as my arm. On his word, and nothin' else to go on, what jury is gonna believe that *disgraziat?* Werner ain't talkin'. And I sure as hell ain't about to fess up to nothin'."

Burke caressed Manri's gelatin-like cheek. "I know you're a stand-up guy, Joe. If anybody knocks on your door, keep everything cool and quiet, and if we come out of this I'm gonna talk to Paulie Vario about you gettin' into his crew."

50

Another fire had started, and I was busy snuffing it out. Marty Krugman, to whom Jimmy had promised $500,000 for coupling us with Louis Werner, was making a pest of himself. He came to my house and banged on my door, ringing the bell and yelling at the top of his lungs.

I had more heroin than blood scurrying through my veins. I unlocked the latch to let him in, and that was a mistake. "What the fuck, Marty! It's 1:30 in the morning. What's going on?" I could feel my eyeballs swiveling in their sockets as if they were loose ball bearings.

Marty stormed in, his whole body radioactive. "Henry, this bastard, Burke, is not paying me my money. He tugged at my shirt collar and seethed, "I earned that money, and I'm entitled to it. Now why isn't that shanty mick squaring up with me? What's with this *goyam*? Can't he honor his obligations?"

"Marty, Marty, it's 1:30. I've been high for almost thirty hours. I gotta get some sleep before I collapse. Tomorrow, I'll go talk to Jimmy. Meantime, stay outta sight. The Gent is under a lot of heat. When he's ready, he'll straighten out with you. OK? Until then, stay the fuck away from him."

"Henry, I'll wait 'til tomorrow, and then whatever happens, happens."

I ran a hand through my hair. I didn't need this. "Marty, don't do anything stupid. Lemme handle Jimmy."

51

Krugman didn't heed Hill's advice and drove to Robert's Lounge. Less pleasantries or greetings, he demanded to speak with Burke. A waitress fetched the Gent from the basement, and the moment his head rose from the wooden steps, Krugman heatedly contested, "When am I getting my money? I delivered my end. You pulled off the job, and now I want what's due me."

"This is not the time and place for this. We're not children. We can work it out," Burke appeased. "Come downstairs."

Krugman trudged down the stairway, its treads bowing under the bookie's feet. At the bottom of the stairs, to his dismay he saw Tommy DeSimone in his black leather jacket, black pleated slacks, and a black turtleneck sweater—an executioner from the feudal ages. DeSimone, his legs apart, feet firmly planted on the floor, was holding in his hands the two ends of a bungee cord. With the might of a boar, he charged Krugman, squeezed him in a headlock, and tightly wound the cord around the bookie's neck until his face was purple.

"You're choking me, you crazy guinea. You're gonna strangle me. Let go . . . let go."

Burke got into the act. He yanked on Krugman's hairpiece and tore it off his scalp. "Don't you come in here and start a commotion ever again, you Jew fuck. This time, I ripped your toupee off your head. Next time, I'll tear your heart out."

"What about my money?" Krugman persisted between gasps. "Why do I gotta pay a *vig* every week to your loan sharks when you got what's mine?"

Burke signaled to DeSimone to loosen the bungee and slapped the brown/gray hairpiece—a bird's nest—onto Krugman's chest. "When I'm good and ready, you'll get what's coming to you. Right now, get the fuck outta here."

In a moment of impaired judgment, Krugman blurted out a warning that should've been left unsaid: "If I don't get my end in forty-eight hours, I'm going to the DA." He adjusted the straw-like toupee onto his head, though off-center, and trudged up the stairway.

"Yeah, yeah, run to the DA, and you're gonna be the first one to get locked up, you asshole," Burke hollered out. He threw a heavy glass ashtray at him, a shower of ashes raining down on Krugman. "The minute you get out on bail—if you even get bail—I'll kill you. Now, *on that*, you can make book."

At the FBI BQ5 Center, the telephones were ringing incessantly with leads from street-level informers that led nowhere. One caller, though, a woman asking to speak to Agent Guevara, proved credible. "Hello, Agent Guevara here."

"My name is Beverly Werner. I'm . . ."

Knowing this had to be interesting, Guevara interrupted her in mid-sentence. "Yes, yes, I know who you are."

"My husband said to me he was behind the Lufthansa robbery."

Guevara's heartbeat accelerated. "Mrs. Werner, was there anyone else present when he admitted to it?"

"No, but he said if I'd talk to anybody about it, he'd kill me. He said I should take him seriously because he's involved with 'the real McCoys.'"

Guevara could hear her sniveling. "I know I had to report this because if I didn't, I was afraid I could get into trouble. Now I'm really scared."

"Mrs. Werner, where is Louis right now?"

"He went outside about two minutes ago. I'm looking through my blinds, and I see his van in the parking lot of my condo. It must be running; I see smoke out of the tailpipe."

"Are you saying he's still there?"

"Yes." More weeping, and a moan of despair.

"Mrs. Werner, listen carefully. Lock your doors and windows, and we'll be right over. If Louis tries to come in, call 911."

Earlier that afternoon, in the course of Gruenwald's deposition, Frank Menna's name had come up again. Carbone sent two of his agents to arrest him. In McDonald's conference room, Menna readily acknowledged having linked Werner to "this fat guy, Joe."

McDonald asked Menna, "What's his last name?"

"He never told me."

"Mr. Menna, we know you're a numbers runner. Who are you working for?"

Menna glanced at McDonald and then at Carbone. "Marty Krugman," Menna said, swallowing hard.

Carbone smirked. "You mean Krugman, the proprietor of the wig salon off Queens Boulevard?"

"Uh-huh," Menna grunted.

McDonald nodded at Carbone to step out into the hallway with him. He closed the door. "Steve, what do you know about this Marty Krugman?"

"He runs a men's wig shop, but it's a front for his bookmaking activity."

"Let's pick him up and see what he can add to Menna's story," McDonald said.

"We'll do it after Ed Guevara interviews Mrs. Werner."

52

Guevara, two other agents, and two uniformed Nassau County cops were knocking on Beverly Werner's front door. BOOM, BOOM, BOOM. "Mrs. Werner, it's the FBI."

Werner's van was not in the condominium parking lot, as Beverly had told Guevara forty-five minutes ago. His pulse raced. "I hope Werner didn't harm her."

They knocked again, this time harder. BANG, BANG, BANG. "We'll give it ten more seconds. If she doesn't answer, we'll jimmy the door lock," Guevara said.

He asked one of the police officers to fetch a crowbar from the trunk of his cruiser. "Get the longest one . . ." But the door opened, and Mrs. Werner, harrowed and barely clad in a blue bathrobe, was standing in the vestibule of the apartment.

"Beverly Werner?" Guevara chanced.

"Yeah, that's me."

Guevara sighed. "Are you all right?"

"*Now* I am. Lou came this close to putting his hands on me," Beverly exclaimed, her thumb and forefinger almost touching, signifying her narrow escape.

"How did the argument start?" inquired one of the agents.

"I pressed Lou for my monthly support payments, and he didn't give me an answer. Then I said I knew he had gotten money from the

Lufthansa burglary, so why can't he get the payments up to date?" Beverly's hand went to her bosom. "Oh, my. I'm so sorry. I didn't ask you in. Please understand, I'm so uptight . . . I'm not myself. C'mon in, won't you?"

"Thank you, Mrs. Werner." Guevara and his troupe entered, and the patrolmen stayed in the parking lot. Inside her home, a scent of burning incense from lighted candles sweetened the air. "What happened next?"

Beverly fluffed her hairdo. "Well, I saw Lou's eyes starting to tic. That's a sign he's about to fly off the handle. Then in his usual bragging way, he came up in my face and went into a tirade." She twisted her mouth and imitated Werner. "That's right, that's right, I did it, I did it. What's it to you, bitch? What are you gonna do now, turn me in?" Beverly paused as if out of breath. "He was spitting through his lips, and his face got deformed. So I backed up against the wall and he said, 'Go ahead, rat me out, you whore. I'd just love for you to do it so I can kill you. I'd love to chop up your body and feed the pieces to the rats in the sewer.' And that's when I called you guys."

The G-men, bemused and mouths agape, looked at one another. Guevara's eyes flitted from Beverly to the agents. "I think it's time we arrest Mr. Werner."

53

My buddy Marty Krugman was more restless than ever. He was phoning me ten times a day.

"When is that fuckin' mick gonna give me my money? I've had it, I've had it!" he bitched.

"Marty, we just got back from Florida. I'm not makin' excuses for Jimmy, but he just took a hit for two hundred and fifty grand."

"I don't give a shit, Henry. I don't give a shit. I want what's due me already."

"Marty, slow down. Give him a chance."

"Give him a chance?! It's been a month. One fuckin' month! And another thing, Who whacked Stacks? What happened to him? I don't like what's going on, Henry, and I'm gonna do something everybody will regret. I mean it . . . I mean it."

Marty was ready to rat out Jimmy for Lufthansa. "Marty, promise me you'll keep your cool, and I'll go talk to Jimmy. OK?" If Jimmy went down, we'd all go down with him.

"All right, Henry. I'm only gonna stand pat until the weekend. After that, well, whatever happens, happens."

54

Carbone and McDonald decided to detain and interview Krugman.

"I checked him out," Carbone informed. "A year ago, Krugman plead guilty to a narcotics charge and was given a suspended sentence."

McDonald stared at Carbone as if something of meaning came to mind. "Interesting." He wagged his forefinger to lead his thought. "If we implicate Krugman in the Lufthansa case, his suspended sentence will be revoked, and we'll have leverage over him."

Glad to learn of this technicality, Carbone nodded. "I think you're right, but before we haul in Krugman, we should put a tail on Werner and see if he goes into a panic. Maybe he'll run to Krugman for guidance."

"Good idea," McDonald assented.

55

I kept my promise to Marty Krugman and spoke with Jimmy. I begged the Gent to negotiate with Marty—if for no other reason than to appease him. "Jimmy, I've never seen Marty so uptight. He says the loan sharks who are floating his gambling book are leaning on him. And he wants to know what happened to Stacks."

"You kept your mouth shut about that, right?"

"Nah, nah. I didn't say nothin'. Then he'd really go berserk."

"Henry, you think Marty talked to his wife about Lufthansa?"

"Marty Krugman's wife is his personal secretary. He don't take a piss without her knowing. She probably holds his dick when he does take a piss."

Jimmy shook his head. "What a dumb fuck."

Twenty-four hours had passed, and the next evening we got a phone call at my house. Karen answered and heard a hysterical woman screaming into the receiver. My wife didn't make out the voice.

"Oh, Karen, it's me, Fran. It's . . . it's 10:30, and Marty hasn't come home. He's never done this before, you should know. Never, never! Oh, I don't know what to think already. I'm . . . I'm so worried!"

Karen rolled her eyes at me and grunted. Innocently, she said, "Fran, don't panic. You know how many times Henry doesn't come home at all?"

"Marty is different. Jewish men don't cheat on their wives."

Karen gave me an angry look, and pointed at the receiver as if I should've been listening to what Marty's wife was saying. I shrugged.

"Fran, maybe Marty is taking care of some business."

"I don't think so. Let me talk to Henry. Maybe he knows something."

Karen practically threw the receiver at me.

"Fran. It's Henry."

"Henry, where's Marty? He called me two hours ago and said he was stopping at the kosher deli, and then he'd be right home. Something is wrong. I've been going nuts. I'm climbing the walls, Henry! He never comes home late, you should know."

Fran was crying, and I was trying to understand what she was saying. Our cranky kids were screaming, too. I stuffed my finger in one ear so I could hear. "Fran, calm down. Please calm down." I waved at Karen to quiet the children.

It dawned on me what had gone down; Jimmy Burke had saved himself $500,000.

"Fran, stop crying and listen to me. I'm gonna go look around. I'll get back to you."

"I want to go with you. Please come and get me."

"No, no, Fran. Lemme look into this on my own, and I'll call you back as soon as I know what's goin' on. Stay calm." I slammed the receiver on the cradle before she could say anything else, my forehead sopping with sweat.

Karen was staring at me, lips tight in her pissed-off look. "What happened, Henry?"

"I think Jimmy had Marty whacked."

"Oh, my God, Henry. Poor Fran."

I drove to Robert's Lounge and found Jimmy in the basement doing paperwork. I got right to it. "What happened to Marty Krugman?"

Jimmy didn't even lift his head from the paperwork. "He's gone. We don't gotta worry about him no more. He's gone."

I froze, cold sweat cooling my face. I didn't ask any more questions and backtracked to my house. Karen had asked a neighbor's daughter to come and watch our two kids so we could go and be of some comfort to Fran. But I didn't know what to say to her.

Marty was my good friend. He'd have given me the shirt off his back, and the Gent whacked him just because he didn't want to pay him the money for Lufthansa.

56

Carbone charged into McDonald's office, startling the assistant US attorney. "Ed, we should've gotten to him yesterday."

Looking perplexed, McDonald squinted. "Who?"

"Marty Krugman. He can't be found anywhere. Either he went into hiding, or he's been murdered."

McDonald banged his fist on the desktop. "I'd bet my last dollar Krugman could've led us to Burke and whoever else had a stake in Lufthansa."

"I assigned three agents to investigate his disappearance. Word on the street is that Burke murdered Krugman."

"Damn! I think we should presume the worst-case scenario and arrest Werner before we lose him, too."

At six o'clock that evening, Werner and his girlfriend, Janet Barbieri, were at the Sterling Bowling Alley in New Hyde Park, Nassau County. Werner's team, the Lufthansa Messerschmitt Bombers, was facing off against the Pan Am Royals. The place was choking with the loud chatter of bowlers and rumblings, cheering spectators, and balls slamming into pins. Werner's bowling was not sharp, his concentration was elsewhere. Janet, a mere spectator, her mind was not on the game either; the Lufthansa investigation was grating her gut. A foreboding sensation shot a shiver down her spine, and she tried not to pay mind to it by engaging in small talk with Peter Gruenwald, who was on the sidelines with an injury.

"How's your wrist, Pete?"

Gruenwald raised the bandaged arm and whimpered, "Ah, it's healing pretty good." He sucked on his teeth, touched the injured wrist with a finger, and made a glum face. "This should be all my problems. It's nothing compared to this . . . this Lufthansa mess Lou got us into."

Janet's complexion darkened to a sickly green. No one, Werner included, knew of Gruenwald's cooperation with Carbone and McDonald. McDonald had instructed Gruenwald not to mention their arrangement and the plea deal they'd consummated: Gruenwald's testimony against Louis Werner as a trade-off for a suspended sentence.

On leaving the bowling alley, Werner and his girlfriend sauntered arm in arm, tightly together to shield from the razor-sharp, subfreezing wind. Werner unlocked the passenger door of his new custom van and helped Janet to climb on board. He walked around to the driver's side, and as he opened the door he heard the shuffling of three or four sets of feet fast approaching. A man's mild voice called out, "Mr. Werner, FBI. You're under arrest." It was Agent Guevara.

A sudden flow of blood pumped in Werner's temples. "For what?"

Agent Corcoran was dangling a pair of handcuffs. "Put your hands behind your back, Mr. Werner."

At the same time, Guevara recited, "You have the right to remain silent. Anything you say will . . ."

Janet began sobbing and jumped out of the van, a wide look of terror in her eyes. "Lou, Lou, what's happening? Where are they taking you?"

"I'm OK. This is all bullshit. I'll see you home later."

"Ms. Barbieri, it's in your best interest to stay out of this," Guevara stressed. "And please sit in your vehicle."

Janet Barbieri, who fashioned her wardrobe after streetwalkers, was rigged in a mid-thigh, buttocks-hugging leather skirt, a sheer blouse with a décolleté neckline, and lots of gaudy costume jewelry. She retreated into the van, bawling and wailing, eyes raining tears, a hand covering her face.

Guevara, ever the gentleman, offered, "Ms. Barbieri, do you want someone to drive the van and take you home?"

Without uncovering her mouth, she nodded gratefully.

57

Ed McDonald was a devoted husband and father, and sadly his weekends dashed fleetingly into Monday morning. With a wife and two elementary school-age children, some chore or another always demanded his time—driving the younger one to a birthday party, or taking the older boy to watch a college basketball game. This weekend was different. From the minute McDonald and Carbone had set to meet with Werner on Monday morning, the hours inched along at a snail's pace. McDonald couldn't shut Lufthansa out of his mind, and the anxiousness to blister Louis Werner had made him as antsy as an expectant father.

Over the weekend, Werner had been confined at the Manhattan Correctional Center (MCC); on Monday morning, his arraignment was about to begin. It marked the first official charges in the Lufthansa case. In the courtroom, standing room only, 90 percent of the spectators were journalists and media-related people. Werner stood to the left of his attorney, a court-appointed public defender. To their right were McDonald and Guevara. It was excessively noisy, and Judge Costantino hammered his gavel.

"Everyone quiet down. This court is in session," he proclaimed, scowling over his eyeglasses. Centered in the wooden tray ceiling of the vast courtroom hung a fifteen-foot diameter alabaster chandelier. The walls were paneled in oak, and the aroma of lemon-scented wood polish wafted throughout.

Following the opening preliminaries, Judge Costantino boomed, "Mr. Werner, in the matter of *The United States vs. Louis Werner*, how do you plead to the charge of conspiracy to commit armed robbery?"

Werner's lawyer, rigidly erect, his chin tilted slightly upward, responded, "Not guilty, Your Honor."

Reading from notes in his hand, enunciating clearly, McDonald applied to the court, "Your Honor, the prosecution requests the defendant to be held without bail." In support, the US attorney argued, "The defendant is a flight risk, and even if he doesn't flee, for his own safety he must remain incarcerated."

The judge flipped through some documents. "Mr. McDonald, why do you believe Mr. Werner will be in danger if released?"

"Two individuals whom the US attorney's office suspected as accomplices in the Lufthansa robbery within the past five weeks disappeared or might've been murdered. And for those reasons we are sure Mr. Werner will abscond or be killed."

Justice Costantino addressed the defense attorney. "Do you have a rebuttal, Counselor?"

"Yes, Your Honor, my client has community ties, and he is a provider to his two children, who are in need of his financial support."

"I see." His Honor's intonation hinted he had already decided. "I'll compromise and set bail at one million dollars: half in cash, half in bond."

In practicality, those conditions were the same as no bail at all. Werner couldn't raise one million pennies, never mind one million dollars. Judge Costantino then finalized, "I'm scheduling a pre-trial hearing for next Wednesday," and remanded Defendant Werner to the MCC house of detention.

McDonald had a request of Werner's attorney: "Counselor, in your presence I wish to confer with your client. Do you oppose having him brought to my office for the three of us to talk this over?"

Werner's lawyer, Greg Lispz, a hunched-back man with bristly hair, replied, "Mr. McDonald, is this an overture to plea bargain?"

McDonald smiled courteously. "I won't say it's an overture to plea bargain, Counselor. I'd call it a couple of minutes of reasoning and assessment of your client's situation."

Lispz pinched his nostrils and tucked a manila file under his arm. "If I'm present, I guess it'd be a harmless meeting. I'll consent, Mr. McDonald."

Three guards ushered the shackled and manacled Werner into the US attorney's suite. Chains clanging, in an orange jump suit and head bowed, the prisoner sat at McDonald's desk. Werner, unshaven, his hair oily, looked as frightened as a mouse cornered by alley cats.

McDonald pointed to a cupboard cabinet. "Would you care for some coffee, Mr. Werner?" The US attorney's guise, a display of graciousness, was disarming, and Werner misinterpreted it as weakness; or that McDonald might be a pushover.

"Sure."

Preceded by a fragrance of fresh baking, a clerical assistant came into the room and placed a basket of buttered bagels on the cabinet top. Werner helped himself, and obviously as hungry as an ape stranded in a desert, devoured three of the bagels. "The food at the MCC sucked," he said, his mouth overfull. "I don't know how anybody could eat it."

"I understand," McDonald said sympathetically. "If you cooperate with us, I can almost guarantee you no longer have to worry about the lousy prison food."

Werner snickered. "What am I gonna cooperate about? I don't know nothin' about what went down with this Lufthansa bullshit."

"Mr. Werner, we have . . ."

"You can call me Lou," Werner interrupted.

Werner had walked in hostile; this gratuity surprised McDonald. "Thank you, Lou. And I'm Ed to you." McDonald clapped his hands once in eagerness to open an earnest dialogue. "As I was saying, we have substantial evidence to prosecute you and *successfully* convict you. We've spoken with several witnesses who could *easily* convince a jury you were the axis of the Lufthansa armed robbery."

Lispz moved in closer to his client. "Lou, before you answer or make any statements, wait for my signal."

Disregarding Lispz's warning, Werner asked, "What's an axis?"

"In this context, it's the center pin of a crime, Lou," McDonald tutored.

He bit savagely into the bagel and slurped the hot coffee. "Like I said, I got nothin' to do with any of that."

Although Werner was testing McDonald's patience, the US attorney curbed his frustration. "Lou, I can feel what you're going through. You don't know how the outcome of this is going to affect the rest of your life. It's all understandable, but, Lou, rejecting hard facts isn't going to make it any easier." McDonald stood and sat on a corner of his desk.

"Lou, have you ever heard of the Hobbs Act?" McDonald posed.

"No."

"The Hobbs Act," McDonald explained, glancing at Lispz, "is an antiracketeering law that empowers prosecutors to charge a party who has committed, conspired, or abetted a robbery and/or extortion with the use of force and duress."

"And what's it got to do with me?" Werner feigned.

"Well, I'll connect the dots for you, Lou." In a priestly way, McDonald clasped both hands. "The Hobbs Act was legislated in 1951 and sponsored by . . ."

Werner interjected. "I don't want a long-winded story. Just get to the bottom line."

"Bottom line? That's a good term for this, Lou." McDonald looked for Lispz's approval. On his nod, the US attorney proceeded. "The bottom line is this: The Hobbs Act enables a federal prosecutor to indict a person who has been *involved* in a theft of interstate or international commerce." McDonald swilled his coffee. "As set forth by this statute, whether an offender committed the physical act of the robbery or simply conspired to abet it, the sentencing guidelines are the same."

The defense counselor returned a consenting gaze, allowing McDonald to complete the loop. "The sentencing guidelines for such an offense are quite rigorous. In short, Lou, even if your complicity is only to the extent of having supplied information to those who perpetrated the robbery, you will not receive a suspended sentence or probation. The court will sentence you to the same lengthy term as if you were one of the holdup men." McDonald stood from the desk and sat in his high-back chair. "Off hand, I approximate fifteen to twenty-five years, depending on the defendant's criminal history. And don't think you'd be paroled after a few years. White-collar criminals are seldom paroled. And that's the bottom line, Lou."

To McDonald's dismay, Werner said, "I don't understand what it all means. I didn't do anything wrong, so all this mumbo jumbo don't mean shit to me."

Outwardly, McDonald held on to a faint smile, but inwardly he was incensed. He lifted the phone receiver and dialed an extension. "Hello, please have Agent Carbone bring in 'Mr. Smith.'"

For a minute or two, Lispz and McDonald talked shop, and Carbone and Guevara walked in with Peter Gruenwald.

Wild-eyed and jaw slackened, Werner shouted, "What the hell are you doing here, Pete?"

Somber as a funeral director, Gruenwald uttered, "They know everything. I gave them the whole story. It's over, Lou. The best thing is for you to make a deal with them."

Despite the crumbling of his façade, Werner shot back with unabashed boldness. He cut into Gruenwald's eyes with a look as though his coworker had lost his mind. "What in the world are you talking about, Pete?" Werner glanced at Lispz, and then at Guevara and McDonald, who couldn't believe these antics. Werner thumbed at Gruenwald and ridiculed, "This guy must be smoking banana peels."

Everybody was speechless. *Why was Werner willing to endure a trial?* He could've confessed, testified against Frank Menna, who in turn might've identified Manri from police mug shots, and started a new life. Instead, Werner was headed to prison.

After Werner's bravado died down, frightening seconds roused an alarming commotion. He went into a shaking fit, his breathing wheezing and gasping, and almost in a whisper said that he was feeling heart palpitations. Werner outstretched his right arm in a desperate reach for someone's hand. Everyone felt a dread, and McDonald took hold of Werner's wrist. "Lou, are you OK? What's wrong?"

"He might be having a heart attack," Guevara guessed. "We should call 911."

Werner's spastic jerking and heaves were escalating violently. Mc-Donald grabbed the pitcher on the table, poured water into a glass, and knelt next to him. "Lou, drink some water."

Werner seemed to be choking, his chest lugging as if an erupting quake were building inside the cavity of his torso.

Fluster threw the room into chaotic movements. Carbone crouched beside Werner. "Let's call the paramedics."

"Somebody call for assistance!" Lispz insisted. "Let's not waste time."

His face ashen, Gruenwald exclaimed, *"Rufen Sie einen Doktor an."* He corrected himself and repeated in English, "Something's going on with him. Call a doctor!"

McDonald went for the phone to dial 911, but Werner's symptoms, whatever spurned them, abated. He rebounded, though his coloring remained blanched. He drank a half glass of water, and his panting slowed. "I'll be fine. Give me a minute to catch my wind." Werner hung his head for a short while. "I don't know how I can help you. I don't know nothin'."

Although in disbelief, there wasn't a soul in the room who didn't have pity for Werner. McDonald, diligent and talented, though kind at heart, mused, *here's a father of two, fighting a felony that will land him in a penitentiary for fifteen to twenty years, and he's too stubborn to understand he's on the road to ruination.*

Werner's character, prognosticated a psychiatrist who had been monitoring the Lufthansa spectacle, was parallel to that of a chronic sociopath, one who believes he can surmount any obstacle and conquer the impossible.

58

Carbone and Guevara were in an FBI-issued Crown Victoria. In the rear seat was a bug man, an installer of surveillance gadgets. The threesome had been tailing Tommy DeSimone, waiting for him to leave his pink Cadillac unattended so the technician could affix a homing beeper on the undercarriage.

Driving the Crown Vic, Ed Guevara decelerated to keep a distance from DeSimone's Caddy. "He's turning into Burke's driveway."

"I'll be damned. Pull over behind that white Ford over there, Ed."

DeSimone locked his automobile and strutted to the front entrance of Burke's house. Fifteen seconds ticked away, the door opened, and he entered the Gent's home.

The bug man was anxious to do his magic. "OK, let me out. I have to work fast. We don't know if he plans on staying for a while, or he might be out in a minute."

Carbone, Guevara, and the electronic wizard hastened out of the Crown Vic. The two FBI agents ducked behind the white Ford parked in front of their car, guns drawn, as the technician, carrying an all-purpose cloth satchel, jogged with light steps to Burke's property and crawled under DeSimone's "pimpmobile."

Their snub-nose .38 Colts cocked, Carbone and Guevara peered at Burke's lighted porch.

The technician's gloved fingers were trembling from nervousness. The below-freezing temperature didn't help either. He unzipped the bag and groped for the tools he needed. He fumbled, and despite the harsh conditions, in less than two minutes he had fastened the bug onto the rear chassis railing.

The FBI agents, eyes locked on Burke's porch, backpedaled to their car. Carbone shut the door softly and faced the bug man in the rear seat. "How'd it go?"

"No problem. Damn cold, though. My spine felt like I was on a slab of ice." He rubbed his palms together and blew on them. "OK, I'm activating the bug. Let's see if it works." He flipped the toggle switch of the twelve-volt receiver. A red indicator light blinked at a rate of four times per second, and then a green one glowed steadily. "Bingo! Good reception."

Guevara turned on the engine, drove three blocks east, and reparked the Crown Vic. "When DeSimone comes out, he won't see us from here."

Weeks and weeks of Carbone and Guevara roving about the five New York boroughs tailing the pink Cadillac, however, yielded zero. DeSimone was shrewd and spoke only of trivialities, and how quickly he could tantalize his new dates into disrobing.

Two months had elapsed since the Lufthansa robbery, and Carbone and Guevara hadn't advanced forward in piecing together the puzzle with which to build evidence against Burke and his Robert's Lounge gang. Desperation was setting in, and Carbone implored McDonald, "Ed, we need a warrant for Angelo Sepe. He's been known to be a braggart, and probably shoots off his mouth in his car. You gotta get me this warrant."

McDonald was reluctant. When a prosecutor applies for a warrant or a subpoena that bears no fruit, the next time around a judge will be less willing to grant it.

"Steve, something has got to give in this case. And it has to happen soon. Right now, we don't have anything to make an arrest that will stick."

"No, we don't, Ed, but I *am* working on stacking the odds against the Burke crew. I'm at it day and night."

Carbone's tendency was to roll the dice. In 1981 a board of psychiatrists had studied six different ethnic groups and tracked a pattern. The inclination to take chances was greater with Italian Americans. Carbone, though, "had a hunch" that bugging Sepe's automobile might yield results.

McDonald massaged his eyelids and groaned. "This is the last warrant I'm going for. Unless you come up with indictable evidence, don't come begging me for more subpoenas."

A week after they'd planted the beeper in DeSimone's Cadillac, on another frosty night, Carbone, Guevara, and the spying expert had repeated the fingernail-biting operation on Sepe's brand new Thunderbird; a gift he had bought himself and paid for in cash.

Sepe, however, had an intuition the FBI had "wired" the Thunderbird, and his countermeasure was simple; he'd raise the volume of the car radio to the maximum, and the eavesdroppers were treated to the latest rock and disco tunes.

Two weeks passed, and McDonald asked Carbone for an update.

"Uh . . . DeSimone is keeping tight lips. Probably on Burke's instructions. Uh . . . as far as Sepe, all he does is turn up his goddamn stereo," complained Carbone.

"That's nice. Real nice! Warrant after warrant, and all we have is a big fat zilch."

Carbone scratched his temple. "I'm going to have the bug technician disable the stereo in Sepe's T-Bird."

"Oh! Steve, you're grasping at straws. Now I've heard it all."

59

I was just waking up when the phone rang. It was Jimmy.

"Hello, Henry. Come down to my joint in an hour. Gotta talk to you."

"What is it, Jimmy?"

"That bastard, Richard Eaton."

I glanced at my watch. "I can be there by one o'clock."

"OK, that'll do. See you then."

I strode into Robert's Lounge and saw Jimmy at the bar, a tense look on his face. I had a pretty good idea what was bothering the Gent.

Richard Eaton was a straw man for Jimmy Burke and the owner of record on the liquor license of Robert's Lounge. Eaton was a smooth conniver, and his targets swallowed his lies. And man, he was as slick as grease.

After Lufthansa, Eaton bamboozled Jimmy into fronting him $250,000 for a cocaine transaction. Eaton was good at making his bull-shit sound believable.

"After I cut the dust, for sure, we're gonna make millions," he'd promised the Gent.

Jimmy invested part of the money from his piece of Lufthansa in the drug deal. Weeks later, the truth came out. Eaton didn't invest Jimmy's money to buy cocaine. He spent it on high-flying women, drugs, weekends in Vegas, and fancy sports cars. Knowing that con artist for a dozen years, Jimmy should've been wiser, but as usual, greed fogged his thinking.

"Can you believe this fuckin' Eaton? I give him a chance to make a score, and he puts it right up my ass," Jimmy vented.

"A quarter of a mill!? I always said you should watch that ass-fucker."

"Found out he's in Florida, Fort Lauderdale. I'm going down there, and I want you to come with me." Jimmy watched my reaction. He pulled a drag on his cigarette, eyes crinkling against the smoke. "I'd ask Tommy, but this Saturday he's gettin' made."

"Shit, I'll go anywhere but Florida," I said. Every time someone mentions Florida, I remember what happened the last time.

Jimmy shooed with his hand. "Henry, this is a different ball of wax."

"All right, but I don't wanna wind up back in Lewisburg."

"Stop acting like a woman, Henry. Nothin's gonna go wrong."

Tommy was about to become a made man, a lifetime diamond-studded milestone. When Tommy had killed his best friend, Stacks, he showed unselfishness and guts. He did it for the Mafia as a whole. And for this devotion, Tommy claimed he deserved to be part of the *Cosa Nostra*. He hocked and hocked Paul Vario to nominate him as a member of the Lucchese family. And Tommy made it known that, even though it had been the hardest thing for him to whack Stacks, as an obedient soldier, he followed orders. He had proved to be a stand-up guy and fought for his button, the imaginary badge of a made man. At last, the rites and rituals, "the christening," was to take place the weekend after Christmas.

We landed in Fort Lauderdale, rented a car, and drove all over South Florida. "That no good prick must've taken a powder, and if I ever find him," the Gent fumed, "I swear, I'm gonna hang him by his nuts with guitar strings."

"Jimmy, you come up with the weirdest ideas. I mean, stringing up Eaton by his balls with guitar strings kind of strikes a chord with me. Get it? Ha, ha, ha."

"It's not funny, Henry."

"Eaton will turn up. They always do. Mark my words."

"Yeah, I just hope he don't turn up dead before I kill him," Jimmy wished.

60

Burke and Hill were losing their minds in Florida hunting for Eaton. Up north in New York Tommy DeSimone was dressing for his acceptance into the Mafia. He donned his double-breasted black Bill Blass suit, a starched blue shirt, and beige silk tie. His hair was trimmed and coiffed, and he could've passed for a Hollywood star nominated for an Oscar. Vario's son, Pete Jr., was en route to DeSimone's house; he'd been chosen to chauffeur the made man candidate to the secret hideout where he'd be initiated into the Lucchese outfit.

DeSimone lived in Ozone Park, an Italian neighborhood crawling with underworld figures. Many of them, DeSimone included, dwelled in unkempt residences built in the spawning 1900s. Despite the squalor they lived in, they bought new Cadillacs every two years.

Pete Vario Jr. rang the bell, and DeSimone's wife, Angela, let him in. DeSimone came out of his room and gave Pete Jr. a high sign. He kissed Angela good-bye and left with his friend. Angela, a gum-chewing, hard-core woman with a permanent of plastered blonde hair, waved to her husband. "Good luck, Tommy. Hope it all goes well. Lemme know if you're coming home for dinner tonight."

"Yeah, yeah. I'll call you after it's over."

Pete Jr. shifted the black Caddy into drive and accelerated moderately. DeSimone fidgeted with his tie, and Pete Jr. glanced at him. "You look a bit nervous, pal. Relax, it's gonna be all right."

Pete Jr. steered toward the northbound lanes of the Cross Island Parkway, heading for the Throgs Neck Bridge. They crossed over Long Island Sound, the Cadillac then stopped at the tollbooth, and Pete Jr. paid the $1.25 fee. As if it were riding on air, the automobile floated along the rutted streets of the South Bronx and in twenty minutes crossed Arthur Avenue.

Blue-collar masses and factions of outlaws were scattered throughout the Bronx. Three-story tenements built in the late 1800s landscaped the residential blocks. Rusting wrought-iron fire escapes attached precariously to the flaking mortar on the brick walls of the housings were an all-too-familiar sight. Cooking flavors spilled into the streets, and drying laundry flapped at the windows— as did the mouths of tenants who frittered time chatting with neighbors on bordering balconies. Clashing and screeching music squawked from everywhere, and Jerry Vale and Jimmy Rosselli recordings blared twenty-six hours a day.

In the flats, you'd run into bragging Italian Americans, the sort who spoke of an uncle or a cousin who was "connected." (Strangely, though, no one ever clarified to what or to whom.) These charlatans bragged of belonging to the Mafia, but in actuality those who do are forbidden to publicize it. And if a made man disobeys this rule, he's subject to severe punishment—a hollow-point .38 into the temple.

Pete Jr. parked the ocean liner–like Cadillac, and he and DeSimone went into an Italian restaurant, Don Vito's. The handful of tables were covered with red and white plaid tablecloths, and one wall was painted with a mural of the Bay of Naples, a plume of white smoke billowing in the foreground from the peak of Mount Vesuvius. In a throwback to the early twentieth century, sawdust was sprinkled on the wooden plank floors. Music played loudly from speakers in the dropped ceiling panels; Luciano Pavarotti's unwavering tenor was belting out a vintage Italian song, "Mamma."

A tanned Dean Martin look-alike wearing a glittering silvery gym suit greeted Pete Jr. and DeSimone. He motioned for the two wiseguys to follow him into a stairway leading to a dimly lit basement, where three older men that, in similarity to wax statues, sat motionless around an octagonal card table.

DeSimone smelled chicken pizzaiola, the bistro's specialty. After the ritual, he'd feast on a bear-size portion of this dish, washing it down with a bottle of red wop.

As was customary at the Mafia christening of a made man, candles glowed on the walls and everywhere. DeSimone, edginess in his look, peered tentatively at those seated. He didn't recognize the faces, and it rippled his nerves. "Is this where I'm gettin' christened?" he asked, caution in his voice.

The elderly gentlemen, their hands wrinkled and dotted with freckles bowed their heads in unison. Unexpectedly, at least to DeSimone, from a doorway materialized the silhouette of a man. Despite the low candle-light, DeSimone identified the figure. It was John Gotti. Everyone was still and silent, except one of the gray-haired men seated at the table. He had the air of a rough, weathered patriarch with savagery in his eyes, and his clan called him the Cardinal. With his hand, thinly and etched with blue veins, he pointed to an empty chair in the center of this crypt-like chamber. In a gruff voice, the Cardinal saluted, "Welcome, Tommy. Congratulations! Pull a chair up to the table and sit comfortably. This is not an ordinary day in your life, I want you to know."

"Yeah, sure. Thanks." DeSimone's fearsome stance was suddenly reduced to the pose of a timid lamb. His eyes had lost their gape of insanity and now had a hollow gawk, a strange submissiveness for a man whose temper ignited as easily as gasoline vapors.

DeSimone sat, and everybody regarded him with somberness. Gotti, slowly stepping closer and closer, his shoes clacking on the tiled floor, stood behind the subject of this ceremony. The presence of the Gambino captain distressed DeSimone. Gotti does not belong to the Lucchese family. Why is he at this Mafia ritual? The moment of enlightenment came within the span of three seconds. Gotti pulled out a silencer-equipped .38 Colt magnum from his inner breast pocket and drilled three bullets into DeSimone's cranium. PAH . . . PAH . . . PAH. DeSimone's head blasted forward, and with the thud of a ten-pound boulder slumped onto the card table, blood seeping and leaching onto the green felt tabletop.

Gotti buttoned his camel cashmere overcoat, straightened the lapels, and with casualness walked out of the room with a vaunting stride. The three geriatrics, as if their witnessing of this execution was mandatory, stared at the forever immobilized DeSimone. Not a word was spoken.

A combination of conflicts had come to a head, provoking the elimination of Tommy DeSimone. The chief reason for the hit was an unsettled beef that had been grating between the Gambinos and the Luccheses.

Furious over DeSimone about to be granted his button, Gotti had asked for a sit-down with Paul Vario. "Paulie, I kept quiet all this time, but now I gotta speak up." Palms at chest level, Gotti tilted his head and looked into Vario's eyes. "Not for nothin', Paulie, but this fuckin' DeSimone whacked two of my top earners, and I let it go for a long time. Now he wants to be made, and I'm not gonna sit quietly. I mean, that's as bad as putting a cactus up my ass. Understan' what I'm sayin', Paulie?"

"John, what do you suppose I should do?" Vario asked, already knowing the answer.

Gotti planted his left forearm on the tabletop and stared at the Luc-chese capo. "Paulie, all I want is what's fair. I wanna whack the bastard, and I want you to give me the green light."

It was not a tough call for Vario. Besides DeSimone's past disregard for a Mafia code of honor—taking it on his own to kill two made men—it was a matter of time before the Lufthansa detectives would soon be shadowing his doorstep. Unmasking his face during the robbery, and now known to the investigators as one of the gunmen, the noose was tighten-ing. More troubling, as Vario anticipated, was an outstanding hazard: If DeSimone had to face spending the duration of his sexual prowess in a federal prison, he might negotiate a plea bargain and "rat out everybody."

Lastly, when Hill was imprisoned for the Florida assault charge, Vario had looked after Mrs. Hill, in more ways than one; he had an affair with her. DeSimone interpreted it as if Karen Hill were free meat for the taking. On a summer morning, he must've waked with a burning libido. He went to Karen's home and made advances to her. She rebuffed DeSimone, and he waved his penis at her. Karen ran to Vario with this, and he swore to her that DeSimone's remaining days would not outlast the life of a mouse. So Gotti's request to murder him was timely and well received.

"I see where you're coming from, John." Vario lay back in the arm-chair, his humongous belly inflating and deflating in rhythm with his heavy breathing. He quieted and tipped his head up and down for effect, pretending to be between a rock and a hard spot. Vario lingered a while longer, and ultimately slapped his knee. "All right, Johnnie Boy." This was Gotti's nickname. "Do what you gotta do. You got my OK, kid. *Mi capisci?*" You understand?

"*Sicuro che ti capisco.*" Of course, I understand.

DeSimone had vanished, and his wife drove to the 113th Precinct, and reported him missing.

The NYPD belatedly informed the FBI, and Carbone could've kicked himself. He'd had grounds to arrest DeSimone, and he damn should have. Two Lufthansa employees had identified him from police mug shots.

Carbone speculated that maybe DeSimone had gone on one of his philandering binges with another woman, and his wife might've been overreacting.

The agent reporting to Carbone squashed that supposition. "I'm afraid not, Steve. Rumors from fairly reliable street informers are saying DeSimone was murdered."

"Are there leads? I mean, who might've done it?"

"According to a recently updated dossier, the shooter had to have been John Gotti."

"OK, thanks." Carbone threw his head back and joggled the phone receiver, as though it had the answer of where to go from here. *I should've had him locked up.*

61

Jimmy and I, downcast and loaded with luggage, lumbered out of the Eastern arrival terminal at LaGuardia Airport, coming back from Florida empty-handed; Richard Eaton, knowing the Gent was on to him, had gone into hiding.

Jimmy's son, Frank, met us at the airport. We threw our luggage in the trunk, and after a delayed and bumpy flight, I couldn't wait to get home. Frank was driving toward the ramp to merge onto the Grand Central Parkway. "Dad, Henry, eh . . . I don't know how to start."

"What? What?" Jimmy asked. "I don't need any more bad news."

"Tommy's gone."

"What do you mean, Tommy's gone?"

From the rear seat, I leaned forward. "What are you talkin' about, Frank?"

"They . . . they whacked him."

I never thought I'd see it: Jimmy burst into tears. Neither the Gent nor Jesus Christ himself could have stopped DeSimone's whacking. The ski mask mishap, a senseless thing to do, had drawn heat on the Robert's

Lounge gang and Paul Vario. Though it left Vario no choice, Jimmy re-sented him for green-lighting the killing of his protégé and friend.

The three of us fell grim for the rest of the ride home.

62

Theresa Ferrara, DeSimone's on-and-off main squeeze, had been dab-bling in selling narcotics. She was a bushy blonde with an un-sensational physique, though her seductive eyes—nickel-size and wide apart—could fog a man's moralities. Theresa was an opportunist who was drawn to hoodlums and gangsters. She cohabited and loaned her affections to the highest bidder until a new, wealthier suitor entered her life. Her hair salon was insolvent, and a Colombo made man, Benny Aloi, who had financed the beauty shop, had been twisting her arm to repay him with sexual favors. Ordinarily, Theresa did not mind amortizing a debt with sex. But Aloi repulsed her. He was grossly fat and thought grooming applied only to dogs and horses.

One afternoon, not long after DeSimone's body had gone cold, Aloi went to the beauty shop, took Theresa by the hand, and led her to the backroom. There on past occasions, somehow, she had managed to stim-ulate his orgasms. It wasn't easy because the fifty-three-year-old Aloi had been on a medication to lower his blood pressure. In spite of this short-coming, Theresa, talented in the art of resuscitating a lazy penis, induced the slovenly shylock's ejaculations—though she loathed physical contact with him. How could Theresa rid herself of Aloi? Never at a loss to invent a lie, she said to him, "Look, Benny, I've been going out with Paul Vario. He's divorcing his wife, and we're gonna get married. And I don't think Paulie's gonna like it if he finds out you're making me have some sort of sex with you once a week."

"Oh, c'mon. You don't gotta tell that fat fuck Paulie about us."

"I already did. Actually, he wants to talk to you and get to the nitty-gritty of how much more I owe you. This damn place is a loser, and I don't want it on my head that either I gotta give you a vig of three points a week, or have sex with you."

In time, when Theresa did apprise Paul Vario of her debt, she and Vario made a pact. If she'd fulfill his libidinal urges, he'd call for a sit-down with her nauseating creditor. "I'll make that filthy prick Benny take a walk, and that'll be the end of it, Theresa."

Theresa hugged Vario, invited him to her apartment, and gave him a sampling of her gratitude. The Lucchese capo did not know she was a Nassau County Police informant, and that her home was wired with snooping electronics. In 1977, the Narcotics Squad had arrested Theresa for peddling marijuana, and to skirt prosecution she joined the cadre of stool pigeons. Burke had caught a whiff of this and assigned Angelo Sepe to observe Ms. Ferrara's daily moves. Sepe spied on her and reported back to the Gent: "For the past three mornings, she spent twenty minutes in the diner across the street from her salon having breakfast with a clean-cut dude in a black suit."

Burke bitterly bit his lips. "You know who the guy is, Angelo?"

"Nah, but I think he's either an NYPD dick or one of those FBI pricks."

"Stay on top of her, Angelo."

"I'd love to be on top of her. Ha, ha, ha."

Burke saw no humor. "Let's keep it straight. This ain't no monkey business."

Theresa Ferrara was a grand-slam informant for the investigators, especially because DeSimone had been loose-lipped and gave her news feeds of the Lufthansa plans.

Steve Carbone had stumbled upon Theresa through another street spy, and assigned rookie agent Christopher Mackey as her handling agent. His youth and inexperience, usually a liability, in this case could be an asset. Mackey was about Theresa's age; Carbone figured it might forge empathy between the two.

Agent Mackey, tidy, athletic, and single, had begun debriefing Theresa, and Carbone's insight was correct; she instantly trusted Mackey.

With the fervor of a novice, eyes blinking, Mackey light-stepped into his boss's office. "Mr. Carbone, I got Theresa Ferrara to commit to a full testimony against Burke, Vario, and Sepe."

"Fantastic! When will you be speaking with her again?"

Mackey spoke rapidly without taking a breath. "Sunday morning. Same place, the diner across the street from her beauty salon."

"Good. Make it happen, Chris."

"You bet, Mr. Carbone. You bet." The phrase "you bet" is not uncommon for Americans from the inland and southern regions of the country, especially those of Irish and English ancestry, to express.

Carbone phoned McDonald. "Theresa Ferrara is ready to cooperate, Ed. You can depose her sometime next week."

A tingle rippled through McDonald's spine. *Could this be real?*

Agent Mackey, by now on a first-name basis with Ms. Ferrara, was poised for the encounter with the witness who knew *everything* about Lufthansa. Angling this mole could put a feather in his cap. He called Theresa to firm up the appointment. The phone rang eight times. Silence. Mackey's heart sped, a blister of heat flaring on his face. At the tenth ring, she answered in a whispery hush. "Hello."

"Hello, Theresa?"

"Hi, Christopher. Paul Vario was here, and luckily, he left as the phone squealed."

Mackey could hear her fast gulps of breaths. "Are you OK?"

"Yeah, yeah. I'm fine. I just can't wait to get this over with, Chris. It's giving me the heebie-jeebies." She had called him Chris. Intimacy between the Brooklyn-born Theresa and the wheat-grown Mackey, as those working with him noted, was warming. If one were to guess, Mackey was growing love-struck, but the street-smart Theresa was too fast for the bland Midwesterner.

"I'm . . . I'm glad you're all right," he said, a pining in his undertone. "Listen, I brought my supervisor up to speed, and he spoke with the US attorney. We're set for tomorrow, Sunday morning. Same time, same place."

"Oh, Chris, I can't wait to get this goddamn monkey off my back. But why on a Sunday morning?"

"Agent Carbone wants to arrange for your safety without wasting a minute." This wasn't totally true. Mackey, the lover boy, his heart throbbing, couldn't wait to see Theresa. "OK? I'll see you tomorrow at 9:30. Have a good night, Theresa. And watch yourself. Please."

Transcending from the courtships of men who competed in pampering and impressing her to waking every morning in the general population of a county jail, would be an incomprehensible adjustment for Theresa. She was afraid of the atrocities, as is common belief, inmates inflict on the weaker, unnerved prisoners. Thus, she ran for cover and didn't need much swaying to become a "stoolie."

On second thought, though, she tussled with her conscience. Theresa's roots had ingrained in her not to snitch, and in a moment of soul-searching the wrath of a betrayer touched her. On the other hand, hadn't Paul Vario sanctioned the murder of her Tommy? And Burke did not stand up for him. Not even that snake Henry Hill had fought for Tommy. And there you have it, they were the Judas, not her. In light of those reflections, Theresa resolved that entering the government's den of backstabbers was not just a bridge to a new life; it was also sweet revenge for her boyfriend's murder.

From a phone booth in Brooklyn on the corner of Rockaway Parkway and Foster Avenue, Burke reached out to Theresa. "Hello, Theresa. It's Jimmy Burke."

"Well, hello, Mr. Burke. Long time no hear."

"I want you to know how sorry I am about Tommy. And I tell you, never in my life did I feel worse."

"Oh, that's so touching, Jimmy," she said dryly. "But you know what bothers me? You did *nothin'* about it."

"Theresa, there was nothin' Henry or me could've done. It was strictly between the Italians. They're the ones who make those calls, and what's done is done. Meantime, if you need me for anything, you know how to reach me."

"Should that make me feel better?"

"Take it any way you want. Listen, Theresa, this is not why I'm callin' you. Paulie asked me to do him a favor and contact you. You know him; he don't talk on the phones. He's got something he wants you to keep for him. Paulie wants to see you tonight at about six o'clock in the parking lot of the diner across the street from your beauty shop."

"Why don't Paulie come to my house like he usually does?"

"He's got some heat on him, and he don't wanna be seen at your apartment. He'll fill you in himself."

She exhaled with heaviness. "All right, I'll be there."

At six o'clock that Saturday evening, Theresa left her beauty parlor and trekked to the diner, her head covered with a plastic rain bonnet, showers pouring and lightning fracturing the darkness. She skipped over fresh puddles, muddy water splashing her ankles, and could see Paul Vario and his pillowy belly wedged behind the steering wheel of his black Lincoln, a cigar rolling between his lips. Preserving the wiseguy tradition, the rear windows of Vario's car were tinted, and Theresa couldn't be sure if he was in the company of anybody else. She yanked open the front passenger door and plopped into the Lincoln, a booming thunder crackling in the drenching skies. The hairdresser leaned in to kiss Vario. Burke and Angelo Sepe, slumped in the backseat, understood she'd seen them and flinched at their presence.

Burke smiled wryly. "Hi, Theresa."

"What're you doing here, Jimmy?"

The Gent veered his lips downward and shrugged as if he'd just come along for the ride. Sepe didn't make eye contact with her and gazed at the beads of rain slashing the window.

Theresa's pulse must've raced; the occupants of the Lincoln could see her throat swelling with unnatural gulps.

"What's going on, Paulie? What's all this sneakin' around?" she pleaded.

Vario started the engine, swished out of the parking lot, and headed west on Burnside Avenue in the direction of Kennedy Airport. "I got some hassles with my wife. I'll explain when we get to Jimmy's place."

Theresa's fingers fluttered, and the Gent watched her face flaring to a flush. She tugged at Vario's wrist. "Paulie, how can you do this to me? It's Saturday night, I have customers coming in. You can't make me miss my appointments. This is my livelihood, Paulie. Please take me back. Please!"

"This will only take ten minutes," Vario mumbled, the cigar bobbing on his lips.

Sunday morning, Mackey went to the diner for his tryst with Theresa. She wasn't there. He checked his watch: 10:31. Ten more minutes and still no sign of her. Mackey hastened to the bank of public telephones near the lavatories and called Theresa's apartment. He let the phone ring fourteen times. No answer. Mackey also phoned the beauty salon. No luck. He ran his fingers through his hair, a razor-cut of blond bristles, and phoned Carbone.

"She'll turn up, Chris. She's probably struggling with her upbringing. I know the type. She's Italian, and from birth they're brainwashed with the number one rule: Never squeal. The next time Theresa goes into frenzy about doing time, she'll turn up."

"I hope you're right, Mr. Carbone." Mackey seemed morose; signs he was burning embers for the lovely Theresa were more and more apparent. She was bubbly and never harassed a man with the taunt of marriage, a perfect mate, thought Mackey. He had been nurtured in a conservative Episcopalian world, and a fancy, fast-flying woman of Theresa's spirit—provocative, yet respectful of men—tempted him. On this morning, though, he felt a twinge in his innards, a sensation that not all was well with her.

The following day, Theresa's employee reported her missing. McDonald was at wit's end. "Steve, you've got to do something to stop this killing spree. This is insane."

Carbone didn't reply, and Mackey was practically in mourning.

Carbone then held his chin and raised a forefinger. "Ed, I'm going to put out an advisory through the informants in the streets for anyone who has any involvement with the Lufthansa robbery to ask for our protection."

McDonald jutted his hand at Carbone. "It's a start, Steve. Do it."

63

The Lufthansa situation was still hot, but I was in my own orbit, higher and higher into the heroin distribution. Jimmy and I were partners in the drug business, and although it was a new game to me, I soon found out how much money we could make. I went to see Jimmy at his house in Howard Beach to give him his cut of the week's profits.

The Gent came out, and I almost fell to the floor. "What the hell are you doing answering the door in your underwear?" I looked behind me and to the sides. "What if it was a woman?"

"I'd fuck her, Henry." He pulled me inside and shut the door. Jimmy put his arm around my neck, happy to see me. "So what're you got for me?"

I was carrying the cash in a child's lunch pail. I took out two rubber-banded wads and handed them to him. "Twenty-two large ones, Jimmy."

"Good going, Henry." The Gent juggled the two bricks of money in the palms of his hands. "You talk to Paulie lately?"

"Yesterday."

"Did he ask you how you're making all this bread?"

Out of habit, I snorted. "Yeah, kind of. I keep tellin' him I have a few scams going with fixed card games, I'm selling stolen cars to a Haitian. Shit like that."

"Does he believe you?"

"Eh, you know. When I give him an envelope with five grand, he changes the subject."

Vario wasn't in tune about Jimmy and me selling narcotics. If I got caught I'd be facing life, and sure as hell, Paulie was not going to chance me cutting a deal and giving him up. So he'd kill me. And this was incentive not to get pinched.

Meantime, guys were getting whacked left and right over Lufthansa, and I had first-hand knowledge Jimmy was the one doing it.

The Gent was high on heroin day and night, plus he drank bourbon from the minute he woke in the morning to the time he blacked out. The booze and drugs added to his paranoia that everybody who knew about Lufthansa was gonna rat him out. I became my own best customer also, and the whole day long I was on another planet.

When Theresa Ferrara went AWOL, I asked Jimmy, "What the fuck happened to Theresa? I mean, you gotta put yourself in check, man. Pretty soon, there ain't gonna be nobody else for you to whack."

Stone-faced, Jimmy looked into my eyes and lashed out, "I don't know nothin' about Theresa. And if I was you, I'd mind my own business. Get my drift?"

64

It had been six days, and Theresa Ferrara never reappeared. Carbone was having lunch in McDonald's office. They had phoned in an order from the German deli five blocks from the US attorney's office. Carbone was chewing on a roast beef hero, mayonnaise smearing his lips and chin, and McDonald was savoring smoked salmon on a sesame bagel.

"Steve," McDonald said, his jaw hacking the bagel. "every time we get close to a potential witness, somehow they're murdered or vanish."

Carbone wiped his mouth. "Well, we know Burke has something to do with it."

"I'm having trouble with a possibility that had me up the whole night." McDonald held up his left palm and cautioned with a tinge of embarrassment, "This is not a personal reflection on you, Steve. Is it *possible* you have a mole among your agents or clerks?"

Carbone's bushy eyebrows turned upward, and he dropped the sandwich onto the paper plate. "What are you trying to say, Ed?"

"This is not a personal offense, Steve. Look, presuming Burke is behind these murders, how does he know whom we're targeting as informants? Unless somebody on your staff tips him off. His timing seems to be right on."

Carbone's eyebrows reshaped to a horizontal line, and he crunched another bite of the roast beef hero. "I can't discount that possibility, Ed." He blew out a long breath. "I'm going to have to expand the surveillance."

Ed Guevara huddled with Carbone over a desk inside the FBI surveillance van, their faces green from the lighted short-wave receiver. Listening into a pair of headphones, Guevara's hand had been scribbling speedily on a yellow notepad. "Steve," he prompted, "hurry, get your headphones on."

Carbone scrambled and pressed a headset to his ear. "I think we're getting somewhere, Ed."

"C'mon, c'mon. Keep talking, keep talking," Guevara said to himself, hoping, Angelo Sepe and the passenger in his two-door sedan might blab on about a homicide presently unknown to the FBI.

The bug in Sepe's Thunderbird had been active for a week. Carbone and Guevara had intercepted Sepe saying he had purchased the automobile for $16,240. An inquiry with the Department of Motor Vehicles revealed the selling dealer, and the salesman recalled, "This hood type, eh . . . his name, I think, is Angelo Sepe. He strolled into the showroom with a duffle bag full of ten-and twenty-dollar bills. Hey, a sale is a sale, and I didn't give it a second thought. It's not my job to figure out how people get their money."

Carbone and McDonald surmised the small, unmarked bills must've been Sepe's cut from Lufthansa. They analyzed the conversations that had come from the mike in Sepe's car and reckoned they had probable cause to arrest him for parole violation, consorting with another parolee—his passenger. Sepe and his friend had vaguely discussed a murder, plus they talked, though garbled, about "buried money."

But McDonald wasn't ready to celebrate. "Steve, the only charge that will stick is Sepe's parole violation. The rest is conjecture, minus indictable evidence."

Carbone, not one to surrender easily, contended, "Even if the arrest is based only on the parole violation, at least we'll have him in custody, and maybe he'll crack under pressure."

"If we cannot muster material evidence implicating Sepe in a Class A felony, or minimally, a preponderance of circumstantial evidence, why would he crack?" McDonald contemplated. "He's a veteran criminal and knows the most he can be imprisoned for a parole violation is sixteen months. And a mere sixteen months on ice isn't going to tempt him to burn Jimmy Burke and Paul Vario because *that* could be a death sentence for Sepe."

McDonald was increasingly troubled; he cringed at the prospect of standing in a courtroom empty-handed and admitting to a judge, *eh, sorry, Your Honor, but we can't proceed to indict.* Throughout his legal tenure, he'd been careful not to dent his reputation. And charging someone with a crime without solid proof to prosecute could blemish the impeccability of McDonald's status as a US attorney.

Carbone fanned his hand at the US attorney's concerns. "Let's get Sepe on the parole issue so he doesn't get lost or get killed. And I'll work on getting together what we need to indict him on a higher felony. I'm sure he'll eventually take us right into the bunker of the Lufthansa perps."

"I don't like it, Steve. If you don't uncover anything new against Sepe, it can backfire and end up in a disaster."

"Ed, I know we'll dig up what we need to collar Sepe. I know it."

McDonald drummed his fingertips on the desktop and stared at Carbone. "All right, if we're going to pick up Sepe, notify the other agencies so we don't trip over each other's feet."

Advising the local police and the borough attorney of the decision to apprehend Sepe was not on Carbone's program. He and George Wells, chief of the Queens BQ5 FBI division and Carbone's boss, sketched ulterior designs. Wells and Carbone were set on catching their prize without the local police forces. Wells said to Carbone, "Set out to do what you and I discussed." Wells winked slyly. "That'll keep them away from the media."

Carbone set his chief's plan in motion and telephoned the NYPD 113th Precinct detective squad commander. "Lieutenant Ahearn, this is Steve Carbone."

"Well, hello, Steve. And to what do I owe the pleasure of hearing from you?" Ahearn said with cynicism.

"A courtesy. I wanted to put you on notice we're going after Angelo Sepe."

It startled Ahearn. "On what charges?"

"I'm not at liberty to go into it, Lieutenant. We want to make sure the information doesn't get into the wrong ears and winds up on the street."

"Carbone, are you implying my detectives are corrupt?" This was a sore wound. The New York City Police Department had been under scrutiny for a corruption virus that had infected many of its precincts.

"Lieutenant, I'm not implying anything. But we'd rather err on the side of caution."

"You son-of-a-bitch. You fuckin' FBI people never change." And Ahearn slammed down the phone.

Ahearn's rude ending thumped in Carbone's ear. Carbone chuckled, aligned his thoughts, and redialed Ahearn's number.

"Hello," Ahearn answered angrily.

"This is Steve Carbone again."

"What're you want now?"

"You should appreciate we have to take special precautions to . . ."

"Oh, stop with your bullshit, Carbone."

"An official from the bureau will be contacting the heads of the NYPD, the borough attorney's detective squad, and you. You'll be briefed when and where we should meet to coordinate Sepe's arrest."

"That's fine, Carbone. I hope you and your fuckin' agents choke on your next line of shit."

Except for a variation of disparagement and choices of curses, similar hostilities were hurled when Carbone reached out to Captain DeGeneste and the district attorney's chief of detectives.

This resentment was the excuse Carbone needed to minimize contact with the other law enforcement branches and muddle communications among them. Carbone, however, wanted to put on the impression he was proceeding in concert with everyone else.

The next morning, a woman at the FBI office, Louise Burrows, dialed in all parties on a conference call and updated them with the day and time everybody should assemble to coordinate the last steps before Carbone's agents would swarm into Sepe's apartment on Utrecht Avenue in Brooklyn. Per Special Agent Carbone, all forces were to arrive at the loading dock of Lufthansa Cargo Building-261 at 4:00 a.m. on Saturday, February 17.

In a broadcast-quality voice, Ms. Burrows said, "Detectives, if Jimmy Burke is tracking the investigators' movements, it will appear as if you are revisiting the crime scene for a reinspection, and this should dispel suspicion of a dragnet closing in on Sepe."

Ms. Burrows wavered and pretended to have forgotten a pertinent fact. "Oh, one last directive, gentlemen," she added, "the FBI task force that'll move in on Sepe will be traveling in a telephone company van. As a decoy, at precisely 4:15, three of *your* unmarked vehicles will then leave Cargo Building-261, separate, and disperse in multiple directions. Do not go . . . I repeat, gentlemen, do not go directly to Mr. Sepe's residence."

"Thank you for the advisory. Veeeery kind of you," Ahearn said scornfully. "I'm confirming my men and I, *and* the personnel from the Port Authority, and the District Attorney's office will be at Building-261 at 4:00 a.m. on February 17th." He terminated the call and reclined in his swivel chair, thinking how pompous Ms. Burrows was. "Bitch. Hope she gets a yeast infection."

This seemingly cooperative effort lessened the tension between Carbone and his counterparts. But not quite. In the predawn of February 17th, a wintry day, the squadron of policemen from the NYPD, Port Authority, and the borough attorney's squad waited with cold breath pouring from their lips, and to everyone's chagrin Carbone and his agents were a no-show.

The FBI had misrepresented the strategy of Sepe's arrest to throw Ahearn, DeGeneste, and Tyson off-track. The false timing paved the way for Carbone and his subordinates to single-handedly collar Sepe, convene the media, and bask in *all* the credit. But there was a downside. If Carbone failed to build indictable evidence to slap Angelo Sepe with a Class B felony, he'd lose his stronghold on him. The FBI would then bear the brunt of the criticism—and the embarrassment.

65

Carbone's men apprehended Sepe, and to the ire of DeGeneste, Ahearn, and the illustrious Francis Tyson, FBI Chief Wells held a press conference and pranced in front of rows of cameras, microphones, and shouting reporters.

"At 4:30 a.m. this morning, FBI agents from the Queens office arrested a suspect believed to have been one of the armed robbers of the Lufthansa robbery on December 11, 1978. His name is Angelo Sepe, a dangerous felon. FBI agents seized him in his apartment on Utrecht Avenue in Brooklyn without incident."

Bulbs flashed, the press corps hollered out questions, and for this media extravaganza Chief Wells was preened and spruced sporting the FBI signature razor cut. He could've passed for a scrubbed-down midwestern farmer. Wells wore a black suit and would've loved to smile broadly and heaped scorn on Ahearn, DeGeneste, and Tyson by injecting a besmirching remark. *See, my FBI men shafted all you wily New Yorkers.* The Bureau had imported Wells from somewhere in the plains of the Midwest, and he was more at home with cattle and pigs than he'd ever be with New Yorkers and their overrated Big Apple.

"That lowlife cocksucker. Carbone and his FBI scumbags played us all for fools," Tom Ahearn vented to DeGeneste. "Those sons of bitches sent us on a wild goose chase. Them fuckers are as low as cockroaches." He was so upset, and unconscious of his fit, he was chewing on the eraser end of a pencil. "Yeah, that's what they did. And that weasel-faced country hick, Wells, made it a point for no one to talk to the press. And there he was on TV telling the world how his agents cracked Lufthansa. I think I'm gonna go personally wring that prick's neck."

DeGeneste, a man with decorum, cautioned, "Tom, that piece of shit Wells ain't worth it. Why should you risk your career for that hick? Let it go. We'll get those FBI fucks when they least expect it."

"You're damn right he ain't worth it. I'll drop it for now. But one day I'm gonna get my hands on that Wells, so help me God," Ahearn swore.

Francis Tyson, too, was flabbergasted. He couldn't believe he was watching Wells's face plastered on the television screen. And to add insult of having been stood up the night before, the FBI was rubbing salt onto the wound by hosting its own show. Humiliated, the publicity-hungry Tyson had been sidelined for this media-chomping sensation, a tremendous setback to his political aspirations. But the Honorable Borough Attorney, unbroken and intrepid, was not one to limp away with the tail between his legs. Instead, he phoned Carbone.

Carbone had prepared for an unpredictable morning and could surely guess who'd be calling with a bombardment of harassment and maligning. "Special Agent Carbone here."

"This is Francis Tyson."

"What can I do for you, Francis?"

"What you can do for me?" Tyson sounded off balance. "I . . . I thought you're a professional, Steve. How could you have deceived me? You played us all for fools."

Carbone had rehearsed the explanation for these sorts of accusations and had the advantage. "I am a professional, and I apologize for the misunderstanding."

"Misunderstanding? There was no misunderstanding. Chief Wells's secretary directed us to convene at the Lufthansa cargo loading dock at 4:00 a.m. My understanding was that from there we were going to Sepe's residence to arrest him." Tyson's diatribe made him bite his upper lip, and he tasted blood on his lips. He wiped them with the back of his hand, and a drop splattered on his monogrammed shirt.

"Maybe that's what you wanted to hear, Francis. Chief Wells's assistant, Ms. Burrows, did not say that detectives and plainclothesmen from all the agencies were to participate in the operation. She said '*the task force*'—the FBI Task Force—was to surround Sepe's residence and grab him." Carbone had full knowledge of Ms. Burrows's clouded message and its true meaning; he had prescripted her memo word by word with deliberate haziness.

"Steve, *that* was not how we had understood it. Now what the fuck went wrong?"

Carbone deflected the barrage. "As I said, Francis, it must've been a misunderstanding on your part. I assure you we did not intend to misinform you, Captain DeGeneste, and Lieutenant Ahearn. Absolutely not!" Carbone paused to slow Tyson's volley. And when his belligerence began rising, Carbone curtailed him. "Hold your horses, Francis. Ms. Burrows simply passed on for you all to meet at the Lufthansa Building-261. Period. She never alluded beyond that."

"Steve, I'm offended because you're taking me for an imbecile. I wasn't the only one who misconstrued your . . ."

"Forgive me for interrupting, Francis," Carbone said. "I *do* have an urgent matter to attend to. We'll keep you posted on any new developments."

Tyson heard the click of the phone and stared at his handset in disbelief. "Sure, sure. The Messiah is coming also."

The Sepe development was, so far, the hottest the investigation had come to scraping at Burke's heels. Sepe's possible meltdown, and him skidding into the arms of the FBI was a nerve-rattler for the Gent. Burke's nerves ultimately loosened when Sepe's wife, through an intermediary, assured him he had nothing to fear; Angelo wasn't talking to anybody. Nonetheless, Burke still couldn't sleep well.

The opposition wasn't having pleasant dreams either; Wells and Carbone's victory scarcely outlasted the lifespan of a fly. And to McDonald's mortification, Carbone had not exhumed any corroborating proof verifying the nuances that the bug in Sepe's Thunderbird had recorded the previous week.

"Now what, Steve?" McDonald ranted, his even-temper no longer, and dying to smash a fist into a wall, or irresistibly, on Carbone's chin. This was the US attorney's self-reproach for straying from his conservative instincts.

Seldom at a loss for words, Carbone remained speechless; he, too, was in a self-blaming mode for the Sepe fiasco. He sought to repair the damage and frowned. "What about the parole violation?"

McDonald sighed, tiredness in his eyes. "That's not within my jurisdiction. It's up to the commissioners on the parole board. At their discretion, they can remand Sepe to jail for whatever time they deem fit *or* cut him loose."

Through an acquaintance of Vario somewhere in the prison system, in less than a month the Department of Corrections released Sepe. He was happy to be home, more so because the Lucchese bosses might surely promote him to a higher rank for clinging to silence.

"Welcome back, Angelo. We always knew you're a stand-up guy," Burke commended. He smiled, and his grin seemed as if it had the blessing of Satan.

Sepe was glad to be free, and at last the Gent could sleep soundly.

In another camp, the atmosphere was not so comfy. "Not only don't we have Sepe, but to add insult to injury you pinched a nerve with Ahearn, DeGeneste, and Tyson," McDonald rambled on, a righteous anger in his voice. "We made enemies out of them."

Hunched over McDonald's desk, Carbone was not about to surrender. "Tomorrow will be a brighter day, Ed. You're too pessimistic. I'll take this case to a closure. You'll see."

"Sure, Steve. If you say so!"

66

Not far from Robert's Lounge, Burke owned a dress factory. And there on this morning, he was brewing a pot of coffee, its aroma in the air. A knock pounded on the door, and he opened it. Two men in overly tight suits flaunted gold badges. Plainclothesmen from the 113th Precinct sent by Lieutenant Ahearn.

"I'm Detective Fitzgerald, and this is Detective Corollo. May we come in?"

"Sure, and call me Jimmy."

"Uh . . . OK, Jimmy. We don't have a warrant or a subpoena. Just a friendly invitation for you to come down to the precinct. Our squad commander, Lieutenant Ahearn, wants a few minutes with you."

"What's it about?"

"We wanna talk about the December 11th robbery at the Lufthansa cargo terminal."

Burke had guessed they were here for Lufthansa. "Sure, sure. I don't think I can be of help. But I'm always willing to cooperate with the cops. Lemme call my lawyer so he can meet us there."

Fitzgerald, Corollo, and Ahearn sat at a table opposite Burke. While waiting for Burke's attorney to arrive, they engaged in elementary talk; the main topic was the walloping snowy winter. The meaningless interchange was dying off, when a uniformed officer ushered in Leon Epstein, Burke's legal counsel. He shed his coat and sat to the right of his client.

Epstein rubbed his cold, purplish hands together. "Gentlemen, why are we here?"

Ahearn glared at the Gent as though they were the only ones in the room. "I don't wanna beat around the bush. What did you have to do with the Lufthansa robbery, Mr. Burke?"

When interrogated by the authorities, suspects ordinarily leave the talking to their attorneys. In Burke's case, he had swum in this pond many a time and was at ease dueling with cunning investigators. "You sure did get right to the point, Lieutenant Ahearn." Burke laughed heartily, and with the candor of a saint asked, "At what time did this robbery happen?"

Ahearn leafed through the pages of his notebook. "Between 3:00 and 3:45 a.m."

Burke chortled, flashing his teeth. "I was sound asleep at the CTC. You know, the halfway house. I gotta turn in there at night. Check the records and see for yourselves." An unshakeable fact.

Ahearn and his two detectives eyed one another, resigned they were not about to extract a confession from the Gent.

Burke read their faces and glanced at Epstein. "Leon, are we done here?"

The lawyer shut his briefcase and stood. "Lieutenant, here's my card. Should you need further assistance from my client, contact me *directly*."

And that snuffed out Ahearn's optimism to squeeze into submission the principal suspect in the Lufthansa theft.

Ahearn had not shared with Carbone his intentions to interview Burke. The lieutenant presumed, rather wished, that if he could trip Burke, it might give him a lead ahead of the FBI. Carbone, however, didn't waste energy on this exercise; Agent Mackey had verified the attendance records at the CTC, and it was a foregone conclusion the Gent would claim his detainment at the CTC as an indisputable alibi.

Lieutenant Ahearn had lost a big round.

67

Stacks, DeSimone, and Krugman, all attached to the Robert's Lounge crew, had departed. And it was a fair deduction their hands might've been stained with Lufthansa's blood. But they'd never tell; Stacks was dead and buried, and Krugman and DeSimone were missing and presumed killed. A stroke of luck, though, might've given rise to a new thread of hope. A CI—a confidential informer—had recounted to Agent Ed Guevara, "I know for sure Burke's boys pulled off the Lufthansa hit." The informer remained nameless, and in the FBI files was cataloged as CI-196. "I ain't guessing, Mr. Guevara. They're the ones who done this."

"What else can you give me that you know for sure?"

CI-196 bent his head in reluctance. "I . . . I don't know. Things are gettin' real bad on the streets. Everybody's gettin' whacked left and right."

Guevara sympathized; an informant was forever aware of the cold-edged sword on his neck. If his cover came to light, death was an inevitability. "You know we at the FBI go to great lengths to protect you. Nothing is guaranteed, but I'd say you're pretty safe with us. So let's have it. What can you give me?"

CI-196 wrung his hands, distress stamped on his face. "I know this guy . . . eh, his name is Cafora. A fat guy, they call him Roast Beef."

Guevara had come across this name. "Louis Cafora?"

"Yeah, yeah, him."

Guevara didn't waste a second running to Carbone.

"Steve, the CI's info adds up. Three of the Lufthansa hostages had said two of the stickup men were grossly obese. One had to have been Joe 'Buddha' Manri, and the other Louis 'Roast Beef' Cafora."

A sunny smile flicked on Carbone's lips. "You're right, Ed. It makes sense. And I bet Manri was the perp Werner dealt with. I'd say go pay Roast Beef a visit. Bring some mayonnaise with you. You may need it. Get it?"

Guevara chuckled. "These Mafia guys have the weirdest nicknames."

Cafora was the proprietor of a parking lot in Astoria, Queens, and state assessors had audited his business for sales tax evasion. Auditors for the state of New York had delivered proof of Cafora's tax fraud to the district attorney, who indicted him. The cash-strapped Roast Beef, smitten and cajoled by his new wife, lived in luxury beyond his means. He traded in his Cadillac every year, dined at exclusive restaurants, bestowed on his bride anything her heart desired, and was mired in a mountain of debt. Was it happenstance that, barely a month since the Lufthansa siege, and here he was squaring up his $68,541 delinquency with New York State? Guevara and Mackey started fishing for the source of Cafora's boon.

A trailer on Cafora's parking lot served as a makeshift office heated by a kerosene heater. Guevara and Mackey arrived unannounced, the acrid odor of kerosene fumes souring their throat. Before asking Cafora to identify himself, Guevara was certain he'd tracked down his person of interest. Not many people were the shape and weight of this Roast Beef oddball. "Are you Louis Cafora?"

Cafora, his mouth full of meatballs he'd bitten off an eighteen-inch hero, was playing poker with the lot attendant. The callers' comportment and attire—black suits, starched white shirts, and bland ties—must've rustled Cafora's innards. His look of surprise was one of uneasiness, dreading the unexpected visitors might be state investigators.

"Depends on who wants to know." Cafora laid down the cards, and his eyes locked on Guevara as if he were a fiend in dark clothes.

Guevara held his badge at Cafora's eye level. "Depends on who wants to know? How about if the FBI wants to know: Are you Louis Cafora?"

Cafora gobbled the meatballs, tomato sauce smearing his mouth, and judging by the sudden redness on his face, Guevara thought, a blood-rushing angst might've gushed up to his head. Roast Beef seemed to be thinking, *is this guy from the state for another sales tax hassle, or is he here for Lufthansa?* Those possibilities, as he admitted later, flipped his stomach upside down, unleashing an avalanching bowel movement.

Cafora nodded at his worker to leave. "Yeah, all right, I'm Louis Cafora. What can I do for you?"

Guevara was glancing down at the shorter, four-foot-wide Roast Beef. "I'm Agent Guevara, and this is Agent Mackey." He shut his wallet with the badge and ID and motioned for Cafora to sit. "We're here for two reasons. One, we want to ask you about your involvement in the Lufthansa robbery at Kennedy Airport."

"Involvement? Aren't you a bit ahead of yourselves? What I know is what I've been readin' in the papers. That's all."

Guevara whistled as if he'd shaken a burden off his shoulders. "Phew! I'm happy to hear that, Mr. Cafora. Because if you truly don't have first-hand knowledge of the burglary, then you have nothing to worry about. We were concerned for you." Guevara then turned to Mackey. "Right?"

"Oh, yes. Glad you had no involvement, Mr. Cafora," Mackey added.

Cafora seemed thrown. "What're you mean you was concerned?"

Guevara expelled a sigh as though a bomb had passed over and hit elsewhere. "Mr. Cafora, we had gotten information you were one of the gunmen in the robbery. Our source, though, couldn't provide us with concrete details. But better to be safe than sorry is why we're here. I guess we were misinformed, and thank God for that. See, Mr. Cafora, we have intelligence reports with an unmistakable pattern."

"What's that?" Cafora asked, his voice quavering.

Guevara weaved an impromptu sting. "Well, you not having been a participant of the Lufthansa robbery, I'm not at liberty to disclose classified intelligence." He raised both palms for effect. "I do guarantee you that if you haven't any knowledge of the theft, you and your family have no cause for alarm."

Cafora's face whitened.

"Oh, Mr. Cafora, one more thing," Guevara pretended casually to recall. "We understand you recently made a settlement with New York State for sales tax evasion."

Cafora wondered how the FBI dug this up. "Yeah, so?"

"Mind telling us where you got the money to satisfy the tax audit?"

"Uh . . . my mother-in-law loaned it to me. Her husband left her a nest egg."

Guevara smiled kindly. "We assumed it must've been something of that nature." He handed Cafora a business card. "If anything comes to mind of importance to us, please call me. Our services are free, Mr. Cafora. Your taxes pay for them." And Guevara winked at Roast Beef.

The FBI agents exited the trailer, leaving Cafora numb and scared. Later, over dinner, he discussed the strange visit with his wife, Joanna, and more haunting, Guevara's lack of persistence. *And why did Guevara readily believe I had no knowledge of this Lufthansa business?* Cafora and Joanna pondered this notion into the night. He usually shared his business with her, which troubled his confederates. A *Cosa Nostra* policy prohibited gossiping about Mafia affairs with the family, *especially* wives.

Paul Vario, sensitive to secrecy and discretion, had invented a proverb. "A husband and wife could be swapping spit today and tomorrow may be at each other's throats. And when that happens," he'd wave his finger, "nobody fights dirtier than a woman. Nobody!"

Worn out by Guevara and Mackey's disquieting visit, the Caforas finished their three-portion dinner of eggplant parmigiana and half a gallon of vanilla ice cream and climbed into bed.

Cafora yawned, the opening of his mouth as large as a lion's. "I'm spent, honey. Let's get some sleep. Tomorrow I'll get to the bottom of this."

"Maybe we should both go and see this Agent Guevara and ask him what the hell he was talking about. You know?"

"Nah, I think it's better I go alone. If he starts asking you about the sales tax money, and who I got it from, it can get sloppy. He might wanna know about your mother's finances. I better go alone."

It'd be unthinkable for a Mafia wife to go along on an interview with a law enforcement agent, and it wouldn't be forgiven. It was viewed as a weakness *and* a hazard.

Two hours into their sleep, they were awakened by thumping noises stemming from the garage. Joanna, short and tubby, tiptoed to the window and peeked through the drapes. "Oh, my God! Louis, wake up, wake up."

"Uh . . . what's wrong?"

"Louis, someone is trying to open the garage door. Come . . . come see."

Cafora sprang out of bed and looked out the window. He saw three silhouettes in dark clothing lurking near the garage. In haste, he lifted open the double-hung window. "Hey, what're you fuckin' think you're doing?" Joanna's new Cadillac was parked in the garage, and Cafora took it for granted these were car thieves.

The would-be burglars scampered, and Cafora, drenched in perspiration, had a scarier thought, a deadlier one than the stealing of Joanna's car. A dozen or so luxury automobiles were parked outdoors along the block. As a burglar, he knew too well that when stealing an auto a thief takes the path of least resistance. Why break into a garage rather than homing in on easier targets on the streets?

Cafora sat on the bed, Joanna kneading his blubbery shoulders, and as if a jackhammer were pounding his head, he mulled Guevara's message.

"Joanna, those fuckin' guys, whoever they were, didn't come to rob the Caddy."

"Then what were they trying to do?" Her eyelashes blinking nervously.

Cafora rubbed his temples. "I think they were gonna hot-wire the car."

Joanna stopped massaging him, her lips fluttering. "What . . . what do you mean, Louis?"

"They probably were gonna put a stick of dynamite under the dashboard, and when I'd start the engine, it'd blow off my balls." Cafora cupped his hands on his face, panting as though he were on a treadmill.

Joanna covered her mouth. "Oh, my God!"

The morning after at 8:30, not even the power of daylight could chase the fright that had spooked the Caforas during the night. Before dressing, Roast Beef glanced at the calling card Guevara had given him. He read it and turned it over as if he were torn between talking and not talking to the FBI.

Joanna, though, pressed, "Call him, honey. Please call him!"

He did.

"Mr. Guevara, this is Louis Cafora. You came to see me yesterday at my parking lot."

"Yes, yes, Mr. Cafora."

"I wanna come talk to you about something."

"Can you be at my office in Queens at 10:30?"

"Yeah."

Carbone, Guevara, Mackey, Cafora, and the out of place Joanna were seated in an interviewing pen at the FBI outpost in Rego Park, Queens.

Following the introductions, Guevara asked, "What do you wish to discuss, Mr. Cafora?"

Cafora gazed meekly at the black suits around the conference table. "Last night we saw three people trying to break into our garage."

Joanna nodded along. Rethinking about the horrid experience pooled her eyes, a pair of turquoise irises under lids crusted with make-up paste.

Guevara's eyes flicked from Carbone to Mackey. "And what do you make of it, Mr. Cafora?"

"I think Jimmy Burke's got me up at bat on the hit parade. I got the feeling that if we hadn't surprised those three fuckers last night, they were gonna plant a bomb in my car."

Though Guevara already knew about the bombing attempt, he feigned shock. "Why in the world did Jimmy Burke wish to harm you?"

The Caforas hung their heads in shame, and for several seconds the room fell into a silence of awkwardness. Guevara broke the stillness. "You had a part in Lufthansa, didn't you?"

Joanna stared at the floor, as Roast Beef nodded.

Carbone picked up a pen and twirled it. "I see. What do you want us to do? We can't react to your complaint without any evidence implicating Burke."

"Well, my wife and I talked it over," Cafora thumbed at Joanna, "and . . . I think I wanna work with you . . . if we can get protection."

Carbone firmed his posture. "That's a different ballgame, Mr. Cafora. In that case, there are provisions for the FBI to enroll you and your family in the Federal Witness Protection Program. Mind you, your full and truthful cooperation is requisite."

"What is *requisite*?" Joanna inquired.

Guevara explained, "It means necessary."

"Oh. I'm willing to play your game." Cafora glanced at his wife, and she stroked his hand approvingly.

"Good. You're making a wise move, Louis." Carbone left the room, and Guevara marked a date and location to debrief the Caforas. Pleased with this turn of events, the occasion everyone had yearned for, Carbone phoned McDonald.

"Ed, it's Steve."

"What's going on?"

"I think this is our lucky day. Wait 'til you hear this."

The news from Carbone spun a mood of happiness, a lighter feeling McDonald had forgotten. His head rocketed into the clouds, and that night was the first sound sleep he'd had in two months.

Guevara recommended the Caforas to continue their daily routines. The objective was not to lend to Burke the slightest suspicion that Louis Cafora was in bed with the authorities. The bureau leased an apartment on Manhattan's Upper West Side for covert trysts and electronic eavesdropping. Carbone and Guevara circled the next Tuesday, March 6, 1979, on the calendar for an appointment with Cafora at that location.

Lufthansa had been a draining and thankless expedition. But at last, as welcome as a farmer's long-awaited rain, McDonald was armed with the witness who'd relegate this nerve-racking investigation to history and put the super criminal Jimmy "the Gent" Burke and his mercenaries on trial.

The Caforas, feeling as if a chunk of lead had been extracted from their stomachs, walked out of the lobby of the FBI field office and strutted three blocks on Austin Street to Joanna's Cadillac. They got into the car, Cafora breathing noisily as he kissed Joanna. "We'll be all right."

Cafora, though, had been tricked. The car thieves who had encroached on his property were not Burke's soldiers. Guevara and Carbone had plotted for three undercover operatives to make it seem as if Burke intended to plant a bomb in Cafora's Caddy—a stunt to terrorize the couple into cooperating. It worked.

The excess flesh on her biceps dangling as she turned the steering wheel, Joanna drove off, and her Roast Beef, stressed out, lay his bull-sized head onto the headrest, his curly, black hair oily and disheveled.

Angelo Sepe, disguised in a brown cowboy hat and wraparound sunshades, was watching from across the street.

68

On hearing the disturbing news, Burke gulped a double scotch on the rocks. "What the fuck could've made Roast Beef so scared all of a sudden and run to the feds, Angelo?"

Sepe shrugged. "Not a clue."

McDonald and Carbone were walking on air. At the first debriefing, Cafora had folded and admitted he was one of the six holdup men. He must've nurtured Burke's confidence, McDonald calculated, or the Gent would not have chosen Cafora as a gunner. Carbone assumed Cafora must know who and how carried out the minute-by-minute steps of the heist.

With that, the FBI supervisor and the US attorney were readying to shake out their newest star. Carbone drove from his home in Brooklyn directly to the FBI secret apartment on the Upper West Side. McDonald stopped by his office and asked a stenographer to come along with him. Cafora was to travel by train to Penn Station on 34th Street. Then a taxi ride to the FBI furtive location was less than fifteen minutes. No escorts, no fanfare.

McDonald and the stenographer entered the apartment. The newly arrived glanced around, taking in the whiff of fresh-brewed coffee. Carbone offered, "Help yourselves. I just made it."

McDonald introduced the stenographer: "Steve, this is Lina Applegate."

Carbone smiled weakly and gave Ms. Applegate his hand. "Pleased to meet you. Get some coffee in your system. We have a long day ahead." He peered at his watch. "It's 9:20. Cafora should've been here by now."

McDonald looked at his gold-plated Omega. Minimizing his concern, he said, "He's taking a train and a cab. The Long Island Railroad to Penn Station is pretty much on time, but to catch a cab in mid-Manhattan at the height of rush hour can be a pain. He'll be here shortly."

The minutes rolled on, then the hours. No Cafora. Carbone called Ahearn at the 113th Precinct to alert him that Louis and Joanna Cafora had dropped off the radar.

Ahearn contested hotly, "You double-crossing bastard. You got some pair of balls. First, you monopolize a possible witness who can break this case, and when you lose him, you call me to find him. Like you guineas say, 'What're you, *stoonat*?'"

"We want to make this a joint effort, Lieutenant."

"A joint effort, my ass! Why didn't you make it a joint effort when Cafora first came to you? Here's where I stand, Carbone. Unless a next of kin to Cafora comes in my precinct and files an official missing person report, you and the FBI can go fuck yourselves." His face contorted with ire, Ahearn thumped the receiver onto its cradle.

"Damn it, Steve. You shouldn't have let the Caforas be on their own without protection." McDonald fumed, but at this advanced and inconclusive stage, he was beyond frustrated.

Carbone smacked his palms together. "Oh, yes, Monday morning quarterback. Should've, could've, and would've."

"I'm sorry, Steve. Everybody's nerves are shot. I'm to blame as well. I should've learned from Krugman's disappearance."

"I thought we had this case clinched."

"So did I. I figured, save the logistics to put on a solid prosecution, we were done with Lufthansa. Now we're back to zero."

Nobody saw or spoke with Mr. and Mrs. Cafora, and three days into the new week, Joanna's mother, panic-stricken, filed a missing persons report on her daughter and son-in-law.

But only Burke and Sepe had knowledge of the Caforas whereabouts: They weren't missing or marooned on a tropical island. "Angelo," Burke chuckled, "did Cafora and his fat wife make bail?"

Sepe grinned and nodded. "Oh, yeah. They made bail, all right."

The idiom "made bail" bears a double connotation. In legal terms, of course, it signifies that an accused has posted bail; in Mafia lingo, it means to crush and "bale" a car—with its owner in it.

Groping for clues, the NYPD and the FBI were left with Sepe, who refuted his implications in anything and everything; Peter Gruenwald, who had never met Louis Werner's liaison to the Lufthansa burglars; and Werner, who pig-headedly continued to proclaim, "Look, Ed, how many times do I gotta say it? I didn't do nothin' wrong, and I know nothin' about this Lufthansa bullshit. Frankly, I don't give a rat's ass about goin' to trial. You ain't got nothin' on me, and in court my lawyer's gonna make an ass out of you and the FBI."

Werner could not post bail and was languishing in the dungeons of the Manhattan Correction Center, and yet he wasn't willing to cooperate and circumvent a trial, one that would result in a conviction and a prison sentence outlasting the life of a Grey African parrot. McDonald could not understand Werner's stoniness, one presumably buoyed by the man's ignorance of the law. Or was he an incorrigible sociopath who truly believed he could win against the ironclad prosecution McDonald and Carbone were preparing to mount? "Louis, how can you look in my eyes, and with a straight face say you're not concerned about going to trial? We have a pageant of witnesses who will easily persuade a jury."

"You think so, Ed? Who've you got? That shit-ass Gruenwald? My lawyer will make him out to be what he is, a loser who's trying to save his own neck." Werner tilted his head with cockiness. "Frank Menna? Who's gonna believe him? He's a convicted felon ten times over. Bill Fischetti? Same shit. He's got all kinds of skeletons in his closet, and my attorney will flush them all out." Then Werner got snappish. "Who else you got, eh?" He stared sneeringly at McDonald, daring him to pull out higher-caliber weapons.

The US attorney's eyes dimmed from sincere pity to repugnance. "I have your girlfriend's testimony to the grand jury whereby she had learned from you about your role as the Lufthansa inside man, Louis. Those are incriminating testimonials that, should she recant them on the witness stand, she'll be committing perjury. And I'll attest she gave me details how you boasted to her, quote, 'I'm the one who pulled it off.'"

"She'll deny it to the end," Werner said with insolence.

McDonald's tolerance was at its redline. "See it any way you want to, Louis, but I promise you that unless you start working with me, you have no way out of this." With a snap of his hand, he irately swooped up his notepad and huffed out of the lawyer conference cubicle, and out of the Manhattan Correction Center, Werner grinning as if he had won a game of chess. Counselor Lispz was holding his forehead, mortified by his client's grandstanding idiocy.

On May 7, 1979, the matter of *United States of America vs. Louis Werner* was in session. The courtroom was overcrowded with an army of journalists and TV legal analysts outnumbering civilians. Werner's defense was flat and feeble, and his attorney's countervailing at the prosecution was limited to groundless challenges of the qualifications and credibility of the witnesses—a futility prickling the audience into chuckles and giggles.

The weather was inordinately warm, and the temperature in the chamber of justice had been simmering. In federal buildings throughout the northeast corridor, the air-conditioning equipment was not operational prior to May 15th. More rankling, the proceedings were dull and uneventful until Janet Barbieri, Werner's girlfriend, took the stand and enlivened the show. She was bedecked in costume jewelry with quartz gems of yellows, purples, blues, greens, and burgundies, a picture as dizzying as eyeing into a kaleidoscope.

McDonald, dapper in a tailored-fit navy blue suit, was on the fourth question of the twenty-two he had lined up for her. "Ms. Barbieri, you appeared before a grand jury in the matter of the *United States of America vs. Louis Werner*. Is that correct?"

Meek as a frightened kitten, in an inaudible hush she answered, "Yes."

"Ms. Barbieri, did you testify under oath that defendant Louis Werner had divulged to you he was an accomplice to six armed men, who at gunpoint on December 11, 1978, pirated approximately six million dollars in cash and jewelry from the Lufthansa Cargo Building-261?"

Ms. Barbieri, in a knee-length, black knit dress with a turtleneck collar, asked, "What does *divulged* mean?"

The judge interceded. "It means to make known, Ms. Barbieri." His Honor gaped at the US attorney. "Proceed, Mr. McDonald."

Feigning struggling to breathe, the witness tugged at the turtleneck of her collar and clutched her neck. Fearful the woman had gone into cardiac arrest, the spectators sighed and burbled. Abashed, Judge Costantino recessed the court. "Ms. Barbieri, are you all right? Bailiff, give her some water."

A female guard rushed to Ms. Barbieri with a flask and a glass. "Miss, are you all right? Here, sip this, please."

The water revived Ms. Barbieri.

Soft-pedaling, McDonald asked, "Are you OK to continue, or do you wish to recess?"

She shook her head.

"If at any time you want to take a break, feel free to do so. OK, I'll repeat my question."

To everybody's dismay, Ms. Barbieri collapsed, and tumbled out of her chair, landing partially on the deck of the witness box and partially on the marble floor, the jurors dumbfounded and wide-eyed. The crowd moaned loudly, "Ahhh!"

The bailiffs darted to Ms. Barbieri's aid and hoisted her onto the chair in the witness stand. One was fanning the woman's face, and the other felt her pulse.

"Ms. Barbieri, are . . . are you in need of a doctor?" the judge asked, glancing curiously at her. "Do you want medical assistance?"

She lurched into a self-induced convulsing fit, her blonde hair, firmed at the nape with a black-velvet bow, unraveling. His Honor called out, "Is there a physician here? She may be on the verge of a seizure."

Rustling and shuffling, a man emerged from the sixth row of benches and raised his hand. "I am, Your Honor."

Judge Costantino waved him on. "Please come forward, doctor. Come forward."

In short strides, the doctor fast-stepped toward Ms. Barbieri and pressed his palms under her chin.

She was biting her tongue, an amateurish act, and Werner covered his eyes. Mouths open, everybody's inhalations hung in suspense, and the courtroom quieted as if it were in the middle of a cemetery. The physician patted Ms. Barbieri on her shoulder and said to the judge, "She's fine, Your Honor. She's excited, and her pulse is racing. I don't see anything going on with her as far as any medical issues. Just excited."

His Honor seemed relieved. "Thank you, doctor, thank you." He then lowered his head down at the witness. "Ms. Barbieri, do you wish to continue?"

Teary eyed, she nodded faintly.

Judge Costantino raised his eyebrows at the US attorney. "You may go on, Mr. McDonald."

Out of habit, the US attorney expelled a throat-clearing cough and wiggled the knot of his tie. "I'm still on the same question, Ms. Barbieri," he said as he looked at the witness. "Ms. Barbieri, did you not testify before the grand jury . . ."

Again, she flew into a spastic frenzy, howling and heaving, and by the look in his eyes, Judge Costantino saw through it this time. Not amused, he'd had it with Ms. Barbieri's antics and asked the prosecutor, "Mr. McDonald, are you done with this witness for the day?"

Bemused, McDonald was speechless and rested an elbow on his lectern. "I guess so, Your Honor."

The judge glowered at Janet Barbieri, his stare riveting and stinging sharper than a blistering sun. "You're excused, Ms. Barbieri." He pointed at her, the creases in his brow deepening. "Tomorrow, I expect you back here and if called to take the stand, should you repeat today's performance I will hold you in contempt." The judge's reproach hadn't registered in Ms. Barbieri's jumbled mind, and she stayed seated in the witness box, her mascara streaking with black tears. "Ms. Barbieri," Judge Costantino shouted, "*I said* you're excused."

As if her legs were buckling, she placed the left hand on her chest, held out the right one for the bailiff to take, and motioned him to walk her out of the courtroom.

McDonald waved a sheaf of bound pages above his head for the jury to see and addressed the court reporter. "Let the record reflect that . . . one moment, please." McDonald leafed through the binder. "I'm quoting from page eleven, Line sixteen, in the transcripts of Ms. Barbieri's grand jury testimony. 'Two or three days after the robbery, Louis told me he was coming into a lot of money, and all his financial problems were going to be over.'"

Attorney Lispz leaped to his feet. "I object, Your Honor. The witness is not present to . . ."

"Overruled, Counselor," His Honor growled, tired of Ms. Barbieri and Werner's nit-picking lawyer. The judge then jerked his chin at McDonald. "The transcripts are duly entered in the record, Mr. McDonald."

Ms. Barbieri, dabbing her nose with a pink handkerchief, disappeared through the courtroom doors.

The trial lasted eight days, and no one was stunned, when a few hours after the defense rested, the jurors found Louis Werner guilty on all counts. The judge ratified the verdict and set the sentencing date for June 19.

Werner's semblance was that of a man facing a firing squad, a dazed glaze in his eyes. "This is insane!" he hollered out at no one in particular, a guard handcuffing him. "This is an injustice. A goddamn injustice! The thieves who mugged Lufthansa with shotguns are out there in the streets, and I'm the one gettin' locked up. It don't make sense."

Lispz might've stored a smidgen of mercy for Werner. "Lou, I'm going to file a motion to reduce bail, and maybe the judge will release you pending the appeal." It was a dull placation. Any lawyer worth his salt knows that, in most cases, a court will not permit a defendant to remain free following a conviction—especially if bail had not been granted at the time of the arraignment.

"Mr. Werner," Judge Costantino clamored, jolting the condemned. "I hereby remand you to detention at the Manhattan Correction Center until sentencing is set." He banged his gavel and pronounced, "Court is adjourned."

That afternoon, as three federal marshals were transporting Werner to jail, Angelo Sepe was en route to an apartment in Maspeth, Queens. It was one of Paolo Licastri's safe houses. Burke had had Sepe and Licastri on standby for an undertaking that had been in the wings as of the day of Werner's arrest.

69

It had been twenty minutes since the jury had returned Werner's guilty verdict, and radio and television stations were spiraling it on the air. Invariably, in any reporting that had to do with Lufthansa, the name Jimmy "the Gent" Burke was the focus of the story. Burke had been in the headlines for the past five months and was rising as the most infamous gangster in the New York Metropolitan area.

It was 12:30 p.m., and the federal marshals had ferried Werner to the Manhattan Correction Center in time for his first meal as an inmate.

Also about to enjoy lunch were Licastri, Sepe, and Burke. The restaurant was Umberto's Clam Bar at Mulberry and Hester Streets in the Little Italy quarter of downtown Manhattan. A dusky complexioned waiter, who spoke limited English, had accommodated the Burke party at a table near a window. The eatery, patronized by Mafia mobsters, was owned by Genovese family *capo regime* Matty "the Horse" Ianniello. In 1972, a hard-bucking Mafia aspirant, "Crazy" Joe Gallo, was dining at Umberto's when four shooters killed him in a hail of bullets. And because of "Crazy" Joe's assassination, the restaurant became a tourist attraction. Go figure!

Burke, slurping a spoonful of lobster bisque, looked straight at Licastri and Sepe, pointing a fork at them, his way of demanding undivided attention. "I made an appointment for tonight in Brooklyn with Manri and Frenchy. But then I made up some bullshit about the FBI tailing me, and it's not smart for all of us to be spotted together. I told them you two are gonna take Manri and Frenchy to where I'm supposed to be waiting for them. Understand?" Unbeknownst to Burke, his tale to dupe Frenchy and Manri wasn't something he had contrived; FBI operatives were, in fact, watching him.

Sepe mumbled, "Uh-huh."

Licastri listened and said nothing.

Joe Manri and Frenchy McMahon had been aggravating Burke with a pestering grievance; they claimed he'd shortchanged them on their percentage of the Lufthansa money. For the same reason, an uprising was simmering among the rest of the Lufthansa marauders. Burke had given them a cut based on Werner's approximated two million dollar haul, and when Lufthansa publicized its actual loss of six million, the Gent's partners were disgruntled. Burke had let it go in one ear and out the other.

More troubling for the Gent, a new liability was creeping on the horizon. Years and years of a prison stretch could weaken Werner's staunchness. True, he'd taken the fall alone, but waking in a cell day after day for months on end, Werner might fold and beg McDonald to help him. Werner could recognize Manri from mug shots, and he, Manri, might throw in the towel and dive for his own salvation.

Burke was not far off the mark.

CI-196, the informant known as Mr. X, reported to Agent Guevara and lighted a renewed outlook on the dusty Lufthansa files. Mr. X had had a casual chat with Manri, and their talks drifted toward the post-Lufthansa massacres. At Guevara's direction, Mr. X sowed a pinch of logic in Manri's ear. If Burke was killing everyone who'd had a hand in the robbery, Manri also might soon be in the slaughtering pool. And perhaps he should place himself at the mercy of the FBI and save his skin. More distressing, Mr. X called to Manri's attention certain whisperings that were fast-spreading in the Mafia grapevine. When Manri began wading in the circles of the underworld, he proclaimed he was of Sicilian descent. Recently, his South American nationality had been uncloaked, and Mr. X pointed out that that sham extinguished the slimmest chance for him to become a *Cosa Nostra* associate. Consequently, the probability of joining the list of Burke's casualties and the *impossibility* for the Mafia to christen Manri as a made man were pushing him to run for shelter with the FBI.

Manri could also embroil Burke, and it'd be the beginning of the end. For that reason, the Gent had to disconnect himself from Manri, and to do so he had to murder him. And while he was at it, why not eliminate Frenchy McMahon; why risk that he might open a dialogue with the Feds?

70

Sepe wore black dungarees, a black sweatshirt, and black wool cap, his standard regalia for a hit. "What time did you say we gotta meet with Frenchy and Manri?"

Burke checked his watch. "Ten o'clock at Mill Basin in Brooklyn. By nine-thirty at night, that neighborhood is as dead as a doornail. Nobody's around. Just the rats."

Tony Bennett had left his heart in San Francisco; Licastri left his in Sicily and wasn't accustomed to sneakers and sweatshirts. He was outfitted in Varese wingtip shoes, gray pleated slacks, and a burgundy Bill Blass hunting blazer—a classily dressed assassin. "What're you wanna do with the bodies, Jimmy?" Licastri's English wasn't easy to understand, though Burke had gotten the hang of it.

"Leave them in their car. Let the cops worry about gettin' rid of the stiffs."

"What are we looking for?" Sepe asked. "I mean, what kind of car will they be drivin'?"

Burke scratched his right cheek. "I'm pretty sure it's a green Buick two-door. I told Frenchy and Manri to park on the corner of Clear Water Road and Bell Point Drive and wait for you. That's right near a canal. Nobody goes there. When you guys get close, leave your car a few blocks down the street, go up to their Buick, and ask them to let you in. Both of you get in the back seat, and the rest, you know what to do."

"No sweat, Jimmy," Sepe signed off nonchalantly.

Unacquainted with American slang, Licastri seemed out of the loop, his eyelids squinting,. "What's 'sweat'?"

Burke eyed him. "That's what you smell like, you fuckin' grease ball."

Sepe rested his hand on Licastri's shoulder and winked at Burke. "I'll explain it to him, Jimmy." He then said to his cokiller, "C'mon, Paolo, let's go to Lenny's Clam Bar in Howard Beach and have a nice plate of scungilli and calamari with hot sauce, eh. It'll give us energy for the job."

71

"I don't care how bad you feel, Henry. Eat it. It'll coat your stomach."

Karen had cooked me three eggs, and the greasy bacon cleared my nostrils. Problem was, I hadn't been eating. The heroin was killing my appetite. "Stop breakin' my balls, Karen. I'll eat when I feel like it." I was vomiting and losing weight by the hour.

It was eleven o'clock in the morning, and Jimmy came knocking.

"Karen, let him in."

Jimmy strolled into my kitchen and threw the *New York Daily News* on the breakfast table. I almost fainted. My vision was fuzzy, but I couldn't miss the headlines.

TWO MEN FOUND IN THEIR CAR SHOT EXECUTION STYLE IN THE BACK OF THEIR SKULLS

I could tell Jimmy was more stoned than me. He tapped the newspaper with his index finger, looked at me, and smirked. "Go ahead, read it."

I read a few lines and flung the paper on the tabletop. I waved to my wife to take the kids to their bedroom. "Holy shit, Jimmy. This is gettin' out of hand, man."

"Well, what can I do?" he shrugged. "You know Werner got convicted yesterday?"

I was taken aback and didn't answer. I'd just read that Frenchy and Joe "Buddha" got whacked, and the man behind this was standing in front of me. "Why, Jimmy?"

"I'll say it again, Werner lost his trial, and he'll be gone for a long, long time. Givin' up Manri would've been his only way out. And then I'd be sweating that Manri might flip on me." The Gent formed a horseshoe with his lips. "I mean, what was I to do, Henry?"

"But why Frenchy?" I cried out in a high pitch.

Jimmy fanned with his hand. "Eh . . . Frenchy's been acting weird lately. I wanna clean up everything 'cause I don't wanna have to deal with any of this bullshit for the next ten years."

"Frenchy acting weird" really meant he'd been hocking Jimmy for a bigger stake of the Lufthansa stash. The Gent figured he was better off getting rid of Manri and Frenchy in a double hit and work out a discount with whomever he'd paid to do the job. And as far as the killers, the more I thought about it, the more I was leaning toward Sepe and that creepy Licastri. Nobody else was left; it had to have been those two trigger-happy scumbags. Not to mention, morning, noon, and night Licastri had been loitering around Robert's Lounge. He was with the Gotti crew, so why else would he have been at our hangout?

Later on, I found out from two FBI agents that I was right. Their recordings were full of hints Burke was sending Sepe and Licastri to wipe out anyone who, in his drug-cooked head, might've been snitching on him—or shaking him down for a larger slice of Lufthansa. The glitch was this: All the FBI gathered were sketchy hints, but couldn't get the nitty-gritty out of Burke's conversations with his henchmen.

72

Reading the bulletin about the executions of Manri and McMahon deflated Carbone's euphoria from last evening. He phoned Ed McDonald. "You must know by now about Manri and McMahon."

McDonald couldn't think of much to say. "Yes, I'm afraid I do."

"What next, Ed?"

"I don't know."

Carbone excused, "I did all I could to get Manri and McMahon to realize the danger they were in, and . . ."

"I'm disturbed by it. But it's water under the bridge, Steve." And McDonald ended the phone conversation.

Carbone, admirably, was undeterred and started working on another angle, Paolo Licastri. Intelligence culled by Guevara brought forth inklings of Licastri as one of the Lufthansa holdup men, and two FBI agents were shadowing him around the clock.

Licastri was dating a Mafia princess of sorts, Lina DiNapoli, the favorite niece of a Bonanno family capo, Carmine Galante. Lina, a brunette with French poodle-like curly hair and a bronzed complexion, invariably wore black clothing. One evening in late April of 1979, she was driving to Licastri's basement apartment in the Bushwick section of Brooklyn.

Due to her overcharged sexual urges, moments of hot flashes often emblazoned the voluptuous Lina. It happened to be an extraordinarily sultry night for the month of April, and she set the air conditioning in her white Cadillac Eldorado to the coldest temperature. "Where are you taking me, Paolo?"

"A specia place, *Tre Amici*. Good restaurant. Very specia. You like."

This restaurant, on the corner of 3rd Avenue and 72nd Street, was indeed an excellent choice, and the Mafia princess gorged with gusto, beginning with an antipasto of mozzarella in carrozza, a croissant with melted mozzarella cheese and anchovies. "Delicious, Paolo."

"I tell you this good restaurant." Licastri put his thumb and index finger together and kissed the tips in contentment. "Uhmmm!"

Upon finishing the last course of this superb northern Italian dinner, Lina's appetite for sex was awakening. She caressed her date's hand and whispered, "Let's go back to your apartment, Paolo."

Their dalliance went on for two months, and her Uncle Carmine grew fond of Licastri, labeling him a model contender as a spouse for his niece. Licastri, above all, was Sicilian and, conveniently, in the extortion business—a perfect suitor for the gorgeous Lina and an asset to Galante's gangland dynasty.

In a matter of weeks, the curvy, five-foot-six Lina ballooned five dress sizes to 198 pounds, dousing Licastri's penchant for her. He ducked her phone calls, and on June 30, 1979, Carmine Galante summoned Licastri to Joey and Mary's, a restaurant in Maspeth, Queens. Over a lunch of buffalo mozzarella garnished with olive oil, parsley, and roasted peppers, Godfather Galante put it to Licastri, "So when're you and Lina gettin' hitched?"

"What ees hitched?" Licastri asked.

"Married," Galante simplified.

Licastri nearly choked on a grissini, a bread stick. "Uh . . . eh, Carmine, Lina and me no talk about marry. We just friends."

"Just friends?" Galante said sourly.

"Yeah, we friends, that's all. I no say I marry Lina."

Galante, a most vicious, stumpy man with a glowing bald head, lunged into the table inches from Licastri's face. A cigar between two fingers, the Bonanno chief pointed at the Sicilian. "Nah, nah, goombah. You've been fuckin' my niece, and now you gotta marry her. Understand?"

It daunted Licastri, uncocking his bravery and fearlessness, and he *hit the mattress*; but Galante's henchmen flushed him out. His charred cadaver turned up in a lot amid a growth of weeds and bramble. The body was so toasted that a gold bracelet Licastri had worn melted onto the skin of his wrist.

Except for the FBI, who had lost another potential snitch, no one grieved Licastri's death, and Jimmy Burke improvised a mock eulogy. "That grease ball had it comin'. May he *not* rest in peace. Amen." He pulled out a stack of cash from his pocket and said to Sepe, "Angelo, here's fifty bucks, go buy a box of Havana cigars and get it to Carmine Galante."

John Gotti, however, felt otherwise. He wore a black band on his sleeve for three months, mourning his boy, Paolo Licastri.

Carmine Galante had hardly digested that mouth-watering lunch in his final company with Licastri at Joe and Mary's when, on July 12, 1979, in a barrage of bullets four gunmen killed him at the same table in the same eatery. A macabre photo of the corpse lying on the ground in a fetal position, a cigar stuck in its mouth, was plastered on the front page of the major newspapers.

73

Long Branch is a summer resort town on the Atlantic along the central portion of the New Jersey shore. Vacationers with deep pockets pay exorbitant rental rates there to lie on pure sandy beaches and line their lungs with the salty mist of the ocean spray. It's a community with multimillion-dollar homes, palaces that their wealthy owners refer to, with modest pretensions, as "summer cottages."

It was the third week of May 1979; the sleepy spring season was waning, giving way to the Memorial Day weekend.

At nine o'clock in the evening, the Thursday before the holiday, Ronnie Venezia, a twenty-two-year-old college graduate freeloading off his parents, parked his 1969 Volkswagen bus on a dead-end street with a pathway to the beach. At this hour, it was deserted, and total blackness extended to the horizon. The only source of light was the silvery iridescent foam cresting the surf. Ronnie and his high-school-age girlfriend, Buffy Blonder, quilts under their arms and a cooler chock-full of wine and beer, trekked to the beach and unfolded the blankets on the ground, a moist bed of sand. A flood tide was swelling, and the sea waves roared louder than hungry lions. The briny scent was invigorating and subtly inebriating.

Eagerly setting an ambiance to mystify Buffy, a childlike sweet sixteen, Ronnie popped the cork of the Chianti and poured the wine into two paper cups. Two-thirds into the bottle, and he started fiddling with the hook of Buffy's bra. She did not protest, and with the smoothness of a pickpocket, Ronnie unbridled her lemon-sized breasts. The kissing and fondling lasted four to five minutes, and Buffy shushed in Ronnie's ear, "Let's take our clothes off and go lie on the edge of the water. That's where I want you to make love to me."

Ronnie saw this request as a heavenly favor. In seconds, he shed his green plaid Bermuda shorts and white T-shirt, and to expedite Buffy's disrobing he lent her a hand. She gripped Ronnie's penis and towed him to where the water was ankle high. Buffy lay back awash in water, Ronnie on top of her. It certainly was innovative, if not daring. There had been shark sightings along the Jersey shoreline, and gossip had it that vaginal fluids attracted those man-eating mammals. Despite this peril, the two lovers slithered together, pre-heating one another's genitals, their blond hair wet and stringy.

A wave rumbled closer and closer, and they felt it rushing in, slightly buoying their bodies. A weighty object plowed into them. It brushed against their legs, receded, and pummeled Buffy's shoulder. The bulky mass sloshed around them, and the couple's bliss ruptured into a scene from a horror film. Hysterical, Buffy sprang to her feet and jumped wildly in the water as if she were stomping out a fire. "Ahhhh!! Ahhhh! Ahhhhh!"

Ronnie's reaction was similar. "Ahhhh! Ahhhhhhhh!"

74

Carbone's assistant rang his extension. "Mr. Carbone, a medical examiner from New Jersey is on extension 4133. He asked for you."

"Hello, Special Agent Carbone speaking."

"Good afternoon, sir. I'm Dr. Rufus Fowler, Trenton medical examiner."

"Trenton, New Jersey?"

"Yes."

"How can I help you, Dr. Fowler?"

"Please call me Rufus. Is a Theresa Ferrara a person of interest to your agency?"

"Yes, she is, Dr. Rufus. I mean Rufus. Do you know of her whereabouts?"

Dr. Rufus Fowler fancied himself a master of one-liners. "I can tell you where half of her is."

"What do you mean?"

"Well, Ms. Ferrara's torso is on one of my operating slabs. I don't know where her lower half is." This trunk, bloated and bluish, was the intruder who had disrupted Ronnie's and Buffy's foreplay.

A recoiling shiver struck Carbone's spine. "How did you ascertain her identity, Rufus?"

"I have an unusual clue, Agent Carbone. The torso underwent a breast augmentation procedure. Breast implants. My staff checked the statistics of missing women, and voilà, we verified Ms. Ferrara's boob job."

Carbone did not appreciate Dr. Fowler's tactless sense of humor. "I see. Agent Christopher Mackey will be contacting you on this matter."

Of the adventurous lovers who had bumped into Theresa Ferrara, Buffy Blonder had not yet recovered from the ghoulish specter on the beach; she was in therapy for mental trauma. Her sex partner, Ronnie Venezia, was in the county jail pending a bail hearing for a sodomy charge; Buffy had been an unwitting minor.

Throughout the fall of 1979, Carbone and McDonald chased butterflies. Burke had disposed of most of his Lufthansa prowlers. And of those who were still on Earth, none could be of enlightenment. Carbone, a devout Roman Catholic, was beginning to believe Burke was the devil's mentor. McDonald, who didn't subscribe to the occult, viewed Burke as a brash, ruthless mobster with one anomaly, astuteness. And a handful of the Gent's friends theorized he might've been a hybrid of Carbone and McDonald's speculations.

The Lufthansa investigators had run out of witnesses, and the investigation was running out of steam. Crimes are the daily viruses of society, and new cases took root on McDonald and Carbone's calendars. And though the Burke murder count was up to eight, the US attorney's office and the FBI, mired in blind alleys, had to retire the Lufthansa probe. And the media, with its highly imaginative workforce, not unlike a traveling circus, folded its tents and moved on to sensationalize new scandals and political corruptions with which to entertain the public. Thus the most captivating heist of all time slumbered to a dormant giant.

Four months into his fifteen-year sentence, Louis Werner could not acclimate to prison life. Wrought with the likelihood he could not survive this punishment, he had renewed thoughts of changing his fate.

McDonald had just settled in his office, removed his jacket, and was pouring fuming coffee into a cup. His extension rang. "Hello."

"Mr. McDonald, there's a collect call for you on extension 318."

A recorded message announced, "You are receiving a collect call from an inmate of the Leavenworth Federal Penitentiary. His name is Louis Werner. If you accept the charges, press one. This call may be monitored."

"Hello, McDonald here."

"Hello, Ed, this is Lou Werner."

"Well, this *is* a surprise."

Werner chuckled, a strenuous put-on. "You never know what can happen next." Another false chuckle. "I wanna work with you. I should've listened to you and cooperated from day one." A suppressed repentance in his voice.

"Lou, I'm appreciative of your wanting to be of help, but with Joe Manri dead, unless you can implicate someone else who can incriminate Jimmy Burke in the Lufthansa robbery, I don't see your testimony bearing any fruits. Had you come forward before Manri was murdered, you could've been freed right there and then."

Indeed, it was too late; except for Manri, Burke had had the ingenuity to insulate himself from Werner. McDonald and Carbone had carved deeper and deeper into that protective lining, and with the cunningness of a hunted wolf Burke thwarted them from tunneling through his protective walls.

75

As I saw it, Jimmy was obsessed with covering his loose ends. He was whacking anybody and anyone who had a mouth and could've gone to the cops. Somehow, word in the streets about Lufthansa and the Robert's Lounge crew had gotten out of hand. I don't know how it spread, but it did. Everywhere I went, I was hearing about Lufthansa. I didn't admit to nothing and made believe I had no idea what everybody was talking about.

Meantime, my drug network was leaching out into New Jersey, Connecticut, and Pennsylvania, and profits were surging beyond my imagination. That took some of the Lufthansa stress off Jimmy; but he was as suspicious as a rattlesnake of anyone who looked at him cross-eyed.

My wife, Karen, was another story.

"Damn you, Henry, you're out of control. You're using more heroin than your customers."

"Karen, leave me the fuck alone. I know what I'm doing." I was sick of her treating me like a child.

"Leave you alone? You're doing stupid things and getting careless. What's gonna happen to me and the kids if you get busted again? This time, they'll lock you up for life."

Deep down, I had some understanding that Karen was watching me self-destruct, as was my girlfriend, Robin. The difference was that Robin used as much drugs as me—and going down as fast as me. Day and night, I was in a constant high. I had so much pressure on me; all I wanted to do was numb myself. And numb I was. Jimmy was still going strong, and every morning I opened my eyes and thought he was gonna whack me next. That's how I lived for six months. And even though Lufthansa was going cold, the FBI kept breakin' my balls. They'd show up and search my house, harass Karen, threaten to arrest me, all to push me to start talking to them about the heist. Luckily, I was pretty sure the FBI was in the dark about my drug hustle, and I was right. Their priority was Lufthansa, Lufthansa, Lufthansa. Meanwhile, right under their noses, I was selling more drugs than a national pharmacy chain.

76

Bobby Germain Jr., an eighteen-year-old, was a nickel-bag marijuana pusher. He had done maintenance and repairs on Hill's house. Bobby, shaggy and thinly, was cheerful and quick with sharply-timed jokes, amusing Karen, who often served him lunch in her kitchen. At times, Bobby Jr. overheard telephone conversations between Henry Hill and his heroin vendors and addicts. In January of 1979, Bobby was arrested for dealing pot, and rather than fight the charges he enrolled in the informants' program of the Nassau County Narcotics Division. He pleaded guilty to eleven counts of controlled substance abuse and signed on Detective Daniel Stahl's stoolies rat pack. In exchange, his three-year sentence was suspended.

Several weeks of talks with Stahl and his field investigators, and Bobby Jr. seemed to be a worthy connection to the drug-polluted streets. Nevertheless, Stahl suspected Bobby Jr. wasn't 100 percent forthright. One day, as a means to shake up the teen, Stahl told him he'd been ordered to debrief him in the presence of Deputy County Attorney Bill Florio.

To a criminal, appearing before a prosecutor or the devil is one and the same. Disquieted, Bobby Jr. wagged his head, gloom on his acne-riddled face. "I don't see why I gotta talk to the deputy county attorney when I'm reporting to you."

"No need to be uptight. DCA Florio is all right. He's not gonna bite you."

The portly Detective Stahl drove his informant to Florio's small office and introduced him. The rusty-haired, freckled-skin deputy county attorney, a short, forty-one year old of unimposing stature, handed the teenager a paper cup filled with coffee. Stahl and Bobby Jr. sat across the desk. Florio's office was more a cubicle than a room, not fit to accommodate three adults. To add to the claustrophobia, it was cluttered with stacks of brownish-red folders stacked against the walls.

Stahl was chewing gum, the muscles in his canine-like jaws flexing. "Bobby, what are we gonna talk about today? It's time you give us a big, meaty bone. I mean, we're keeping you from going to the can, and this Friday we gotta report to the judge on your case and let him know the progress we're making with you. Otherwise, he has to carry out the sentencing, and it's bye-bye Bobby."

Grateful, yet wary, Bobby Jr. rotated his eyeballs from Florio to Stahl. He gulped the coffee. "Mind if I have a cigarette? It'll help my nerves."

Stahl waved a hand in consent.

Bobby Jr. lit a Lucky Strike and ingested a drag. "I don't know if this means anything or not."

Florio and Stahl inched to the edge of their chairs, and the novice informant took in a long breath. "I know this drug dealer. He deals big time. He's with some Mafia people."

"What's his name?" Stahl asked with keenness.

"Henry Hill."

A wide grin flashed out Stahl's tobacco-brown teeth, and he opened his notepad. Bobby Jr. said he had overheard Hill on the phone talking "drug dealings" and had no qualms supplying Florio and Stahl the address of this "heavyweight dealer." Bobby Jr., seemingly wanting to please, went on and on for two hours. And if the proportion of Hill's distribution network, as estimated by Bobby, was accurate, it'd be the largest drug bust in the history of Nassau County. DCA Bill Florio, a man with a boyish mien and flitting eyes, flounced about as if he'd won a lottery. "This can be an arrest of epic scale." Imagine the publicity; it'd splash his face in the living room of every Nassau County voter, a public figure's dream of dreams.

Content with the wealth of statistics Bobby Jr. had coughed out, Stahl dismissed him, at least for then.

Stahl was burning with anxiety. "Let's get a subpoena to wiretap Hill's phone." His eyes had an I-told-you-so look. A week ago, Stahl had mentioned to Florio how valuable Bobby Jr. might be, and at the time the deputy county attorney had gauged that assessment as an overstatement. It isn't uncommon for detectives to embellish a not-so-indictable case to prosecutors, and Florio had sat on the standpoint of show-me-and-I'll-believe-it.

"This, eh . . . what's his name again? Bobby, right? He seems believable." Florio conceded as he popped a pistachio in his mouth. "We'll make a motion for a court order to wiretap Hill's lines. I'll draft the documents and get them to Judge Ritter's law clerk. With luck, Ritter will sign the order tomorrow."

Drafting the subpoena to eavesdrop on Hill's telephone, Florio predicted, might eventuate to his magnum opus as a deputy county attorney. All the while, Stahl and his investigators were amassing devastating facts surrounding Hill's interstate narcotics operation. They had learned that Hill and the Pittsburgh marijuana trafficker Paul Mazzei—Hill's accomplice in the Boston College basketball point-shaving gig—again had been up to no good. The core of this partnership was drugs, and Burke was the secret financier of the Hill-Mazzei pharmaceutical emporium. And an emporium it was; their inventory of controlled substances was geared to satisfy the appetites of users from all shades of life: the ghetto drug addict, the white-collar professional, the Wall Street broker, and so forth.

Three months of round-the-clock wiretapping, and Stahl had piled on Hill's back sufficient evidence to indict and convict him for a string of lofty felonies.

One morning in February 1979, Stahl brushed the snowflakes off the lapels of his gray overcoat and, wipping his scuffed shoes on a mat to rid them of mud, trudged into Bill Florio's work space. He hurled a file on the DCA's desk and nodded at it. "We got all we need to grab Hill and make the narcotics charges stick. It's all in there. Hill's airline receipts when he went back and forth to Pittsburgh to pick up cash from his partner, Paul Mazzei; transcripts of phone conversations of Hill, Mazzei, et cetera." Exhausted, Stahl released a breath of air. "Bill, a lot of footwork and time went into this. It wasn't easy, you should know."

"Nothing is easy, Dan. But if we get Hill convicted, it could springboard me to a high political post and you to a higher rank. Isn't that why we're doing all this?" Florio posed, feeding more pistachios in his disproportionately small mouth, his lips as thin as the line of a pencil.

77

You'd think otherwise, but my arrest was un-sensational.

I had a couple of last-minute errands to run, and then I'd be going to LaGuardia Airport for a flight to Pittsburgh. Paul Mazzei had a package of heroin for me to pick up. I had just gotten in my car and was about to back out of my driveway.

A moment later, "Freeze! Keep your hands on the steering wheel."

I twisted my head to the left, and my eyes met the muzzle of a semi-automatic, the barrel sticking through the open window of my Chevy Monte Carlo. In a split second, slightly crouched in combat positions on both sides of the car, a bunch of cops who could've been a SWAT team were aiming artillery at me. I didn't see any of them in the front or rear of the Monte Carlo. When catching a suspect who's behind the wheel of a car, not to risk getting run over, law enforcement people never stand in front or behind the automobile.

One of my drug couriers and one-time mistress Marley Carr was in the passenger seat. She lunged into hysterics as a cop dragged her out of the car. "Let go of me, you dick-less prick! Let go." Marley's pink beret fell on the ground, her short red hair all tangled, and she kicked and twisted as two plainclothesmen cuffed her skinny wrists.

I got out of the Monte Carlo and put my arms behind my back for the shackling, five officers closely huddling around me. With sorry eyes, I looked at Marley. "Stay cool, baby. It's OK. I'll straighten out all this."

Marley went into a crying spell. Two fucking officers took the 115-pound woman by the arms and manhandling her, practically lifted the poor thing into a van. I looked on helplessly. "Where are you taking her? She's got nothin' to do with this. Let her go."

One of Stahl's detectives laughed. "Yeah, sure. When they get arrested, everybody's innocent. And you ain't even man enough to stand up and take your lumps."

The damned cop who cuffed me made the shackles too tight, and my wrists were killing me. The bastard shoehorned me into the back seat of an unmarked Crown Victoria for the ride to Central Booking in Mineola, an April drizzle misting the car windows.

Stahl had a grasp on my bicep, and he hauled his catch—me—into the ground floor of the Central Booking Police Precinct. I got booked—fingerprinting, mug shot, strip search; they took my wallet, money, belt, jewelry, and shoelaces. As always, the hecklers were on hand—those lousy cops who check in a new prisoner—and the hissing started. "Hey, Hill, they say you snort more lines of coke than you sell. So how do you make a profit?"

If only I could've gotten my hands on those motherless sons of bitches!

An obese cop with a squashed nose and a bald pate as shiny as a chromed dome teased, "Hill, is it true your dog does drugs, too?"

Everybody had to get into the act.

Marley, still bawling—the mascara running down her cheeks, making her look like a spider—was also booked and charged with conspiracy to transport wholesale quantities of contraband, a Class B felony. The charges against me were way worse; I was looking at a thirty-year sentence. But my problems didn't end there.

In a processing room, as they called it, the head honcho who was gunning for me, Detective Stahl, was sitting across the table. He was holding a document and turned it around for me to see.

"What is it?" I asked, knowing it couldn't have been good.

Stahl widened his eyes and beamed like a snobbish asshole. "It's a deposition from an informant whose name I can't give you."

"So?"

"*So*, is all you got to say, Mr. Hill?" Stahl pointed at the typewritten paper. "What's in here, based on our informant, is that your wife, Karen, played a role in your narcotics network. And that means we're gonna have to arrest her as an accessory. When she gets convicted, she'll wind up doing ten to fifteen years."

My heart raced, and nausea crept up my in throat. I stared at Stahl in disbelief and tried to raise a palm to make a point in Karen's defense, but my wrists were chained to the waist. I listed my neck to the right and copped, "Wait a minute, Detective Stahl. Let's slow things down here. My wife's got nothin' to do with my business. I swear. She's too busy taking care our two kids."

Stahl , his voice sounding as if he were gurgling, shook his head and sneered. "Well, I don't wanna disappoint you, but that doesn't match up with the testimony of our source." Stahl slid the document toward him and sucked on his teeth. "Oh, one more thing. You're girlfriend, Robin Cooperman, has problems, too. We got quite a bit on her. In fact, before the week is over, Ms. Cooperman will be indicted because she's one of your associates." Stahl smiled as if he'd just won an easy bet. "So I'd say you got some serious thinking to do, Mr. Hill. If I were you, I'd work out a plea deal. That is, if you wanna save your women."

"But you're not me," I snipped, perspiration on my brow. "You're a cop, and you should stick to that. Don't give legal advice. I got a lawyer for that." *Piece of shit*, I said under my breath.

"Suit yourself, Mr. Hill. It's your funeral."

The insinuation of Karen winding up as my codefendant was the most upsetting part of my troubles. What would happen to the children, our home, and the family furnishings? And I couldn't ignore that my *commara* might get indicted for a drug felony. This hard-on, Detective Stahl, would throw her into the fire. Anxiety churned my stomach.

By law, my wife could not testify against me. This wasn't the case with my girlfriend. She'd sure as hell would turn state's evidence and hand over my head on a silver platter. And Marley Carr—who had ferried my heroin, cocaine, amphetamines, and pot across state lines—frightened and unstable, could tell Stahl a mountain of crimes to lock me up for and chuck the key into an alligator swamp.

And how could I face my children? They'd be terrified knowing their daddy was going to prison. The thought of them growing up missing their father sickened me.

From a reckless and carefree lifestyle, in a few hours my life tripped on a mine field. I gotta admit, I couldn't blame anybody but myself for having landed in a tub of shit. The drugs, alcohol, and the debased orgy marathons in my home—which Karen herself had known about—siphoned the senses from my mind and flooded it with embalming fluids—or that was how it felt. A shrink might've found that for the past year I'd been brain-dead.

Meantime, never mind that my women—Karen, the wife; Marley, the courier; and Linda, the mistress and master heroin cutter—were all on the verge of nervous breakdowns, I couldn't post the $150,000 bail. But this turned out to be a blessing in disguise—I was safer in the county jail. I was in the medical unit, but had I been in the general population, the animal pit, I might've been a dead man.

"I'm not sure I wanna make bail and get out," I said to my lawyer, Richard Otto, in a conference stall of the visiting area. "I mean, Jimmy's probably pissed at me for gettin' sloppy and gettin' caught, and I can just imagine Paulie. Paulie . . . must wanna kill me. I lied and swore to him I'd never deal drugs." Feeling as miserable as a man who had his nuts cut off, I ran a hand through my hair, curls that used to be a sandy color, and now were graying faster than a pile of burning ashes.

It was all looking dark, and Otto said, "Your tear glands are about to gush tears."

Richard Otto, who always had a white carnation in his lapel, was counselor to the gangsters, and Paul Vario was his principal client to whom he owed the highest allegiance. I must've looked so fucked that Otto reached across the gray metal table and placed a hand on my shoulder. "Not that it matters now, but why in hell did you get started in drugs knowing how strongly Paulie objected to it?"

Six conference cubicles were one next to the other, and the loud chatter around us made it impossible to speak discreetly. I was groveling for words. "Rich, it was the money. My whole life I hijacked trucks, and I had to steal a fifty-foot tractor trailer loaded with swag to make a tenth of what I can make with a ten-inch brick of heroin. You understand?"

"There's no need to rehash it. It's too late. The question, is how do you want to go forward with your defense?"

"I don't know, Rich. I gotta think it out. Right now, thanks to you, they put me in a one-man cell, and I never leave it. Unless somebody poison's my food, I feel safe here."

"I know. That's why I begged the judge to direct the deputy sheriffs to place you in isolation."

"Karen's parents are working out a deal with the bail bondsman to put up their house for collateral, but as I said, I'm not all that anxious to get out of here. Besides, I need some time to get my body and mind clean of drugs."

Skimming his notes, Otto said, "I pray they don't indict Karen for complicity." He pointed at me and said in a whisper, "Inferring you might cooperate, I've been stalling Florio to move forward with arresting your wife and your *commara*, Linda. And only because I've got him believing there's a good chance you'll inform on your associates." Otto collected his papers, tapped them on the table surface into a neat packet, and stuffed them in a tan briefcase. "We have to notify your parole officer. What's his name?"

"Jimmy Fox."

The lawyer wrote down Fox's name on a pad. "You may want to consider having me work out a plea deal with Florio. And if you do, I'm sure he'd want you to testify against anybody you can—Burke, Vario, and all the big shots you can finger." Otto let this last sentence float and fixed a bitter stare on me. "Of course, I know you'd never cause problems for your friends. Would you? After all, they've been good to you." Again, the attorney stared into my eyes, probing to read my thoughts. Damn well knowing that Otto's best interests were with Vario, I kept my stony face on and withdrew into myself.

Otto stood as if he'd run out of time. "Let's face it, Henry. This November, there'll be a local election, and our *dear* county attorney will not want the voters to think he's cutting loose a criminal who's littering the streets with addictive drugs. He has to show his voters—the people he's bound to protect from felons—that by forfeiting your case, he can prosecute much, much heavier hitters. That's why DCA Florio will only consider a plea deal if you help him hang the big tunas." Otto nodded up and down and grinned, a subtle warning in his eyes. "It's all about politics, my friend. It has nothing to do with justice . . . just politics."

The Mafia lawyer paused and cocked his head. "Here's what I'm getting at, Henry. If you're only willing to cop a plea without handing over Burke and Vario—and *I know* you won't give up your friends—Bill Florio will push and push until you're sentenced to thirty years. Then he can dance in front of the cameras and give the impression he's the public's savior who got rid of the sewage." Otto leaned in face-to-face with me. "See what I'm saying? You gotta take your lumps—like the stand-up man that I know you are—and sit it out for a long haul behind the wall."

I dropped my head and looked upward at Otto—a short, stubby wiseass of a man in shiny, silk suits that changed color as he moved. I nodded in silence for a few seconds and bullshitted him, "I realize I got no choice but to go down alone. I could never hurt Jimmy and Paulie."

Otto zipped his briefcase, and we shook hands. "Well, it's settled, Henry. I felt it in my heart you'd do the right thing. Paulie will be pleased to hear this. Remember, if you do good, then good comes to you. If you do bad . . ." Otto turned up his palms. "Well, you know what happens."

The attorney unhooked the white carnation from his lapel and laid it on the table. "Good luck, Henry. May this rose brighten your day," and he left, blending into the crowded visiting room. Hoping Otto had believed me, I let out the breath I'd been holding in for the past ten minutes.

Two days passed, and in the same interviewing pen I was hosting federal parole officer James Fox.

"Henry, you're caught between a rock and a hard place," Fox said.

"Mr. Fox, I don't have anybody to turn to. They'll kill me. I know they'll kill me, and there's no one who can help me. That's why I gotta keep quiet, and whatever it is, it is."

"Henry, I'm surprised at you. You should be wiser. Whether you turn against them, or accept your punishment and not squeal, you're a *dead* man. Your associates will murder you in prison. They're not going to chance that maybe one day, feeling miserable in your cell, you'll say to yourself, *I want to be free again.* And you'll rat out your partners in crime. So either way, you're a dead man. Don't you see?"

78

In June 1980, the Lufthansa investigation had run its course. McDonald shifted his attention to newer cases, as did Steve Carbone. One morning, due to flooding rains, the normally rush-hour crawl was slower than ever, and McDonald was late getting to work. As he bustled into his office, the phone was ringing.

"Hello ... McDonald here," his words choppy with winded breathing.

"This is Parole Officer Fox. Jimmy Fox."

"How can I help you, Mr. Fox?" McDonald asked, his speech now steadier.

"One of my parolees was arrested and charged with six drug-related felonies. He's afraid his cohorts will snuff him out to keep him quiet. He's interested in striking a deal, and it seems to me he may have information you want."

McDonald's heart raced. "Such as?"

"Lufthansa." Fox tarried in silence for McDonald to digest that magic topic.

"What's his name? Where's he being held?"

"Henry Hill. He's at the Nassau County Jail. He hasn't yet made bail."

McDonald's thoughts were racing as fast as his heart. "Can you give me some background on this individual, Mr. Fox?"

"Hill's got a long criminal history and affiliations to the Lucchese faction, and he's also a protégé of Jimmy Burke."

McDonald weighed the significance of this last sentence, a sudden uplift of hope. Feeling weightless, he called Carbone. "I think we got a gift out of nowhere."

McDonald's upbeat mood made Carbone envision the tides swinging in their direction. "What about, Ed?"

The US Attorney repeated to Carbone his conversation with Fox.

Carbone moved the phone receiver away from his ear and stared at it as if he didn't believe McDonald's words. "This *is* a gift. I'll go there and see what I can shake out of this Henry Hill."

"Please keep me posted, Steve."

"Sure will, Ed."

Hill hadn't yet made bail, and Burke was more distrustful of anyone than ever before. Sepe, Frank Burke, the Gent's son, and Hill were the remaining survivors of all who had knowledge about Lufthansa. Burke understood that Sepe, despite having been arrested and potentially convicted for Lufthansa, did not crumble under McDonald and Carbone. The Gent had confidence that Sepe would go to the grave before he'd cause harm to his idol and guru.

On the other hand, because Hill's future was doomed Burke could no longer depend on him to be a stand-up guy.

Aside from his extramarital affairs, Hill had a faint attachment to a tradition, the unity of a family. Should his wife be imprisoned, it'd be a tragedy for the Hills. Burke would've wagered that Hill was dead-set on preventing Karen's incarceration—at any cost. Hill was bound to buckle and undoubtedly emerge as the centerpiece in the prosecution of Vario, Burke, and his Robert's Lounge pips. This eventuality was clearer than clear to the Gent.

Hill consulted with his parole office and was set on speaking with the FBI. And although he had promised Stahl and Florio to assist dismantling the Lufthansa mystery, he cleverly opted to play both sides to gauge where the safest haven was, with the Nassau County authorities or the FBI.

Karen was bathing her daughter, and the telephone rang. She left the child in the bathtub and, drying her hands, ran to the phone. "Hello."

"Karen, it's Jimmy. How'r things goin'?"

On hearing Burke's voice, Karen's knees weakened. He was trawling to fish out if her husband had been released on bail, and more gut-ripping, if he were clinging to his sanity or on the brink of flipping. "Everything's the same, Jimmy. And no, Henry didn't make bail yet."

Burke phoned the Hill residence four to five times per week with the same inquiries. *"Is Henry keeping calm?" "When is he getting out?" "Does he need anything?" "Are you and the kids OK?"* This was Burke's excuse to stay in touch with Karen so he could be abreast of the latest developments.

As for Vario, ordinarily unfazed, Hill's possible defection had him biting his nails; and he, too, relentlessly called Karen, who, responding hazily to his questions, feigned to be withering emotionally. And it was a godsend that Vario was in the dark about Burke having financed Hill's narcotics enterprise. Had that not been the case, the Gent wouldn't need to fret over the possibility of Hill siding with the investigators; the Lucchese capo might've reserved a burial plot for Burke. Paul Vario enforced his policies, and they were strict. Business was business and rules were rules, and he did not tolerate insubordination, nor did he give leniency to those who, intentionally or not, drew the interest of the law to him. In doling out punishment, Vario's sentencing guidelines were consistent. Death!

To sniff out if Vario had an inkling of the Burke/Hill narcotic partnership, the Gent dispatched Sepe to the Euclid Taxi Stand in Brooklyn, a company owned by Vario and his brothers, Lenny and Tuddy. The stated purpose of Sepe's errand was to fill Vario in on Hill's status.

Lenny Vario saw Sepe trotting through the garage doorway of the cabstand and rushed to greet him. "Hey, Angelo. *Che si dice?*" Lenny hollered out. He thrust his club-like forearm for a handshake, a gold-banded watch glistening on his hairy wrist.

"Nothing new, Lenny." Sepe was jumpier than ever, on pins and needles over the pickle Hill was in. "Jimmy wants Paulie to know Henry is still in the joint. And . . . well, Jimmy thinks Henry should get whacked as soon as possible. Jimmy's got the feeling Henry's gonna give us all up."

Lenny studied the greasy cement floor of the garage, a darkish cave with an odor of dirty motor oil. "Yeah, my brother, Paulie, is shittin' about it, too. That fuckin' Hill is an asshole."

"Oh, yeah. He's an arrogant prick," Sepe said.

Lenny motioned Sepe to follow him. "Why are we standing out here like a couple of *chitrools?* Let's go in my office and talk."

Calling it an office was the same as naming a thirty-dollar-a-night motel The Ritz. Everything was smudged with greasy handprints, and *Playboy* centerfolds were thumbtacked to the paint-crackling walls. Empty cups with dry coffee rings inundated Lenny's desk, and a tinny-sounding radio at a whispery volume was perched on a narrow shelf. It was tuned to an oldies rock station, Roy Orbison crooning: *Pretty woman, walking down . . .*

Sepe sat on a milk crate and opened the zipper of his Adidas blue sweat suit, the customary apparel of low-level Mafia hoods. "Yeah, Jimmy don't think Henry started talking to the cops yet, but who's not to say he already might've, right?"

Lenny nodded. "You're right, and I guess Jimmy wants to play it safe. I don't blame him."

Sepe lit a cigarette and sucked in a puff, flicking ashes on the floor. "Yeah, I mean, this fuckin' Henry could flip anytime. And if Paulie goes along with it, I'll find a way to whack the fuck in the county jail. If Henry thinks nobody can get to him in there, he'll get the surprise of his life."

A cup of hot coffee in hand, Lenny was impressed with Sepe's audacity and eased the cup from his lips. "You think you can get to him inside the joint, Angelo?"

With the smugness of a jockey in a fixed race, Sepe gave Lenny a long nod. "For a carton of cigarettes, I can have somebody cut Hill's throat. This dude, Sammy DiGennaro, an inmate I know in there, he's the man."

"But I thought Hill is in a one-man cell in the medical unit and not in the general population. How's this guy gonna get to him?"

"Easy. Sammy's job in there is to clean toilets. When he goes to mop the bathrooms, that's when he can slice that son of a bitch's throat. See," Sepe expounded, "the cells in the medical unit don't have toilets and sinks out in the open. They have enclosed bathrooms. And as Sammy is cleaning the john, he'll call Henry in there with an excuse like, *there's something on the floor that might be yours.* When Henry steps in the john, Sammy can whack him, and nobody will see a thing."

"Ha, ha, ha," Lenny belched out. He saw Sepe's scenario to get to Hill as hilarious. "Ah, ah, ah." Lenny's laughter was boisterous, and not to swell his inflamed appendix he wrapped both arms around his waist, a blubbery roll of dough. When the laughing seizure quelled, he dabbed at his cheeks with his wrist. "Angelo, it's a great plan. My brother's gonna love it." He drank the coffee, and content as a pig lying in mud, sank low into his chair. "I'm gonna see Paulie tonight, and I'll bring him up to speed. Paulie is pissed at Hill for lettin' him think he wasn't into drugs. So I'm sure Paulie will OK whacking him. Tell the Gent we'll let him know."

79

My ears hurt from the noise in the visiting room, a loud, cramped space with inmates and visitors outshouting each other. It was depressing, and everybody had misery in their eyes. Karen hated to come here; she had to go through a degrading strip search, and the worst was for her to take off her bra in front of a half dozen female correction officers. And who knows how many perverted male guards might've been peeping? The whole place smelled of cleaning chemicals and cheap cologne the younger inmates splashed on themselves. These jerks weren't much older than nineteen. The majority were in for drug abuse, a misdemeanor carrying a maximum of twelve months in the county jail. Convicts sentenced to longer than a year go to state prisons.

Her hair held in a brown clip, Karen looked above the one-inch Plexiglas divider, her chin barely reaching the top, and in a sea of orange picked me out in my carroty jumpsuit. Prisoners are not allowed to stand in the visiting area. Karen propped a chair under her and pressed an open hand against the glass to meet with mine. She saw a palm print on the divider, and it grossed her out. She pulled her hand from the glass and shook it. "Oh, Henry, this is full of germs." She stuck out her tongue. "How disgusting. Don't they ever clean it?"

"Karen, this is not the time to talk about germs." Frustrated, I looked away from her. "I don't understand you, Karen. I'm looking at a thirty-year stretch. Paulie and Jimmy are probably plotting to kill me, and you're thinking about germs. Let's talk about something else. What's happening with the bail money? I gotta get out of here, Karen. I got a bad feeling. I'm afraid to eat. Anybody can poison the goddamn shit they call food."

Karen fixed the top button on her white blouse. "I'm going through a lot, too. You have no idea." And seeing my name on the jumpsuit set Karen off, her eyes squinting with dampness. "You don't know how lonely I feel, Henry. Not knowing what's going to happen to you, and the children constantly asking where their daddy is. Oh, it's awful."

"OK, OK. What about the bail money?" I asked, impatience and, even command, in my question.

"Oh, God! My parents are doing all they can to take a loan on their house, but they're not millionaires, Henry. The bank said the appraisal came in too low, and my sister is getting another appraiser she knows. She went out with his son, and maybe he'll fudge the numbers."

I gritted my teeth and punched the glass divider. "Oh, that's just great. And how long is this gonna take? The longer I stay in this rat hole, the more time they'll have to figure out a way to whack me." I was getting louder and agitated, and the guards were watching, and ready to pounce on me.

"What do you want from me?" Karen whined, ripping into sobs. "I don't know what you expect of me! Maybe you should get your girlfriend to help you. Why don't you have that tramp sell herself and raise your bail money? On second thought, her body isn't even worth enough to bail a dog out of the pound." Karen snatched her Gucci purse from the ledge and exploded off the chair. In seconds, she was gone, her high heels clicking on the tile floor.

"Karen, come back. Don't leave me, come back." She was gone. I stood and screamed, "Kaaaaaren!"

Two correction officers charged toward me. I must've turned into a demented man on the verge of murder. They handcuffed me and hustled me to my cell. It all seemed to happen in a split second.

It had been twenty-two hours since Karen high-tailed it out of the visiting room. I was in my cell lying idly on the three-inch padded bunk. I was lost in thought, and the clunking of the door lock broke my lull. I saw the gray uniform pants of the guard through the glass window on the lower part of the door, and I got tense.

"Hill," said the deep voice of the black correction officer, "let's go. You got visitors."

Oh, Karen is back, I assumed, loosening my nerves. I zipped up my jumpsuit, and slipped my feet into a pair of plastic flip-flops, compliments of the county jail. The guard and I went to a segregated section of the floor, then into the elevator, and down to the ground level of the jailhouse. I couldn't wait to get out of the piss-stinky elevator. It stopped with a thud, and the door opened. "To the left, Hill," the officer directed.

Surprised, I asked him, "Where the hell are you taking me? I thought you said we're going to the visiting room."

"I didn't say that. I said you got visitors, special company. I'm taking you to the attorneys' conference pen."

I got scared shitless and couldn't imagine what the hell to expect. Every hair-raising scenario raced across my chest. On entering the cubicle, two men in black suits came toward me to shake hands. The shorter of the two gave off an aroma of aftershave so strong it overpowered the stink in the air.

"I'm FBI Special Agent Steve Carbone, and this is Agent Ed Guevara."

"What . . . what the fuck are you guys doin' here? You wanna get me killed?"

"Calm down, calm down, Mr. Hill," Carbone said. "We're here to help you. That is, *if* you want to help us."

"Calm down! Are you fuckin' kidding me? You couldn't have been more discreet. If it gets back to Burke or Vario that I'm meeting with the FBI, they'll have somebody here drown me in a toilet bowl. And you're telling me to calm down!"

"In here, nobody can get to you," Guevara consoled.

I smacked my forehead and looked at the ceiling. "I don't believe this. Agent Guevara, when were you born, last night? A monkey with Alzheimers knows they could whack me in a prison just as easily as they can get to me on the outside."

80

Burke sent his son, Frank, to pick up Angelo Sepe and drive him back to their Howard Beach home. Robert's Lounge was off-limits. The Gent was certain it was under police watch and, most likely, swarming with undercover investigators posing as comatose drunkards. Speaking on the telephone was chancier—Burke was sure the FBI had tapped his lines.

What if Angelo asks me why you want him?" Frank said.

"Just say I gotta talk to him. Get going."

Frank Burke found Sepe in his apartment tending to his menagerie of critters, nursing a newborn white and brown rabbit. Sepe's existence and sole contribution to society was violence, but he hosted an unconditional affection for animals, an incongruity.

Sepe, who lived in the basement of a two-family home, answered the knock on the door. "Hey, Frank, how'rr you doin'?"

"Listen, man, my father needs you. C'mon, I'll take you to my house. He's waiting."

"What's it about?"

"I'm not sure, but if I were to guess, I'd say it's about Henry."

Sepe snickered, and the pimply skin on his cheeks stretched with creases.

Once in Burke's den—a room furnished with colonial furniture upholstered in a brown-tan plaid and a handwoven American Indian area rug—the Gent offered, "How about a cold beer, Angelo?"

"It'll hit the spot, Jimmy."

Burke said to his son, "Frank, get a few Schlitzs. The cold ones are in the back of the fridge." Oddly, the Gent, a proponent of antiestablishment standards, had hanging above his fireplace a two-foot statue of an eagle clutching an American flag in its talons.

This was Sepe's first visit to Burke's home. In awe, he browsed about the den and nodded enviously. "Nice pad. So what's happening, Jimmy?"

Burke spoke with straightforwardness and did not double-talk. "Angelo, I don't know what's going on in Henry's head. I can't get to talk to him, and Karen is tight-lipped. It's real strange he didn't reach out for me. Not even to ask for bail money. It's three weeks he's been locked up, and not a sound out of him. If I don't get to speak to him by this Friday, he's gotta go. By the way, Angelo, I got Paulie's OK to whack him. So you don't gotta answer to nobody."

Burke pointed to his chest, then at Sepe. "I got the OK, and I'm givin' *you* the OK. Understand?"

Sepe took pleasure in the Schlitz and smirked.

81

Carbone and Guevara made more trips to see me at the Nassau County Jail, and it pissed me off. The possibility of an inmate squealing to Jimmy about my huddling with the FBI gave me diarrhea. It'd be a given I had jumped ship and turned on my closest friends. And to create a smoke screen, when the correction officers took me to the interviewing cubicle, I kicked, yelled, and grappled with the guards, making believe I was resisting going there.

The second time Carbone and Guevara came, as I was let out of my cell I saw an inmate looking me over as if he wanted to make sure I was *the* Henry Hill. He hustled to the recreation room and dialed the pay phone. I got scared shitless. It turned out he was just curious. He'd seen my picture in the newspapers and on TV and wanted to brag to his girlfriend that he happened to be in the medical unit with a famous drug dealer.

I had become a celebrity overnight. Nonetheless, I let fly at the two agents. "You fuckin' guys are gonna get me killed in here. Why the fuck can't this be done without the whole world knowing that I'm talkin' to you?"

Carbone pumped the air with his palms. "All right, Henry. Tomorrow we're going to arrange to privately have you driven to the US attorney's office. OK?"

"I might be dead by tomorrow." My face got cold, and it must've been as white as an eggshell.

"Before we leave here," Guevara said, "we're going to recommend to the deputy sheriff to assign round-the-clock guards to watch over you."

"Oh, you're a big sport, Guevara. Am I supposed to feel better now?"

Carbone began hammering out negotiations for me to surrender to the FBI and the US attorney and fade into the Federal Witness Protection Program (FWPP).

"Henry, we'll do everything we can to keep you alive," Carbone assured. "*You* have to do whatever is necessary to help us convict Jimmy Burke and Paul Vario for Lufthansa."

"Yeah, yeah. I can throw facts at you that'll make your hair stand up," I claimed, "but pleeeease don't come back here ever again." My heart beat so fast I put my hand on it as if I could slow it down.

82

Carbone and Guevara appealed to the jail administrators to be on the alert, for Hill could be in grave danger, but the agents' pleadings didn't buy him any sympathy. The two FBI men left the Nassau County lockup and went to see McDonald. It was the last week of May, and as they traveled westbound in mid-afternoon on the Brooklyn-Queens Expressway, Carbone and Guevara crawled along in dense traffic, orange sunrays glinting through the windshield. Six miles ahead reigned the Manhattan skyline, an unrivaled lineup of skyscrapers with glass façades, luminous as though they were a wall of gigantic mirrors reflecting the sunlight.

On reaching the office of the US attorney, Carbone flounced to McDonald's desk, soaring with the thought of buttoning up Lufthansa. "Ed, good news."

"I could use it. Let me have it."

"Hill is ready to talk. An issue has to be worked out, though. He feels in danger when we go see him at the county jail, so we'll have to transport him here tomorrow."

"Great news, Steve," McDonald blared. He scanned his calendar and said, "Nope, tomorrow won't work for me. I have to depose a witness on another case. Let's do it the day after tomorrow."

"Done," Carbone said. "The day after tomorrow is Friday. We'll drive Hill here, say, at ten o'clock?"

"Perfect. Friday morning it will be, Steve."

83

The day following my last powwow with Carbone and Guevara, Karen's parents had clinched a home equity loan and sprang me out of the county jail without the FBI, McDonald, Stahl, and DCA Florio knowing it. I had been stressed out for almost five weeks and stayed alive by fine-tuning my built-in radar. I rarely left my cell and ate only pre-packaged food. I did my own housekeeping, and when I needed a shower, instead of going to the common stalls I bird-bathed in the lavatory of my cell. It was a hell of an inconvenience, but compared to the day-by-day chances of getting shanked, it might've saved my life.

Driving home to Rockville Center, Long Island, I was withdrawn as if I were a freshly released POW. Grateful, I thanked my mother-in-law. Her husband, a lazy homebody, had stayed in his now double-hocked house.

Karen caressed my neck; her pale complexion of lately had gotten some color back. "You must be dying for a good meal, Henry."

My mother-in-law, the type you wanna strangle, fanned a hand, her pink-lacquered fingernails glowing in the dark. "You lost weight," she criticized. "You look worse than before. Somebody might take you for a scarecrow. Tonight you should buy us all dinner. It's only fair after what my husband and I just did for you. You may have rotted in jail until somebody killed you."

In the front seats, Karen and I glanced at one another, she signaling me to ignore her. I must've had the look of wanting to attack the nagging bitch.

"All right, Ma! Enough already. Give Henry a break. He's been through a lot the past month."

My mother-in-law, fluffing her bluish-white coif of hair, tsk'ed. "That's no fault of mine. It's all his doing. And I always said it. These *goyims* are not worthy of a nice Jewish girl. Look at the situation he's got you in. And when I think about those poor grandchildren of mine. Ach! What's the use already?" She stared at her fingernails, turned her hands over, and I had the feeling she was thinking of another insult to throw at me.

"And you, my dear daughter, you're always making excuses for him. He should've married his own kind, a shiksa."

"Maaaah! I said enough already."

It was getting dark, a stinging chill running through me, and my mother-in-law's irritating welcome wasn't warming the reunion. Well, I became a wild man and grabbed the steering wheel out of my wife's hands. I screamed out, "I'M DONE!!!!! Stop the fuckin' car, Karen! Stop the fuckin' car. I wanna get out. Or else I'm gonna choke her."

Karen's mother, forehead creased and eyebrows arched, squawked, "Ahh! This is how you thank us for putting up our house to get you out of jail? I always remind my daughter she should never have married you. Now she's stuck with a lemon. She should've married her own kind, and none of this would've happened."

Aside from my mother-in-law's insults, I was glad to have shed the orange jumpsuit. I was bound for home, and though no one from the Robert's Lounge gang or Paul Vario's clan had gotten wind of it, I wondered how safe I'd be, or if my days were numbered. Maybe, I wondered, I might've been better off in jail.

We got rid of that nagging, nosy mother-in-law of mine, and Karen and I were figuring out where to go from here. In our kitchen at the dinette table, we were chewing a pot roast that Karen had burned and made it get dry and tough. The mashed potatoes weren't too appetizing either. Karen had no talent for cooking and diluted the potatoes with a heavy hand of skimmed milk and watery gravy, a soupy liquid I thought came out of a can of Alpo. But this was the least of our problems. We were getting sick, worrying what might happen to us as a family. And was all this going to scar our kids?

"What are you going to do, Henry?"

I threw the fork and knife onto my dish of mystery meat and restlessly ran a hand through my hair. "I don't know yet, Karen." I blew out a breath of air and squeezed my temples. "Jimmy went straight for Stacks . . . well actually that dumb *mouleenian*, may he rest in peace, deserved to get whacked, but whacking Marty Krugman was uncalled for. I mean, Jimmy could've worked out a fair cut with him."

"Yeah, that was terrible. And that poor Fran, I always think about how she must feel, losing her husband that way."

I put up three fingers and counted. "The next one who went was Tommy, and that was Paulie and John Gotti's doing." I started massaging my eyelids. My body was as stiff as a board from sleeping on the hard bed in the county jail. "Although, I can't blame Jimmy for whacking Louie Cafora and his wife. He found out those two were ready to sing to the FBI."

I pushed aside my plate; talking about what had gone down over the past two months, I was in no mood to eat.

"The next ones to go were Frenchy and Joe Manri. And I'll never understand why Jimmy did it."

"For the same reason he murdered everybody else. He's covering his tracks to make sure there's no one left to squeal on him."

"Karen, all Jimmy had to do was to give them a little bit more money from Lufthansa."

I dropped my head into my hands. "And what about Tommy's girlfriend, Theresa? Jimmy had her body chopped to pieces? All he had to do was to plant a painless slug in her head and let her family bury her in one piece."

Karen didn't seem to know what else to say, and I slumbered in thought. I was under a thick pile of legal troubles, kicking and struggling to swim to the surface, blurs of the faces of those who got killed flashing in my head.

Karen touched my hand. "So what do you make of all this, honey?"

"What I make of all this? I'm probably next."

The phone shrilled. I signaled for Karen to answer it.

"Hello."

"Hi, Karen, it's Jimmy."

"Hold on." She sighed and covered the mouthpiece. "It's Jimmy. You want to talk to him?"

I got up from the table and took the receiver from her. "Hello, Jimmy."

"Henry! You're home. I'm so happy. Why didn't you reach out for me? We were all worried about you."

"A lot of shit is goin' on. I was fighting to raise bail, and all kinds of hurdles were gettin' in the way."

"I could've helped you with the bail, Henry. I wish you had called me. Anyway, listen, pal, I want to know from you what's going on. Let's have breakfast tomorrow morning. All right?"

"I don't know, Jimmy. I got so much to do. I gotta go see my lawyer."

"Nah, nah. That'll wait. Meet me in the morning at the Airport Diner at around nine."

I stalled. Then I thought, what harm could come to me at a busy diner? "All right, I'll see you there at nine."

I saw an unsettled look in Karen's eyes. "Is it safe for you to meet him there?"

I tried to make her feel at ease, but my voice must've sounded shaky. "I guess I'll be safe at the diner. I have to see Jimmy in person to read what he's got in his crazy mind."

The Airport Diner, always lively with people, on this morning was nearly empty. Strange. Could Jimmy be behind this? The Gent couldn't possibly control how many customers were here. Or could he? Unlikely. It was probably an off day, though those smells of slimy frying oil were in the air, and it meant everything was normal.

I spotted him in a booth reading a newspaper. He was wearing a gray tweed sport jacket and a shirt with an open collar. "Hi, Jimmy," I said in a daze.

He dropped the paper on the table, removed his glasses, and stood. He embraced me and kissed me on the cheek. "Sit down, sit down. So how'rr you holding up, kid? Lost a couple of pounds, eh?"

I sunk my eyes and gaped at the Formica tabletop. "I don't know. This whole thing don't look good. I'm gonna go see my attorney after I leave here, and I'll hear his take on my situation."

The Gent nodded with a letdown stare. "See, you got too careless." He shrugged and said, "Eh, what's done is done. Here's what I wanna tell you. I found out the bastard who ratted on you is Bobby Germain's son, Bobby Jr. The kid who used to hang around your house."

I leaned into the table, and my jaw dropped. "You gotta be kiddin'. How'd you know this?"

"Never mind how I know. Bottom line is Bobby Jr. gotta get whacked. Period. He'll be one less witness you gotta deal with. Understand?" Jimmy looked through me as if to X-ray my head. "By the way, Paulie's *done* with you. But you expected that."

Jimmy's determination to whack Bobby Jr. unnerved me. You'd think he was doing it to rescue me. No way. It was *self*-preservation. The smaller the odds of me crumbling under the narcotics charges, the lesser the motive I'd have to turn against him and Vario. This is what must've been going through Jimmy's mind, and I was afraid he wasn't done with the wave of the Lufthansa killings.

84

Carbone and Guevara drove to the Nassau County Jail to deliver Henry Hill to the US attorney's office. For McDonald and the FBI men, the long-awaited wish of having Hill in their control to debrief him about Lufthansa seemed too good to be true.

On arriving at the county jail, Carbone requested for Hill to be consigned to him. The deputy warden chuckled. "Agent Carbone," he said chidingly, "you FBI guys are sleeping on the job."

"What do you mean?"

The deputy warden loosened his grip on the empty coffee cup he was holding and let it fall into an overfilled wastebasket. "Yesterday, inmate Henry Hill was released on bail."

"He was *what?*" Carbone exclaimed. Forty-eight hours ago, the reward for those months of dead ends had materialized; and the last hope, Henry Hill, who could've put to rest this Lufthansa insanity, was on the loose. And all that remained was a disheartening presumption: Hill was a fugitive forever lost in a jungle of deserters. Or, if he hadn't yet absconded too far from his haunts, Burke and Vario would surely kill him. Carbone had no faith he might see Hill ever again. "Hill hasn't been able to make bail for the past five weeks," he asked. "So how is it possible that all of a sudden he raised the money for the bond?" No sooner Carbone had let this out of his mouth, he wished he could take it back.

The deputy warden patted his chest and answered with cynicism, "Agent Carbone, all I can tell you is Hill is out on bail. It's not my job to figure out how prisoners make bail."

"Eh . . . may I use your phone?"

The deputy warden pointed to a workstation in a corner of the reception room. "Yeah, use that one over there."

Carbone phoned McDonald. "Ed, it's Steve," his words slow and glum.

"Yes, Steve. What time are you coming with Hill to my office?"

"We're not. Yesterday, he was released on bail. Can you believe it?"

"Released on bail! Hill?"

"Yes, Hill." Carbone answered dolefully. "Where do we go from here, Ed?"

"Place him under observation. That is, if he's still around and doesn't get killed. Send some of your agents to see if he's in his neighborhood. Meantime, I'll file a material witness motion. Judge Costantino, remember him?"

"Yes, the Werner trial."

"Right. He'll grant the motion."

"I'm sure he will. I'm just praying Hill hasn't flown the coop."

"Even if he did, Steve, once I get the order to arrest him, there'll be a warrant and a nationwide hunt for him."

Within three hours, Carbone's agents were outside Hill's home spying on him. It was a hot morning and, the air conditioning equipment operating, all windows and doors were shut—a hindrance for Carbone's stakeout team to hear or notice activity inside the house.

A lucky moment came when Hill stepped outside onto the stoop of his side door to toss a bag of garbage in a waste bin. He hadn't yet fled, and McDonald, who had already typed the motion to rearrest him, hurried two floors below his office to the federal courthouse and into Judge Costantino's chambers. The judge had left his door ajar to circulate fresh air. McDonald, tie unraveled, craned his neck inside the room, perspiration darkening the armpits of his shirt. "Excuse me, Your Honor."

Judge Costantino, white-haired and pink-skinned, was engrossed in Cindy Adams's gossip column in the *New York Post*. His Honor folded the tabloid on his desk, a paper-strewn jumble, and removed his reading glasses, squinting at McDonald. "Ed, come on in. Please sit. What can I do for you?"

McDonald sat, anxiousness in his movements. He rested the motion on his lap and tapped it. "Judge, I have here a motion for an order to arrest a material witness in the Lufthansa case."

Judge Costantino flung his glasses on his nose. "Ah! The elusive Lufthansa saga. What have you got, Ed?"

"Well, this individual, Henry Hill, purports to have vital information regarding the Lufthansa case. Unfortunately, yesterday he was released on bail for an unrelated matter, and before he skips or gets murdered by one of his cohorts, I want to rearrest him."

Amused, Judge Costantino dipped his head understandingly.

McDonald, pleased at His Honor's keenness, got to the core of the apple: "I'd wish for you to grant this order, Judge. The problem is . . . well, every second heightens the likelihood Hill will either abscond or turn up dead. What I'm asking is, and I hate to impose, if you could review this at the earliest."

Judge Costantino reached across the desk for the brief and practically tore it out of McDonald's hands. "Oh, sure, I agree. You have to dispatch him to the marshals at the MCC immediately. Here give me the motion. Hell, I'll sign it right now. Is this soon enough?" He picked up his ballpoint pen, a Mont Blanc that a defense lawyer had gifted to him for brownie points. "Let's see, where's the page requiring my John Hancock?"

McDonald, ethics and forthrightness always before ambitions, was stumped. "Eh . . . Judge, shouldn't you first read it?"

"No, no. It won't be necessary. I trust you, Ed. I trust you. Besides, as you said, we can't waste a minute apprehending Hill." And Honorable Costantino scribbled his signature on the warrant, clearing McDonald and Carbone to recollar Henry Hill.

McDonald thanked the judge and, feeling as light as a feather, traipsed out of the halls of justice. The minute he was out of sight, Judge Costantino reopened the *New York Post* and engrossed himself in the gossip column.

85

June 1979.

Confidential Informant Bobby Germain Jr. had done a stellar job in helping to indict Henry Hill and whomever else he might lead to the police. In gratitude, Detective Stahl gave Bobby Jr. a bone, a one-month sabbatical from his weekly reporting. Bobby Jr. frittered a good part of this "vacation" in a dingy watering hole, The Barrel, on the corner of Hillside Avenue and 199th Street in Jamaica, Queens.

On a sweltering June afternoon, Bobby Jr. was there at the bar cooling his innards with ice-cold beers. The tavern was darkish, and the low light came from three or four neon signs. A red Budweiser lighted sign, an illuminated yellow clock with a mouth-watering picture of a tall glass of blond beer, and a black and brown plaque advertising *Jim Beam is the Smoothest* were a few of the colorful fixtures inside the stark gin mill.

A short, scrawny man with unruly black hair trundled into the bar and sat next to Bobby Jr. He wore tan jeans with a collage of brown and black stains that from afar could've been mistaken for psychedelic patches in vogue in the sixties. Imprinted on the front of his T-shirt was a palm with outstretched fingers, the emblem of the Sicilian Mafia. The bartender, a 280-pounder scruffy type, panted between words. He spotted the newly arrived, who seemed thirsty for a frosty ones. "What . . . zzzz . . . will you have, buddy? Zzzz . . ." The customer, mean-eyed and nervy, said, "Eh, gimmie a scotch on the rocks."

"You got it."

This newcomer—whose eyes hadn't yet adjusted to the darkness, incessantly kicked his shoes on the foot-rest of the barstool as if he were restless. He pivoted to face the drinker next to him. "Hey, man, my name's Angelo. You come here a lot?"

Bobby Jr., happy to have "someone to shoot the breeze with," put out his right arm for a handshake. "Hi, Angelo, I'm Bobby Jr. Yeah, I'm in here every afternoon. Nice joint, and the drinks are pretty cheap. The bartender is Butch. Nice guy. Looks out for his people. Every other drink is free."

Angelo nodded in the direction of the bartender. "Cool, cool. What'd you say his name is?" He was slapping the top of the bar as though he were playing a set of imaginary bongos to the beat of Latin music.

"Butch. You'll like him. And later, around nine o'clock, a bunch of hookers come in here to hang out. Fun girls."

Angelo wasn't listening to his drinking mate's gibberish. He glanced right and left and moved elbow-to-elbow with Bobby Jr. "Listen, man. I got some dynamite pot I wanna sell. Interested?"

Bobby perked up; Angelo might be another delicious catch for Detective Stahl. And he'd be proud of Bobby Jr. He shielded his mouth with a hand in case someone could read his lips. "How much pot you got?"

"I don't wanna get into it here, man. I have it stashed in my apartment. A few minutes from here. If you want, we can take a ride. I got my car outside."

Angelo did have a car parked not far from The Barrel, but it wasn't his. The automobile, a metallic-brown Datsun 240Z, belonged to a Continental Airlines stewardess. The owner, a sprightly blonde, lived in Kew Gardens, a sector of Queens midway between Kennedy International Airport and LaGuardia Airport. In Kew Gardens a multitude of the inhabitants are employed by the airlines. There, on the previous night, Angelo had stolen the car from a lightly trafficked street. He jimmied the door lock and hot-wired the Datsun without fearing the flight attendant might see him. Angelo's contact at Continental Airlines had scoped out her itinerary for the month; she was flying a six-day leg somewhere in Europe.

Angelo, a big sport, paid Bobby's bar tab and his own, and they ambled out of The Barrel. The new friends strolled around the corner and ducked into the low, sleek Datsun. Angelo shifted the five-speed transmission into first gear, popped the clutch, and they were off, tires screeching and rustling pebbles.

The zippy acceleration pinioned Bobby's neck to the headrest. "This is a mean machine. I think I'm gonna get me one. Tell me, how much pot you got, Angelo?"

"Plenty. And it's good stuff."

The Datsun sped onto the westbound entrance ramp of the Grand Central Parkway, and in seven to eight seconds it was traveling at eighty-five miles an hour, blurring past the landscape.

Bobby Jr. leaned to his left and peeked at the speedometer. "Wow! This car has the feel of an airplane taking off. I got some money coming to me. I'm definitely gonna buy me one of these." He sniffed the scent of a woman's perfume. "Hey, I bet you've had a few broads in this car, eh?"

"Oh, yeah! This is a hell of a pussy mobile."

Angelo steered into a tranquil neighborhood one block west of Queens Boulevard—neatly landscaped quarters with English Tudor-style apartment buildings of the art deco era—and parked it in the same space he had stolen it from the night before. "We're here, Bobby."

"You live in a nice area, Angelo. Selling pot pays, don't it?" Bobby Jr. was feeling high, and not from the beers he'd chugged back at The Barrel. He was about to net a big tuna for Detective Stahl. Angelo could turn out to be another pawn for which "the hard-nosed Stahl" might reward Bobby Jr. and possibly discharge him as an undercover operative. He'd be a free man.

"Bobby," Angelo said, "wait in the car. I'm gonna check to make sure there's no narcs or nothin' funny going on in the lobby of my building."

"Go ahead."

Bobby Jr. was admiring the creature comforts in the interior of the Datsun 240Z and the eight-track tape deck encased in the dashboard, a sound system of this period that fomented the envy of young drivers. He had lost himself in a dream of owning a car of this status, when fast-on-coming footsteps shook him out of it. Angelo was jogging back.

Bobby Jr. lowered the window. "Everything OK?"

"Oh, yeah. Everything's clear." Sepe neared the Datsun from the passenger side, a hand behind his back. Swiftly, he stopped short, knelt slightly, outstretched his right arm—at the end of which was a Berretta semiautomatic—aimed at Bobby's face, and fired a high-velocity round, shattering the informant's skull into a dust of fragments.

Mouth open, blood dribbling, Bobby's head listed into the center console of the sports car, his left temple leaning on the stick shift. Angelo Sepe raised the windows shut and strutted three blocks south to where his Thunderbird was parked.

At the end of her six-day tour of duty, the owner of the Datsun, Lorraine Weaver, did not return home. Lorraine's boyfriend, the captain of the flight—married with children and living in Arizona—had reserved for him and Lorraine a ten-day vacation in St. Maarten. In the airline industry, it's a commonality for female stewardesses to be in romantic relationships with pilots, married or not.

In total, Lorraine had been out of New York for two and a half weeks, while Bobby's body was decomposing in the Datsun—and he wasn't exactly looking his best.

Once back home, Lorraine inserted the key in the door lock of her Datsun and was immediately thrown off kilter; the lock was mangled. A thief had broken into her car. "Damn it," Lorraine cursed. "No street is safe anymore. I bet some fucker ripped out my tape deck." In the late '70s, *fucker* was a disparaging profanity broadly used by women in the age range of twenty to thirty years old.

Lorraine yanked open the door, and the sight of swarming flies buzzing over a dead man frizzed her into shock.

And more angst wrung the homecoming flight attendant into a panicky wreck; detectives could not believe her seemingly far-fetched explanations of how the insect-dotted corpse of a police informant found itself in her car.

"I don't know . . . maybe somebody put him in my Datsun. Or maybe he was trying to steal my car and someone shot him." Distraught, she insisted, "I didn't kill anybody. I didn't do this, I swear."

Lieutenant Joe Berardi, though—a closed-minded detective longing to take credit for solving a homicide—twisted this uncanny situation in Lorraine's disfavor and moved to charge her with murder. But Berardi's superiors, not as dogmatic, sorted out the facts and cut her loose.

Who killed Bobby Jr.? wondered Detective Stahl and DCA Florio. They'd lost their star witness against Henry Hill, and at the 113th Precinct a consensus had formed; Lieutenant Ahearn and a dozen of his detectives all swore on a stack of bibles that the Gent had signed off on the Bobby Jr. rubout.

Until this latest homicide, second thoughts zigzagged through Henry Hill's soul. Was it right and morally correct for him to cuddle in bed with the authorities, and jail the people who had nurtured him? Or was he a selfish traitor? Well, Burke's murder of Bobby Jr., emotionless and cold-blooded, quickly unstained Hill's conscience.

Bobby's demise underscored Burke's unlimited prowess to safeguard his freedom and his money. Bobby Jr.—hardly nineteen years old—had met an untimely end. And the irony was that his murder was in vain.

Had he not betrayed Hill, it might not have made any difference. Hill, self-destructive, and indiscreet, would've been caught one way or the other. Jimmy Burke's critics viewed the killing of Bobby Jr. as an unjustified travesty.

The Gent's homicidal propensity awakened Hill to ensure the safety of his loved ones—girlfriends included.

Hill had tentatively agreed to enter the Witness Protection Program while aiding Carbone and McDonald in their pursuit of Burke and Vario. But this path had a downside for Hill; the invasive twenty-four hour scrutiny by the FBI and the US attorney. But it was a question of time before he'd be killed. With this in mind, Hill came to his senses; he needed government protection. Period. Maybe, he considered, he might've had a second choice. First, though, Hill had to free himself from the narcotics indictments, the guillotine that was hanging over his head. But from the minute he'd been out on bail, Stahl and Florio had been coaxing him to turn state's evidence. Perhaps, this was the answer. Hill, however, wasn't quite sold on the premise that the Nassau County police and deputy county attorney wielded the means to safeguard him from his enemies. And as any clever consumer does, he shopped for the best deal.

In June 1979, Hill resolved to contact Stahl and Florio to evaluate their offer, and choose with whom to seek refuge: the Nassau deputy county attorney or the mighty American eagle.

86

The night was wearing on, and I snorted a couple of lines of cocaine. No heroin. I wanted to keep it light, and at 11:30 I fell asleep. The next morning, another hot day, I called Stahl.

"I wanna talk to Detective Dan Stahl."

"Please state your name and the nature of your call."

"My name is Henry Hill."

"Spell your surname, please."

"What's a surname?"

"Your last name."

"Oh. H-I-L-L."

"Please hold, Mr. Hill.

Thirty seconds later. "Detective Stahl speaking. May I help you?"

"This is Henry Hill." I had a throat full of phlegm, and my voice was gravelly and tense. "I wanna talk things over with you, Detective Stahl."

There was a pause. "Mr. Hill! Well, well, well. I understand you got out on bail."

"Yeah, two days ago."

"Congratulations," Stahl said with typical blue-collar cop sarcasm. "So what're you wanna talk about?"

"We can start with Lufthansa."

"Glad you're comin' around, Mr. Hill. You wanna come to my office?"

I paused to think. "Eh . . . I could be there at eleven o'clock."

"You know where my office is?"

"Yeah, I know where you are. But honestly, I'm afraid to leave the house."

"Are you staying at the same address where we arrested you, Mr. Hill?"

"Yeah, why?"

Courteous the way a salesman sucks up to a customer, Stahl volunteered, "I'll send two uniformed officers to pick you up. How's that?"

"That's fine. I'll be ready at eleven. I gotta go, someone's at my door." I hastily hung up the phone and BOOM, BOOM, BOOM, another round of knocks but harder. *What the fuck,* I said to myself. I'm going for the door, and BANG, BANG, a third knock heavier and louder. I freed the deadbolt, and the door practically blew open as if a stick of dynamite had been lit.

"FBI, FREEZE! Put your hands up and don't move. You're under arrest." In a heartbeat, half a dozen men stormed into my split-level. In their uniforms of black pullovers, gray pants, and knee-high boots, these six commandos were a hell of a sight, and add to it the heavy weaponry, well, you'd figure these dudes were from *The Terminator*.

I froze owl-eyed. The moment the door had opened so violently, my split-second dread was that my time was up; Burke and Vario's executioners had come. And looking back, those shouts of, "FBI, FREEZE!," felt relaxing as when a doctor tells a cancer patient the biopsy test was negative.

87

Two strapping marshals and I, one in front of me and one behind, single filed into McDonald's office. A frank smile budded on the US attorney's lips as if turned on by a people-detecting sensor. "Mr. Hill, please be seated."

The federal officers muttered in low voices, saying they'd wait in the hall, and McDonald swung his attention to me. "I'm the prosecutor in charge of the Lufthansa investigation, and hopefully, I'll lead the prosecution of the perpetrators. I'm eager to work with you and hope to get to the bottom of all the facts related to this case."

McDonald seemed to be eyeing me up and down; the glassy eyeballs, a three-day grayish stubble, uncombed hair, and a stinky plaid shirt with a worn collar. I was a defeated, sad-faced hood reduced to begging for mercy, a far cry from the swanky, silk-suited gangster profiled by the FBI. I could see McDonald, out of kindliness, disregarding how disgraceful I must've looked.

"Mr. Hill, we're relying on you to fill in the blanks of the Lufthansa riddle."

"Call me Henry. My throat is dry. Any chance I could have a cold beer?"

I shouldn't have said that. McDonald covered both eyes with a hand and shook his head. He must've wished he hadn't gotten involved with me. He was polite and had the patience of a saint.

"Thanks for letting me call you Henry. Now it's time to establish some rules. Special Agent Carbone, his subordinates, and I will be debriefing you. And those sittings will not be informal chats as if we're friends at a bar having cocktails."

"Oh, sure, Ed. Just that I haven't had anything in my mouth since I woke up, and I'm thirsty."

"I didn't say you can call me Ed."

"I'm sorry, Mr. McDonald."

"It's OK. You can call me Ed. Back to the beer. I certainly understand you can be thirsty. How about some water?"

"Water! Water makes metal rust and sinks ships. Just think what it does to your stomach. Ha, ha, ha."

McDonald buzzed an assistant on the intercom and asked for a pitcher of water. "Henry, the immediate order of business is to make sure you and your family are protected."

"Yep, I'd say that's a good start."

"Temporarily, I'll have to place you in custody at the MCC—the Manhattan Correction Center. And not in the general population. I'll see to it that the marshals confine you to the third floor. And your wife and children will remain at your home under round-the-clock protection until the marshals can make arrangements for you to go to a safe house." McDonald's smile never wavered.

"What's on the third floor of the MCC?"

McDonald seemed uncomfortable with my question. "It's . . . it's a section exclusively designated for informants."

"You mean that's where they keep the rats caged up so nobody can get to them."

McDonald nodded, a bit of embarrassment on his face. "Yes, if you will. It's . . . it's a secured area of the MCC." Anxious to change the subject, he said, "Anyway, the approval of your admission into the Federal Witness Protection Program may take a month or two. In the interim, we have to situate you in a place that's secure from anyone who wishes you dead."

This was going too fast, and I put up my palms. "Whoa, whoa, Ed. I gotta think all this out. I mean, I wanna know what you're gonna do for me. Another thing, I gotta talk it over with my wife, 'cause if she don't wanna go into the program, I ain't goin' either."

"Henry," McDonald said tolerantly, "if you don't enroll in the witness program, the only other place you'll be going is to your grave. And that's guaranteed!" McDonald slid the telephone toward me. His smile melted. "Henry, listen and listen good. Get on the phone and tell your wife FBI agents will go to your house and drive her here so we can all discuss the steps you have to take."

I called Karen, and she didn't wanna hear it. She said there was no way she'd go into the witness program. And she hung up on me. Karen could be as stubborn as a mule with amnesia. That night, in my cell at the MCC, I didn't sleep too well. I was unsure of the proposal McDonald had put on the table. How was it possible for my drug indictments, like magic, to get quashed?

The hours dragged on, and near dawn a guard, a redneck with a heavy southern drawl, woke me. "Git up, Hill. We gotta git you ready and transport you to the federal buildin' in Brooklyn. You got an appointment with the US attorney and some o' the big boys up there."

McDonald leaned on the backrest of the swivel chair behind his desk. On the opposite side, Carbone, Guevara, and I were seated in a semicircle. "Mr. Hill," Carbone opened, "we reviewed your case, and the allegations are very, very serious." He arched his black eyebrows to add to the graveness of my dire straits—as if I didn't already know the pile of shit I was in.

Guevara tightened his jaws and nodded grimly to play up Carbone's sad song. I had heard this funeral march a hundred times before. "I know. I know the score." I straightened up. "Question is, what can you do for me?"

In a loose-fitting black suit and red tie, Carbone cocked his full head of hair and turned up both palms. "Mr. Hill, your question is premature. We can't guarantee you much unless you give us a prelude of the depositions you'd be giving us in conjunction with Lufthansa." Carbone glanced at Guevara and McDonald, and they dipped their heads up and down, reminding me of those bobbleheads in the mid-sixties on the dashboard of Puerto Ricans' cars.

Baffled, I squinted. "What the hell is a prelude? You didn't mean Quaaludes, did you?"

Swallowing a chuckle, McDonald eyed Carbone and cut in, "Agent Carbone meant we have to have an idea of the merits of your testimonies."

With the tell-them-whatever-they-want-to-hear embellishment of a used car salesman, I bragged, "Lemme say this. I can give you accounts of the craziest situations that in your careers as G-men you've never seen. Besides Lufthansa, I got dirt on some big, big names."

A veteran at hearing tantalizing but bullshit-coated yarns, Carbone, unmoved, replied, "Give us an example, Henry."

Knowing I had an audience, I got my second wind. "You want a name? How about Paul Vario? And here's more: Jimmy Burke, John Gotti, Tommy DeSimone, Stacks Edwards, Louis Cafora, Angelo Sepe, Frenchy McMahon, Joe Manri, Marty Krugman, Theresa Ferrara?" These were people tied to Lufthansa, names that, though the FBI had already suspected, only an insider could've known. I smirked the way a wiseass makes a point.

Carbone and Guevara seemed thunderstruck. They must've figured I had a lot of information to give them.

Two weeks earlier, having been freed on a $150,000 bond, I had kissed off my loyalties to the Mafia and jumped on the side of the Nassau deputy county attorney. And here I was, shrewdly backing out and teaming with the FBI, an agency invested with authority far beyond that of the local cops and county attorneys.

I had tricked Stahl and Florio.

88

While Hill agonized at the MCC, his wife was at home; on a twenty-four hour rotation, four federal marshals were guarding her and the two children. The bodyguards were 250-pounders, and it seemed as if the Hills' house had shrunk and became too cramped for the four bulky men.

Her instinct for hospitality kicking in, Karen offered them coffee. She opened the pantry, and there wasn't any. Shuffling her feet as a child does when holding in urine, she fussed, wringing her hands. "We don't have eggs for breakfast in the morning. No coffee either. I'll go to Waldbaums and get some things."

Lorne, one of the marshals, raised his palm, his eyes shooting a warning. "No, no, Mrs. Hill. We don't want you leaving the house."

At that moment, Karen's little girl, her brown hair in pigtails, came running noisily into the room. "Mommy, mommy, can you make me hot chocolate?"

"Not now, Gina," Karen said, shooing the child to her room and reverting to Lorne. "I want to go pick up . . ."

"No, no, no. Please stay put. Take care of your children," Lorne said with finality. "Make a list of what you need, and one of us will go and get it. Besides, you should be starting to pack and getting ready to leave here. I don't know what your husband and the FBI are working out, but you sure as hell can't stay here."

Overcome with sadness, Karen let herself plunge onto the couch. Tears streaming, she began bawling, her shoulders heaving. "I know Henry has to go into the witness program. Me . . . I don't think I can go through with it. I can't leave my whole life behind as if it never existed. I'm sorry I'm crying, but I can't let go of everything and everybody I know. I just can't . . ."

"There's no other way out, Mrs. Hill," Lorne said pity-eyed, though his gargantuan companions gaped indifferently at her.

She went to the kitchen, pulled a napkin out of its flowery dispenser, and dabbed her cheeks. Karen gazed emptily out the window over the sink, the orange sun resembling a burning ball, sinking beyond the horizon, the sky varying from blue to red.

Burke was climbing the walls. Hill hadn't responded to phone calls and messages, an ominous sign.

"Angelo," Burke said to Sepe, "I want you to do some prying around Henry's house. See what cars are parked there and check out anybody who could be a cop." Burke stared distantly as if he were trying to define the clouds. "Look for anything unusual. It's strange that Henry doesn't step foot past his front door. Strange, very strange."

Sepe smacked his left palm with the right fist. "I'll wait 'til dark and make a few passes around Hill's neighborhood." Clad in a black turtleneck with moth holes and a Yankees baseball cap, Sepe reveled, "I'd love to put a hole in that son of a bitch's skull."

"Don't you make a move on Henry unless I say so. Get it?"

"I was just thinkin' out loud, Jimmy."

"Next time, think to yourself."

Sepe returned from his reconnaissance of Hill's house. "Jimmy, I saw two Crown Vics parked in Hill's driveway. Definitely unmarked cars. Could be anybody. Maybe Nassau County cops, Port Authority, or FBI. But whoever was there stayed in the house the whole night."

Not a good sign, Burke contemplated. Hill seemed to have flipped. "He's gotta be singing to the cops. Shit!" Burke bit his lower lip. "Angelo, go give Pete Vario the scoop that Henry is ratting so he can let Paulie know immediately. We have to figure out what to do—*and* fast."

A few weeks earlier, when Stahl had arrested Hill for the drug felonies, the detective, ever-ambitious and motivated, hadn't terminated the eavesdropping on Hill's telephone. Stahl continued to listen in, and one late evening he was staggered when Hill spoke of an unimaginable scandal that, evidently, had been on going up to the day of his bust.

Baffled, the detective rewound the tape recordings over and over and thought he was hallucinating. Discussing drug dealings in coded terms, on numerous occasions Hill had mentioned, "the big Irishman up in Albany." Pondering this, Stahl remembered that back in 1974 New York Governor Hugh Carey's campaign ads had promoted him as "the big Irishman." The governor's mansion is in Albany. It suddenly clicked in the detective's mind; Carey had to have been "the big Irishman in Albany" Hill alluded to.

Ensnaring a governor partnering in a drug ring, "a big catch," made Daniel Stahl twist and turn the entire night. The next morning, he dashed into Bill Florio's office. "Bill, you are *not* going to believe what we picked up on Hill's phone yesterday."

His eyes enlarging with wonder, Florio leered at Stahl.

Stahl dragged over a chair and dug his elbows on the deputy county attorney's desk. "Are you ready for this? We decoded talks of a big Irishman in Albany."

"Who's the big Irishman?" Florio shrugged.

Eyes fatigued and bloodshot, and his psyche so enraptured, Stahl fumbled with the words. "Bill, it's . . . it's a code name for Hugh Carey, the governor."

Florio's mouth plunged to a gaping hole. "You gotta be kidding, Dan. If this is true, short of the president of the United States, we have the biggest fish we could ever hook and prosecute." He unconsciously chewed on his lip and fantasized, "I can just see the headlines all over America: *New York State Governor Hugh Carey Nabbed in a Heroin Ring.* Unbelievable!"

And this, apparently, was all Bill Florio saw, the vision of prosecuting a governor and the prominence and laurels that came with it. And under the assumption that Hill's cryptic references to the "the big Irishman" meant Hugh Carey, DCA Florio was willing to dismiss Hill's indictments provided he, Hill, testified against the governor. Florio's head glided into the stratosphere; for a prosecutor this is the jackpot of a lifetime.

89

Screaming and cursing, shoving and pushing, eyes red from crying, my wife came to terms with a realization: She had no choice but to join me in the witness program. If she refused, as McDonald had told her, unless I backed out of ratting out on Jimmy and Vario, *they'd* get to her and the children.

"Besides, Karen," McDonald stressed, "DCA Florio will indict you in Nassau County as an accessory to Henry's narcotics trafficking." He spread his arms and warned, "There are no alternatives."

As though she were a new widow, Karen hung her head and sniveled. "It feels as if our lives are over."

"Correction, Karen," McDonald said, waggling his index finger. "Your lives are over as *you led them.* And that's not to say you can't start over with a clean slate. Hopefully, on the right foot."

That said, Karen and I jumped onboard the McDonald rocket to freedom and safety.

90

Florio and Stahl were in a sweaty frenzy, certain Hill had skipped town. In mid-May of 1980, he hadn't appeared at a pretrial hearing in Nassau County District Court. The courthouse, a fortress-like limestone edifice surrounded by a lawn expanding to a suburban block, is on Old Country Road in Mineola, a town one mile north of Garden City, Long Island.

The telephone operator rang McDonald's office. "Mr. McDonald, a deputy county attorney from Nassau County is on line four, and he's *demanding*, to talk to you."

"Demanding to talk to me! Put him through, please." McDonald guessed the nature of this call. "McDonald here." Whenever he spoke by phone, he had a smile on so not to sound bitter or angry.

In contrast, the caller's tenor was in a fury. "This is DCA Bill Florio from Nassau County. Where *is* Henry Hill?"

"Good morning to *you*, Mr. Florio," McDonald said. "I had Mr. Hill rearrested on a material witness order, and he's now in federal protective custody."

"Needless to mention, Mr. McDonald . . ."

"Please call me Ed," the US attorney said with softness.

"Eh, thank you," Florio replied uncomfortably. "Hill is a defendant under my jurisdiction, and I'm ready to prosecute him for his outstanding indictments."

"I'm aware of it, Bill. Oh, forgive me, please. May I call you Bill?" McDonald instinctively shed formalities.

"Eh . . . yes."

"I meant to notify your office of Hill's present status. He'll be cooperating with our investigation of the Lufthansa robbery. Naturally, I hope we can agree to certain stipulations for your office and mine to share him as a potential witness. And it won't be limited to *my* Lufthansa case. Hill may be of assistance to you in indicting suspects unrelated to Lufthansa."

"In principle," Florio said wryly, "I'm agreeable. When might it be convenient to discuss it in person?"

McDonald flipped through the pages of his calendar. "Thursday, the day after tomorrow, at my office will be fine with me. And the reason we have to meet at my office is because I have an on going grand jury inquiry, and I must be available on a minute-to-minute basis."

"I have to check my diary." A pause. "Thursday will work for me. Say, at ten o'clock. Is that OK?" Florio said tersely.

"That'll work. Looking forward, Bill," McDonald bid cheerily.

Florio didn't relish sharing Henry Hill with Ed McDonald. The idea of going head to head with a federal prosecutor, especially one who belonged to the Special Organized Crime Task Force, roused butterflies to Florio's stomach. And clear on the certainty that McDonald could've and *would've* fought for access to Hill, in consolation to his scraped ego Florio saw the US attorney's compromise as a concession he could digest.

Thursday, June 9, 1980, was swamped in a thundering, muggy, downpour, and Florio was en route to the Brooklyn Federal Court complex. Delayed in stifled rush-hour traffic, he was fussing to see through the windshield of his blue Jaguar XJ12 convertible. The westbound lanes of the Long Island Expressway, certified by disgruntled motorists as the world's largest parking lot, were at a near standstill. The convertible top of Florio's vintage Jaguar was leaking water, wetting the left side of his head and shoulder, splotching his tan jacket. The defogging system was inadequate in clearing the windows of fog and humidity, adding havoc to the hair-whipping rain. It had been a stressful drive, an hour and a half longer than usual, and when Florio reached the federal court he was a ball of nerves.

He let his overstuffed briefcase drop onto the gray marble tiles in front of the reception booth and closed his eyes for a second. He hissed out a pent-up breath of air. "I'm Bill Florio, and I have an appointment with Mr. McDonald."

The receptionist, a freckled redhead with a squeaky voice, greeted him. "Mr. McDonald's in a grand jury room. He should've been out by now. But there may be delays."

His balding head still soaked, Florio pounded the redhead's desk and complained loudly, "What do you mean? I have a ten o'clock appointment with him. I drove through hell for two and a half hours."

Skillful at placating, the receptionist replied, "I understand, Mr. Florio, and I do apologize. Sometimes these sessions go on unexpectedly. Why don't you have a seat? Maybe you could use some coffee or tea. May I get you something?"

Feeling as if he'd been demoted to a minor league, Florio brooded. He couldn't believe that he, a deputy county attorney with a splendid future, was at the mercy of a measly assistant US attorney. To add insult to injury, here he was, about to soar and ascend to national stardom by prosecuting a New York governor, and this prissy missy, who didn't look older than a girl who just survived the agony of her first menstrual cycle, had taken a stab at pacifying him. Florio wiped his brow and asked with impatience, "How long before Mr. McDonald is back?"

The redhead noticed the wet beads on Florio's head beginning to boil. "Sir, it's hard to say. Mr. McDonald could return in five minutes, or it may be an hour. Why don't I get you a cup of warm coffee?"

For an hour, Florio paced frantically in the reception area, huffing in exasperation; his damp jacket was somewhat drier, though his skull looked steamier and redder. At last, McDonald appeared at the end of the hallway, a thick brown manila folder under his arm. Strutting briskly in the direction of the reception desk, arm prematurely stretched out for a handshake, and his smile turned on to the highest setting, McDonald ventured, "Bill Florio?"

"Yes, a *mad* Bill Florio. You must be Ed McDonald."

The lateness wasn't McDonald's fault—his supervisor had assigned him to a case of epic proportion, which he'd had to present to a grand jury. Nonetheless, McDonald switched to his specialty mode, extinguishing explosive fuses. "I'm sorry for my lateness, Bill. I'm overloaded with cases and hadn't foreseen this major one winding up in front of a grand jury this morning." Sensing Florio's fury losing steam, McDonald turned on his graciousness. In a toasty warmth he said, "Let's go to my office and relax. Looks like you had a rough commute."

Drinking hot coffee and breathing slower, Florio's inflamed mood had cooled, and his jacket and shirt were drying. McDonald tilted back in his chair and folded his arms across his chest. "I believe Hill will cooperate with you in whatever way he can render himself useful. In return,

I must tell you, he'll want nothing short of walking away from your pending narcotic charges."

Florio didn't belabor the point and adhered to his professionalism. "Is Hill represented by legal counsel?"

"He is, for the moment," McDonald answered laughingly, "but he will dismiss him."

Florio looked uncertain. "Why?"

"Hill's lawyer, Richard Otto, is also Paul Vario's attorney *and* close friend."

"I get it. Hill is afraid that whatever deal he strikes with you or me will be covertly fed back to Vario and Burke. And those two will see to it that Hill doesn't testify against them."

"That's a fair assessment, Bill."

McDonald's goal was for Hill to be a worthy informant and ward off Florio's drug prosecution so he could take cover in the Witness Protection Program and assist in the Lufthansa probe.

In the course of that afternoon, McDonald and Florio drafted a pact, which included Hill giving oral and written affidavits that, at day's end, was to sweep the streets clean of Vario and Burke, and most important to Florio, for him to collar "the big Irishman in Albany," Governor Hugh Carey.

It wasn't a tough sell for Florio to persuade his superiors to meet Hill's demands. The entire staff of the county attorney's office was infatuated with the sweet notion of arresting and placing Governor Carey behind bars. "Bill," Florio's boss said passionately, "Hugh Carey! Th . . . this . . . can be big, really huge. This . . . this only presents itself once in a blue moon."

"I know, I know," Florio acknowledged hungrily. "So do we give Hill immunity and a walk?"

Bill Florio's supervisor urged on, "Sure, sure. Prepare a plea agreement, have Hill's attorney agree to it, and we'll get a judge to approve it."

A district court judge ratified the written covenants between Defendant Henry Hill and the People of the State of New York. In simple terms, this accord specified for Hill to lay bare the inner workings of his tristate narcotics operation and identify his co-conspirators. In exchange, Florio consented not to prosecute Hill for the Nassau County indictments, consigning him exclusively to McDonald. Florio was content with this. Thanks to Hill, they were about to land the big prize, Governor Carey. The rest of Hill's partners in crime, whose necks he could line up on the deputy county attorney's butcher block, were small-fry compared to parading a handcuffed governor before television cameras. As for Lufthansa, Florio wasn't interested because it belonged to the FBI and the US attorney.

All parties came to terms and sketched out Hill's duties as a government witness on the local and federal levels. Florio added Hill to his den of informants, and when they'd convict Governor Carey, the reward would be a dream come true. Carbone and his FBI team would get credit for solving "the greatest robbery of the century," jettisoning them to national notoriety. Books and movie deals, or a variety of lucrative offers from the private sector might come knocking.

Last but not least, McDonald's wish to jail Jimmy Burke and his delinquents promised an exhilarating reward. He visualized headlines from New York to California touting him as one of the cleverest and most esteemed assistant US attorneys in the country. Simply put, it was a win-win situation for all sides. Everyone was now sailing under blue skies with fair winds and a following sea.

Formally in the Federal Witness Protection Program, Henry Hill, Karen, and their two children were shrouded by a posse of US marshals who moved them from location to location in New York, Connecticut, and Pennsylvania. This roving was a necessity. The government hadn't yet chosen a suitable site to relocate permanently the Hill family. Secondly, Hill had to be in proximity to Nassau County; it had been agreed for McDonald to avail Hill whenever Florio required him as a witness against his past associates, Governor Carey ranking the highest. The third reason for shuffling Hill from safe house to safe house was one of immediacy. The turncoat's former clan had managed to hone in on "the rat," setting off Hill's nerves-knotting dreads about the torture they'd inflict before killing him.

Initially, the US marshals zeroed in on East Hampton as a temporary hideout. This township is one of the Hamptons' summer resorts, a world-renowned playground of the wealthy, spanning forty miles on the southeastern ocean shore of Long Island. The Hamptons personify exclusivity, and during the summer months, vacationers from all over the United States and Europe flock to those seaside hamlets. Many are politicians and entertainers, two diverse societies that most often reverse roles and somehow excel at either one. And because groves of authors, television, and Hollywood personages are regulars in the Hamptons, this retreat is dubbed Malibu on the Atlantic. There you won't find tall buildings, malls, mega shopping centers, and gaudy neon signs—just sleepy, shady streets lined with poplars and large-trunk spruces. Over decades, developers have expanded the post–World War II summer cottages into palaces secluded behind walls of hedges. Miles and miles of sparkling beaches, where basking in drier weather is a marvel, buffer this taste of paradise from the mighty Atlantic. And to think of this splendor as a hideout for Hill, the product of Mafia upbringing, well, it connoted a mismatch—the jester of the Crimson Court on the king's throne.

91

"Hey, I can get used to this," I told the federal marshals as I chucked my blue blazer on a cotton-covered couch in the East Hampton safe house.

One of the marshals, Jake, slipped the soggy cigar from his lips and said in his Texan twang, "Don't get too damn cozy 'cause we ain't stayin' here too darn long."

"Why, this is the life, Jake." I took in a gulp of sea air gusting in from an open window and stared at the sheer white curtains blowing in the wind.

Jake pointed the cigar at me, smoke swirling and polluting the room. In a drawl, sounding as if it came from a tape recorder running at a slower speed, he said, "If one of your pals finds out you're here, Hill—and by the way, we're only a hundred miles from your old neighborhood—it ain't too safe here."

My stay in East Hampton was supposed to last until Florio finished with me. He found my snitching valuable, and he and his boss couldn't have been happier.

But the party soon ended, and Florio's smooth sail ran aground. I was in his office when the plea agreement we'd worked out fell apart. Out of the blue, Florio jumped up like a maniac and screamed out, "What do you mean, Jimmy Burke is not *the big Irishman?*"

The way he yelled at me took me by surprise. "Yeah, as I told you we used to call Jimmy Burke the big Irishman. Who'd you think we meant?"

"We understood your reference to the big Irishman to be Governor Hugh Carey."

I burst out in a gut-ripping laugh. "Governor Carey? How . . . how the hell did you come up with that?"

Florio's face drew a blank. He sifted through his paperwork as if the answer to contradict what I had said was in there. "It says here . . . eh, the big Irishman is . . . is Hugh Carey."

Grinning, I shook my head in amazement. "I don't know where you're gettin' this."

Florio's cheeks heated to an apple red. He pushed himself away from the desk and tossed his pen on a pile of papers. "Let's back up here for a minute, Henry. *What* do you mean, Carey is not the big Irishman?"

"I mean just that. As I said, the big Irishman I was talkin' about with my runners is Jimmy Burke."

Florio fished a white handkerchief from a pocket of his trousers and wiped his forehead. "You're saying Governor Carey had no complicity in your narcotics distribution?"

I couldn't believe Florio's far-out idea. "I don't even know the man, and I didn't even vote for him."

Florio, so enraged, started to pant. "Then I'm afraid we have to scrap this whole arrangement and proceed with the indictments. You aren't able to furnish us with anything of substance."

"Whaaaat!" I yelled out, my lips curled in a snarl. "I told you whatever I know, and that's all I'm supposed to do. It's not my fuckin' fault you thought this big Irishman was Hugh Carey. I never said he was."

"This was not my understanding."

Then he dropped a bomb. "I'm sorry, but I'll have to rescind the plea agreement."

92

On learning of Florio's reneging on his arrangement with Hill, McDonald objected. "Bill, you can't do this."

Florio tensely chewed on his pen and wriggled in his chair. "Hill did not provide us with substantive testimony or indictable facts."

"Hill complied with *and* met his commitment to the best of his ability. And the key term is, *to the best of his ability*. You can't rescind the agreement and go forward with prosecuting him because you misconstrued who *the big Irishman* is. It's not Hill's fault."

"We can't even use Hill as a witness against Burke. So we're also screwed on that end," Florio lamented.

"The testimony of an accomplice is not sufficient to convict in this state. It's elementary in criminal law, and you damn well knew it before you executed the plea agreement."

"Well, my supervisor wants to annul the deal and put Hill on trial, and I'm in accord."

A rare surge of temper made McDonald's eyebrows come together. "I'll oppose it and let a judge decide this issue."

The settlement that had been forged—a reasonable resolution equitable to Florio, McDonald, Carbone, and Hill—was crumbling faster than a sand castle awash in a surf. Everybody's stakes were floating out to sea. Florio had lost the "once-in-a-lifetime chance" to destroy a governor. McDonald's last resort at nailing Burke and Vario for Lufthansa was evaporating; Carbone's chance at succeeding J. Edgar Hoover was now as bleak as the prospect of getting rich selling bikinis in the Arctic Circle. And the miracle for Defendant Hill to skirt fifty years behind bars seemed as though the angels were copping out.

Carbone was baffled by Florio. This zealous prosecutor had overreacted and was blaming Hill. "This is an abomination, Ed," Carbone proclaimed. "How . . . how can Florio not honor the agreement he made with Hill? If he convicts him, Hill won't have any incentive to work with us, and there goes Lufthansa down the drain." He squeezed his temples with his thumb and forefinger as though he were massaging a headache. "Do we have any options?"

McDonald thought for several seconds. "I'll talk to my supervisor, Tom Puccio. I'm pretty sure there's a provision in the New York State statutes to petition for a hearing on whether a prosecutor is inescapably bound to uphold an executed plea bargain."

Carbone leapt off his chair. "Well, let's do it."

"Steve, I said I have to speak with my supervisor. And it'd be wise to research the state laws and make sure there aren't any loopholes Florio can invoke to automatically void his deal with Hill."

At the Nassau County District Court in Mineola, Judge John McElhone was set to hear arguments with respect to Hill's plea agreement. Six federal marshals had transported Hill from the Hamptons' safe house. This was his first public appearance as a "Mafia rat," and the escorts, armed with heavy artillery, were ultra cautious with impenetrable security.

Five minutes into the hearing, mudslinging among the lawyers began, and voices grew louder. "Come to order." Honorable McElhone, his head hairless, grimaced at the attorneys. "Let's get to the crux of this." He glared heatedly at DCA Florio. "You may begin."

Florio sidled to the lectern, and rambled on, "Defendant Hill failed to supply the Office of the Nassau County Attorney with concrete evidence and particulars of prosecutable merit." In a whimpering appeal, Florio summed up, "Your Honor, simply put, Defendant Hill has been of no use to me and my superiors."

Judge McElhone, cheeks pale and silvery, removed his glasses and in slow motion polished them with a paper tissue. "Mr. McDonald," he said, "your rebuttal, please."

McDonald stepped forward with importance. "My contention is that the defendant, to the best of his ability and recollection, did fulfill the stipulations of his plea covenants with the deputy county attorney. I therefore submit, Your Honor, Mr. Hill has been truthful and forthright with Mr. Florio and his investigators. The county attorney's office, how-ever, had presumed incorrectly that Governor Hugh Carey was a certain individual whom Mr. Hill named as *'the big Irishman'*—and whom Mr. Florio misconstrued to have been Hill's coconspirator in his drug ring. It was an unprofessional misjudgment on the part of Mr. Florio, and the defendant should not be penalized."

McDonald's opening statements seemed to have awakened Judge McElhone as though he'd been splashed with a bucket of ice water. "Governor Carey!? What does he have to do with this case?"

With a citric smile, McDonald turned to his right and faced Florio. "Absolutely nothing, Your Honor, other than the suspicions of the re-spected assistant county attorney."

The judge couldn't have looked more confounded, and the crowd ruptured into a laughing fit. Only Florio saw no humor in this. He shut his eyes tight and winced.

McDonald swung in the direction of the defendant's table and, re-garding Hill kindly, petitioned, "I therefore request, Your Honor, for this court to uphold the plea agreement entered into by the county attorney and defendant Henry Hill."

Unceremoniously, the judge decreed, "Fine. I'll reserve judgment, and all parties will be notified. Court is adjourned." Judge McElhone rapped his gavel and stepped down from the bench, head shaking, his black robe fluttering as he burrowed through the oak-wainscoted door leading to a private chamber.

McDonald, Guevara, and Carbone walked briskly out of the courthouse, an anticipated victory in their bounce. Enlivening the day, was the mid-fall season, bedecking the topography of the courthouse grounds with natural colors. The leaves breezing on the 65-foot elms had shed their green and mutated to a prism of orange, red, violet, and yellow high-lighted by a blue sky as if it were a canvas backdrop—a marvel of a vista on Long Island.

Hill's outlook was not as sprightly. "Maybe," he suggested to his con-science, "while I still got the chance, it might be time to seriously think about skipping out."

93

Two days after the hearing before Judge McElhone, another azure sky hosting a crisp air was burning through the morning haze. McDonald walked out the door of his home, glanced up, and sucked in a breath of air. The balminess seemed to symbolize a triumph, though he couldn't predict how, when, and where. On reaching his office, he whisked past his receptionist, and she handed him a message. "Oct. 18, 8:56 a.m. Doug Feuerbach called and said Judge McElhone dismissed the charges against Hill and for him to be in the custody of the Federal Witness Protection Program. You should receive the memorandum in about two to three days." Feuerbach was law secretary to Judge McElhone. McDonald stripped off his trench coat and tossed it sloppily on one of the chairs near his desk.

Florio was humiliated. The career-making event, the capture and incarceration of a crooked governor, had been a figment of his imagination. And bucking all odds, Hill had slipped out of Florio's noose, stealing a headlining drug prosecution from the deputy county attorney.

And there were other sorry souls. Lieutenant Ahearn and Captain DeGeneste were not destined to see their names in print for capturing the Lufthansa perps. On this day, the winners' circle belonged to McDonald and Carbone—and the ultimate winner, Hill. Who could have imagined that he, the underdog least expected to dodge Burke's carnage, and who had harrowingly shirked the loss of his liberty, resurfaced, not only unscathed, but free as a bird—the luck of the Irish, *me lad.*

94

When I got the good news from McDonald, I thought I was dreaming. "It feels good to see Florio—the worm that he is—left with nothing but his dick in his hands."

"Florio was just doing his job. Nothing personal, Henry."

"Easy for you to say. The rope wasn't around your collar," I said, stroking my neck as if to make sure the noose wasn't really there.

McDonald said, "We're going to take a break for the rest of the week. It'll give you and Karen a chance to settle into the safe house. On Monday, I'll have the marshals drive you to my office, and we'll get back to work. Meantime, hope you have a relaxing weekend in the Hamptons."

"What a difference forty-eight hours makes," I said to Karen. "From looking at fifty years in the joint, and most likely gettin' killed in there, to hanging out in the Hamptons."

I was barefoot and in white tennis shorts, strolling lazily with Karen on the warm sand of Main Beach in East Hampton, a mild wind ruffling our hair. I squinted at the sun, touched my mouth, and kissed the sky. On a thankful note, I sang out, "Only in America!"

We walked along the water, our feet wading in the waves. Karen hooked her arm around my waist and tilted her head on my shoulder. "Henry, I'm sorry for putting up a big fuss. I didn't wanna leave everything I've known. I couldn't think of never seeing my parents and my sister ever again."

She tightened her hold on me and, teary-eyed, admitted, "Now, I'm kind of glad we're getting away from the insanity we've been living in. I'm actually anxious to start over in a new city, a different neighborhood, a new home."

Karen then let go of my waist and took a step back. "And . . . and no more girlfriends, Henry. You promised me! No more Lindas, no more Marleys, and who knows who. Got it?"

I gazed into the salty mist hazing the water line and paid her no mind. Karen stopped, feet slightly apart, head bent to the side. She winged both arms on her hips and hollered, "Henryyyy! You *got it?*"

I got close to Karen, pulled aside the collar of her pink blouse, and kissed her neck, the surf swishing around our ankles. "I got it, I got it." I smiled and read her insecurities for the silliness of a woman. For weeks on end I had shacked up at my mistress's apartment, not seeing it as a marriage-stressing issue. Then, after all that had happened, I saw our situation differently. To redeem myself, I was willing to stop running around with broads. "What're you worried about, Karen? I'm here with you, ain't I?"

She tugged at my ear, gnashing her teeth. "You wanna know what I'm worried about? Let me list a few: Linda, Marley, Lynn, Carol, Michelle, and . . ."

"All right! All right! Knock it off. That's all in the past. We're starting a new path. It's gonna be just you and me, baby. Just you and me. And the kids."

"It better be, Henry, or else I'll pack Gina and Greg and go back to my parents. And I mean it. And before I leave you, I'll shove my foot up your balls." Karen feigned a kick to my groin and waded into the water until she was knee-deep, her blue cotton skirt soaked and sticking to her juicy thighs.

Life was good again. Or so I thought.

A week had passed since our stroll on the beach, and I was in a convoy of three vehicles, black Ford Crown Victorias, cruising westward on Route 27. In the second Crown Victoria—the one in the middle of the motorcade—four federal marshals were escorting me to my first commute from the East Hampton safe house to the US attorney's office in downtown Brooklyn.

The two hour and forty minute drive was scenic, a trip I couldn't have envisioned. I'd never been in these parts of Long Island, and vineyard after vineyard astonished me. I thought only California produced grapes and wine. The marshal sitting to my left must've been reading my mind. "Henry, depending on the year, the local burgundies put the California brands to shame."

Then we passed hundreds of acres of fruit orchards—peaches, apricots, plums. Two or three miles ahead, I saw strawberry patches. At the age of thirty-seven, I got to know the eastern end of Long Island, surprised to see it isn't just about the Hamptons, but it's also where you can get homegrown fruit and damn good wine grapes.

I licked my lips. "I'd sure love a glass of red wop right now."

"That's gonna have to wait, Henry," one of the marshals said, the car slowing to a crawl, traffic congesting the exit ramp. "We gotta get you to Mr. McDonald clean and sober."

Tapping the steering wheel, the driver grumbled, "Hope this clears up soon, or we may not get into Brooklyn until the afternoon."

The marshal riding shotgun twisted his neck toward me and chuckled with a smoker's gurgle. "Who cares when we get there? We're getting paid no matter what, you included, Henry. Right?"

On the two-lane exit ramp, the traffic was rolling at five miles per hour. The third Crown Victoria was now in the left lane, tailing the one I was in by forty to fifty feet, and the three marshals in this last vehicle were watching something odd going on.

In the right lane, a green SUV with tinted windows was creeping next to our car. I found that strange, too. The left rear window of the fucking SUV started sliding down, and I thought I caught the shadows of two black-hooded heads, eyes blinking nervously, though from my angle I couldn't get a good view of them.

95

The marshal in the third car radioed us. "Come in, Barry. This is Eddie. Over."

Barry was sitting next to the driver, Ralph. The radio crackled as Barry talked into the mike. "This is Barry. Over."

"Barry, tell Ralph to drive away from that damn green SUV next to you. Either get ahead of it, or fall back a bit. There's something funny going on in there."

Me and my four bodyguards looked to our right and spotted the black barrels of two shotguns through the open window of the SUV, a paralyzing sight. "Get away from this fuckin' SUV. Turn left onto the grass, turn left, God damn it," I shouted, pounding on Ralph's headrest. "God damn it! Move over to the left, Ralph. We're about to get shot at. Move over, Ralph!"

Wild-eyed, Barry and two of his coworkers fumbled to cock their weapons, shotguns they'd had resting on the floor between their legs. In a split-second, two ear-deafening blasts with an orange flash detonated from inside the SUV, shattering the windows on the right side of the Crown Vic. The two deadly forces of pellets and shards of glass crashed across the passenger side, literally tearing off the right shoulder of the marshal to my right, and shredding Barry's jaw and upper neck.

Ralph panicked and, his face and uniform splattered with Barry's blood, steered onto the grassy shoulder and into a ravine where the automobile bumped along for a hundred feet or so, ultimately smashing into an electrical pole. A millisecond prior to the shooting, I had bent forward, and the stray pellets missed me. The bleeding marshal, breathing spastically, his gray shirt saturated with blood, had slumped over on my back. In the front seat, Barry's torso had fallen forward, his head wobbling on the dashboard. Of five passengers, the gunmen had shot two of us, though everyone was bloodied, making it confusing to see who was wounded and who wasn't. Red was everywhere, on the seats, the carpets, the headliner, the beige vinyl door panels. Everywhere!

The SUV sped off, tires ripping and raising smoke, leaving in its wake the stench of scorched rubber. The vehicle zigzagged in and out of the clusters of stalled cars. Many of them had collided into one another in the chaos, blocking access to the exit lane. The marshals from the tailing Crown Victoria piled out and fired rifle shots at the SUV, but none hit it. In seconds, the runaways raced to an elbow curve at the end of the exit ramp and disappeared. I was still on the floor in the rear of the torn-up automobile, and not to chance leaving me unprotected, in case back-up ambushers might've been nearby in another car, my entourage didn't give chase to the snipers.

It was mayhem. Unaware the assailants had escaped, the bystanders locked themselves inside their vehicles. The marshals were the only ones who could call for assistance, thanks to their two-way radios. Ralph switched his portable to channel nine and contacted the Southampton police. "This is federal marshal Ralph McDermott. I have an emergency. A shooting. Over."

There had been ten marshals, including the two injured. Ralph and three colleagues stayed close to me; my skin must've been whiter than snow. The rest of my protectors had spread among the stalled traffic, calming everyone. One lane of the ramp had to be cleared for the much-awaited response personnel.

The attempted bushwhack was as close as I had ever come to meeting death. One of my enemies, most likely Jimmy, somehow had pinpointed the general whereabouts of the safe house, and this breach was the newest headache for the Feds. They had to relocate me and my family, and fast. So much for bumming on the beaches of the Hamptons.

As the madness and commotion quieted, a nerve-gripping thought got my heart racing. "My wife! My wife and kids!" I yelled out. "We gotta go back to the safe house. Those bastards could've gotten to them. Let's go, let's go!"

Amazingly collected and unruffled, Ralph did a 360-degree scan. He then waved on everyone else.

My guards, mouths open, looked at one another, concern in their eyes, and Ralph cried out, "Damn right. Let's go."

We all squeezed into the two Crown Vics—the third one with the shattered windows was left behind for a flatbed to tow away—and rushed back to East Hampton, the sights not as pretty as they'd been on the way out. Scared, I was seeing the surroundings as colorless, black and white.

96

On the one lane Route 27, pushing way beyond the forty-five mph speed limit, Ralph weaved in and out of the shoulder of the road, passing red lights. The Crown Victoria with the rest of the marshals was right behind us, almost tailgating.

My clothes had started out as a black, long-sleeved shirt and pleated beige slacks, and now they were unrecognizable. Blood and chunks of raw flesh stained my designer threads like a butcher's apron. I was a nervous wreck; with every clicking minute, the odds of us finding Karen and my kids unharmed were getting slimmer. Grief over the two fallen marshals had dampened everybody's mood. We didn't know how bad the damage from the shotgun pellets was, but it didn't take a doctor to understand the graveness of the injuries, or more accurately, mutilations.

The speeding Crown Vics whizzed through Hampton Bays, then Southampton, Watermill, and Bridgehampton. We were crossing Wainscott, and my heart was beating faster than the cars, my knees and feet twitching. "How much longer, Ralph?"

Clutching the steering wheel, Ralph glanced in the rearview mirror, and his green eyes met mine. "We should get into East Hampton in ten minutes."

"Step on it, Ralph. Step on it, please."

We made it to Hildreth Lane, the street where the safe house stood, a cedar-shingled, tiny home that was actually a bungalow. Ralph steered into the driveway, tailed by the other Crown Victoria, gravel crunching under the tires. The automobiles stopped, and all four doors popped open, as though sprung by a powerful mechanical force. With me in the lead, we sprinted up to the porch. I yanked on the wooden screen partition, unlocked the door, and rushed into the house.

I turned my neck in all directions, eyelids flickering and hysterics out of control. "Karen, Karen." No answer, but the stereo was on: *Riders on the storm . . .*

On a two-tiered cabinet, a brown-stained stand, stood a television and a stereo tuner with green, red, and orange blinking indicator lights. In a stomping trudge, I ran to the cabinet, and in a moment of madness I kicked the tuner. It tumbled onto the planked floor, quashing the music. "Damn it! She must've been dragged out of here in a hurry."

Everybody spread out on the ground floor, tearing from room to room. Ralph called out, "Greg, Gina. Are you here?"

Skipping steps, I bounded up the stairs; all the windows were open, curtains fluttering. "Karen. For Christ sake, answer me. Karen, goddamn it, where the fuck are you?"

I checked the bedrooms, bathroom, and closets, slamming doors and kicking chairs. On the ground floor, the eight marshals were grouped by the front door, everyone breathless. Ralph was checking the lock on the door. "I don't see signs of forced entry."

Lonny, the tallest of the marshals, shook his head, frowning. "That means nothing, Ralph. The perps could've knocked, and Karen might've let them in."

Distraught and on the verge of tears, with quavering fingers I lit a cigarette. I puffed out a cloud of smoke. "Nah. If she was alone, she wouldn't have opened the door. Maybe she went to Waldbaums for groceries. Let's go there."

"We should call Agent Carbone and fill him in on the sniping incident and the casualties," Ralph said.

97

Over the phone, Ralph explained to Carbone what was going on.

I was standing close to Ralph and could faintly hear Carbone's voice in the receiver. "Ralph, I'm glad most of you were unharmed. But I feel bad about your two colleagues. I'm sending a few agents out to you immediately. They'll be there in two to three hours. Meantime, stay close to Hill, and exercise caution. And before we press the panic button, inquire with the neighbors if they might've seen or spoken with Karen. It's possible she may have gone to the beach or something."

"Will do, Mr. Carbone."

I pushed on, "Let's get going and find my wife and kids."

Outside, everyone scuttled to knock on neighbors' doors. No one had seen Karen or the kids. Back into the cars, we drove to Waldbaums on Newtown Lane, and looked through the inside of the supermarket. We went to other stores in the area, storming in and out like a bunch of crazies who had escaped from a cuckoo house. I was a wreck, and Lonny consoled, "Henry, take it easy. Don't jump to conclusions. As Agent Carbone suggested, maybe they're at the beach."

"I hope you're right. If Jimmy hurt my family, I swear I'll personally fuckin' whack him." I spat on the ground and wiped my eyes. If any harm came to my family, I'd be so guilt-ridden that after killing Jimmy, I'd put a gun to my own temple.

Main Beach in East Hampton stretches for three miles, and on a flood tide the surf can rise up to ten feet, a surfer's wish. On summer weekends, bathers lying on oversized towels, roasting in the sun, pack every square foot of sand. But it was a Monday, and we didn't have to search long to be grimly let down at the no sight of Karen and the two tots.

Bleak-faced, Ralph patted down his reddish-blond hair that was ruffling in the wind. "Where do we go from here?"

On the lonely beach, the bunched marshals, stocky and overly tall in their scary gray and black uniforms, were attracting the attention of the sparse beachgoers. "Let's get out of here," Lonny said.

"Hey, what about the beach on the sound inlet? The one she went to with the kids a couple of days ago," Ralph suggested.

"Devon Beach," I said. "Let's go, let's go."

We all piled in the Crown Vics and sped there. Before we came to a full stop in the parking field, the doors sprang open. We jumped out and scampered frantically here and there from one end of the beachhead to the other. The pebbled shoreline is a mere five hundred feet long, and on this weekday, it was deserted. No Karen.

It was getting hopeless, and the marshals thought we should go back to the safe house and call the East Hampton Police Department so it could join in the search.

I was shaking from head to toe. "Where the hell could she have gone without a car? I mean, how far could she get?"

"If Karen and the kids were abducted," Ralph said, "say, sometime after we left the Hamptons earlier this morning, by now they could be in another state."

"Thanks, Ralph," I said, fright in my voice. "Let's just get back to the safe house and call the cops."

Jake, one of the bodyguards, a quiet type, said, "Mr. Carbone's agents should be getting out here pretty soon. We should let them call the next shot."

The Crown Victorias turned into the driveway of the safe house. The front door of the homey cottage, white paint flaking off, was slightly ajar. Panicked, I bolted toward the cedar porch, and Ralph firmed his hand on my shoulder. "Henry, hold it. Let us go in ahead. Somebody could be inside waiting to open fire. Stay outside."

Jake signaled his colleagues to arm their rifles, and he and three of them tiptoed to the porch, rustling gravel beneath their boots. Two of the marshals and I crouched behind one of the cars some sixty feet from the barn, one door hanging loosely off its top hinge. Holding the rifle with the right hand, Jake raised his left arm, a sign he was ready to storm the house. Shoulder first, he threw his 230 pounds into the door, and it slammed into the foyer wall.

I couldn't resist following them. Lonny had soft-stepped inside, his rifle aimed into the room. Ralph and Jake followed, eyes darting left and right. I stayed back about ten feet, and a stinging reek pricked my nostrils. Someone was in the house, and Karen's voice sounded off in the kitchen.

She was screaming, "No, no. Stop it! Please don't put it on my face. Please don't! Doooon't!"

"I smell ether, the gas dentists use," Lonny hushed. "They're choking her with it. Let's move in on them. Everybody ready?"

They nodded in unison, jaws clenched and lips tight. "We'll charge in on three," Jake whispered. "One, two, three."

Lonny, Jake, and Ralph stormed into the kitchen, me right behind, to find Karen at the dinette table, removing her nail polish, and little Gina fooling around with a cotton ball. She was dabbing her mother's lips with it, wanting to wipe off the lipstick.

On seeing this SWAT team, Karen's eyes widened in terror, her body stiffening. In a jerky reaction of surprise, she gulped and sighed. "What's going on?" Then she sat back. She patted her chest and huffed out a breath of air. "Whew. It's . . . it's you fellows. You scared the hell out of me. What . . . what are you doing back here?"

Relieved to see my wife and children, I burbled, "Where the hell have you been? We've been goin' nuts lookin' for you."

"I don't understand. Why are you so upset? We went to a hiking trail and then to the drugstore on Main Street. What's the big deal, Henry?"

"What's the big deal? Karen, there's all kinds of people wanting to whack us, and you're runnin' around town as if we're on vacation at a resort."

"I thought you said we're safe here?"

"We ain't safe anywhere, Karen!"

98

The scare of almost having gotten whacked had numbed to I-wish-I-could-forget that nightmare. The government moved us to a coal-mining town in western Pennsylvania, and McDonald, Carbone, and I got back into the debriefing routine. My stories—escapades with Jimmy Burke, Paul Vario, and the rest of my criminal friends—were spinning McDonald's head. My collection of hard-to-believe scoops opened a book of thieveries and scams dating back to the early 1950s and ending twelve weeks ago at the time of my drug bust.

Nearly purged of drugs and alcohol, I relaxed in an armchair, my elbows lodged on the conference table, and McDonald, sitting across from me, poured water from a bottle of Poland Spring into a glass.

I put up a palm. "Forget water. Why don't you send somebody for a couple of bottles of wine?"

"I don't drink, Henry," McDonald said.

An Irish who don't drink? I remember thinking.

He jotted today's date on a yellow notepad and touched the tip of his nose with the left thumb. "Today we're going to begin with when and how the idea to burglarize Lufthansa came to your attention."

I shifted in my seat. "Well, let's see." My memory sputtered. "Marty . . . Marty Krugman the bookie. He came to me with the whole idea. And to tell you the truth, I didn't think it could be done. By anyone!"

My mind cleared because I truly reveled in recounting the Lufthansa heist. I got into it, and not just as an informant; I was swimming in a sentimental period of my life that I dearly missed. But despite my straightforwardness in recounting the details—those I could remember, at least—McDonald was up against the same problem that had burst Florio's bubble.

Jimmy had killed anyone and everyone who'd been entangled in Lufthansa, except me. But my testimony against the Gent, by itself, was not enough for a jury to hang him. I had been a co-plotter of the crime, and for me to drag Jimmy into it I had to give McDonald a lot more; for example, a second witness. But who? Anybody who had knowledge of the robbery, save Angelo Sepe, was dead. And Sepe would take a bullet before he'd rat on Jimmy.

99

"I'm beginning to regret we got Hill out of hot water with the Nassau County attorney," McDonald begrudged. "When all is said and done, he has little to contribute to the Lufthansa investigation."

McDonald reviewed this dead end with Tom Puccio, the supervising US attorney.

Puccio said bitterly, "This Hill character duped us along with Florio. I now see he's a lot smarter than I imagined." He chortled and chanced, "Maybe you can depose Hill on crimes unrelated to Lufthansa. His depositions don't have to be restricted to Lufthansa. We're so engrossed in this case that we can't see the forest for the trees."

"I concur," McDonald said.

"Maybe we should concentrate on building a case against Governor Carey. I wonder if Hill can help us there," Carbone joked.

Everyone broke into hilarity, diluting the acid in Carbone and McDonald's stomachs.

The upcoming sessions with Hill, the FBI, and the US attorney were not productive, frustrating McDonald and maddening Carbone. The incompleteness of Hill's allegations of Burke and Vario's illegal businesses were hearsay and inadmissible in a courtroom. Carbone and McDonald were at wit's end.

"You were right, Ed," Carbone conceded. "We made a mistake in giving Hill transactional immunity."

100

I stepped into the conference room, and McDonald and Carbone didn't look too happy. In my jolly manner, I said, "Hey, I was taking a piss and something came to mind."

"What about it?" Carbone asked offhandedly.

"You know, under the bocce court in the basement of Robert's Lounge, Jimmy ditched the bodies of a few guys he whacked."

Carbone's eyelids shrunk to thin slits, and he scrunched his lips. "Do you know what you're saying? Why would Burke keep evidence on his premises that could get him indicted for multiple murders?"

"You should ask him," I said. "I'm telling you it's true."

I'd babbled on with so many sensations of wilder than wild accounts linked to underworld figures, and at this point Carbone and McDonald couldn't separate fiction from truth. And sure, Jimmy's reputation was that he might've been the devil's son, but with this latest story they figured I was bending their ears.

"Henry, you're saying that if I apply for a warrant to excavate in the basement of Burke's bar, we're going to find bodies?" McDonald asked with reservation.

"That's right!"

Carbone gazed at McDonald, shook his head, and pointed at me. "Ed, this man is out of his mind."

McDonald didn't answer Carbone. "Henry, you have to be sure of this," he cautioned. "I'd be in a difficult position to ask a judge to sign a court order to dismantle Burke's basement floor on the premise we believe we'll discover bodies. After the judge laughs until he swallows and chokes on his dentures, he'll look at me as if I lost my senses. So I need good cause. And if I'm wrong, I'll never get a judge *anywhere* in the country to sign another warrant." McDonald scratched the back of his neck and glanced at me. "Not to mention, I'd be the laughing stock of the legal profession."

"You can do whatever you want. *I know* for a fact Jimmy buried two or three people under the bocce court. One of them, believe it or not, is Marty Krugman."

"Why did you wait so fuckin' long to tell us this?" Carbone seethed. "We've been spinning in an empty circle for the past two months, and you didn't mention a hint of stashed bodies in Burke's basement, you stupid fuck."

McDonald raised his palms. "All right, all right, Steve. Take it easy. We have to keep our heads straight. OK?"

Eyes bleary and spittle whitening the corners of his mouth, Carbone said, "I know, I know, Ed. I apologize. This case has been haunting me day and night. I can't even get a couple hours of sleep before I wake up."

I butted in. "I don't know why you're losing sleep. You're gettin' paid no matter what. Rain or shine, or whether you solve a case, your salary is guaranteed. When it comes to federal employees, the eagle shits every damn month, and you never miss gettin' paid. Right or wrong?"

That did it for Carbone. He lunged at me from across the table, and his hands around my throat were tighter than a vise. The room went black.

101

Had it not been for McDonald severing them, Carbone might've rung Hill's neck until his face turned the shade of an eggplant. As it was, he just about passed out. The fray lasted one or two minutes, and McDonald managed to untangle Carbone from Hill.

McDonald straightened his tie and caught his breath, his face tinged pink. He mulled over Hill's far-out statement about bodies under the bocce court and, with reluctance, took him at his word. But rather than going out on a limb, McDonald passed it on to the Queens County prosecutor, Francis Tyson. Foreseeing a swarm of journalists who, like buzzing bees at honey, would flock to cover the search, Tyson leaped at the opportunity. He didn't doubt Hill's rumor and gladly petitioned for the warrant. And why not? Tyson pondered: Who'd think Burke hid the bodies of those he murdered in his own place of business?

The NYPD contracted with an excavating company to dig out the flooring in the subterranean level of Burke's bar, and Tyson huddled with his public relations specialists.

"I want all newspapers, magazines, and TV networks to telecast this search, beginning with the serving of the excavation warrant on Jimmy Burke to the removal of the corpses. Every minute of it, got it? I scheduled the process server to arrive at Burke's doorstep next Wednesday at seven. I want it to coincide with the evening news."

The nine million New Yorkers would note the publicity, establishing the name Francis Tyson as a political brand. He gloated in a bubble of happiness. At last, the Lufthansa spotlight was about to shine on Queens County Prosecutor Tyson, and this time he, and not those FBI bullies, would be the star of the press conferences, clinching his reelection.

The process server, flanked by photographers, journalists, lights, and cameras, tramped into Robert's Lounge and accosted Burke, who was smartly dressed in a black velvet sport jacket, and a burgundy shirt with an open collar, gray chest hair sprouting out of it.

A barrage of photoflashes lighted the dingy tavern as Burke read the warrant. "Go ahead, be my guest," he said invitingly, bowing with a hospitable sway of his hand. "You're welcomed to dig all you want. I'll take you downstairs. Follow me."

The detectives were surprised by Burke's nonchalance. Once in the basement, however, a sinking feeling stopped them cold. The cellar was dank with the mustiness of an underground cave, and oddly, the excavators saw a freshly dug six-foot wide hole in the floor that was covered with plywood, dirt strewn over it.

Tyson made a grand entrance in the company of his staff, a gallery of cheerleaders. The reporters bombarded him with questions all at the same time, jamming microphones in his face.

"How many bodies do you expect to find, Mr. Tyson?"

"I'm not at liberty to comment."

"Mr. Tyson, Mr. Tyson," called out a short, thinly female crime writer. "Could you give us the names of whoever is buried in this building?"

Tyson waved her away as if he were a king brandishing a scepter. "You'll soon find out. You're going to have to be patient. No more questions, please. We have a job to do. This is not a bazaar for anybody's entertainment." Tyson was right; this happening was not a bazaar. It was a three-ring circus.

Suddenly, a stabbing thought occurred to Tyson. "Where are the FBI rodents? And where's that US attorney, McDonald? I didn't think they'd miss this for the world."

"We didn't see them, sir," said a detective, one of Tyson's minions.

He blocked out the racket and commotion and dwelled, *why aren't the FBI and the US attorney here to stick their mugs in front of the cameras?*

They had opted to warm the sidelines and watched the Francis Tyson Revue on television. Carbone and McDonald's rationale was, if no cadavers turned up Tyson would be the sole buffoon.

Meanwhile, the diesel engine of the excavator groaned, and the ground vibrated from the weight and thuds of its plow. The television vans, CBS, NBC, ABC, and CNN antennas extended thirty-five feet into the air, were broadcasting Tyson's peacock prance. News programs were scoring the highest ratings since the weeks shortly after the Lufthansa robbery. Thirty minutes sped by, then an hour, then two. Dirt and rocks were piling and piling in the parking lot. But no stiffs, no skeletons, just stones and sand. Tyson was pacing in circles, a cameraman shadowing him closely.

A pudgy reporter, whose beetle-hair style was flying in the wind, stuck a microphone inches from Tyson's mouth. "Sir, what's going on down there? How many bodies have your men found so far?" Tyson turned his back to the camera and pretended to speak with a subordinate.

The wind was gusting stronger, and the reporter, a hand on his head to hold the mop-like hairdo from blowing wildly, harassed, "Mr. Tyson, us media people out here are getting restless. Do you still believe there are bodies down there? Or is this a hoax?"

Seconds later, Tyson's chief of detectives came up from the basement. "Sir, they found some bones, and a deputy coroner is examining them."

Tyson's face brightened, and he fast-strutted toward the rear door of Robert's Lounge. "Oh good, good. Tell the excavators to keep going. Where there's smoke, there's fire."

102

Deputy coroner Keith Grimes had updates on the excavation and walked over to Tyson, who excused himself from the press corps. "What have you got, Keith?"

"We found some bones."

"And?"

"They're animal bones, Mr. Tyson. Probably sheep."

"What do you mean, animal bones? Why are they animal bones?"

"Well, sir, see all this?" Grimes waved his arm in an arc far into the distance. "At the turn of the century, the southern section of Queens County—including where Kennedy Airport lies—used to be farmland. Animal farms, and . . ."

"Farmland? Keep digging, keep digging. There's got to be more than animal bones. KEEP DIGGING, GODDAMN IT!"

Laborers ferried buckets and wheelbarrows of sand and rocks, cops climbing up and down the stairs of the cellar, supervising the search. But the journalists were getting bored, and impatience thickened the air. Burke was the only one having fun. A bottle of beer in hand, he'd been taking delight in the slow transformation of Tyson's swagger to a glum, hunched stagger.

The night wore on, and the media sharks, disillusioned and tired, shut down their lighting rigs, pulled up stakes, and one by one vacated the parking lot.

Inside Robert's Lounge, Burke instructed his bartender to pop the champagne. He sent a waitress outside to let everyone know his gin mill was open for all to patronize, and to inform Tyson he and his toadies were also invited to belly up to the bar—even though this courtesy wasn't a compliance of the search warrant. Just good sportsmanship on the part of the Gent.

The waitress raised her chunky arms, the excess flesh under the biceps shaking loosely, and hollered, "Bar is open. Mr. Burke says drinks are on the house for everybody. That means you too, Mr. Tyson."

The detectives were tempted, and if their boss, Tyson, hadn't been around they might've dove at Burke's favor. Tyson shot a sizzling look at the flabby woman and motioned his men to clear out.

McDonald and Carbone had watched the broadcast from the comfort of their living rooms. Afterward Carbone phoned McDonald. "Ed, it's Steve. What did you think?"

McDonald chuckled through his nose. "We sure made the right call to let Tyson take out the warrant, and am I glad I wasn't there."

"You're not kidding. This Burke must have a contact at Tyson's office. How else could he have known to beat Tyson to the punch and gotten rid of the bodies."

"There's no doubt about it, Steve. Which brings me to my point. You should caution your agents that henceforth, anything pertaining to the affairs of Burke and his associates must not be within earshot of Tyson's office."

"I will." An idea then budded in Carbone's mind. "I'm going to bring in Marley Carr for questioning. She may be able to pry open Hill's drug-rotted memory."

"Sounds good, Steve."

The next day, Carbone, Guevara, McDonald, and Puccio, all in black suits, sat Ms. Carr and Mr. Hill in an interviewing room. The hosts and guests assembled around a centered table, an oblong, dark-stained mahogany piece.

103

When the marshals walked me into McDonald's conference room, I was shocked to see Marley Carr, my old flame and courier. They brought her in, hoping she could help me remember whatever I might've missed. Marley's frizzy hair, short and tinted a wacky violet blue, must've had everyone there thinking where the hell I had found this dizzy broad. She was wearing a purple blouse opened down to her mini cleavage, partly showing her mini breasts. Carbone introduced Marley to Puccio, Ed Guevara, and McDonald, and she didn't as much as offer her hand.

The formalities out of the way, McDonald opened a fresh notepad. "Ms. Carr . . ."

The right arm dangling over the back of her chair, she interrupted him, "Call me Marley."

McDonald gave her a superficial smile. "OK, Marley." He turned to me. "First, I want to ask *you* a question, Henry."

I also had one of my arms resting on the back of my seat as if I were lounging under a cabana on a beach. "Go ahead, Ed."

"Where were you, and what were you engaged in for most of the month of December 1978? I mean just prior to the Lufthansa robbery."

The heist had happened fourteen months earlier, and for me to remember where I might've been that long ago was a tall order. I petted my newly grown goatee and concentrated. You could almost smell my brain overheating. "I'm not sure."

Marley cut in. "You and I were in Boston from the end of November 'til the third week of December."

"Yeah, yeah. She's right, that's where we were," I said.

McDonald scribbled on his pad. "What were you doing in Boston? Did it have to do with peddling heroin?"

"Nah." I shook my head and giggled. "We was involved with three players on the Boston College basketball team, and they were shaving points for us. Burke, Vario, and me betted against the odds. Know what I mean?"

Puccio and Carbone seemed puzzled. Puccio gazed around the table and asked, "What does it mean, they were shaving points for you?"

McDonald was familiar with shaving points, and his face got beet red. "What did you say?" He said it as if he were ready to kill me.

I was taken aback by McDonald's sudden change of attitude. "Yeah, we had a little scheme going on," I said. "The players made sure the score wound up less than the point spread and . . ."

McDonald sprung to his feet like a maniac. He banged wildly on the tabletop and leaned into it, going for my throat. Last week, Carbone had wanted to strangle me; today it was McDonald. "You did what?" he repeated, foam bubbling on his mouth.

Puccio, Carbone, and Guevara couldn't understand what got him to freak out.

At that moment, Ed McDonald, so unbecoming, could've choked me with his bare hands. This infuriated guy, a six-foot-one athletic bulk burning to pounce on me, threw me off balance. Why did he snap? Well, it turned out McDonald had graduated from Boston College and had a short stint as a player on the Eagles.

Puccio calmed McDonald, and Guevara poured him a glass of water. "Here, Ed," Guevara said, "take a sip, and don't make it personal."

McDonald sat, Carbone patted his shoulder and looked at everybody in the room. "We're going to attack this investigation step by step. This point shaving thing might be the ax we've been waiting for." He walked to the side of the table where Marley was and stared at the weird-looking broad. She was chewing gum, and Carbone stole a glance at her tongue— she'd had it pierced. He thumbed at me without breaking eye contact with her. "Is this true about the point shaving?"

Still chewing, she nodded. "Uh-huh."

McDonald also was glaring at Marley. "I can't fucking believe it."

"For Christ sake, he cursed," Carbone and Puccio exclaimed, both saying it at almost the same time. McDonald sounded unnatural spewing curse words.

Anyway, I gave McDonald and Carbone the lowdown of how Paul Mazzei, the Perla Brothers, three corrupt players, and me had faked the Boston College basketball scores. It raised Carbone's eyebrows. Naturally distrustful of witnesses, he and Guevara glanced at me with a look that said, *is this another one of your fibs?*

"For the US attorney to impanel a grand jury and indict Burke, in addition to your testimony, you'd need proof he conspired in the scheme," Carbone recapped.

"I got proof Jimmy Burke was in this deal up to his eyeballs. What're you think, I'm gonna waste your time?"

"OK, then, please impart to us in detail this . . . this so-called proof you have, Henry," McDonald said, rolling his hand in circles to goad me on.

I straightened and touched my shirt collar with my chin. "Did . . . did you say 'take apart' the proof?"

McDonald threw his head back sighed. "I said *impart*. It means to relay."

"Oh, to relay. I get it."

"So let's hear it, Henry," Carbone pressed with a mean look.

I shifted on my ass and licked my lips. "Any chance you can send for a frosty beer?"

"NO! Continue." McDonald had lost his patience.

"See, if I have a couple of beers, I relax, and my memory loosens up."

Unknowingly, I was testing McDonald. He was heading the investigation of the decade, and me, I couldn't function without a buzz. He dug hard in the pocket of his trousers, fingers shaking, and yanked out a crumpled wad of one-dollar bills, daggers shooting out of his eyes. McDonald trudged heavy-footed toward Guevara and stuck the money in his palm. "Ed, do us all a favor and send somebody to get this hopeless drunk some beer. And put hydrochloric acid in it."

Ed Guevara looked at the US attorney in a funny way. "Hydrochloric acid?"

"I was kidding," McDonald replied miserably.

Carbone, also out of tolerance, yelled, "Go ahead, go ahead, Ed. Get this nut some damn beer."

As Guevara headed for the door, I hushed to him, "Hey, tell whoever is going to get a six-pack of Pabst Blue Ribbon and one of Schlitz."

Carbone couldn't resist flinging a ball of paper at me.

McDonald unbuttoned his shirt sleeves as if he was ready to fight. He flipped his notepad to a clean page. "We're getting your beer. You happy now? Now let's hear a taste of the proof linking Burke to the Boston College point-shaving fix."

I was counting the seconds for the beer runner to walk through the door. "After the games I had to pay the players their graft, and Burke wired me the money. And I'm sure you can get copies of those transfers from Western Union."

McDonald, Carbone, and Guevara were scribbling excitedly on their yellow pads, and Chief Puccio seeming pleased.

After hours and hours of babysitting me, I had at last steered them onto a less bumpy road.

A brunette, hips swinging, light-stepped into the room carrying a brown paper bag; her sexiness and what I hoped was inside the bag flustered me. She placed it on the table and lifted out two six-packs, Pabst and Schaefer. No Schlitz, but no big deal. My memory was getting clearer and clearer. "Another thing came to mind. Jimmy used to call me in Boston three or four times a day. Those long-distance calls you can verify with the phone company. Right?" I winked and chugged a half can of Pabst.

McDonald chewed on the tip of his pen and regarded Carbone. "Interesting."

Carbone lifted his eyes from the notepad. "You're right, Henry, the beer does work."

A vision of nailing Jimmy "the Gent" Burke stirred McDonald's adrenalin. He drummed on the table surface with his pen and stood. "I'm impressed, Henry. These facts are of great value. Can you give us any corroborating details that will strengthen all this?"

I popped open the second beer, drank a third of it, and burped.

"C'mon, Henry," Guevara remarked, "there's got to be more. "How about some witnesses outside this scam who can swear Burke was in Boston during that same period?"

"Why don't we break for lunch and send out for some sandwiches?" I said.

In a split second, Carbone became the picture of a crazy man who wanted to tear my heart out.

"In a few minutes, we'll order food," McDonald appeased. "Right now, concentrate on Agent Guevara's suggestion. "

"You mean if there's anybody who saw Jimmy in Boston with me?" I touched my left temple and closed my eyelids. "Come to think of it . . . I got friendly with someone up there. Neil. I think his last name is Pendergrass. Yeah, Neil Pendergrass. He's the conscientious at the hotel I was staying."

"The *conscientious*? What the hell is a *conscientious*?" Carbone remarked.

Everybody in the room glanced at each other, and McDonald asked, "Henry, did you say *conscientious?*"

My face must've showed confusion as well. "Am I missing something here? You people don't know what a hotel conscientious is? You know, the man at the front desk who gives out information to the guests."

McDonald's chest heaved. "You mean a *concierge?*"

"Yeah, a conscientious."

"OK, we understand. So his name is Neil Pendergrass?"

"Yeah, we bullshitted about bettin' on horses and numbers, and I told him we were fixing the basketball games. He asked me if I could place guaranteed bets for him. And once or twice when Jimmy flew up for one of the games, I let him meet Neil. Matter of fact, we brought Neil to see the Boston-Fordham game in December of '78."

To McDonald and the FBI, this was a sweet melody. Western Union wire transfers, telephone records, a witness with knowledge of the point-shaving operation who had been with Jimmy and me at the scene of the crime—the Roberts Center Arena in Chestnut Hill, Massachusetts. Jimmy had violated five or six federal statutes, and I was stitching together a case for McDonald that he'd win hands down. And this final blow *should* take down the Gent and whoever else remained standing. Though with the slippery Jimmy Burke, it wasn't done until it was done.

104

At the federal court in Brooklyn, the trial of the *United States of America vs. James Burke, Paul Mazzei, Anthony Perla, and Rocco Perla* had begun. Henry Hill, unfazed by the icy eyeballing from his coconspirators, testified that, in concert with those defendants, he had fixed the Boston Eagles basketball games.

McDonald and Carbone were pleased with Hill's performance and prayed for the second witness to be as effective. The media barreled into the courtroom with the same franticness it had invaded the Louis Werner trial; the public saw it as a sequel to the Werner saga.

Preened and polished, McDonald stood, hands in the pockets of his navy blue pleated and cuffed pants. The courtroom quieted, and his new black winged-tip shoes squeaked as he approached the lectern. "Sir, please state your name for the record."

The witness cleared his throat and peered fleetingly at Burke, who, perfumed and donned in a gray tweed Italian suit, was seated at the defense table staring fiercely at him. Ashamed to be a squealer, the informant lowered his eyes and seemed to want to hide inside the witness box. "Eh, my name is Neil Pendergrass."

McDonald walked up to him and was overcome by the man's body odor. "What is your occupation, sir?"

Pendergrass peeked about the courtroom as if he were a critter afraid to come out of its warren. "Eh, I'm a hotel concierge at the Boston Sheraton."

"Where in Boston is that hotel located?"

Disquieted by Burke's menacing stares, the tips of Pendergrass's shoes were pattering the floor. He coughed and glanced up at the judge as if to beg for protection. "It's on the corner of Dalton and Belvedere."

"How long have you been employed at the Boston Sheraton?"

Pendergrass jiggled his blue tie. "Six years."

So far, the questions had been harmless protocol.

His arm outstretched, indicating Burke, McDonald asked the perspiring Pendergrass, "Are you acquainted with the defendant?"

"Eh, yes."

McDonald swiveled in the direction of the jury. "Mr. Pendergrass, please acquaint this panel on how you and the defendant, James Burke, met."

His tie suddenly too tight, Pendergrass subtly tugged at it. "Eh . . . Henry Hill was a guest at the hotel I work at, and he got friendly with me." He glanced sneakily at the defendant and stammered. "Eh, then . . . eh, Mr. Burke came to visit Mr. Hill a few times, and uh . . . Mr. Hill introduced him to me."

Despite the overcrowded courtroom, it was so quiet you could hear a mouse squeal.

"Is it fair to say, Mr. Pendergrass, you soon developed a relationship with Mr. Hill and Mr. Burke?"

"Well, not really."

"I'll rephrase the question. Did Defendant Burke and or Mr. Hill pay you any favors?"

Pendergrass sensed it was going to get muddy, and he gulped. Again, he wiggled the tie for air to cool his neck, his tan shirt collar dank with sweat. "I don't understand the question, sir."

Smiling weakly, McDonald said, "Did Defendant Burke and/or Mr. Hill perform any services or pay you any form of compensation?"

"Yes," Pendergrass answered in a whispery hush.

Pointing with his finger McDonald directed the witness to where Burke was seated. "Please describe the favors you received from the defendant and/or Mr. Hill."

"They . . . they placed bets for me on college basketball games."

"Why did Defendant Burke or Mr. Hill bet on your behalf? Do you have impairments or physical disabilities preventing you from placing your own bets?"

"Eh . . . no, I don't, sir."

"Then why were Defendant Burke and Mr. Hill handling your betting on the college basketball games, Mr. Pendergrass?"

The spectators listened intently to the exchange. Reluctance slowing Pendergrass, he flitted his glances from Burke to McDonald, and then up at the judge, who commanded tersely, "Please answer the question, Mr. Pendergrass."

Pendergrass unbuttoned his brown blazer and mustered the courage to come clean. "Mr. Burke and Mr. Hill fixed the games, and they told me my bets were a sure thing."

Burke did not flinch, his eyes leering at Pendergrass, and the crowd let loose a deafening roar. Journalists and photographers jumped to their feet, cameras clicking, flashes blinding the jurors. The judge, frail and elderly, hammered his gavel. "Silence, silence. Bailiffs, confiscate all photographic equipment." A coughing spell interrupted him. When it ended, he reproved, "At the commencement of these proceedings, I ordered everyone in this courtroom not to take pictures. And I meant it. I want all the cameras." His Honor's head, so tiny, seemed as if it were about to disappear inside the collar of his loose-fitting robe. He flailed his arms and scolded, "Go on, bailiffs, go on. What are you waiting for, hell to freeze? Round up those cameras. Now!"

Too late; the paparazzi scurried out of the courtroom like roaches running into the floor crevices when the lights are flicked on.

The jury deliberated for five and a half hours. The five women and seven men took their seats in the jury box as the judge watched them file in. "Foreman of the jury, have you reached a verdict?"

The foreman stood and in a stentorian voice said, "Yes, we have." He handed an envelope to the bailiff, who passed it to the judge.

"Foreman of the jury," His Honor called out, "how do you find Defendant James Burke?"

"Guilty on all charges."

The same verdict came down for Burke's three codefendants, the Perla Brothers, and Paul Mazzei.

At sentencing, the judge meted out a seventeen-year sentence to Burke and variations of it to Mazzei and the Perlas.

Of the three Boston College Eagles players, in a separate trial Rick Kuhn was convicted and sentenced to ten years, and Earnie Cobb was acquitted. Jim Sweeney was not tried and, somehow, skated clean.

Although Burke was imprisoned, McDonald and Carbone did not forsake taking advantage of Hill's deep-rooted knowledge of the Lucchese Mafia family's inner workings. From Hill's ramblings McDonald elicited a trove of sins authored by Burke and Vario, deeds far more serious and violent than the Boston College sting. The problem was a fundamental one; Hill could not substantiate much of it, though he outlined the incident when Vario set up a bogus job for him and falsified documents to comply with parole conditions. This was a Class B felony, and compounded by the bogus paperwork Vario had submitted to the Lewisburg parole board, the jury convicted the Lucchese capo. The court incarcerated him for five years.

Vario's prison sentence was a far cry from the punishment he really deserved, nonetheless, it was the rising of justice. Perhaps, Hill might pry more hidden offenses from his past, and the government will score additional indictments against Vario and Burke.

105

After going round and round, I'd become a dry sponge. McDonald had squeezed everything out of me that I could remember.

"We're disappointed in you, Henry," McDonald complained. "I went out of my way to fight on your behalf for you not to be indicted in Nassau County on the drug charges," he said harshly. "I endorsed you in the witness program, and all we got is a gambling conviction on Burke and a document falsification on Vario. And these two subjects are the most dangerous felons this side of the Rockies, mind you."

I clammed up. Carbone stepped in and sat on the table facing me, letting his left foot dangle. "Here's what we'll do, Henry."

"Nice shoes, Steve. Italian made?"

Carbone snarled, "Never mind my fuckin' shoes. We'll call it a day, and we'll start over tomorrow morning. And you better come up with something we can sink our teeth into. Understand?" After a while, everyone started talking my lingo.

I looked at the air conditioning vents, and as if forgotten days began sifting out of them, I stood and touched my temple. "Hey, this should grab you. Yeah, Richard Eaton!"

"Who?" Carbone asked.

McDonald couldn't wait to hear *this*.

I drew a long breath. "Eaton was a straw man for Jimmy. He was on the liquor license of the Gent's bar, Robert's Lounge. The ocean would part before they'd give Jimmy a liquor license. Know what I mean? Anyway, after Lufthansa, Eaton conned Jimmy into fronting him three hundred and twenty-five grand for a cocaine deal. And the Gent took some of the money from his piece of Lufthansa and invested it in Eaton's drug deal."

McDonald listened with baited breath. I lay back in my chair and began to feel helpful.

"And here's the thing: Eaton didn't buy cocaine with Jimmy's $325,000. He spent it on high-flying women, narcotics, weekends in Las Vegas, luxury cars, and all that. Jimmy should've known better, but greed pushed him into a fog."

I had McDonald and Carbone's interest and went into details about Jimmy and I chasing Eaton in Florida and coming back empty-handed.

McDonald and Carbone were stunned. Again! After months of working with me, how could I not have mentioned this?

I stuck another Marlboro between my lips and lit it. "We never saw or heard from Eaton. And knowing Jimmy, he'd never forget about him. Sure enough . . ." A coughing fit shook me into spasms, and Carbone poured me water. The cough stopped, and I went on.

"A couple of months after Lufthansa, one of John Gotti's boys spotted Eaton in a Manhattan restaurant. To make a long story short, it got back to Jimmy, and he told Angelo Sepe to tail Eaton."

"Get to the point," Carbone growled.

"I'm gettin' to it. Relax. Anyway, Sepe found out Eaton lived in one of those roachers somewhere in Greenwich Village."

"What's a roacher?" McDonald asked.

"Those old, smelly tenements downtown New York with roaches crawling on the floors and walls."

"I see. Go on."

"Jimmy and Sepe paid Eaton a visit and gave him the beatin' he had comin'. I don't know the full story, but rumors were that things got out of hand, and they broke Eaton's neck. Then the Gent and Sepe dumped Eaton in the Gravesend Bay area of Brooklyn. They figured Eaton was as good as dead, and the idiots didn't realize he was alive. Gravesend Bay is near New York Harbor, and a lot of streets are marshy."

I gazed at McDonald and Carbone to make sure they were listening. "Some of those blocks are abandoned—weeds and garbage all over the fuckin' place. At the southern end of Gravesend Bay stands a creaky wharf. It's probably a hundred years old, and from there you can take in the Verrazano Bridge in a way you never saw it before."

I could see Carbone was losing his temper. "Henry, what's all this got to do with Richard Eaton and Burke?"

"I'm gettin' to it. Christ, give me a chance. As I was saying, Gravesend Bay had been home to celebrities. Marilyn Monroe's last husband, the guy who wrote plays, Arthur Miller, was born there. Some shady people also lived in this . . ."

All of a sudden, Carbone's teeth were sticking out of his lips, and he screamed, "Stop! Stop this crap, goddamn it. We're not interested in the history of Gravesend Bay. We want to know what happened to Eaton."

106

My stomach was making noises. "We've been at it for hours. Let's take a break and have some lunch."

"Nah, nah," Carbone said. "We're not recessing until you finish what you started." As if he were aiming a rifle, he pointed two fingers at me and warned, "And the ending better be good. Where's Eaton now?"

"I don't know all the details. What I remember is that in the northeast, the last few days of that February were the coldest in twenty-five years."

Wilder than a hungry boar, Carbone rapped on the table with both fists, and the floor vibrated as if an earthquake were shaking it. "God-damn it! We don't care about the weather statistics. Finish the fuckin' story or you're going to leave here on a stretcher. I'm sick of you."

"Jesus, you guineas are all hot-headed."

"Henry, how is the weather related to Richard Eaton?" McDonald asked, a jittery suspense in his voice.

"I'm gettin' to it, Ed. Man, you're all so uptight." I held my chin and paused. "That whole week was twenty degrees, and when Jimmy and Angelo Sepe left Eaton unconscious—I think they dropped him off in a trailer—he froze to death."

"And what happened to his body?"

Palms up, I shrugged. "How the hell am I supposed to know? This happened a while ago."

107

Twenty months previously, on a February morning, as snow-fluffed clouds were sinking two homicide investigators from the 111th Precinct in Brooklyn had stumbled on a frozen mass on the plank floor of a rotting box trailer.

"What the fuck?" blurted Detective Don Shea, back-pedaling two or three steps, hands dangling at his hips, fingers stiff and fanned out. "Look at this, look at this, Bob. Jesus, Mary, and Joseph!"

On analyzing the six-foot-long icy bulk, it became apparent it was a corpse. Enfolded in a bloodstained cloth, solid as if it were a chunk of stone with a dusting of flaky white frost, reminded the two cops of an ice sculpture. Detective Kohler, eyes blinking and mouth shut, opened his pocket knife, knelt next to the ghastly sight, and scraped at the surface. On grating a layer of frostiness, they could see the cadaver was rolled in a blue blanket. Kohler buttoned the collar of his tan trench coat, vaporized breath swirling around his nose. "Don, he's frozen so hard we can't even take that blanket off him."

Arms tight at his sides so as not to let body warmth escape, Shea's eyes roved, examining the victim, frigid winds howling. "It's so cold. There's nothing we can do in here. It feels like a freezer."

Kohler retracted his neck into the coat collar and kneaded his chill-purpled fingers. "I'm gonna call the medical examiner's office and let them handle this."

"Wonder how long it'll take to defrost."

Kohler knocked his fist on the block of human ice. "I'd say at least forty-eight hours."

He wasn't far off the mark. The body thawed in two and a half days, at which time the coroner informed Kohler and Shea it was available for their inspection. Moreover, the medical examiner ruled the death as a homicide, and the deceased was a Richard Eaton. The two detectives raced to the morgue. When he had met his fate, Eaton was wearing a brown leather jacket. Sewn inside the lining he'd hidden a beige leather-bound telephone book. Shea scanned the pages, so worn they felt as supple as chamois cloth. On the third page, something rapt him. He snickered at Kohler, who was bent over the gurney, looking for bullet punctures on Eaton's abdomen, the skin a phosphorus white tinted an eerie blue. Shea held the phone book above his head. "Look at this! Jimmy Burke's address and phone numbers."

108

McDonald was mixing coffee and cream. "OK, Henry. Let me back up for a minute. Where did you say Burke and Sepe had brought Richard Eaton after beating him unconscious?"

My eyes went to the light fixtures, and I ruffled my hair, dandruff sprinkling like snow. "They left the poor bastard in the Gravesend Bay area. Someplace around there. Or maybe Coney Island. Anyway, it was near the water."

"Most of Brooklyn is encircled by water," Carbone said snobbishly.

"What're you want from me? I'm doing my best trying to remember," I shot back. "It was around Gravesend or Coney Island. Or maybe it was in Sheepshead Bay."

109

McDonald telephoned four precincts in the Gravesend Bay and surrounding neighborhoods: Bensonhurst, Borough Park, Sheepshead Bay, and Canarsie. Navigating by phone ultimately led him to the 111th Police Station, the command post of the two detectives who had discovered Eaton's body.

McDonald gave Shea and Kohler a glimpse of why he was contacting them and suggested they fix an appointment to meet at the earliest. He intimated Henry Hill might be of assistance in unscrambling the Eaton puzzle; Shea and Kohler were appreciative yet mistrustful. NYPD cops are burdened with an old chafing rash; US prosecutors align themselves with the FBI and do not share statistics with competing law enforcers. Then why, as Shea and Kohler racked their logic, was *this* US attorney untypically gratuitous, lending his informant to the New York City police? The answer was not a complicated one. Had it not been for their overly sensitive skepticism, the detectives would've realized the Eaton homicide was in the jurisdiction of New York State and not under the authority of the federal government.

The detectives strutted into McDonald's conference room with a walk that said *we're here, but we know it's a waste of time.* Their faces were locked in a serious look, jaws taught and clamped. The US attorney shook hands with the mustachioed cops. Shea, six-foot and robust with a round belly and a mop-like of salt and pepper hair, wore a brown polyester suit and a three-dollar burgundy tie, the standard costume of NYPD detectives. Kohler was shorter and stout, his hair combed back in a dense bush of graying blond—the mane of an aging lion. Both men, emitting vibes of apprehensiveness, carried the mannerisms of the Blue-collar class, and were patently rustled by the environment of the federal surroundings. FBI agents and NYPD detectives have forever been archrivals.

It was time for McDonald to switch his holy demeanor to its highest setting. "Detectives, it doesn't matter to me who gets credit for what; I just want to see justice prevail. If the Eaton case is not in my power to prosecute, I'd rather be of help to your department and see Jimmy Burke—if in fact he's guilty of murdering Richard Eaton—punished."

It seemed McDonald had unwound Shea and Kohler's tensions, but they still couldn't understand why a US attorney was volunteering to collaborate with the NYPD; it must've been a sting, they conjectured.

110

Guevara came to the outer reception room to get me. Over the past month, I had been hitting the liquor and had gone back to the heroin. I was in bad shape. I strolled into the conference room with the lazy walk of a person who had given up on life. The instant Detectives Shea and Kohler saw me, they both held their heads as if a headache was coming on. My body language and wacky appearance, they must've assumed, explained why the feds wanted to get rid of me and turn me over to the local cops. Shea and Kohler were probably convinced this was a hoax. I had the droopy eyes of a drug addict in need of a fix. My hair was oily, eyes bloodshot, hands trembling, a cigarette stuck at the side of my mouth, and my clothing was unforgettable: a canary yellow shirt unbuttoned to my belly button, and red and blue striped pants. I was either a giant parrot or a hobo.

Eyes wide and mouths agape, Shea and Kohler looked insulted. They were about to leave when a female receptionist walked in balancing a tray of beverages, coffee and cream, seltzer, soda, and a can of beer for me. I swiped it off the tray, popped the lid, and chugged it. The detectives glanced at one another. Kohler wagged his index finger at me and addressed McDonald. "*This* is the man who's gonna be key in convicting Jimmy Burke for the Eaton murder?"

McDonald smiled. "Allow me to make the proper introductions." He nodded at me. "Detective Shea, Detective Kohler, this is Henry Hill."

The police officers, staunch and aloof, didn't shake my hand; I gave them a sleepy gaze that said I didn't give a shit, one way or the other.

McDonald smoothed the rough start. "Gentlemen, please help yourselves to some coffee, soda, or whatever you want."

The detectives didn't want to take anything, and McDonald got into the core of it. "I can personally attest Mr. Hill has been reliable and effective on the stand. Needless to say, he has to be coached and prepared thoroughly. At a trial, anyone who testifies for the prosecution must be guided and rehearsed with patience." McDonald gulped his coffee and eyed Shea and Kohler over the rim of the paper cup. "I predict Mr. Hill will make a compelling witness, if for no other reason but for his tremendous fear of Jimmy Burke." In five minutes, McDonald had chased away the notion that this was a staged prank, and reshaped the detectives' opinions of me from a hollow-headed alcoholic to a credible witness.

Believing they'd made a new ally, Shea and Kohler were at ease. Everybody shook hands, and the detectives got up from their chairs, Shea pulling up his baggy pants; they'd almost fallen below his testicles that, because of his bloated stomach, he probably hadn't seen in many, many moons.

To Henry Hill's credit, the indictment and trial of Jimmy Burke resulted in another win for the people of the state of New York and lifted the weight of a meteor off Hill's shoulders. Burke landed a twenty-five-years-to-life confinement in a state penitentiary, and by the script of destiny, Burke's final gasps would be weak wheezes of prison air, an atmosphere tainted with hostility and darkness that permeates behind the walls of the penal structure.

With Burke gone, Hill's blood pressure was out of the red zone, and for the first time in two years he could muster an erection. Karen took advantage of it and lured her husband to their bedroom—an austere eight-by-ten closet. Filtering through the white venetian blinds, the dawn sun shone horizontal yellow lines on a wall above their queen-sized bed, wiping out the blackness of the night—and perhaps, symbolically—obliterating the ominous shadows of the Hills' past.

111

My spine was getting crushed; Karen was hugging me so tight.

"Oh, Henry, it's been so long. So long. Stay inside me," she shushed, her skin a sheen of moisture, a fringe of hair strands matted on her forehead.

In the heat of passion, Karen clutched my scrotum.

I jumped off her. "Ouuuuch. Whoa! Your nails are digging into my balls. What's wrong with you? I'm gonna get an infection." I flicked on the shade lamp, a water-stained relic on a wobbly nightstand, and looked over my bruised testicles. "Damn those nails of yours, Karen. Gotta be more gentle with my balls."

"I will. Next time, I'll bite them off."

"Yeah, and you'll get indigestion."

Lying on a metal-frame bed, shaky and creaky, Karen stared at the ceiling, its paint peeling and cracking, and she got nostalgic; gone were the fancy automobiles, and gone were those wads of hundred dollar bills. The ten-thousand-dollar shopping sprees, the vacations in the tropics, and the Las Vegas gambling binges were fast-fading memories. It depressed us all. But losing the good life outweighed getting a temple full of lead, though losing it all hadn't been easy.

In February of 1984, Paul Vario was up at bat to be reindicted. He was about to finish a thirty-eight month prison stretch for fixing my no-show job, and he'd be back on the streets in seven weeks—too soon for my comfort. Hand-in-hand with the FBI and the US attorney, we worked to bust Vario, and this time Carbone staked, "We'll put him away for good."

Beginning in 1983, McDonald had been the head of the Federal Organized Crime Strike Force in an anti-Mafia operation dubbed "Kenrac" (Kennedy Racketeering). In launching Kenrac, the Strike Force went on a crusade to cleanse Kennedy Airport of extortion, theft, and truck hijacking. Paul Vario's successors had been shaking down freight and shipping companies for millions of dollars—ongoing rackets dating back to the late 1950s when the airport was called Idlewild. They gave in to the extortion while the NYPD and Port Authority closed their eyes to the racketeering. Why? Graft. The club of dirty cops was rampant. Even New York City politicians were on the take, and the wheel of fortune spun and spun.

By now, Ed McDonald and I were on friendly terms. I was glad he'd been promoted to chief of the Organized Crime Task Force. But McDonald had to move fast to indict Paul Vario for the Kenrac violations.

"Henry," McDonald asked, squaring up four hundred pages of my depositions into a neat packet, "did my assistant give you a copy of this?"

I craned my neck to read the title on the stack of papers. "You mean my deposition on Vario?"

"Yes."

"Yeah, I got a copy."

"I want you to read it over and over until you practically have memorized all the answers in there. This is our last shot at getting rid of Vario."

"I understand. I know what I'm doing," I said faintheartedly.

McDonald held his forehead and seemed to have suddenly fallen deep in thought. "Henry, we can't afford to have Vario skate on this." He stared at me, his left eyebrow higher than the right one. "*You* can't afford for him to be acquitted on the Kenrac indictment."

Seeing me looking at the floor, not saying anything, McDonald slumped in his high-back chair. The stillness hung there. "Henry, you're not getting cold feet, are you? It's normal to feel intimidated. It happens to every witness, especially if it involves prosecuting a former associate or friend. Perfectly normal."

My eyes lifted and met McDonald's. "Perfectly normal! Fuck, it's easy for you to say. If something goes wrong and Vario walks free, I'm a dead man. Ain't I?"

McDonald pulled himself into his desk and sat up straight. "That's my point. When I call you on the stand, you've got to make sure your testimony is flawless. No mistakes, no fumbles. No inaccuracies."

"Did I ever fuck up before?"

"Ho, ho, ho," Carbone cut in. "Let's not go there, Henry. When you were in the witness box, my heart was in my mouth."

"Whadda you mean? I testified at five trials, and I think I done pretty damn good. So far, everybody got convicted. So what the hell are you talkin' about, Steve?"

McDonald stuck to diplomacy. "Henry, to be fair, yes, you did well. Then again, because of your vagueness and lackluster delivery, if we didn't present overwhelming evidence your testimony might've been the weak link. So this time, you have to be better than just good. OK?"

"Look, I wanna get Vario out of my life—I'm scared shit of him. I'm stayin' off drugs so I can read up on the questions and answers we've gone over, and I'll do whatever I gotta do to be crisp."

Although I had it in my gut all along, it was now a bowel-loosening reality that if Vario was ever freed, I'd be a marked man, and the hit would not be a question of if, but when.

The Kenrac trials commenced, Paul Vario in center stage, and despite frightening stare-downs from his black, killer eyes, rather than curling into a stance of intimidation, I let those threatening looks pump up my courage to blast him with my destroy-all testimony. Italians the likes of Vario took revenge at *any* cost; their greatest reward was vengeance. With this in mind, I rose to the occasion. On the witness stand I fired off with sharpness without barring any holes. I sank Vario with the might of a torpedo ripping through the hull of a ship.

Carbone and McDonald had achieved a trouncing victory, even though there was no closure to Lufthansa. Carbone placed his hand on my shoulder—this shocked me—and gave me an affectionate pat. "Well,

Henry, I admire your conscience. I must admit, you rebounded the way a champ does. I now know you've got more common sense than all those goombahs who think they're geniuses."

"Fuck them and their *Omertà* bullshit," I said to Carbone. "Them Sicilians and that other bunch of cutthroats, the Neapolitans, will cut their noses to spite their faces. It's *Omertà* this and *Omertà* that. Oh, they'll say, *you gotta be a stand-up guy, no matter what.* Meantime, they kill each other and leave families to fend for themselves. That's why once I found out Vario and Burke were ready to whack me, why shouldn't I have gotten them before they hit me? For what, so that I'd go to my grave as a hero? Fuck that and fuck them grease balls."

With my help, Kenrac got rid of the moths at Kennedy Airport, and it filled Ed McDonald's cap with a lot of feathers. Vario drew twenty years in a maximum-security penitentiary. And that was the end of his hope for revenge. Instead, the fuck died in the joint.

As for Jimmy Burke, he never again saw his stomping grounds. Worse yet, the prison barbed wire walls could not stop cancer from scaling them, riddling his body, and reducing it to ashes.

112

The loss of Burke's fatherly guidance for the ever-loyal Angelo Sepe was emotionally devastating and financially crippling. He was too stubborn to join any of the other crews. *Why pay protection money for muscle?* And though he himself was a thug, he could hardly afford a basement apartment—not to mention the care and maintenance of his menagerie of animals.

Sometime in April of 1984, in the lull of a sleepless night Sepe was wracking his wits how to raise the past-due rent. A brilliant whim bloomed in his mind. This newly hatched idea was for him to make "a lot of cash by robbing drug dealers." Why? Those individuals often carry large sums of money and, if mugged, are in no position to run to the police. Sepe sold himself on his brainstorm and took action.

The initial tryouts were a snap, and his future couldn't have been more promising. "Soon, we're gonna be rolling in dough, baby," he said to his twenty-year-old girlfriend, Donna, a chubby Italian-American with tawny skin and a tightly harnessed figure. A pasta mama.

Sepe's immediate success gave her slight encouragement. "Are we gonna get married and finally get out of this boiler room we're living in and buy one of those nice houses on the canal in Howard Beach? That's where all your friends have their homes? How come you can't afford one there?"

This was a sore subject with Sepe, and he consulted John Gotti about taking Donna as his bride. The Gambino lieutenant drew his advice from experience.

"Angelo, this broad of yours reminds me of the classic guinea woman who's drawn to wiseguys like us," Gotti schooled. "She'll keep a figure with just enough meat and curves, yet slim, and she'll push for a fast marriage so she can stop watching her weight. And when she blows up, tough shit on the husband. That's the mentality of the Italian American wives. We ought to marry Jewish broads; they never get fat."

Buoyed by the simplicity of his new line of work, Sepe studied the peculiarity of a Mexican drug dealer, Henriquè Velasquez. In winter or summer, Velasquez moved around wearing a heavy insulated coat. Distrustful of his roommates, he stuffed his working capital—thirty to forty thousand dollars—in the inner linings of the thick blazer. To Sepe, Velasquez was a mobile vault, an easy mark. On one summer evening, Sepe assaulted the drug dealer, stripped him of fourteen thousand dollars, and slipped a diamond-paved Patek Philippe off his wrist, leaving him for dead in the gutter of an alley. And here's how Sepe explained it to the full-bodied Donna: "Baby, it was as easy as taking candy from a child," and this wasn't far from the truth.

But it had been a misjudgment, after all. As a safeguard against the Angelo Sepes of the underworld, Velasquez, who had survived the beating, had paid dues to a Colombo made man, Vic Orena, known as Little Vic. In the aftermath of the bone-crushing assault, full of morphine to anesthetize the pain of nine fractured ribs, Velasquez phoned Little Vic from his hospital bed and apprised him of his misfortune. Little

Vic assured him, "Henriquè, my friend, you get yourself healthy, and I'll straighten out this Sepe prick."

One night at 12:30, an obnoxious knock awakened Sepe. Donna, snoring from the aftermath of a cocaine trip, didn't hear anything.

Sleepy and yawning, Sepe shuffled to the door. "Who is it?"

A gruff voice from outside answered, "Angelo, it's Benny. Open up, man. Sorry to come so late. I gotta ask you a favor."

Sepe didn't unlock the door. "Benny who? Benny and the Jets?"

"C'mon, don't be funny, Angelo. I'm Benny, Little Vic's driver. Remember me?"

"Oh, yeah, right." Sepe opened the door, and Benny and another man, a short, cylindrical-shaped roughneck, ducked their heads to step through the low entryway. They both produced .44 Magnum Smith & Wessons. Benny rammed the barrel end of the revolver against Sepe's forehead. "Time's up, Angelo."

In a series of rapid frames, Benny's companion trekked over to the bed. Sepe stepped back and, out of instinct, reached for his semiautomatic, though all he felt was the waistband of his boxer shorts. "Hey man, what the fuck . . . ?"

The second gunman, on the bed straddling Donna's waist, fired a round into her forehead, the black-haired beauty's brains coloring the white pillowcase.

Amidst the fracas, Benny plugged Sepe's neck and stomach with three bullets. The torque and speed of the Magnum projectiles joggled Sepe off his sandaled feet and chucked him into the oil burner, his 140 pounds dislodging it from its base, sparks flying out of the boiler.

Sepe's death finished the elimination of those who'd had an involvement with Lufthansa, flaming out any further considerations for Ed McDonald to re-open the probe. The irony was that Lufthansa had saved the Hills' lives by opening the gates to the Federal Witness Protection Program, but it rendered Henry Hill ineffective to McDonald in achieving the grand prize. This, however, wasn't Hill's fault. Burke had killed everyone attached to the robbery. His son, Frank, had not been in the execution lineup, but didn't die of old age either. He was fatally shot in 1987 for attempting to fool a drug dealer. Frank was cutting cocaine with baking flour and swearing, "This coke is as pure as a virgin's pussy."

113

The Silver Eagle long-range bus was cruising southbound on I-85, due east of Birmingham, Alabama. The rain had been falling in buckets, and the windshield wipers were beating in synch to "Sweet Home Alabama" playing on the radio in the motor coach.

The bus was to arrive at its destination in less than one hour. Eight passengers were on board: the driver, Henry Hill, Karen Hill, the couple's boy and girl, and three federal marshals, chain-smokers riding shotgun, the stench of tobacco choking the air. The children's faces were stuck to a window at the rear of the motor coach, watching the rain-sodden landscape smearing past them.

That night, they'd slumbered into a sound rest, and in the morning Henry Hill, serenity about him, was clad in a Hawaiian shirt, khaki shorts, and sneakers. The silk suits and Italian shoes of bygone days were a dimming memory, as were the gold rope necklaces, the diamond pinky rings, the thick bracelets, and the diamond-encrusted Piaget.

It was 10:00 a.m., and Hill seemed a bit nervous behind a lectern, shifting his stance from the left foot to the right one, hot stage lights on him, sweat glistening on his brow. He was before 344 spectators.

"And that's been the journey of my screwed-up life," he said into the microphone, his voice reverberating in the auditorium. "Yeah, sounds like a cool way to live, but trust me, you don't wanna go through what I went through. And all the hassles I created for my family. Forget about it." He waggled his finger and continued, "Keep this in mind: All those wiseguys put their loved ones through hell. That's right, they all do." Hill scanned the audience, a sea of faces staring at him. "That road ain't what it's cracked up to be. There's no peace. On any one day, you never know if one of your own is gonna whack you. And every time you look over your shoulder, some cop or FBI agent's got a tail on you. I tell ya, it was always somethin'.

"You can keep your lives on the right track, and I hope three weeks from now, when you graduate from here, you'll get into a college and learn a legit way to make a living. And I know you can do it." He paused to read from his script. "You know, I thought the law and the American justice system were my worst enemies. But guess what? They turned out to be my best friends. They saved my life. So do the right thing and don't disappoint me. You hear me?"

The high school seniors rose from their chairs, exploding to a rumbling applause. Misty-eyed, Hill waved to them, rows of clapping hands booming on.

Back on the bus, Hill asked one of the marshals, "Where are we goin' tomorrow?"

"Paul W. Bryant High School, in Tuscaloosa, Alabama."

"Where the hell is Tusca-what?" Hill wondered.

"Henry, if we get on the road by seven in the morning, we'll get there in time for your nine o'clock talk."

Epilogue

Daniel Simone has buoyed Henry Hill's legacy in this book. Henry amassed fans all over the world, though some people view him as pariah because, in the end, he became "a rat." Those dissenters, however, may not know that unlike most Mafia turncoats, he didn't inform on his associates merely to save himself; rather, he was slated to be killed whether he held to his silence or not. The FBI secretly recorded Paul Vario and Jimmy Burke plotting to murder him. Hence, Henry was a dead man no matter what.

Henry was not of violence; he loved fun, and most of all he loved delighting anyone and everyone. He never refused an autograph or posing for a photo. But of greater importance, he redeemed himself with his eagerness in attending fundraising events and host dinner affairs less any compensation. He genuinely wished to be of service to society. He made peace with his family and even with a few of his enemies. Henry couldn't walk past homeless persons without giving the unfortunates whatever money he had in his pockets.

Daniel, I believe, understood Henry's inner self, and as they collaborated on this book, I watched their friendship grow into a seamless mold. And Daniel's portrayal of Henry is Henry.

May he rest in peace.

—Lisa Caserta

Afterword

It is hard to believe that more than three decades have passed since I, Ed Guevara, was assigned to work the largest robbery of the century as a young special agent of the FBI.

"Signal 2896 report immediately to the Lufthansa cargo building at JFK," squawked the Brooklyn-Queens radio operator. The events and the aftermath surrounding the December 11, 1978, robbery have been written about, discussed, and analyzed in the media worldwide; depicted in countless books; made into movies; and exposed in documentaries. Yet the story holds improbable fascination. The events leading up to it, the charismatic characters, the brutal homicides, and the ultimate betrayal by one of their own captivate people's minds and tickle their curiosity. But no one has so adroitly told this story and masterfully interlaced the known facts with the lingering mysteries as the author Daniel Simone. He has done an artful job at weaving the events, crafting the gaps, and capturing the essence of the characters while adding the what-ifs, the unknowns, and the could-have-beens in such an intriguing fashion. I should know. I was there.

—Ed Guevara, retired FBI agent, New York BQ Office

Notes and Sources

My quest and unwavering aspirations to publish a book about the 1978 Lufthansa affair, as I named that stupendous crime, began swirling in my mind in the spring of 1979, a few months following the robbery. And though on numerous occasions over the past decades I'd steal fragments of time to delve in this project, the relentless demands of life's daily routines seemed to throw hurdles in my path—until I met Henry Hill.

In the countless hours of debriefing Mr. Hill, he relayed to me the majority of facts and details relevant to the characters, their planning and execution of the Lufthansa robbery, and the events that unspooled in its aftermath. Mr. Hill, instinctively talkative, reveled in recounting his bravura and the sensationalism of his associates' affront on Lufthansa. Moreover, he retained a keen memory, rattling off names, dates, and places.

Henry's last wife, Lisa Caserta, was instrumental in tracking down many of the individuals—the bad guys, the good guys, and those in between—who had a hand in helping me fit together the pieces of the various sides of this story.

The reader must be mindful that the value of the US Dollar in 1978 adjusted to present value amounts to approximately four-hundred percent greater.

It should also be noted that at that period cell phones, computers, fax machines, GPSs, or sophisticated electronics only existed in *James Bond* films.

Henry Hill's coconspirators in the Boston College basketball point-shaving scheme, Paul Mazzei, and the Perla brothers, Tony and Rocco, eagerly filled in the gaps in the segments of the sports scandal where Mr. Hill had not been present. It is of great importance to point out that two of the players believed to have conspired in the Boston College fix, Jim Sweeney and Earnie Cobb, were not convicted for their participation and, as of this writing, steadfastly maintain their innocence.

349

Former deputy US attorney Edward McDonald provided comprehensive information regarding his perspective of the crime and the attempted prosecution of the suspects presumed to have partaken in the audacious burglary. Mr. McDonald described the frustrations stirred by the elusive alleged perpetrators, whom their leader, Jimmy "the Gent" Burke, was systematically killing just as the investigators were scraping at their heels, dampening the momentum of the investigation. Among a wealth of particulars he imparted, Mr. McDonald recalled his efforts to negotiate plea bargains with the only two individuals charged in connection with the burglary. One of them, Louis Werner, a Lufthansa shipping clerk, dubbed "the inside man of the robbery," dogmatically refused to cooperate, and following his conviction was sentenced to a lengthy incarceration.

Thomas Puccio, former chief US attorney in charge of the New York Eastern District Organized Crime Task Force, contributed his practical analysis of how a squad of illiterates carried out such a daring robbery with the unwitting assistance of the unsuspecting Lufthansa administrators.

The two principal FBI operatives in the trenches of the investigation, Supervisor Stephen Carbone and Agent Ed Guevara, supplied their experiences and disappointments in the unrelenting pursuit to zero in on the robbers. They were candid about the behind-the-scenes rivalry with the NYPD and Port Authority detectives, who jousted with the FBI to assume the dominating role in the case, a high-profile crime of national proportion, a cause célèbre. Mr. Carbone conveyed to me the difficulties he encountered with Henry Hill as a government witness, and his ultimate disenchantment when he, Hill, couldn't proffer any information of value with respect to Lufthansa. (By the time Hill decided to defect and align himself with the FBI, Jimmy Burke had murdered everyone attached to the robbery.)

Ed Guevara, who also spearheaded the investigation of the Boston College basketball point shaving scheme, was most helpful in attempting to sift out the truth from fiction of that infamous sports scandal, which thirty-seven years, later still lingers in a haze of debates and controversies. Agent Guevara suffered through the same struggles as his colleague, Agent Carbone, met upon relying on Henry Hill, who at times, laboring under his alcohol and drug-ravaged mind was disoriented and ineffective.

I was also privileged with the vivid recollections of certain parties, who, on condition of anonymity, disclosed to me a fountain of specifics related to the Lufthansa affair and the protagonists of the story. One such person was a retired NYPD first grade detective from the 112th Precinct in Queens County. He gave me his version of the constant battle with the FBI for the center stage of the *Lufthansa Revue* and the deceitful tactics devised by the Feds to veer off course competing law enforcement agencies.

A records clerk at the Brooklyn Federal Courthouse, allowed me access to certain transcripts, documents, and recordings with which I reconstructed decisive moments that unfolded during several crucial legal proceedings.

A former Queens deputy prosecutor revealed his supervisor's ploy to take charge of the Lufthansa prosecution and his determination to undermine the ambitions of the FBI.

An ex-police recognizance technician availed to me his remembrances of surveillance strategies that culminated in the arrest of Henry Hill for multistate drug distribution.

A typist, who worked at the Nassau County Narcotics Squad, clarified an absurd misinterpretation on the part of detectives while eavesdropping on Hill's cryptic telephone conversations. This misunderstanding whirled to euphoric proportion, confusing the prosecuting attorney to mistakenly immunize Hill for his narcotics felonies.

A limo driver, who often chauffeured a Mafia lieutenant and his guests shared their word-for-word discourses touching on the Lufthansa topic.

Three restaurateurs who frequently hosted Jimmy Burke, John Gotti, and Paul Vario enlightened me with intriguing tales of their underworld patrons.

Two former Lufthansa shipping clerks took me on an insight tour of Cargo Building-261 and rendered their speculations about the physical aspect of the robbery.

Years prior to setting sail on this project, I had casual, off-the-record conversations with others who were directly and indirectly entwined in Lufthansa. One such individual was Louis Werner, who spoke with me reluctantly. Mr. Werner was key to my reconstruction of his dialogues with his ex-wife, girlfriend, gambling associates, his cohort, Peter Gruenwald, and the bookmaker to whom he was indebted, Marty Krugman.

Bill Fischetti, a compulsive gambler and aspiring gangster, spoke to me about his affair with Mr. Werner's estranged wife, Beverly. Mr. Fischetti was Werner's friend and drinking companion who bragged to him about his plans to rob his employer, Lufthansa. In turn, Mr. Fischetti confirmed that he had told his paramour, Beverly, about Mr. Werner's complicity in Lufthansa, and that she, in revenge to her ex-husband's alimony delinquency, alerted the FBI.

Since my teens, I've had a peculiar hobby: I accumulated data and movements of notorious Mafia personages. During the late spring of 1979, I devised ways to engage a rebellious and ruthless gangster, Carmine "Lillo" Galante, into a series of interviews, focusing on his underworld and the undesirables associated with him. In the course of those sessions, Mr. Galante, who was aggressively in the midst of assuming control of the Bonanno family—murdering rivals in the process—spooled out a trove of Mafia rituals and traditions, opening a portal into a dark society. Mr. Galante further claimed to have held a rather unusual gripe against one of the Lufthansa armed robbers, Paolo Licastri. Although the authorities never confirmed who bore responsibility for Licastri's demise, I theorize it was Carmine "Lillo" Galante.

In the early eighties, I chanced upon a Colombo associate, Benedetto "Benny" Aloi. He operated a limousine service out of Middle Village, Queens, a front for his illegal activities. He expressed a grievance over the Lufthansa caper; he'd demanded a share of the haul, but Jimmy Burke rebuffed him. Mr. Aloi saw this as deliberate disrespect and "would've loved to have taught Burke a lesson," though he refrained. Mr. Aloi must've known that Jimmy Burke had the support and protection of far more powerful Mafia made men, chiefly *capo regime* Paul Vario and Gambino lieutenant John Gotti. Thus Mr. Aloi wisely opted to walk away. He also chatted freely about his financial/sexual stint with Theresa Ferrara.

Lastly, I retrieved a multitude of FBI interoffice memos filled with substantiating essentials and particulars respective to the Lufthansa case.

In addition to the myriad of media sources, I gleaned bits of information on this subject from dozens of print publications and a torrent of television coverage, which I compared to corroborate some of the facts I had already gathered.

Independent Media Sources

2014 documentary, *Playing for the Mob*, directed by Cayman Grant and broadcast by ESPN

2012 documentary, *Jimmy the Gent Burke*, broadcast by the Biography Channel

2004 documentary, *Perfect Crimes: The Lufthansa Heist*, broadcast by the History Channel

2002 documentary, *The Real Goodfella (Henry Hill)*

Crime Library Episode by Alan May

Wikipedia articles on the Lufthansa Heist, Jimmy "the Gent" Burke, Henry Hill, John Gotti, and Paul Vario

March 15, 2014, *Boston Globe* feature story, "When Goodfellas Collided with Boston College Basketball," by Bob Hohler

Wiseguy, a nonfiction book by Nick Pileggi

Gangsters and Goodfellas, a nonfiction book by Gus Russo

Glossary of Italian Slang

Achità: Heartburn

Approved errand boy: An individual entrusted by the five New York Mafia factions to deliver interfamilies messages.

Baccalà: Italian name for codfish. It is also a slang alternative for a senseless person, a lout.

Brasciol: Italian recipe of thin slices of beef rolled and filled with parsley and parmesan cheese. This term is also used to call someone a good for nothing.

Buona salute: Italian well wishes for good health.

Button: Mafia term for *made man.*

Cafone: Italian slang for a lowly, ill-mannered person.

Capish: Italian dialect meaning understand.

Chase car: Vehicle that follows the getaway car after a hold-up. Its purpose is to block a pursuing police car.

Che si dice?: Italian for "What'r you say?"

Chitrool: Italian slang for a senseless person.

Collione: Italian slang for testicles.

Commara: Italian slang for mistress.

Coornuto: Italian slang for a disloyal, untrustworthy person. Also, the equivalent of a *cuckold,* a man whose wife is unfaithful.

Dick: American English slang for detective.

Disgraziat: Italian slang for a disrespectful human being.

Fattà nah camminat: Italian slang meaning, *Take a walk and get lost.*

Guinea: American/English slang for an Italian.

Goyim: Yiddish term for a non-Jew.

Grease ball: American/English slang for an Italian.

Goombah: Italian slang for a boy's godfather. Also a reference to an Italian/American gangster.

Guinea red: Slang for red wine.

Ho Capito: Italian for I understand.

Horse: Euphemism for heroin.

Kraut: American/English slang for a German.

Kvetching: Complaining. (Yiddish)

Madonn: So help me Mary.

Mammalook: Italian slang for a nitwit.

Meshugna: Yiddish term for dumb.

Mick: American/English slang for an Irish.

Minghia: Italian slang for male genitals.

Mouleenian: Italian slang for African/American.

Mule: Drug carriers and runners.

Omertà: Mafia precept prohibiting a member to testify against your own and cooperate with the authorities. If breached, the penalty is death.

On the lamb: Mafia term for hiding out.

On the mattress: Mafia term for hiding out.

Paesani: Italian for landsman or nationals of the same country.

Pasta e fasool: Coarse peasant dish of pasta and black beans.

Pizzaiola sauce: Sauce cooked with the combination of anchovies, cherry tomatoes, capers, and olive oil.

Puttana: Italian slang for a whore.

Runners: Individuals who pick up bets from gamblers.

Saloot: Toast that translates to "To your health."

Scaronnia: Italian slang for a jinx.

Scemoneet: Italian slang for a dazed person.

Schickster: Non-Jewish woman.

Schivies: Italian slang for dirty underwear.

Schmendrick: Yiddish slang for a patsy.

Schmuck: Yiddish slang for stupid.

Schwarzers: German slang for blacks.

Shylock: Yiddish slang for a loan shark.

Stand-up guy: Man or woman who would obey the *Omertà* Mafia Law and never testify against his or her associates or ever cooperate with the authorities.

Stoonat: Italian slang for someone who seems to be in a mental coma.

Stroonz: Italian slang for feces.

Test'e minghia: Italian slang for a dickhead.

Transactional immunity: This type of immunity completely protects an informant or a witness from future prosecution for crimes related to his or her testimony.

Troia: Italian derogatory reference to a lewd and disrespectful woman by associating her to Helen of Troy, who'd renounce her lovers and husbands for a mate of greater means.

Twenty-footer: Woman whose beauty diminishes as one gets closer than twenty feet in distance.

Uhpazz: Italian slang for a crazed person.

Vah fangool: Italian slang for fuck you.

Vig: 1. Usurious interest rates charged by loan sharks. 2. Ten percent of the winnings bookmakers charge their bettors.

Zoccolà: Italian slang for a slutty woman.

INDEX

A

Ahearn, Thomas: and Jimmy Burke, 228–29; and Louis Cafora, 237–38; Lufthansa heist investigation, 136, 151–52, 158, 159, 163–64, 222–23, 225

Air France: money storage room, 1–2, 4, 5, 8, 25–26; private detectives, 22, 23–24, 27; robbery in 1967, 7–11; transporting of US currency from Europe, 9

Airport Diner, 54, 84, 85, 86, 145, 277

Aloi, Benny, 213–14

American G.I.s in Viet Nam, 41

Applegate, Lina, 237

Aqueduct Racetrack, 70

Atlanta Federal Penitentiary, 47

B

Bamboo Lounge, 1, 5, 7

Barbieri, Janet, 180, 181, 196, 197–98, 240–42

Beck, Hans, 132–33

Berardi, Joe, 284

Blonder, Buffy, 250–51, 252

Boone, Jay, 48–50

Boston, MA, 81

Boston College basketball fixes, 76–86, 95–97, 146–50, 322–23, 324–28

Boston Garden, 96

Boston Sheraton Hotel, 81, 96, 146, 327

Brinks, 144

Bronx, 208–9

Burke, Frank, 121, 125, 126, 167–68, 212–13, 270, 342–43

Burke, Jimmy "the Gent": and Angelo Sepe, 227, 264–65; as an outlaw, 21; and Bobby Germain, Jr., 277, 284, 285; bodies buried in the cellar of Robert's Lounge, 21, 316, 318–19, 320; Boston College basketball fixes, 84–85, 86, 96, 146, 147–48, 323–26; and Casey Rosado, 33–38; court trial, appeals, and federal prison for extortion conviction, 38–39, 42–43, 47, 51, 59–60; court trial for Boston College basketball fixes, 326, 327–29; died of cancer while in prison, 340; drug dealing, 218–19, 265, 330–31; and Frenchy McMahon, 244, 245–46, 247; and the halfway house, 98–101; and Henry Hill, 246–47, 265, 266, 271, 276–77, 291–92, 316–17, 323–26; and Joe Manri, 188–89, 244, 245–46, 247; and Louis Cafora, 236; and Louis Werner, 244; Lufthansa heist, 62, 66–75, 88, 90, 91, 92–

93, 97–98, 124–26; and Marty Krugman, 59, 190, 194–95, 196; and Paolo Licastri, 250; and Paul Vario, 13, 29, 59, 146, 213, 217, 265–66; planning for the Lufthansa heist, 62, 66–75, 88, 90, 91, 92–93, 97–98; prison sentence, 336–37; questioned by Thomas Ahearn about the Lufthansa heist, 228–29; and Richard Eaton, 206–7, 212, 330–32, 336–37; and "Stacks" Edwards, 88–90, 167–68; suspect in the Lufthansa heist, 152, 154, 157–61, 174; and Theresa Ferrara, 214, 216–17, 219–20; and Tommy DeSimone, 212–13; traits and personality, 28–29; the unholy trinity, 32

Burrows, Louise, 223–24, 226

C

Cafora, Joanna, 232–34, 238
Cafora, Louis "Roast Beef": his murder, 238; Lufthansa heist, 99, 100, 101–3, 105, 106–7, 110–15, 116–19, 120, 121; suspect in the Lufthansa heist, 230–35
Carbone, Stephen: and Angelo Sepe, 205–6, 220–24, 227; and Francis Tyson, 226–27; and Frank Menna, 191–92; and Henry Hill, 270, 271–73, 278–79, 289–90, 316, 317, 323, 324, 330–32; and Kennedy Airport, 134; and Louis Cafora, 235, 236, 237–38; and Louis Werner, 177, 202, 239; and the Lufthansa heist, 135–36, 140–41, 151–55, 157–58, 161–64, 172–75; and Marty Krugman, 194, 196; and Peter Gruenwald, 177, 186–87; and Theresa Ferrara, 214–15; and Tommy DeSimone, 203–4, 205, 211–12
Carey, Hugh, 292–93, 297, 300, 303
Carlin, George, 14
Carr, Marley, 80–81, 258, 259, 260, 321–22
Chestnut Hill, MA, 85–86, 326
Ciaccio, Johnnie, 33, 36–38
Cobb, Earnie, 96–97, 149–50, 329
Community Treatment Center (CTC), 100–101, 154–55
Costantino, Judge, 198–99, 240, 241–43, 279–80
Cooperman, Robin, 260, 261
Cosby, Bill, 14

D

DA investigators, 22, 29, 41, 47, 129, 224
Dangerfield, Rodney, 14
DeGeneste, Henry: arrest of Angelo Sepe, 225; Lufthansa heist, 129–34, 135, 136, 151–152, 159, 223
Department of Corrections, 227
DeSimone, Angela, 208
DeSimone, Tommy: after the Lufthansa heist, 151; Air France robbery, 7–14, 22–25; as an outlaw, 21; at the halfway house, 98–101; hijacks, 34, 41, 57; joins fight at Robert's Lounge, 89–90; and Louis Werner, 63;

the Lufthansa heist, 103, 104–5, 107, 108–9, 110, 111, 119–20, 121, 122; and the Mafia, 207–11; murdered by the Mafia, 210–11; planning for the Air France robbery, 1–6; planning for the Lufthansa heist, 72–73; robbed by hookers, 17–19; and "Stacks" Edwards, 165–67, 168, 175–77, 207; suspect in the Lufthansa heist, 152–53, 154, 159–60, 203–4

DiGennaro, Sammy, 267

DiNapoli, Lina, 247

Don Peppe's restaurant, 70

Don Vito's restaurant, 209

E

East Hampton, NY, 299, 305, 312

Eaton, Richard, 206–7, 212, 330–34

Edwards, Parnell "Stacks": attacked at Robert's Lounge, 88–89; gigs at Robert's Lounge, 90; his murder and funeral, 176–77, 182–83, 207; Lufthansa heist, 90, 124, 125; repercussions after leaving evidence after the Lufthansa heisting, 126–28, 157, 161, 164–67

Eirich, Rudi, 108, 109, 111–15, 116–19, 129–31, 156

Ellis Island, 16

Epstein, Leon, 229–30

F

FBI, 128–29, 133–34, 140–41, 154, 163, 171, 235, 290

Federal Bureau of Prisons, 48, 100

Federal Organized Crime Strike Force, 169, 172, 338

Ferrara, Theresa, 213–18, 251, 252

Feuerbach, Doug, 304

Fischetti, Bill, 178–79

Fischetti, Frank, 188

Florio, Bill, 255–57, 262–63, 292–93, 294–95, 297, 300–303, 304

Fowler, Rufus, 252

Fox, Jimmy, 262, 263, 264

G

Galante, Carmine, 248–49, 250, 252

Gallo, Joe "Crazy Joe," 244

Gambino family, 59, 90, 91, 93, 95, 210, 341

Genovese family, 244

Germain, Bobby, Jr., 255–56, 277, 280–85

Glenn, John, 154

Gotti, John, 90, 91–95, 103, 124, 125, 209–11, 250, 341

Graff, Fred, 136

Grimes, Keith, 320

Gruenwald, Peter: arrested and questioned, 184–87; employee of Lufthansa Airline, 52; imprisoned in Nassau County Jail, 187–88; and Louis Werner, 137–40, 143–44, 145–46, 188, 197, 202, 203; planning the Lufthansa heist, 52–53, 56; served with a material witness subpoena, 181–82, 185; suspect in the Lufthansa heist, 173–74, 177, 178, 181–82

Guevara, Ed: and Angelo Sepe, 205, 220–21; arrest, arraignment, and questioning of Louis Werner, 202, 197–98; arrest and questioning of Peter Gruenwald, 184–85, 186; and Beverly Werner, 191, 192–93; and CI-196 (a confidential informer), 230, 245; and Henry Hill, 270, 271–73, 278–79, 325; and Louis Cafora, 231–32, 234–35, 236; and Louis Werner, 177–78; and Tommy DeSimone, 203–4

H

Hill, Henry: Air France robbery, 7–14, 19–20, 22–25; as an outlaw, 21; arrested for drug trafficking and imprisoned at the Nassau County Jail, 258–63, 297–98; arrested for the Florida assault charge, 211; attempted murder on him, 306; bail money, 262, 268–69, 273; Boston College basketball fixes, 76–77, 79–86, 95–97, 146–49, 150–51, 322–26; and Casey Rosado, 34–38; court trial, appeals, and federal prison for extortion conviction, 38–39, 42–43, 47–50; and crooked cops and politicians, 41–42; drug dealing, 41, 85, 146, 148, 150, 218–19, 254, 255; Federal Witness Protection Program, 285, 288–89, 293, 298; as a government informant, 285–86, 288–90, 298, 314–17, 322–26, 329–32, 334, 336, 339; and the IRS, 47; and Jimmy Burke,

246–47, 276–77, 316–17; and Joey Rossano, 29–31; and John Gotti, 90, 91; in Las Vegas, 19; and Marty Krugman, 40–41, 51, 189, 193–96; owner of The Suite, 32, 33; and Paul Vario, 29; planning for the Air France robbery, 1–7; planning for the Lufthansa heist, 58–63, 68–69, 71, 92; plea deal with Bill Florio, 300–305; rearrested with a material witness motion, 286; and Richard Eaton, 206–7, 212; robbed by hookers, 17–19; and "Stacks" Edwards, 90, 182–83; and the unholy trinity, 32; and union administrators, 33

Hill, Karen, 43–45, 50, 59, 211, 259–60, 290–91, 313–14

Hobbs Act, 201

Hychko, Mike, 104–5, 113, 119, 134–35, 151, 152–53, 154

I

Ianniello, Marty "the Horse," 244

Improv, The (comedy club), 11, 14

J

Jade East motel, 3, 23–25

K

Kennedy Airport, 6, 33, 41, 51, 59, 103, 338, 340

Kenrac (Kennedy Racketeering), 338

Kohler, Detective, 333, 334–36

Krugman, Fran, 56, 195, 196

Krugman, Marty: Boston College basketball fixes, 76–77, 96–97,

146–48; demands his share of the money from the Lufthansa heist, 189–90, 193–94; and Frank Menna, 191; his murder, 196; and Louis Werner, 39–41, 44, 51–52; Lufthansa heist, 52–61, 63, 69, 75

Kuhn, Rick, 78–79, 80, 81–82, 83, 86, 95–97, 149–50, 329

L

Las Vegas, NV, 149

Leno, Jay, 14

Lewisburg Federal Penitentiary, 48, 49, 50

Licastri, Paolo: his murder, 249; and Jimmy Burke, 244; Lufthansa heist, 103, 105, 107, 114, 118, 121, 122–23, 124–25, 126; murder of Joe Manri and Frenchy McMahon, 244–45; suspect for the Lufthansa heist, 248

Lispz, Greg, 199–200, 202, 203, 243

Long Branch, NJ, 250

Lucchese family, 13, 29, 59, 175, 207, 210, 227, 329

Lufthansa Airlines, 52, 58, 87, 111, 129, 143, 164

Lufthansa heist (1978), 102–21

M

Mackey, Christopher, 154, 214–15, 218, 231–32

Mafia, 13, 32, 91, 207–10, 233, 245

Manhattan Correctional Center (MCC), 47–49, 198, 199, 200, 288

Manri, Joe "Buddha": as a criminal, 62–63; defends Stacks Edwards, 88–90; his murder, 345–46; and Jimmy Burke, 244, 245; and Louis Werner, 63, 64–66; Lufthansa heist, 60, 63, 66–68, 73–74, 87–88, 97–98, 103, 104, 106, 107, 108–20, 121–24, 126; suspect in the Lufthansa heist, 230

Manriquez, José Miguel. *See* Manri, Joe

Marchesi, Nadine, 172

Maxwell's Plum restaurant, 46–47

Mazzei, Paul: Boston College basketball fixes, 76, 79–81, 82, 83, 147, 148–49, 150–51, 323; drug dealing, 257; trial for the Boston College basketball fixes, 326, 329

McClaren, Lloyd, 131–32

McDermott, Ralph, 308–11, 312–13

McDonald, Edward A.: and Angelo Seppe, 205, 221–22, 227; and Bill Florio, 301, 302–3; in the Eastern District Organized Crime Strike Force, 169–70; and Frank Menna, 191–92; and Henry Hill, 278–79, 287–90, 294–95, 297, 314–15, 316–17, 322–26, 330–32; and Louis Cafora, 237, 238; and Louis Werner, 197–98, 199–203, 239, 240–42, 253; and Marty Krugman, 194, 196; and Paul Vario, 338–39; and Peter Gruenwald, 181, 185–88; and

Stephen Carbone, 171–75; and Theresa Ferrara, 215; trial for Boston College basketball fixes, 326–28

McElhone, John, 302–3, 304

McMahon, Robert "Frenchy": Air France robbery, 7, 9, 19–21; his murder, 245–46; and Jimmy Burke, 244, 245; Lufthansa heist, 103–4, 106–7, 110–11, 114, 115–21; and Marty Krugman, 51; planning for the Air France robbery, 1–4, 5–7; suspect in Air France robbery, 19, 21, 22–28

Menna, Frank, 64, 188, 191–92, 202

Murray, John, 108–10, 111–12, 119, 120, 123, 134

N

Nassau County District Court, 294, 302

Nassau County Jail, 187–88

Nassau County Narcotics Division, 255, 351

New Hyde Park, 141, 196

New York State Tax Treasury, 47

New York state troopers, 129

Nolan, Mike, 2–3, 24, 25, 28

NYPD: Air France robbery, 32; Kennedy Airport, 338; Lufthansa heist, 128–29, 134, 136, 173, 222–23

O

O'Malley, Brian, 25–27

Orena, Vic "Little Vic," 341–42

Otto, Richard, 261–63, 297

P

Pendergrass, Neil, 325–26, 327–28

Perla, Rocco, 78–79, 80, 81, 82, 83, 323, 326, 329

Perla, Tony, 78–79, 80, 82, 83, 149, 323, 329

Port Authority, 21, 27, 29, 120, 129, 134, 135, 224, 338

Prudenti's Vicin' O'Mare restaurant, 90–91

Pryor, Richard, 14

Puccio, Thomas, 169–71, 302, 315

R

Rebmann, Rolf, 105–6, 108, 110, 119, 134, 151, 152–53, 154

Regina, Vincent, 142

Rivers, Joan, 14

Roberts Center Arena, 85, 326

Robert's Lounge, 21, 66, 88, 206, 270, 316–18, 330

Robert's Lounge Gang, 21, 41, 154, 167, 205, 254

Rosado, Casey, 33–38

Rossano, Joey, 29–31, 32

Roth, Cy, 39, 42–43

Ruppert, Wolfgang, 110–11

S

Salerno, Anthony "Fat Tony," 30–31, 32

Sal the Shank, 30–31, 32

Santiago, Marie, 155–56

Sepe, Angelo: accomplice in Stacks Edwards murder, 176–77; after the Lufthansa heist, 151; arrested and later released for the Lufthansa heist, 224–25,

227; and Henry Hill, 266–67, 291–92; and his murder, 142; and Jimmy Burke, 244; Lufthansa heist, 72–73, 102–3, 104, 105–6, 114, 118, 119, 121–22, 123–24; murder of Bobby Germaine, Jr., 281–83; murder of Joe Manri and Frenchy McMahon, 245–46; and Richard Eaton, 331, 332; suspect in the Lufthansa heist, 153, 205, 221; and Theresa Ferrara, 214, 217

Shea, Don, 333, 334–36

South West Florida FBI outpost, 37–38

Special Organized Crime Task Force, 295, 338, 350

Spikey, 51–52

Stahl, Daniel, 255–56, 257, 259–60, 285–86, 292–93

State Tax Commission, 47

Sterling Bowling Alley, 141, 196–97

Stratton (nightclub), 75–76

Suite, The, 29, 30, 32, 33, 41–42, 47

Summer, Donna, 46

Sweeney, Jim, 80, 81–83, 86, 95–97, 146, 149–50, 329

T

Temple Terrace Lounge, 36

Tyson, Francis, 136–37, 140–41, 158, 161–62, 225–27, 317–21

U

Umberto's Clam Bar, 244

United States Justice Department, 168

United States of America vs. James Burke, Paul Mazzei, Anthony Perla, and Rocco Perla, 326–29

V

Vario, Lenny, 266–67

Vario, Paul "Big Paulie": Air France robbery, 13; Boston College basketball fixes, 86, 96, 146; as a criminal and protector of other criminals, 29, 32–33, 39, 59, 79; and Henriquè Velasquez, 341; and Henry Hill, 265–66, 267; his death in prison, 340; incarcerated for document falsification, 329–30; Kenrac trials, 338–39; Lufthansa heist, 70–71; prison term, 337–38, 340; and Richard Otto, 261; and Stacks Edwards, 90, 175–76; and Theresa Ferrara, 213, 217; and Tommy DeSimone, 207, 210–11, 213; and the unholy trinity, 32

Vario, Pete, Jr., 208, 209

Vario, Tuddy, 266

Velasquez, Henriquè, 341–42

Venezia, Ronnie, 250–51, 252

Visconti, Remo, 77–78

W

Waiters and Commissary Workers, The, 33

Weaver, Lorraine, 293–94

Wells, George, 222, 224–25, 226

Werner, Beverly, 179–80, 188, 191, 192–93

Werner, Louis: the arrest, arraignment, and questioning for the Lufthansa heist, 197–203; cooperates with authorities on the Lufthansa heist, 253; debts and Marty Krugman, 51–52, 53; employed at Lufthansa Airlines, 51, 52–53; found guilty for the Lufthansa heist and sent to the Manhattan Correction Center, 242–43; and Joe Manri, 64–66, 73–74; at Leavenworth Penitentiary, 253; and the Lufthansa heist, 105, 117; and Peter Gruenwald, 138–40, 143–46; planning the Lufthansa heist, 52–56, 60–61, 65–66, 87–88; questioned by Edward McDonald, 200–202; sent to the Manhattan Correction Center, 199, 238; steals twenty-two thousand dollars from Lutfthansa, 145–46; suspect in the Lufthansa heist, 130–31, 132, 144–45, 173–75, 177–80, 191, 238–39; the trial for the Lufthansa heist, 239–43

Y

Yost, Walter, 133–34, 135–36, 140

ABOUT THE AUTHORS

The late **Henry Hill** entered the Federal Witness Protection Program in 1980 and assisted the government in building cases against forty-six top Mafia associates, severely wounding the major five gangland organizations. He collaborated with author Nick Pileggi on the book *Wiseguy*, which became a *New York Times* #1 best seller. In 1990, Pileggi and Martin Scorsese adapted *Wiseguy* to a screenplay, and with Henry Hill's guidance, Mr. Scorsese directed the film. Until he died in 2012, Henry Hill toured the country on speaking engagements, lecturing high school students not to emulate his past life and career.

Daniel Simone has cowritten autobiographies and published numerous shorter pieces on prominent figures in film, theater, and fiction. He created and wrote a monthly feature for *Long Island Pulse* magazine called "Between the Lines," in which he interviewed and profiled renowned novelists. In September 2012 he appeared in the one-hour Biography Channel documentary *Mobsters: Jimmy the Gent Burke*, which centered on the life and career of Jimmy Burke.